Programmer's Technical Reference: Data and Fax Communications

Programmer's Technical Reference: Data and Fax Communications

Robert L. Hummel

Ziff-Davis Press
Emeryville, California

Editor	Deborah Craig
Technical Reviewer	Bob Flanders
Project Coordinator	Sheila McGill
Proofreader	Cort Day
Cover Design	Tom Morgan/Blue Design, San Francisco
Book Design	Peter Tucker
Technical Illustration	Cherie Plumlee Computer Graphics & Illustration
Word Processing	Howard Blechman, Cat Haglund, Allison Levin
Page Layout	Anna L. Marks, Bruce Lundquist, M.D. Barrera
Indexer	Ted Laux

Ziff-Davis Press books are produced on a Macintosh computer system with the following applications: FrameMaker®, Microsoft® Word, QuarkXPress®, Adobe Illustrator®, Adobe Photoshop®, Adobe Streamline™, MacLink®*Plus*, Aldus® FreeHand™, Collage Plus™.

Ziff-Davis Press
5903 Christie Avenue
Emeryville, CA 94608

ISBN 1-56276-077-7

Manufactured in the United States of America
10 9 8 7 6 5 4 3 2 1

Communications technology advances at a continually accelerating pace. It does so, however, only through the anonymous efforts of theorists, technicians, and engineers. It is to these selfless providers of grist for the mill of progress that this book is dedicated. Thanks for the nice work.

☰ CONTENTS AT A GLANCE

◰ TABLE OF CONTENTS

⊒ Acknowledgments

SIMPLY PUT, THIS BOOK WOULD NOT EXIST IF NOT FOR THE HARD WORK OF A large number of dedicated people at Ziff-Davis Press. In particular, Deborah Craig's ability to bestow clarity upon convoluted prose is beyond question. I'm also grateful to Bob Flanders and Michael Holmes, whose unbridled enthusiasm at pointing out technical errors has to be experienced in order to be fully appreciated.

My thanks also go out to those in the communications industry who were gracious enough to share their time and expertise with me. In particular, my gratitude goes to Dennis McKenna of AT&T Paradyne, Dave Rasmussen of Datastorm Technologies, Tony Zucharino of Rockwell International, and Lawren Farber of Sierra Semiconductor.

This manuscript was written and prepared using WordPerfect 5.1. Notwithstanding the alleged virtues of other products, without WordPerfect 5.1's ability to create and edit tables and complex equations effortlessly, creating most of this book, and the appendixes in particular, would have been nearly impossible.

 INTRODUCTION

> I'm afraid, Dave. Dave, my mind is going. I can feel it.
> —HAL, in the movie *2001: A Space Odyssey*

THE INTERSECTION OF MODERN COMMUNICATIONS TECHNOLOGY AND THE personal computer has produced a wealth of information. Identifying and locating a particular portion of this information, however, can be a time-consuming task. My goal in writing the book was to provide a single reference text that covered the essential aspects of applied communications technology.

It has been my experience that programmers tend to concern themselves with only one thing: getting the job done. As such, ancillary topics such as the development of telephone systems or the relative merits of the RS-232 interface standard don't receive much coverage in these pages. Instead, this book is designed to present the information you need to understand and program serial and fax communications.

Inside *Programmer's Technical Reference: Data and Fax Communications*, you'll find information on a wide variety of communications topics, including the basics of serial communications, modulation methods, and the principles of facsimile operation. Practical information on programming the UART, the IBM PC serial port, and CRC calculations is also included. Finally, the detailed reference on modem AT commands and S registers will aid both your programming and the analysis of interfacing to modems.

Much of the information presented in this book is independent of the type of computer system being used. Serial communication and modem commands, for example, are not characteristic of a particular computer. Where the information in this book is system specific, it is based on the ubiquitous and popular IBM PC-compatible systems.

How to Use This Book

How to best use this book is up to you and will depend on your particular need and programming experience. You could read it from beginning to end to get an overview of communications—from the essentials of serial communications to modulation methods to fax modem instruction sets. Or you could skip to a chapter that interests you or has a solution for a particular problem you're trying to solve.

Fast access to reference material is essential for any programming book. You'll find that this book contains comprehensive guides to the AT commands and S registers defined for modems available from a wide variety of modem and chip set manufacturers. I think you'll find that the design of Appendices A and B makes it easy to look up an instruction and find the information you need. A thorough index is also provided as a quick reference.

Conventions

New terms and symbols will be defined and explained as they are encountered in the text. You'll also see the following conventions throughout the book.

Number Systems

The byte is the quintessential unit of data exchange in PC-based communications. Typically, byte values will be shown as two hexadecimal digits. Numbers that have the letter "h" (in either uppercase or lowercase) as a suffix are to be interpreted as hexadecimal (base 16) numbers. The number 21h, for example, should be interpreted as a hexadecimal number equivalent to the decimal number 33.

Bit streams, on the other hand, will be shown as a series of binary (base 2) digits and will normally have the letter "b" (in either uppercase or lowercase) as a suffix. In many instances, using a binary number is more convenient than other notations. The byte that encodes a fax machine's capabilities, for example, is more easily understood when presented as a binary number.

Note that a b suffix will not normally be included after the binary digits that are shown in register and HDLC data structures. These structures are typically shown as figures with bits numbered or grouped together.

Reserved and Undefined Fields

In representation of some structures, such as the HDLC frames used in fax communication, some bits or bit fields are not specifically defined as having known values. These fields may be marked reserved or unused. They should not be used for any undocumented purpose nor should their values be considered reliable. The value in a reserved field cannot be depended on to be consistent between different versions of hardware or software implementations.

Latin

CCITT specifications are numbered separately with a group that is designated by a single letter. The V.21 standard, for example, is specification 21 of the V group that addresses data communications over the telephone network.

Occasionally, new specifications are issued that use the same letter and number designation as an existing specification. These extensions are distinguished by the use of the suffix *bis* (secondary) or *ter* (tertiary) in the designation. It's important to note that these new specifications are independent of existing ones with the same designation and do not replace the original version.

1
Architecture of Serial Communications

TO HEAR A TYPICAL DESCRIPTION OF SERIAL COMMUNICATIONS, YOU MIGHT believe it to be some peculiar mixture of witchcraft and alchemy—and far too complex for ordinary programmers to understand. In many ways, these beliefs seem justified. Most discussions of serial communications are couched in complex terms and acronyms and are obscured by archaic terminology. This chapter begins, therefore, by introducing communications technology using some simple analogies and defining some basic vocabulary.

I'll start with simple examples that illustrate some complex ideas. (Indeed, the examples are so simple that I hope you'll grin and enjoy them with me.) In these examples, I'll introduce some communications terminology. Most importantly, I believe that you'll undergo the same line of inductive reasoning that has led to the current state of serial communications technology. (If you're already a communications guru, you may wish to skip directly to the next chapter.) After establishing a working understanding of communications principles, we'll develop a working description of the architecture of serial communications.

Communication Basics

For the purposes of this chapter, I'm defining *communication* simply as the movement of information from one place to another and the path through which this information moves as the *channel*. This information can take many forms: numerical codes representing characters, digitized images, facsimiles, or even voices moving across telephone lines. At this point in the discussion, the exact nature of the information being transmitted is not significant. To keep the discussion simple, we'll consider all information as *data*.

Transmission Systems

A simple communications system is illustrated in Figure 1.1. This example shows two stick figures, A and B, located in two separate rooms, 1 and 2. The stick figures want to communicate by moving information from Room 1 to Room 2. The only channel available between the rooms is from a switch in Room 1 to a lamp in Room 2. (For simplicity, we'll neglect the issue of power sources.)

FIGURE 1.1

A simple communications system

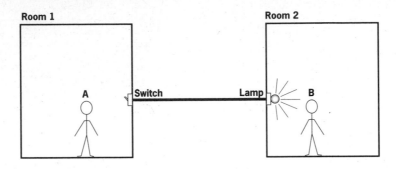

Let's assume that the stick figures have agreed on the following procedure. The lamp is normally extinguished. When the lamp illuminates, stick figure B is to proceed to Room 1. Thus, when stick figure A wishes to transfer the information, "Come here, B, I need you," it simply turns the switch to the ON position.

Note that in this example, the method used to convey the information is the change of state (modulation) of an output device (the lamp) from one distinct and recognizable state (OFF) to another distinct and recognizable state (ON). This form of modulation is the most fundamental type of modulation available and remains an important part of many forms of communication, such as manual telegraphy (Morse code).

Parallel Transmission   The width of the channel through which information passes can control the rate of information flow as well as influence the form of the information itself. To illustrate this, let's modify the previous example to include an additional lamp circuit and two additional stick figures as shown in Figure 1.2.

FIGURE 1.2

Parallel transmission

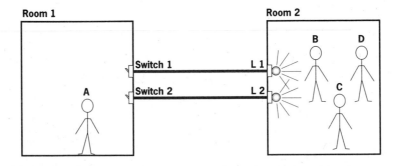

The stick figures have agreed that when only lamp L1 is ON, stick figure B is to respond to Room 1. Similarly, when only lamp L2 is ON, stick figure C is to respond. Finally, if both lamps L1 and L2 are ON simultaneously, only stick figure D is to respond. Thus, stick figure A can send the four distinct messages shown here:

Lamp L1	Lamp L2	Message
OFF	OFF	None
ON	OFF	Stick figure B respond
OFF	ON	Stick figure C respond
ON	ON	Stick figure D respond

Note that this method of information transfer uses a separate dedicated data path in the communication channel for each signal element that makes up the message. This type of communication is known as *parallel transmission*. As more parallel wires are added and the width of the channel increases, more signal elements can be sent in a single message.

Parallel transmission has the advantage that the time required to transmit a complete message is essentially independent of the number of signal elements in the message. Its biggest drawback, however, is that a separate transmitter, data path, and receiver must be provided for each element of the channel. This lamp analogy requires two lamps, two switches, and two separate parallel runs of cable to connect them. In practical circuits, the use of parallel channels is generally limited to short point-to-point data transmission.

Serial Transmission   Assume now that the stick figures find themselves limited to a single data path (for budgetary reasons, perhaps), as shown in Figure 1.3. It should be clear that the simple ON/OFF scheme used in Figure 1.1 is now inadequate for their needs. To solve this problem, stick figure A proposes the following message system:

Lamp Sequence	Message
OFF	None
One Blink	Stick figure B respond
Two Blinks	Stick figure C respond
Three Blinks	Stick figure D respond

By assigning each message a unique series of blinks, the stick figures have created an *encoding* system whereby four distinct messages can be conveyed over an information channel that supports only two distinct states (ON and OFF). This technique also has the useful property that the number of possible messages can be expanded simply by defining additional sequences of blinks. Note that the signal elements making up the message arrive as a series of elements over a span of time. In other words, this communications system employs *serial transmission*.

FIGURE 1.3

Serial transmission

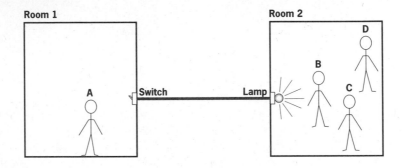

Of course, the stick figures in Figure 1.3 could easily have devised many alternate encoding systems to solve their problem. For example, they might have used blinks of different lengths, alone or in combinations, to represent different states. (Morse code is one example of this type of encoding.) For all practical purposes, the number of possible encoding schemes is infinite. (And left to themselves long enough, the stick figures would inevitably form an overseeing committee to devise and publish communications standards defining the proper blink length, rate, shape, and duration.)

Serial transmission's major advantage is that the number of signal elements in a message can be set independently of the width of the data channel. The trade-off for this flexibility, however, is the time required to send an entire message over the channel, one element at a time. In practical circuits, the flexibility of serial transmission overcomes this disadvantage, making it the preferred system for both short- and long-distance communication.

Parallel-to-Serial Conversion   As mentioned, parallel circuits are typically employed over short distances where a separate signal path can be dedicated to each message element. Serial circuits, on the other hand, are more suited for communication over longer distances. Many communication systems combine the advantages of both transmission methods by including parallel-to-serial and serial-to-parallel converters. This principle is illustrated in Figure 1.4. Here, the stick figures have hired two additional stick figures whose sole job is to convert their messages first from parallel to serial, then from serial back to parallel.

FIGURE 1.4

Parallel to serial to parallel conversion

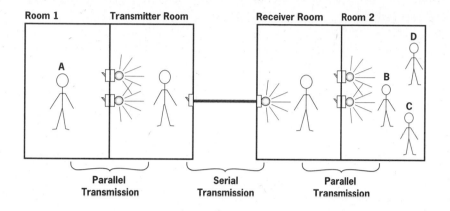

Synchronization

Up to now, all the stick figure examples have sidestepped an important consideration: How does a receiving stick figure know that a message is about to begin or that a message has ended? A one-blink message followed immediately by a two-blink message, for example, might be misinterpreted as a single three-blink message. For a communications system to be useful, it must include an unambiguous method to determine when the start of a message occurs and when to assume that a message has been completed.

In the situation pictured in Figure 1.1, simply extinguishing the lamp is enough to establish that the current message has ended and to prepare the receiver for the next message. But the situation isn't so simple for the stick figures in Figure 1.3. To function predictably, the communication requires some form of *synchronization* (literally, the concurrence of events in respect to time) to keep the sending and receiving ends in step.

Synchronous Transmission A modified version of the serial data transmission system is shown in Figure 1.5. In this case, the stick figures have worked out the following agreement or *protocol*:

- The transmission of a message shall begin exactly at the start of each minute.

- Each message shall consist of six signal elements.

- The individual elements of the message shall be transmitted one per 10-second period (0–10 seconds, 10–20 seconds, …, 50–59 seconds).

- Each signal element shall hold its value for 10 seconds.

- During the time allotted for each signal element, the lamp must assume one of two values: OFF or ON.

- The value of a signal element shall be measured by the receiver at the middle of its active period (5 seconds, 15 seconds, ..., 55 seconds).

FIGURE 1.5

Synchronous transmission

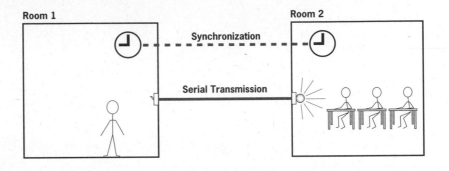

As a result of this agreement, precisely once a minute (8:00, 8:01, and so on), the stick figures in Room 2 know unambiguously that the previous message has terminated and a new message is beginning. During both the transmission and reception of the message, the timing of the signal elements is tied to an independent clock. This type of communication is known as *synchronous*, meaning that the flow of information has a fixed relationship to external (real-world) time.

As shown, however, a serious problem is inherent in this scenario. If the clocks in the two rooms do not display the same time to the precision required by the protocol, the incoming messages will not be interpreted correctly. Even if the two clocks are initialized to the same time by some method, it's reasonable to expect that other factors will eventually put them out of synchronization over a long period of time. Examples of such factors include minor differences in the clock mechanisms, variations in the frequency and voltage of the clock power sources, and so on. Clearly, for synchronous transmission, it is not enough that the clocks be synchronized. They must be periodically resynchronized as well.

The stick figures could implement several systems to keep their clocks synchronized. They might, for example, slave their clocks to each other, or to a common master clock, using a direct connection. This technique would, of course, require a separate communications channel to carry the timing information and would probably be practical only over short distances.

A more general solution might be to develop a protocol whereby the required timing information would be transmitted over the primary communications channel itself. The stick figure in Room 1, for example, might light the lamp continuously for 60 seconds exactly at each hour. The stick figures in Room 2, anticipating this signal, could then use this information to set their clock.

We'll define *synchronous communication*, therefore, as the flow of information through a data channel as directed by the timing signals that keep the transmitter and receiver synchronized to external time. Note that synchronous communication also requires the transmitter and receiver to agree on the protocol by which the data and timing signals are exchanged.

Asynchronous Transmission   As we've seen, the main concerns with synchronous transmission are the need to keep the transmitter and receiver clocks synchronized and the need to periodically transmit synchronizing information over the communications channel. Because these requirements are based on the use of a clock, we can avoid these problems by simply removing the clock, as shown in Figure 1.6. Of course, a receiving stick figure must still be able to unambiguously determine both the start and end of a message.

FIGURE 1.6

Asynchronous transmission

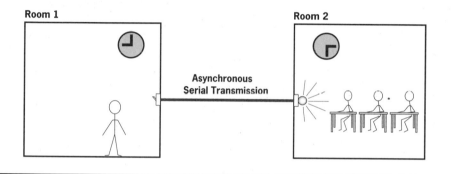

As an alternative to synchronizing the start of their messages to external time, the stick figures agree to develop a protocol in which each message is self-synchronizing. They might modify their previous protocol, for example, to read as follows:

- The start of transmission of a message shall be signaled by a period of 5 seconds during which the light shall be illuminated continuously (ON), followed immediately by a period of 5 seconds during which the lamp shall be extinguished (OFF).

- Each message shall consist of exactly six signal elements.

- The individual elements of the message shall be transmitted one per 10-second period immediately following the message start signal.

- Each signal element shall hold its value for 10 seconds.

- During the time allotted for each signal element, the lamp must assume one of two values: OFF or ON.

- The value of a signal element shall be measured by the receiver at the middle of its period.

Note that synchronization is still an important factor in the reception of the message. Once the message begins, each of the signal elements has a fixed duration and has to be decoded at the proper time. The major difference is that the synchronization must hold only over the period of time occupied by a single message, not an entire string of messages. Each new message that is transmitted resynchronizes the transmitter and receiver. As a consequence of this protocol, the time that can elapse between messages has no upper limit. These self-synchronizing messages remove the restrictions placed on the message by the clock dependency of the synchronous protocol.

In communications terms, this self-synchronizing protocol is called *asynchronous*, meaning that the events (signal elements) making up the message are not coincident with specific moments in external time. (Bear in mind that *asynchronous* is not the same as *unsynchronized*. Unsynchronized data transmission is more aptly termed *garbage*.)

Watching these stick figures evolve their communications standards should help you to acquire an understanding of some problems inherent in information transfer. At this point, we could continue with the stick-figure analogies until we'd covered every aspect of communications theory. It is far better and easier, however, to turn now to the real world and begin to fill in more communications specifics.

Asynchronous Architecture

In the previous discussion, we postulated a simple definition of communication. We then proceeded to illustrate some mechanisms and protocols by which communication might occur in a theoretical environment. In all cases, the use of analogies required that we avoid specifics and limit discussion to an overview of the subject. In the following sections, we'll step decisively into the real world by introducing the terminology and principles that will provide the basis for most of the discussions throughout the remainder of this book.

The study of asynchronous serial communication can often result in a bizarre culture shock for many computer programmers. Having successfully conquered the world of bits and bytes, RAM and ROM, and interrupt service routines, this otherwise knowledgeable group finds itself suddenly thrust into a world that is based on the technology of the 80s—the 1880s, that is. The terminology used to describe the inner workings of serial communication has been appropriated, nearly unchanged, from the earliest communications systems based on the manual telegraph. Much of the terminology and many of the techniques are still in use today, in the telegraph and teleprinter fields as well as in radio communication services.

Channel Description

In its most general form, asynchronous communication can be accomplished using a data path comprising only two wires. In the asynchronous switch and lamp system shown in Figure 1.6, for example, the communication channel was an integral part of the circuit and carried the current required to light the lamp. The communication channels you may be most familiar with also take place over what is essentially a two-wire system: the general switched telephone network (GSTN).

Signal Levels   The goal of even the earliest commercial communication systems was the automatic production of printed characters at the receiving end. As such, the earliest telegraph systems employed a pen-and-paper system that automatically recorded the information being transmitted through the channel. (Literally, the word *telegraph* means "to write at a distance.") The bias of this outlook is reflected in the descriptive terms given to the signals.

Consider the system shown in Figure 1.6. To modify this system to operate like early telegraph systems, for example, you could replace the lamp with a pen. When the signal flowed in the wires, the pen device on the receiving end would be actuated, making a mark on a moving paper. Consequently, when in the ON state, the line is said to be *MARKING*. When the signal was removed, the pen would lift from the paper. This state is known as *SPACING*.

In the same example, we defined the idle state of the transmission line as "lamp OFF." The problem with this convention is that a transmission-line failure (such as a broken wire) isn't immediately obvious. It may be normal, for example, for the system to undergo prolonged periods without transmitting a message. To avoid this problem, an unused transmission line generally idles at MARK. The receiver is then able to flag a prolonged period of SPACE (called a *BREAK*) as an error or a condition requiring attention.

Figure 1.7 shows a representation of information flow during serial communications. In this example, the transmission line is shown idling in the MARK state. Next, the digits of the binary number 0101101b are transmitted. By convention, the MARK state indicates a binary 1 and the SPACE state corresponds to a binary 0.

FIGURE 1.7

Serial data transmission

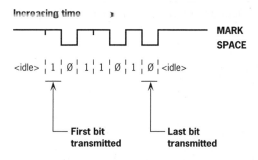

Note that the signal elements representing the binary digits are shown in left-to-right order with respect to increasing time, as might be seen if the transmission line was monitored on an oscilloscope. The first bit transmitted (the least significant bit) appears first (leftmost) on the time axis. Because the least significant bit usually appears in the rightmost position of a number, this convention makes the bits appear as if they're backward in the figure.

Signaling Rate   The terms *baud* and *bit rate* are often used interchangeably; to do so, however, is incorrect. The two terms describe fundamentally different properties of the communication channel as explained here.

The *baud* of a communication channel is an expression of its primary electrical signaling rate. Baud is defined as the number of potential state changes that can occur in the channel per unit of time—regardless of the number of states or their interpretation. As such, baud rate is a physical characteristic of the signal itself and bears no fixed relationship to the data being transmitted by the signal. Each potential change of state is called a *symbol* or *event*, and the baud of a channel is expressed in symbols per second (symbols/sec); 1 baud = 1 symbol/sec.

In contrast, the *bit rate* of a channel is the number of bits of information the channel can carry, expressed in bits per second (bps). The bit rate measures a fundamentally different characteristic in that a single symbol can represent more than one bit.

Consider, for example, a modulation scheme that defines four possible states for a single symbol. Each state is then assigned to one of the four possible combinations of a pair of bits. Using this encoding scheme, a 600-baud channel could carry 2400bps. Similarly, a system that defined 16 symbol states could encode four bits per symbol and achieve a bit rate of 9600bps over the same channel. The baud of a channel is numerically equal to its bit rate only when 1 bit is encoded per symbol.

To avoid confusion throughout this book, I'll use the term *baud* when speaking of the signaling rate of a channel. When describing information transfer, I'll use the term *bit rate*, expressed in bps.

Data Flow   From a communications point of view, the flow of information over a channel has two important characteristics: quantity and direction. So far, all the examples have shown information flow in a single direction only. Such a system, with the capability to transmit information solely in a single direction, is termed a *simplex* system.

In most cases, however, the goal of communications is the exchange of information. A channel capable of carrying information in both directions, but not simultaneously, is called *half-duplex*. The direction of information flow over the channel is reversible, and the reversal is performed by some mutually agreed-upon signal exchanged between the communicating devices. (In half-duplex radio communication, for example, it is customary for the transmitter to say "over" to indicate to the receiver that their roles are about to reverse.) This operation is known as "turning the line around." Because the characteristics of a channel are not affected by the direction of information flow, transmission in both directions has the same signaling rate capability.

A channel capable of carrying information in both directions simultaneously is called *full-duplex*. Full-duplex communication based on a four-wire channel, for example, uses each two-wire pair to carry data in one direction only. To accomplish the same effect with only two wires, the channel is divided, using half of the signaling rate capability to carry information in each direction. Modern systems, using echo cancellation, can use the full signaling rate of the channel simultaneously in both directions.

To be properly termed full-duplex, a system must have the same signaling rate capability in both directions. If different rates are present, the channel is duplex with a one-way primary channel in one direction and a one-way secondary channel in the opposite direction.

For the sake of simplicity, we'll call a channel that is capable of carrying more than two signals simultaneously (regardless of direction) a *multiplex* channel. Most modern communications systems use some form of multiplexing to increase the number of signals that can be carried on their channels. The total signaling rate of the channel, however, remains the same.

Asynchronous Data Format

For the transfer of information to take place, both the transmitter and receiver must agree on the format of the data being exchanged. Asynchronous transmission requires not only the transmission of the characters that compose the message, but also that each character be transmitted with its own synchronization information. The method by which this system generates the required synchronization and why that information is required is explained below.

The Data Bits   The term *character*, used in this context, represents a collection of bits that are transmitted as a single unit. In typical PC information systems, a character may be 5 to 8 bits in length. In a system that uses elementary modulation techniques, each bit of a character is encoded into one symbol, then transmitted over the channel.

Prior to its transmission, a multibit character must be decomposed into a string of individual bits. This process and its complement are known as *serialization*. When the serialized data is transmitted over the channel, the least significant bit is always sent first. The remainder of the bits are then sent in order of increasing significance. On the receiving side, the original character is reconstructed by the complementary operation.

In theory, serializing, transmitting, and reconstructing a character is a straightforward process. In reality, however, the problem of synchronization comes back to haunt us. Figure 1.8 shows a representation of how the signal on a transmission line might appear during the transmission of the 4-bit character 1011b. (A 4-bit character is used here to keep the examples simpler.) By convention, the line is shown idling at the MARK state before the character has been transmitted; it returns to the MARK state when transmission is completed. Time increases as you move from left to right.

FIGURE 1.8

Data on a serial transmission line

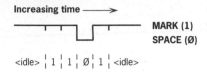

It's easy to identify the individual bits making up the character in the annotated diagram because we know what to look for. It's not so easy, however, for the receiver. The first two bits that are transmitted have the value 1—the same value as the line's idle state. Unless the receiver has some foreknowledge that it should read a bit value at the specific time indicated, it will be unable to distinguish these data bits from the line's idle state. Clearly, some form of synchronization is required.

The START Bit At the beginning of this chapter, we saw that an alternative to synchronizing the start of a message to an external time reference was to make each message self-synchronizing. In Figure 1.8, the message is a single character, so this requirement is easily met by transmitting a synchronization signal, or *START bit*, prior to the transmission of the data bits making up each character.

In Figure 1.9, a START bit has been prepended to two instances of the 4-bit character 1011b. As shown, the START bit is simply an ordinary data bit with a value of SPACE. Its ability to provide synchronization stems from the fact that the use of a START bit requires all valid characters to begin with one bit of SPACE. When a SPACE bit is detected on an otherwise idle line, it indicates that the bits making up a character follow immediately. The receiver simply reads the expected number of bits, then awaits the start of the next character as signaled by the next START bit. The flowchart in Figure 1.10 shows this logic.

FIGURE 1.9

Character synchronization with START bits

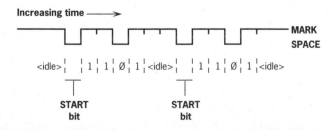

FIGURE 1.10

START bit synchronization logic

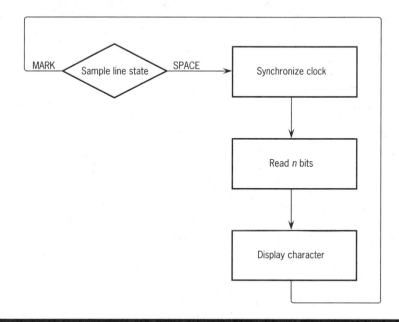

Although the START bit seems to solve the problem of identifying the start of a character, it is neither infallible nor sufficient. The receiving logic synchronizes itself by assuming that any SPACE bit that occurs on an idle line or after the completion of a valid character signals the start of a new character. On a perfect line, this would be true. But if the START bit is corrupted during the transmission process, errors in decoding can occur.

Figure 1.11 shows the transmission of the same 4-bit characters as in Figure 1.9. In this case, however, the second START bit is garbled during transmission and interpreted as MARK instead of SPACE. The receiver mistakenly interprets the garbled START bit and the first two data bits of the second character as a continuation of the idle line state. The third data bit is then misinterpreted as a START bit, whereupon the receiver reads 4 bits from the line and creates an erroneous character.

In Figure 1.11, the line is shown idling after the second character for a period greater than 3 bits. If, instead, additional characters had followed more closely, the single garbled START bit would have caused the misinterpretation to continue indefinitely or until a fortuitous arrangement of bits allowed the receiver to regain synchronization. At no time, however, would the receiver be able to detect that it had interpreted the data incorrectly.

FIGURE 1.11

Data transmission with a garbled START bit

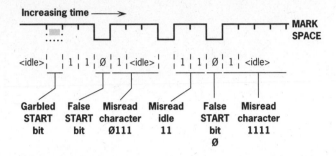

The STOP Bit   As we've seen, the synchronization effect of the START bit can be completely defeated by a single error on the transmission line. Even worse than the error itself is the fact that the error is undetectable by the receiver. To help correct this situation, a STOP synchronization bit (with the MARK value) is transmitted following each character. This combination of START, data, and STOP bits is called a *frame*.

In Figure 1.12, a STOP bit has been appended to two instances of the 4-bit character 1011b. As shown, the STOP bit is simply an ordinary data bit with a value of MARK. Its ability to provide synchronization stems from the fact that the use of a STOP bit requires all valid characters to end with one bit of MARK.

FIGURE 1.12

Transmission with START and STOP bits

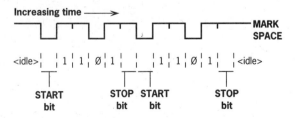

Each time a START bit signals that a character is being transmitted, the receiver reads the bits, but accepts the character as valid only if the STOP bit is sent correctly. If not, the character is discarded or signaled as an error. The flowchart in Figure 1.13 shows this logic. Errors resulting from a bad START or STOP bit are called *framing errors*.

Under the right circumstances, a framing error in START/STOP synchronization may eventually resynchronize itself. The top portion of Figure 1.14 shows a series of 4-bit characters encoded with START and STOP bits as they would be sent by the transmitter. In the bottom portion of the figure, a single error is introduced by garbling the second START bit.

FIGURE 1.13

START bit synchronization logic

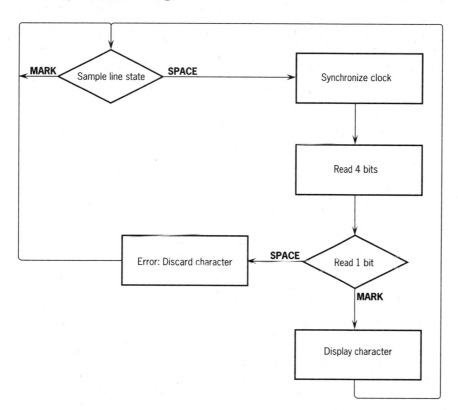

FIGURE 1.14

STOP/START resynchronization after an error

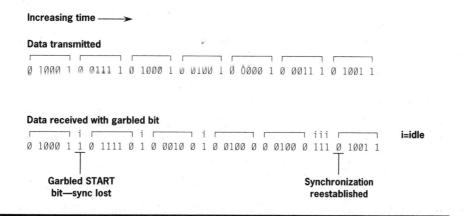

Increasing time ⟶

Data transmitted

Ø 1ØØØ 1 Ø Ø111 1 Ø 1ØØØ 1 Ø Ø1ØØ 1 Ø ØØØØ 1 Ø ØØ11 1 Ø 1ØØ1 1

Data received with garbled bit

      i   i   i   i i i   **i=idle**

Ø 1ØØØ 1 1 Ø 1111 Ø 1 Ø ØØ1Ø Ø 1 Ø Ø1ØØ Ø Ø Ø1ØØ Ø 111 Ø 1ØØ1 1

Garbled START   Synchronization
bit—sync lost   reestablished

Following the algorithm given in Figure 1.13, the first character is interpreted correctly. The garbled bit is then misinterpreted as a period of idle line. The next four "characters" decoded are declared invalid because the STOP bit is not at the MARK level. Finally, the transmitter and receiver reestablish synchronization on the last character.

Although automatic resynchronization is a useful property, you should note that it is not always established as quickly or as easily as shown in this example. In general, data streams composed of long characters with few 1 bits take longer to reestablish synchronization. The data itself also influences if and when resynchronization takes place. The 4-bit characters used in this example were generated randomly and converged quickly. Had a continuous stream of 0000b values been transmitted, for example, the receiver would never have resynchronized. (Communications systems often include specialized hardware to prevent this situation, however.)

The ASCII Character Set

When IBM designed the PC, it chose to imbue the machine with the 7-bit code known as the American Standard Code for Information Interchange (ASCII). The official definition of ASCII is contained in the American National Standards Institute (ANSI) standards document ANSI X3.4-1986 "Coded Character Set— 7-Bit American National Standard Code for Information Interchange." The International Telephone and Telegraph Consultative Committee (CCITT) has a corresponding standard, T.50, titled simply "International Alphabet No. 5."

The ASCII code, shown in Table 1.1, provides 128 character combinations corresponding to the decimal values 0 through 127. (The chart shows the character values in both binary and hexadecimal digits.) Many of the codes in the ASCII alphabet are used for control and communication signals and do not necessarily correspond to printable characters. Expanded definitions of the abbreviations for these characters are given in Table 1.2.

Although the ASCII character set is *based* on a standard, that in itself doesn't imply that there is a *standard* ASCII character set. In fact, the ASCII standard designates many of the character positions as subject to redefinition at the whim of the implementor. (The CCITT specification is even more flexible.)

The IBM PC Character Set

When IBM designed its original PC, it created a character set that, for the most part, was based on the ASCII standard. In addition to the basic ASCII characters, however, IBM defined printable characters for the first 32 control code positions. The ASCII alphabet was then extended to 8 bits, and 128 new characters were defined for the values 128 through 255. This new character set (which is used throughout this book), termed *extended ASCII*, is shown in Table 1.3.

TABLE 1.1

The ASCII Code

	b7 b6 b5 (First Hex Digit)							
b4 b3 b2 b1 (Second Hex Digit)	000b (0h)	001b (1h)	010b (2h)	011b (3h)	100b (4h)	101b (5h)	110b (6h)	111b (7h)
0000b (0h)	000 NUL	016 DLE	032 SP	048 0	064 @	080 P	096 `	112 p
0001b (1h)	001 SOH	017 DC1	033 !	049 1	065 A	081 Q	097 a	113 q
0010b (2h)	002 STX	018 DC2	034 "	050 2	066 B	082 R	098 b	114 r
0011b (3h)	003 ETX	019 DC3	035 #	051 3	067 C	083 S	099 c	115 s
0100b (4h)	004 EOT	020 DC4	036 $	052 4	068 D	084 T	100 d	116 t
0101b (5h)	005 ENQ	021 NAK	037 %	053 5	069 E	085 U	101 e	117 u
0110b (6h)	006 ACK	022 SYN	038 &	054 6	070 F	086 V	102 f	118 v
0111b (7h)	007 BEL	023 ETB	039 '	055 7	071 G	087 W	103 g	119 w
1000b (8h)	008 BS	024 CAN	040 (	056 8	072 H	088 X	104 h	120 x
1001b (9h)	009 HT	025 EM	041)	057 9	073 I	089 Y	105 i	121 y
1010b (Ah)	010 LF	026 SUB	042 *	058 :	074 J	090 Z	106 j	122 z
1011b (Bh)	011 VT	027 ESC	043 +	059 ;	075 K	091 [	107 k	123 {
1100b (Ch)	012 FF	028 FS	044 ,	060 <	076 L	092 \	108 l	124 ¦
1101b (Dh)	013 CR	029 GS	045 -	061 =	077 M	093]	109 m	125 }
1110b (Eh)	014 SO	030 RS	046 .	062 >	078 N	094 ^	110 n	126 ~
1111b (Fh)	015 SI	031 US	047 /	063 ?	079 O	095 _	111 o	127 DEL

TABLE 1.2

ASCII Control Signal Definitions

ASCII value	Signal name	Definition
0	NUL	Null
1	SOH	Start of header
2	STX	Start of text
3	ETX	End of text
4	EOT	End of transmission
5	ENQ	Enquiry
6	ACK	Acknowledgment
7	BEL	Bell
8	BS	Backspace
9	HT	Horizontal tab
10	LF	Line feed
11	VT	Vertical tab
12	FF	Form feed
13	CR	Carriage return
14	SO	Shift out
15	SI	Shift in
16	DLE	Data link escape
17	DC1	Device control 1
18	DC2	Device control 2
19	DC3	Device control 3
20	DC4	Device control 4
21	NAK	Negative acknowledgment
22	SYN	Synchronous idle
23	ETB	End of transmission block
24	CAN	Cancel
25	EM	End of medium
26	SUB	Substitute (character)
27	ESC	Escape
28	FS	File separator
29	GS	Group separator

TABLE 1.2

ASCII Control Signal Definitions (Continued)

ASCII value	Signal name	Definition
30	RS	Record separator
31	US	Unit separator
127	DEL	Delete

TABLE 1.3

The IBM Extended ASCII Character Set

Second Hex Digit

First Hex Digit	0	1	2	3	4	5	6	7	8	9	A	B	C	D	E	F
0		☺	☻	♥	♦	♣	♠	•	▪	○	◙	♂	♀	♪	♫	☼
1	►	◄	↕	‼	¶	§	▬	↨	↑	↓	→	←	∟	↔	▲	▼
2		!	"	#	$	%	&	'	(	)	*	+	,	−	.	/
3	0	1	2	3	4	5	6	7	8	9	:	;	<	=	>	?
4	@	A	B	C	D	E	F	G	H	I	J	K	L	M	N	O
5	P	Q	R	S	T	U	V	W	X	Y	Z	[	\	]	^	_
6	'	a	b	c	d	e	f	g	h	i	j	k	l	m	n	o
7	p	q	r	s	t	u	v	w	x	y	z	{	¦	}	~	⌂
8	Ç	ü	é	â	ä	à	å	ç	ê	ë	è	ï	î	ì	Ä	Å
9	É	æ	Æ	ô	ö	ò	û	ù	ÿ	Ö	Ü	¢	£	¥	₧	ƒ
A	á	í	ó	ú	ñ	Ñ	ª	º	¿	⌐	¬	½	¼	¡	«	»
B	░	▒	▓	│	┤	╡	╢	╖	╕	╣	║	╗	╝	╜	╛	┐
C	└	┴	┬	├	─	┼	╞	╟	╚	╔	╩	╦	╠	═	╬	╧
D	╨	╤	╥	╙	╘	╒	╓	╫	╪	┘	┌	█	▄	▌	▐	▀
E	∝	β	Γ	π	Σ	σ	μ	τ	Φ	Θ	Ω	δ	∞	φ	∈	∩
F	≡	±	≥	≤	⌠	⌡	÷	≈	°	•	·	√	ⁿ	²	■	

$2.$ Errors, Detection, and Correction

ALL DATA TRANSMISSION SYSTEMS ARE SUBJECT TO ERRORS. HOW SERIOUS AN impact the errors have depends on both the type of data and the situation in which the data is generated. The transmission of a simple text message, for example, can often tolerate quite a few errors. In the message "Meet mf fpr luxch at noom," the meaning is easily derived from the context.

Other transmission situations are quite different and require that the data received matches the original data exactly. A single-digit error made while updating your checking-account balance, for example, could prove inconvenient. In cases like these, the data must be examined to ensure that errors do not pass unnoticed. In this chapter, the types and sources of errors are examined, and an overview of the techniques used to detect and correct errors is presented.

Error Origins

All communication channels are subject to errors. Generally speaking, these errors can be categorized according to their source relative to the channel (internal or external) and their type or duration (static or transient). Depending on the source and duration, the effort required to compensate for an error can range from trivial to impossible. Table 2.1 shows some errors that have been categorized according to their type and duration. Bear in mind that many errors fall into more than one category, defying simple classification.

Static internal errors, often called *systemic errors*, are caused by imperfections in the communications system. Examples of systemic errors include transmission-line loss, propagation delay, and distortion—all errors defined by the design of the communications system itself. Because these errors have no time dependency and their effects are easily measurable, compensation for static systemic errors (using repeaters, echo cancelers, frequency equalizers, and so on) is relatively easy to design into a system.

At the opposite end of the spectrum are errors caused by external transient events. The errors caused by these events are unpredictable in both time and magnitude. A lightning strike, for example, can produce radio frequency disturbances or voltage spikes in a power supply, or induce anomalous signals directly into a transmission line. Mechanical contact noise, such as that produced by an electric motor, an engine, or a faulty relay, can completely mask the desired information signal.

TABLE 2.1

Error Types and Sources

Duration	Source Internal	External
Static	Transmission-line loss Propogation delay Distortion Thermal noise	Steady-state noise Atmospheric absorption
Transient	Relay noise Signal reflections Local and far echoes Crosstalk	Impulse noise Electrical glitches Atmospheric disturbances Channel switching by carrier

The analysis and prediction of errors represents an entire department of study within the discipline of information theory. For the purposes of this book, however, it's less important to know the exact source of an error than to know that an error occurred. Consequently, some of the methods used to detect and correct errors during data transmission are discussed briefly in the following sections.

Error Detection

In Chapter 1, the ability of the STOP/START protocol to detect and flag framing errors was demonstrated. In this section, we'll examine situations where the characters are received without framing errors—but without any other guarantee as to their accuracy.

All methods of error detection and correction—regardless of their sophistication or efficacy—rely on redundancy. By sending more information than strictly necessary to specify the data, they incorporate the potential to detect and possibly correct corrupt data. Sending redundant data reduces the bit rate throughput of a system, but can often improve its overall performance by reducing the number of retransmissions required to acquire the data.

Character Parity Check

One of the simplest forms of error detection is the *character parity check*, also known as the vertical redundancy check (VRC). In this system, an extra bit, called the parity bit, is appended to each character to aid in error detection. The value of the parity bit is set to either 0 or 1 depending on the number of 1s in the character and whether ODD or EVEN parity is being implemented.

For example, if the communications system is using EVEN parity, the transmitter chooses the value of the parity bit so that the total number of bits set to 1 in the character/parity combination is even. The character and parity bit are then transmitted. On the other end, the receiver recalculates the parity bit from the character bits and compares it to the received parity. If the calculated parity bit and the received parity bit do not match, an error has been discovered. Similarly, ODD parity requires that the number of bits set to 1, including the parity bit, be odd.

Although convenient to calculate and easy to implement in hardware, the character parity check can hardly be characterized as a robust error-detection method. In Figure 2.1a, a 7-bit character is shown with an EVEN parity bit appended. All 8 bits are then transmitted. When the character is received, the parity bit is recalculated from the 7 data bits and compared with the received parity bit, as shown in Figure 2.1b. If the character and parity have been received correctly, the two parity bits will match. In Figure 2.1c, an error has corrupted one of the bits in the original character (the incorrect character is shown in bold). When the parity is recalculated and compared with the transmitted parity bit, the mismatch indicates the error.

FIGURE 2.1

The character parity check

(a) Character transmitted with EVEN parity bit appended

```
1000001 0
```

(b) Recalculated parity matches received parity

(c) Single-bit error; recalculated parity doesn't match received parity

(d) Double-bit error undetected by parity check

So far, character parity check has performed well. The situation illustrated in Figure 2.1d, however, shows its weakness. In this case, *two* bits of the character have been received incorrectly. Character bit 6 (the leftmost bit) has changed from 1 to 0, and bit 1 has changed from 0 to 1. But because there is still an even number of 1s in the character, the parity check is satisfied and the error is not detected.

The simple parity check is therefore unable to detect all errors that affect an even number of bits. And although it will detect errors that affect an odd number of bits, it gives no indication as to the extent of the corruption. When used in a 7-bit START/STOP asynchronous transmission, a parity bit represents an overhead of 10 percent. Clearly, for the level of error detection provided, the character parity check is a poor choice.

Block Parity Check

The idea of the character parity check can be logically extended to provide error detection for blocks of characters. This method is known as *block parity check* or, equivalently, the longitudinal redundancy check (LRC). Using this scheme, an agreed-upon number of characters, each with its own character parity bit, is treated as a block of data. A parity bit is then calculated across the block for each bit position in a character. These block parity check bits are then appended to the end of the block as if they were a normal character.

Figure 2.2a shows an example of how a block parity check might be implemented. In this example, the agreement between transmitter and receiver is that a block will comprise seven 7-bit characters, each character shall include its own EVEN parity bit, and the data characters will be followed by an EVEN block parity character. Just as the character parity bit establishes the parity across one character, each bit in the block parity character establishes parity for one bit column in the block.

Recall that the character parity check was unable to detect errors involving an even number of bits in a single character. This situation is shown in Figure 2.2b, where the double-bit error in the first character is undetected by the character parity check. The block parity check, however, is able to detect this error. The double-bit error in the first character is converted to two single-bit errors when the parity is calculated for the rightmost two data columns. Because the recalculated block parity character does not match the received block parity character, an error is reported.

Although the block parity check represents an improvement in error detection (with a commensurate increase in overhead), it too suffers from the inability to detect certain errors. Figure 2.2c illustrates the problem. Here, a double-bit error has occurred in both the first and third characters. As expected, the errors are not detected by the character parity checks. But because each of the errors extends across an even number of rows, the block parity check fails to detect them as well.

The block parity check suffers from the same shortcoming as the character parity check: the inability to detect all errors. Although the character parity check is typically implemented automatically by communications hardware, the block parity check is not. Because of this and its overall poor performance, the block parity check is seldom seen in asynchronous communication.

FIGURE 2.2

The block parity check

(a) Data transmitted as block with block parity character appended

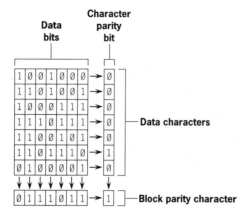

		Data bits						Character parity bit

1	0	0	1	0	0	0	→	0
1	1	0	1	0	0	1	→	0
1	0	0	0	1	1	1	→	0
1	1	1	0	1	1	1	→	0
1	1	0	0	1	0	1	→	0
1	1	0	1	1	1	0	→	1
0	1	0	0	0	0	1	→	0

— Data characters

| 0 | 1 | 1 | 1 | 0 | 1 | 1 | → | 1 | — Block parity character |

(b) Data received with a double-bit error in one character

1	0	0	1	0	**1**	**1**	0	Double-bit error undetected by character parity
1	1	0	1	0	0	1	0
1	0	0	0	1	1	1	0
1	1	1	0	1	1	1	0
1	1	0	0	1	0	1	0
1	1	0	1	1	1	0	1
0	1	0	0	0	0	1	0

| 0 | 1 | 1 | 1 | 0 | **0** | **0** | 1 | Error detected by block parity character |

(c) Data received with a double-bit error in the same column of two characters

1	0	0	1	0	**1**	**1**	0	Double-bit error undetected by character parity
1	1	0	1	0	0	1	0
1	0	0	0	1	**0**	**0**	0	Double-bit error undetected by character parity
1	1	1	0	1	1	1	0
1	1	0	0	1	0	1	0
1	1	0	1	1	1	0	1
0	1	0	0	0	0	1	0

| 0 | 1 | 1 | 1 | 0 | 1 | 1 | 1 | Errors undetected by block parity character |

The Checksum

Although the block parity check is a poor performer, it serves to introduce the concept of block-level error checking. A more common block-level check is the arithmetic *checksum*. Quite simply, the arithmetic checksum is calculated by adding the value of each character in the block to form a single sum. This sum is then appended to the block and transmitted along with the original data.

(Unfortunately, the term *checksum* has become broadened to mean any value calculated for a block of data as part of an error-detection protocol. Unless explicitly noted, however, the term *checksum*, when used in this book, refers exclusively to the simple arithmetic checksum.)

For example, the checksum for seven 7-bit binary characters is calculated as shown here:

```
    1001000
+   1101001
+   1000111
+   1110111
+   1100101
+   1101110
+   0100001
  _____
= 1001100011
```

The number of bits required to hold the resultant checksum varies, depending on the values of the characters being summed. In the preceding example, 10 bits are required to hold the checksum. To append the checksum to the data block, the bits of the checksum must be split between two 7-bit characters and reassembled on the receiving end.

The larger the character size in bits and the more characters in the block, the more bits are required for the maximum possible checksum. The maximum checksum for a block of 256 7-bit characters, for example, would require 17 bits and have to be transmitted as three characters. In many cases, the checksum is forced to fit some predetermined number of bits (usually a multiple of the character size) by discarding the high-order bits.

As with the previously discussed error-detection methods, the checksum has some inherent weaknesses that limit its usefulness. Foremost among these is its insensitivity to an even number of bit errors in a single column. Consider the two checksums shown in Figure 2.3a. Clearly, the data in the two cases is markedly different, yet both cases produce an identical checksum. By extension, the checksum is also insensitive to the order in which the characters appear within the block. An example of this is shown in Figure 2.3b.

FIGURE 2.3

Errors not detected by the checksum

(a) An even number of bit errors in the same column are not detected

```
  1111111        1010101
+ 0000000      + 0101010
= 1111111      = 1111111
```

(b) Transposition of data within the block does not produce an error

```
  0000011        0110000
+ 0001100      + 0001100
  0110000        0000011
= 0111111      = 0111111
```

The Cyclical Redundancy Check

So far, it's been shown that parity bits, parity characters, and the arithmetic checksum are relatively easy error-detection schemes to implement. Unfortunately, their inability to detect common errors severely limits their usefulness. If our toolbox of error-detection techniques were limited to only these, data transmission would be in sorry shape indeed. Fortunately, more effective techniques exist that lend themselves easily to implementation (although not necessarily to explanation). Foremost among these is the *cyclical redundancy check* (CRC).

Compared to the error-detection techniques presented thus far, the CRC is vastly superior. The CRC implementation used in the popular XMODEM-CRC file-transfer protocol, for example, detects all single-bit and double-bit errors, and all errors with an odd number of error bits. Furthermore, it can detect all burst errors 16 bits or fewer in length, 99.9969 percent of burst errors exactly 17 bits in length, and 99.9984 percent of all longer burst errors.

The CRC, like the checksum, is a form of block-level error detection. Instead of being based on the simple addition of character values, however, the CRC is based on a form of division and multiplication of polynomials. In a sense, the CRC is a hashing algorithm. A *hashing algorithm* maps (hashes) the elements of a large set (the data set) onto the elements of a smaller and generally more manageable set (the hash set).

By its nature, the hashing process loses information. A simple analysis shows why: Although each member of the data set maps to one and only one member of the hash set, the reverse is not true. The CRC hashes the large set of all possible binary numbers onto the smaller set of all possible CRC codes. By definition, a 16-bit CRC can represent only 65,536 unique values. Given a set of 65,537 unique data blocks, for example, at least two different blocks must produce the identical CRC. (The upshot of this is that the CRC is very good at detecting changes in data blocks caused by typical errors occurring during serial transmission. When used to detect corruption of disk files by a virus program, however, the CRC is not a complete defense against a savvy programmer.)

A rigorous mathematical explanation of how the CRC works and why it is so effective isn't relevant to this book. (If you're interested, however, several references you may wish to consult are cited in the bibliography.) So after a quick review of some CRC basics, I'll concentrate on their application and implementation.

Polynomial Notation Formally defined, a *polynomial* is a linear combination of products of integral powers of a given set of variables with constant coefficients. As an example, consider how the decimal number 511 can be decomposed into a polynomial, as shown here:

$$511_{10} = 5 * 10^2 + 1 * 10^1 + 1 * 10^0$$
$$= 5z^2 + 1z + 1 \quad \text{(where } z=10\text{)}$$

Note that because 10 was chosen as the value of the polynomial value, the coefficients of the polynomial, taken in order from highest power to lowest power, form the number 511.

There was nothing significant about choosing 10 as the value for the variable z. A number can just as easily be expressed as a polynomial to a different base. To express the decimal number 498 as a polynomial to the base 8, simply change the value of the polynomial variable as shown here:

$$498_{10} = 762_8 = 7 * 8^2 + 6 * 8^1 + 2 * 8^0$$
$$= 7y^2 + 6y + 2 \quad \text{(where } y=8\text{)}$$

Notice again that the coefficients of the polynomial are simply the individual digits 7, 6, and 2 of the original octal number.

CRC calculations are performed in binary. Conceptually, the individual characters in the message block are concatenated to form one large binary number. This result is then expressed as a polynomial combination of powers of two. For example, the binary number 10100101b is shown here expressed as a polynomial to base 2:

$$10100101b = 1*2^7 + 0*2^6 + 1*2^5 + 0*2^4 + 0*2^3 + 1*2^2 + 0*2^1 + 1*2^0$$
$$= 1x^7 + 0x^6 + 1x^5 + 0x^4 + 0x^3 + 1x^2 + 0x^1 + 1x^0 \text{ (where } x=2\text{)}$$

It should come as no surprise that the coefficients of the polynomial form the digits of the original binary number.

It's also obvious that, notationally, this expression is somewhat awkward. Fortunately, by its nature, the coefficients of a binary polynomial must be either 0 or 1. Because the terms with a 0 coefficient contribute nothing, they can be dropped from the expression. All the remaining coefficients must therefore be 1. Simplifying further, these 1s can be omitted, leaving only the variable and exponents. Finally, the term x^0 is reduced to its equivalent, the digit 1. The resulting numerically equivalent (and much more compact) expression for the preceding polynomial is shown here:

$$10100101b = x^7 + x^5 + x^2 + 1 \text{ (where } x=2)$$

Polynomial Operations   Of course, the binary number that was converted to a polynomial in the previous example contained only eight bits. As such, it isn't representative of the polynomials used in typical data communications. A data block comprising 128 8-bit characters, for example, would be represented as a polynomial containing up to 1,024 terms. Similarly, a 1,024-byte block would require 8,192 terms. Clearly, attempting to literally represent these polynomials in the text would not serve to illustrate any point.

In polynomial operations (of which the CRC calculation is a derivative case), the number formed by concatenating the entire data block is called the *data polynomial* (or message polynomial) and is represented by the symbol $D(x)$. The data polynomial is then divided by an agreed-upon polynomial called the *generator polynomial* $G(x)$. This division produces a *quotient polynomial* $Q(x)$ and a *remainder polynomial* $R(x)$.

Looked at another way, $R(x)$ is simply the binary number that, when subtracted from $D(x)$, results in another polynomial that is then evenly divisible by $G(x)$. The result of this division is the quotient $Q(x)$. In general, the quotient is discarded and the remainder term, $R(x)$, is known simply as the CRC. This relationship between the polynomials is shown below:

$$D(x) = Q(x) * G(x) + R(x)$$

Or, equivalently,

$$Q(x) = \frac{D(x) - R(x)}{G(x)}$$

One important property of generator polynomials is that the number of bits in the remainder is directly determined by the number of bits in $G(x)$. To understand why this is so, recall that by definition, the remainder of any division operation must be less than the divisor. Choosing a generator polynomial of n binary bits guarantees a remainder polynomial with no more than $n-1$ binary bits.

In general, the selection of a generator polynomial is driven by two considerations: the size of the desired remainder (as discussed above) and its ability to detect errors. A discussion of the mathematical analysis required to evaluate the effectiveness of one generator polynomial over another is not within the scope of this book. Nor, fortunately, is it strictly necessary. Several generator polynomials have been extensively evaluated, enjoy nearly universal acceptance, and have been endorsed by international standard-setting organizations.

Common CRC Polynomials   One of the most familiar generator polynomials is documented in the CCITT V.41 specification, under the title "Code-Independent Error-Control System." It is the same CRC polynomial used in the XMODEM-CRC and derivative file-transfer protocols. This polynomial produces a 16-bit remainder polynomial and is expressed as

$$x^{16}+x^{12}+x^5+1$$

Throughout this book, this polynomial is called the CCITT-16 generator polynomial. Another name commonly used to refer to this polynomial is CRC-CCITT. Take care, however, not to confuse the CCITT-16 polynomial with another popular 16-bit polynomial called simply *CRC-16*. The latter gained widespread notoriety as part of IBM's binary synchronous communications protocol. It is also specified in an alternative procedure in Annex A to the CCITT V.42 specification "Error Correcting Procedures for DCEs Using Asynchronous-to-Synchronous Conversion." The CRC-16 polynomial is expressed as

$$x^{16}+x^{15}+x^2+1$$

As mentioned, the CRC is a hashing algorithm with a limited number of unique hash values. Increasing the number of unique values can be accomplished simply by increasing the number of bits used for the CRC, and this by the selection of a different generator polynomial. The CCITT-32 generator polynomial produces a 32-bit remainder and is also defined in the CCITT V.42 specification. The 32-bit remainder increases the set of unique hash (CRC) values to over 4 billion. The CCITT-32 polynomial is expressed as

$$x^{32}+x^{26}+x^{23}+x^{22}+x^{16}+x^{12}+x^{11}+x^{10}+x^8+x^7+x^5+x^4+x^2+x+1$$

One final generator polynomial you may run across is the CRC-12 polynomial. CRC-12 is used in situations where fewer bits are available for the CRC or where the higher precision of a longer CRC isn't required. The CRC-12 polynomial is expressed as

$$x^{12}+x^{11}+x^3+1$$

16-bit CRC Calculations   In a theoretical 16-bit CRC calculation, the individual bits of the message are concatenated to form the coefficients of the data polynomial. The high-order bit of the first byte of the data is the coefficient of the high-order term of the data polynomial. The low-order bit of the last byte of the data is the coefficient of the term x^0.

Before division, the data polynomial is multiplied by x^{16}. This has the effect of appending 16 zero bits to the end of the original data polynomial. The data polynomial is then divided by the generator polynomial. Note, however, that ordinary arithmetic division is not used to calculate the CRC. Instead, modulo-two (no carries or borrows) arithmetic is used. In practice, this is implemented using the exclusive-OR (XOR) function. The 16 extra zero bits serve to flush all the message bits through the division operation. The remainder of this division is the desired CRC.

In practice, the CRC algorithm is rewritten so that the trailing zeros aren't required but the CRC produced is the same as would have been produced by the original algorithm. Note also that in hardware and software implementations of CRC calculations (as opposed to traditional polynomial division), it isn't necessary to include the high-order term of the generator polynomial in the operation. The CCITT-16 polynomial, for example, is employed simply as the 16-bit quantity 1021h.

In this section, several different but functionally equivalent implementations of the same CRC calculation are presented. The subroutines shown here have been written to demonstrate how to calculate a CRC, not necessarily how to perform the fastest CRC calculation. Use these routines as a guide to write your own. Remember, regardless of the language in which a CRC algorithm is implemented, its most important quality is speed. A 14.4kbps communications channel may waste a lot of time if it has to wait for an application's slow CRC routine.

Listing 2.1 shows an assembly language implementation of the bitwise CCITT-16 algorithm. Listing 2.2 gives the equivalent C version. The bitwise algorithm implements the longhand version of the CRC operation. Even when fully optimized, execution is slow, but the technique is shown here because it illustrates the CRC algorithm.

LISTING 2.1

Bitwise 16-bit CRC in assembly language

```
;================================================================
; CRC16_BIT
; Folds a byte into a 16-bit CRC one bit at a time.
;----------------------------------------------------------------
; Entry:
;       AL = data byte
;       BX = 16-bit CRC generator polynomial
;       DX = CRC accumulator (Ø for initial call)
; Exit:
;       DX = updated accumulator
;----------------------------------------------------------------
; Changes: AX CX DX
;----------------------------------------------------------------
CRC16_BIT       PROC    NEAR
        ASSUME  CS:CSEG, DS:NOTHING, ES:NOTHING, SS:NOTHING

                MOV     CX,8            ;Number of bits to process
C_1:
                MOV     AH,DH           ;Move CRC to AH and XOR with
                XOR     AH,AL           ; data byte to set SF

                CLC                     ;If CF=Ø, RCL works the same
                RCL     DX,1            ; as SHL, but doesn't change SF

                JNS     C_2             ;If MSB of XOR was 1, SF=1
```

LISTING 2.1

Bitwise 16-bit CRC in assembly language (Continued)

```
                XOR     DX,BX           ;XOR CRC with generator poly
C_2:
                SHL     AL,1            ;Move next data bit to MSB
                LOOP    C_1             ;Repeat for each bit

                RET

CRC16_BIT       ENDP
```

LISTING 2.2

Bitwise 16-bit CRC in C

```c
/*=========================================================
 * int CRC16_Bit(int, char*, int)
 *
 * This function calculates the 16-bit crc of a data block
 * using the bit-method.
 *
 * The first argument is the initial crc value.
 * The second argument is a pointer to the data block.
 * The third argument is the number of bytes in the block.
 * The function returns the 16-bit CRC as an integer.
 *
 * Be sure to define CRC_POLY with a statement such as
 * #define CRC_POLY 0x1021
 =========================================================*/
int CRC16_Bit(crc, msg, msg_len)

int  crc     ; /* starting value for crc, 0 for first call */
char *msg    ; /* pointer to message block */
int  msg_len ; /* number of bytes in block */

{
    int j, data ;

    while(msg_len-- > 0) {

        data = *msg++ << 8 ;  /* Move data to high byte */

        for(j = 0; j < 8; ++j) {  /* check each bit */

            /* if msb of data xor crc is TRUE */
            if( (data ^ crc) & 0x8000)
                crc = (crc << 1) ^ CRC_POLY ;  /* shift and XOR */
            else
                crc = crc << 1 ;  /* else just shift */

            data <<= 1 ;  /* check next bit */
        }
    }
    return (crc & 0xFFFF) ;  /* return low-order 16 bits */
}
```

The operation of the bytewise algorithm is somewhat faster, but less obvious. In this case, the data byte is XORed with the CRC accumulator only once. But the result must still be shifted and possibly XORed with the generator polynomial once for each bit. Listing 2.3 shows this algorithm expressed in assembly language, and the C version is presented in Listing 2.4.

LISTING 2.3

Bytewise 16-bit CRC in assembly language

```
;========================================================================
; CRC16_BYTE
; Folds a byte into a 16-bit CRC one byte at a time.
;------------------------------------------------------------------------
; Entry:
;       AL = data byte
;       BX = 16-bit CRC generator polynomial
;       DX = CRC accumulator (Ø for initial call)
; Exit:
;       DX = updated accumulator
;------------------------------------------------------------------------
; Changes: AX CX DX
;------------------------------------------------------------------------
CRC16_BYTE      PROC    NEAR
        ASSUME  CS:CSEG, DS:NOTHING, ES:NOTHING, SS:NOTHING

                XOR     DH,AL           ;XOR data with hi byte of accum

                MOV     CX,8            ;Number of bits to process
C_1:
                SHL     DX,1            ;Always shift crc accum
                JNC     C_2             ;CY = discarded bit was a 1

                XOR     DX,BX           ;If so, XOR accum with gen poly
C_2:
                LOOP    C_1             ;Repeat for each bit

                RET

CRC16_BYTE      ENDP
```

LISTING 2.4

Bytewise 16 bit CRC in C

```
/*============================================================
 * int CRC16_Byte(int, char*, int)
 *
 * This function calculates the 16-bit crc of a data block
 * using the byte-method.
 *
 * The first argument is the initial crc value.
 * The second argument is a pointer to the data block.
 * The third argument is the number of bytes in the block.
 * The function returns the 16-bit CRC as an integer.
 *
 * Be sure to define CRC_POLY with a statement such as
```

LISTING 2.4

Bytewise 16-bit CRC in C (Continued)

```
* #define CRC_POLY Øx1Ø21
=========================================================*/
int CRC16_Byte(crc, msg, msg_len)

int  crc      ; /* starting value for crc, Ø for first call */
char *msg     ; /* pointer to message block */
int  msg_len ; /* number of bytes in block */


{
    int j ;

    while(msg_len-- > Ø) {

        /* XOR data byte with high byte of accumulator */
        crc = crc ^ (int)*msg++ << 8 ;

        for(j = Ø; j < 8; ++j) /* check each bit */
            if(crc & Øx8ØØØ)    /* if MSB = 1 */
                crc = crc << 1 ^ Øx1Ø21 ; /* shift and XOR */
            else
                crc = crc << 1 ;          /* else just shift */
    }
    return (crc & ØxFFFF) ; /* return low-order 16 bits */
}
```

The principal disadvantage of both the bitwise and bytewise algorithms is the large number of shifts, XORs, and conditional jumps that must be performed for each bit in the message block. By analysis of the CRC algorithm's operation, however, it is possible to separate out the effects of these multiple operations and resolve them to a single value.

Under this method, the high-order eight bits of the accumulator are XORed with the data byte to form an intermediate result that is often called the *combining value*. Next, the CRC of the combining value is calculated and combined with the low-order bits of the accumulator to form the new CRC.

At first, it might not seem that this algorithm represents any improvement. But note that the CRC calculation is performed only on the intermediate value and that there are only 256 possible immediate values. Because of this, the entire CRC calculation can be reduced to a table-driven operation. A table-driven version of the 16-bit CRC calculation is given for assembly language (Listing 2.5) and for C (Listing 2.6). Note that in these examples, a separate subroutine must be called to generate the table before a CRC calculation is performed. Alternately, the table calculation could be avoided by encoding the combining values as data.

LISTING 2.5

Table-driven 16-bit CRC algorithm in assembly language

```
;===================================================================
; GEN_CRC16_TABLE
;
; Generates the table of CRCs of the 256 possible combining values.
; Uses the CRC16_BYTE procedure to generate these CRCs.
;
; Alternately, these values could be encoded as literals.
;-------------------------------------------------------------------
; Entry:
;       BX = generator polynomial
;-------------------------------------------------------------------
; Changes: AX DX SI DI
;-------------------------------------------------------------------
CRC16_TBL       DW      256 DUP (Ø)
CRC16_TBL_END   EQU     $-2

GEN_CRC16_TABLE PROC    NEAR
        ASSUME  CS:CSEG, DS:CSEG, ES:CSEG, SS:CSEG

                MOV     SI,256                  ;Number byte to process
                MOV     DI,OFFSET CRC16_TBL_END ;End of table
                STD                             ;Move backward
GEN_1:
                DEC     SI                      ;Put this value
                MOV     AX,SI                   ; in AL for CRC

                SUB     DX,DX                   ;Clear CRC

                CALL    CRC16_BYTE              ;Get CRC of byte

                MOV     AX,DX                   ;Save in table
                STOSW

                OR      SI,SI
                JNZ     GEN_1

                CLD
                RET

GEN_CRC16_TABLE ENDP


;===================================================================
; CRC16_TABLE
;
; Folds a byte into a 16-bit CRC using the table-lookup method.
; The table must be generated before this procedure is called.
;-------------------------------------------------------------------
; Entry:
;       AL = data byte
;       DX = crc accumulator (Ø for initial call)
;       DS:BX -> CRC table
; Exit:
;       DX = updated accumulator
;-------------------------------------------------------------------
; CHANGES: AX DX DI
;-------------------------------------------------------------------
CRC16_TABLE     PROC    NEAR
```

LISTING 2.5

Table-driven 16-bit CRC algorithm in assembly language (Continued)

```
        ASSUME  CS:CSEG, DS:CSEG, ES:CSEG, SS:CSEG


            SUB     AH,AH                   ;clear ah
            XOR     AL,DH                   ;combining value

            MOV     DI,AX                   ;Make DI into
            ADD     DI,DI                   ; word index

            MOV     DH,DL                   ;SHL DX,8
            SUB     DL,DL

            XOR     DX,[BX][DI]             ;XOR from table

            RET

CRC16_TABLE     ENDP
```

LISTING 2.6

Table-driven 16-bit CRC algorithm in C

```c
int CRC16_TBL[256] ; /* CRCs of combining values */


/*===========================================================
 * void CRC16_Gen_Table(void)
 *
 * This function generates a table of CRCs of the 256
 * possible combining values.
 * Uses the CRC16_Byte function to generate these CRCs.
 * Alternately, these values could be encoded as literals.
 ===========================================================*/
void CRC16_Gen_Table()
{
    int j ;

    for (j=0; j<256 ; j++) {
        CRC16_TBL[j] = CRC16_Byte(0, &(char)j, 1) ;
    }
}


/*===========================================================
 * int CRC16_Table(int, char*, int)
 *
 * This function calculates the 16-bit CRC of a data block
 * using the table-lookup method.
 *
 * The first argument holds the initial crc value.
 * The first argument is a pointer to the data block.
 * The second argument is the number of bytes in the block.
 * The function returns the 16-bit CRC as an integer.
 ===========================================================*/
int CRC16_Table(crc, msg, msg_len)
  int  crc     ; /* starting value for crc, 0 for first call */
  char *msg    ; /* pointer to message block */
  int  msg_len ; /* number of bytes in block */
{
    int cval ;
```

LISTING 2.6

Table-driven 16-bit CRC algorithm in C (Continued)

```
    while(msg_len-- > Ø) {
        /* get combining value */
        cval = ( (crc >> 8) ^ *msg++) & ØxFF ;
        crc = (crc << 8) ^ CRC16_TBL[cval] ; /* new crc */
    }
    return (crc & ØxFFFF) ; /* return low-order 16 bits */
}
```

32-bit CRC Calculations   The calculation of a 32-bit CRC is a simple extension of the 16-bit case and can be performed using the bit, byte, and table-lookup methods. Some implementation differences, however, require an explanation.

The calculation and use of the CCITT-32 CRC in data transmission is described in the CCITT V.42 recommendation. In the following excerpt, the CRC is called the *frame check sequence* (FCS), a fancy term for the CRC check value.

> As a typical implementation at the transmitter, the initial content of the register of the device computing the remainder of the division is preset to all 1s and is then modified by division by the generator polynomial...of the address, control, and information fields; the ones complement of the resulting remainder is transmitted as the FCS.
>
> As a typical implementation at the receiver, the initial content of the register of the device computing the remainder is preset to all 1s. The final remainder, after multiplication by x^{32} and the division (modulo 2) by the generator polynomial ... of the serial incoming protected bits and the FCS, will be "1100 0111 0000 0100 1101 1101 0111 1011" (x^{31} through x^0, respectively) in the absence of transmission errors.

Procedures to implement the 32-bit CRC calculation are given in assembly language (Listing 2.7) and in C (Listing 2.8). Upon examination, however, these examples of 32-bit CRC code may appear to operate "backward" compared to the description above and to the earlier 16-bit examples. The message data, for example, is introduced to the CRC accumulator in the *low* byte rather than in the high byte, and the shift operations are to the right instead of to the left. The CRC accumulator is initialized to all 1s instead of all 0s. Finally, the CCITT-32 generator polynomial, 04C11DB7h, is reversed bitwise and appears as EDB88320h. (Note that the high-order 1 bit in the polynomial is eliminated *before* the bit reversal.)

In a sense, the CCITT-16 CRC calculation is a software emulation of the operation of CRC hardware. In contrast, common implementations of the 32-bit CRC calculation take a more software-oriented approach, lending themselves more easily to programming. Most software, the popular PKZIP archiving program, for example, uses the CRC-32 calculation method shown here. Note that as long as the operations remain consistent with themselves, this reversing of the CRC calculation has no effect on its operation.

LISTING 2.7

Table-driven 32-bit CRC algorithm in assembly language

```
;========================================================================
; GEN_CRC32_TABLE
;
; Generates the table of CRCs of the 256 possible combining values.
; Uses the CRC32_BYTE procedure to generate these CRCs.
;
; Alternately, these values could be encoded as literals.
;------------------------------------------------------------------------
; Entry:
;       EBX = generator polynomial
;------------------------------------------------------------------------
; Changes: EAX EDX ESI DI
;------------------------------------------------------------------------
CRC32_TBL       DD      256 DUP (Ø)
CRC32_TBL_END   EQU     $-4

GEN_CRC32_TABLE PROC    NEAR
        ASSUME  CS:CSEG, DS:CSEG, ES:CSEG, SS:CSEG

                MOV     ESI,256                 ;Number byte to process
                MOV     DI,OFFSET CRC32_TBL_END ;End of table
                STD                             ;Move backward
GEN_1:
                DEC     SI                      ;Put this value
                MOV     EAX,ESI                 ; in AL for CRC

                SUB     EDX,EDX                 ;Clear CRC

                CALL    CRC32_BYTE              ;Get CRC of byte

                MOV     EAX,EDX                 ;Save in table
                STOSD

                OR      SI,SI
                JNZ     GEN_1

                CLD
                RET

GEN_CRC32_TABLE ENDP


;========================================================================
; CRC32_TABLE
;
; Folds a byte into a 16-bit CRC using the table-lookup method.
; The table must be generated before this procedure is called.
;------------------------------------------------------------------------
; Entry:
;       AL = data byte
;       EDX = crc accumulator
;       DS:BX -> CRC table
; Exit:
;       EDX = updated accumulator
;------------------------------------------------------------------------
; CHANGES: AX CX EDX DI
;------------------------------------------------------------------------
```

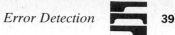

Table-driven 32-bit CRC algorithm in assembly language (Continued)

```
CRC32_TABLE     PROC    NEAR
        ASSUME  CS:CSEG, DS:CSEG, ES:CSEG, SS:CSEG

                SUB     AH,AH                   ;clear ah
                XOR     AL,DL                   ;combining value

                MOV     DI,AX                   ;Make DI
                ADD     DI,DI                   ; into
                ADD     DI,DI                   ; dword index

                MOV     CL,8
                SHR     EDX,CL

                XOR     EDX,[BX][DI]            ;XOR from table

                RET

CRC32_TABLE     ENDP


;=====================================================================
; CRC32_BYTE
;
; Folds a byte into a 32-bit CRC one byte at a time.
;---------------------------------------------------------------------
; Entry:
;       AL = data byte
;       EBX = 32-bit CRC generator polynomial
;       EDX = CRC accumulator
; Exit:
;       EDX = updated accumulator
;---------------------------------------------------------------------
; Changes: AX CX EDX
;---------------------------------------------------------------------
CRC32_BYTE      PROC    NEAR
        ASSUME  CS:CSEG, DS:NOTHING, ES:NOTHING, SS:NOTHING

                XOR     DL,AL           ;XOR data with lo byte of accum

                MOV     CX,8            ;Number of bits to process
C_1:
                CLC
                RCR     EDX,1           ;Always shift crc accum
                JNC     C_2             ;CY = discarded bit was a 1

                XOR     EDX,EBX         ;If so, XOR accum with gen poly
C_2:
                LOOP    C_1             ;Repeat for each bit

                RET

CRC32_BYTE      ENDP
```

LISTING 2.8

Table-driven 32-bit CRC algorithm in C

```c
#define CRC_POLY ØxEDB8832ØL    /* CCITT-32 polynomial */

unsigned long CRC32_TBL[256] ; /* CRCs of combining values */

/*===========================================================
 * void CRC32_Gen_Table(void)
 *
 * This function generates a table of CRCs of the 256
 * possible combining values.
 * Uses the CRC32_Byte function to generate these CRCs.
 * Alternately, these values could be encoded as literals.
 ===========================================================*/
void CRC32_Gen_Table()
{
    int j ;

    for (j=Ø; j<256 ; j++) {
        CRC32_TBL[j] = CRC32_Byte(ØL, &(char)j, 1) ;
    }
}

/*===========================================================
 * unsigned long CRC32_Table(unsigned long, char*, int)
 *
 * This function calculates the 32-bit CRC of a data block
 * using the table-lookup method.
 *
 * The first argument holds the initial crc value
 * The first argument is a pointer to the data block.
 * The second argument is the number of bytes in the block.
 * The function returns the 32-bit CRC as a long.
 ===========================================================*/
unsigned long CRC32_Table(crc, msg, msg_len)
  unsigned long crc ; /* starting value for crc */
  char *msg        ; /* pointer to message block */
  int  msg_len     ; /* number of bytes in block */
{
    int cval ;

    while(msg_len-- > Ø) {
        /* get combining value */
        cval = ( crc ^ *msg++) & ØxFF ;
        crc = (crc >> 8) ^ CRC32_TBL[cval] ; /* new crc */
    }
    return (crc) ;
}

/*===========================================================
 * unsigned long CRC32_Byte (unsigned long, char*, int)
 *
 * This function calculates the 32-bit crc of a data block
 * using the byte-method.
 *
 * The first argument is the initial crc value.
 * The second argument is a pointer to the data block.
 * The third argument is the number of bytes in the block.
 * The function returns the 32-bit CRC as a long.
```

LISTING 2.8

Table-driven 32-bit CRC algorithm in C (Continued)

```
===========================================================*/

unsigned long CRC32_Byte(crc, msg, msg_len)

unsigned long crc ; /* starting value for CRC */
char *msg    ; /* pointer to message block */
int  msg_len ; /* number of bytes in block */
{
    int j ;

    while(msg_len-- > 0) {
        /* XOR data byte with high byte of accumulator */
        crc = (crc ^ *msg++) & 0xFF ;

        for(j = 0; j < 8; ++j) {              /* check each bit */
            if(crc & 1L)                       /* if LSB = 1 */
                crc = (crc >> 1) ^ CRC_POLY ; /* shift and XOR */
            else
                crc = crc >> 1 ;               /* else just shift */
        }
    }
    return (crc) ;
}
```

The calculation of a 32-bit CRC for transmission, therefore, requires the following standard steps:

- Initialize the CRC accumulator to FFFFFFFFh (–1).

- Process each byte of the message through the CRC algorithm.

- Perform a one's complement on the CRC accumulator. This may be done either by the logical NOT operation or by XORing the accumulator with FFFFFFFFh. The resulting value is the frame check sequence (FCS).

- Append the FCS to the message.

The receiver, on the other hand, has several valid alternatives for processing the resulting data and FCS. Processing the data and the FCS as a single string, using the steps shown here, is the simplest approach, as it doesn't require the receiver to distinguish between the data and the FCS.

- Initialize the CRC accumulator to FFFFFFFFh (–1).

- Process each byte of the message through the CRC algorithm.

- Process the four bytes of the FCS through the CRC algorithm. Result should be DEBB20E3h.

Unlike the 16-bit CRC, however, if no errors occurred during transmission, the result will not be 0. Instead, the result will be DEBB20E3h if no errors are detected. This result is a by-product of initializing the CRC accumulator to FFFFFFFFh instead of 0 and of the one's complement operation performed on the original CRC to produce the FCS. (Note that this result is simply a bit-reversed version of the no-error result described in the previous CCITT excerpt.)

It may be programmatically desirable to have the receiving algorithm produce a 0 result if no errors are detected. This can be accomplished using the steps shown here:

- Initialize the CRC accumulator to FFFFFFFFh (–1).

- Process each byte of the message through the CRC algorithm.

- Perform a one's complement on the CRC accumulator.

- Process the four bytes of the FCS through the CRC algorithm. Result should be 0.

Note that the value produced in the CRC accumulator in the third step above is simply the FCS itself. Rather than run the received FCS through the CRC algorithm, it may be simpler just to compare it to the calculated FCS. If the two values are equal, no error has been detected.

Error Correction

Three phrases often encountered when discussing error-handling protocols are error detection, error control, and error correction. Don't fall into the trap of employing these terms interchangeably, as is often done in many computer publications. The three terms are distinct in meaning as well as in operation.

Error detection usually refers to a check on the integrity of the transmitted data. Examples include parity, checksums, and the CRC. These codes may vary in their effectiveness at detecting errors, but detecting an error is the limit of their ability. A good error-detection scheme tells you, for example, that the data you have received is corrupt.

The term *error control* is usually applied to a protocol, an agreement between the transmitter and the receiver. To control errors, an error-control protocol must naturally include some form of error detection. Once it has detected that the received data is corrupt, however, the protocol is able to initiate some action—requesting retransmission, for example—to ensure that a correct copy of the data is eventually received. Error control is damage control, not damage prevention.

In the XMODEM protocol, for example, the receiver must examine the data for errors. If no errors are detected, the receiver sends the transmitter a message indicating that the data has been received intact. If an error is detected, however, the receiver asks the transmitter to resend the corrupt data. Assuming that the error was caused by a transitory problem, this protocol eventually results in an error-free transfer.

The final term, *error correction*, describes a form of data encoding that not only detects errors, but also allows the receiver to correct the errors without data retransmission. This process, known as *forward error correction* (FEC), is typically employed in situations where retransmission of data is impossible or inconvenient and the integrity of the data must be protected.

All error-correcting codes (ECCs) rely on redundant coding—using more than the minimum number of bits required to encode the information. Because these redundant bits convey no new information, they simply lower the effective throughput of a system when included in an error-free transmission. In a situation where errors occur, however, the redundant bits are used to *correct* the errors.

Three popular error-correcting codes are the Hamming, Reed-Solomon, and Bose-Chaudhuri-Hocquenghem codes. The study of ECCs could easily fill several volumes. In the following section, I'll present an example using the Hamming code. If you desire more information about ECCs, a few references in the bibliography will get you started.

The Hamming Code

The Hamming code is an error-correcting code described by R. W. Hamming in *The Bell System Technical Journal* (April 1950). The Hamming code is capable of detecting and correcting all single-bit errors in a character. It is most effective when dealing with small character sizes—4 to 8 bits, for example. As character sizes grow larger, the chances of incurring a multiple-bit error, against which the Hamming code is powerless, increase.

Assume, for example, a character size of 4 bits where the character is represented as the digits *abcd*. Three additional bits are then defined as follows:

$$e = a + b + c$$
$$f = a + b + d$$
$$g = a + c + d$$

where the operations are performed modulo 2 and produce a single binary digit as a result. The three new bits are then appended to the original four bits and the resulting 7-bit character is transmitted as *abcdefg*.

At the receiver, bits e, f, and g are recalculated from the received character bits *abcd* and compared to the received values for bits e, f, and g. If all three bits match, the data is presumed to have been received intact. If the values do not match, however, the information in Table 2.2 is used to determine which bit is in error. The bit value is then complemented to correct the data.

Examining the chart, it's easy to determine the number of data bits that can be protected by a given number of Hamming bits. Using n Hamming bits allows 2^n possible unique combinations to be generated. One combination of bits must always be reserved for the no-error condition. One combination must also be reserved to indicate an error in each of the Hamming bits themselves. The remaining bits are then available to indicate errors in the data bits. This relationship can be expressed by the following formula:

$$m = 2^n - n - 1$$

where n is the number of Hamming bits used and m is the number of data bits that can be protected.

TABLE 2.2

3-bit Hamming Code Interpretation

e	f	g	Bit in Error
			All bits okay
		X	g
	X		f
	X	X	d
X			e
X		X	c
X	X		b
X	X	X	a

x = bit did not match

3 THE UART

IN CHAPTER 1, WE SAW THAT SERIAL COMMUNICATIONS IS SIMPLY THE CONVERsion of data to some form of signal, the movement of that signal through a channel, and the signal's subsequent reconversion to data. Although cumbersome, a processor can perform the serial I/O required for serial communications by using instruction loops to determine timing and by toggling I/O port bits on and off to change output levels as required. Indeed, some specialized communication interfaces (programs designed to send and receive morse code, for example) are still implemented in this fashion.

A high-level programming language is designed to conceal the details of manipulating the underlying microprocessor. Not surprisingly, this concept of a high-level interface has also been applied to serial communications. The result is a specialized microchip that collects the details of managing serial I/O communications into a single package known as a Universal Asynchronous Receiver/Transmitter (UART).

The UART is often depicted as mysterious and difficult to program, but this isn't the case. In perspective, a UART is simply a separate microprocessor with its own (extremely simple) instruction set. Once you've learned the underlying concepts of serial communications, you'll have no difficulty programming the UART.

This chapter will present an overview of the internal architecture of the UARTs commonly found in IBM-PC standard personal computers. I'll begin with a hardware level examination of the structure of a UART, and then explain the theory of operation of some of its subunits and internal structures. Next, a discussion of the register set available for each UART is presented. Finally, a short utility to identify the type of UART installed in a system is presented.

UART Operation

The UART is a complex array of logic and timing circuits that automates the execution of serial communications. The exact operation of the UART in any particular situation is controlled by externally supplied parameters. In general terms, however, the operation of the UART during transmit and receive operations can be outlined as described here.

When transmitting a character, the UART must perform the following tasks:

- Accept a character (as parallel data) from the PC
- Convert the character to a series of bits (serialization)
- Form a frame by adding START, STOP, and parity bits as required
- Transmit the bits of the frame to the interface at the required signalling rate (baud)
- Indicate that it is ready to accept the next character

When acting as a receiver, the UART must perform the complementary tasks described here:

- Receive the serial data from the interface
- Verify that the frame has a valid structure: START, data, parity, and STOP bits; if not, report a framing error
- Verify that the parity, if any, is correct; if not, report a parity error
- Convert the data bits to a character
- Make the character available (as parallel data) to the PC
- Indicate that a received character is available

The 8450 and 16450 UARTs

The original IBM-PC system board contained no specialized circuitry for implementing serial communications. Instead, all support was provided on a separate adapter card called the IBM Asynchronous Communications Adapter. The major component on this adapter was the National Semiconductor INS8250, a single-chip UART fabricated using large scale integration (LSI) circuit techniques.

Since its introduction, the INS8250 has undergone several revisions. The current version is the INS8250-B. In recent years, National has changed the chip's designation; the INS8250-B is now called the PC8250C. For the most part, all revisions of the 8250 perform identically. Some early versions of the INS8250, however, although performing within documented specifications, fail when programmed to operate at signalling rates in excess of 38,400 baud. These early chips are typically found in older PCs and on older asynchronous expansion cards. If the 8250 is installed in a socket, replacing the chip with a newer version will fix any speed problems.

The PC16450C (previously designated the NS16450) is functionally equivalent to the NS16450 and INS8250A components. The PC16450C has improved timing specifications and is fabricated using CMOS technology—facts of interest solely to hardware designers. Because these two UARTs are virtually identical from a programmer's point of view, I'll refer to all National Semiconductor

8250 and 16450 UARTs, equivalent UARTs made by other manufacturers, and devices that emulate these UARTs simply as 8250s.

Features and Capabilities

By design, the 8250 lends itself easily to interfacing between the PC's address/ data bus and a modem or other external device. And the 8250's high level of integration allows a complete serial communications adapter to be constructed using a minimal number of external parts. This section will examine only the UART, however. Chapter 4 provides a discussion of PC-specific implementation.

In operation, the 8250 removes much of the burden of performing serial communications from the processor. Framing bits, for example, are added, checked, and removed automatically by the UART. Similarly, parity bits are generated automatically during transmission and checked on receive. Any parity errors are detected and reported to the processor. The 8250 provides separate indicators for the state of transmit and receive operations as well as reporting the line and data set (modem) status. These indicators can be read by the processor and can also be programmed to generate interrupts. Built-in hold and shift registers for both transmit and receive operations also eliminate the need for precise synchronization between the processor and the serial data.

The 8250 includes a programmable baud generator that divides an external timing reference (8 MHz, maximum) by a divisor from 1 to 65535. The resulting signal provides a 16x clock to drive the internal transmitter logic. The same 16x clock can optionally be used as the input for the independent receiver clock, ensuring that adequate sampling of the incoming signal takes place.

To facilitate hardware design and provide a consistent programming interface, the 8250 includes modem-control signal handling logic that is tied into its interrupt system. The 8250 monitors modem-control signals and can be programmed to report changes using interrupts. The chip's built-in self-test capability includes loop testing to diagnose the communications link and simulation of break, parity, overrun, and framing errors.

Block Diagram

Internally, the 8250 can be visualized as a collection of timing circuits, control and selection logic, and 11 accessible registers. Taken together, these subunits form an interface between the internal logic of the PC and the external world of serial communications. This idea of a physical interface is carried into the 8250. The subunits can be represented as two separate areas joined by a common data bus over which information is exchanged. This functional division is illustrated in Figure 3.1 as a simplified block diagram of the internal structure of the 8250 UART. This diagram shows the relationships between subunits and some of the signals that typically pass back and forth.

FIGURE 3.1

8250/16450 UART block diagram

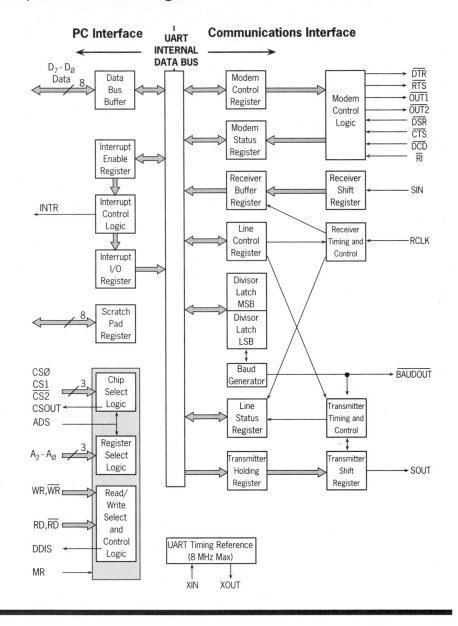

Register Descriptions

All 8250 UART operations, including transmission and reception of data, are controlled through its registers. By reading from and writing to these registers, the programmer can exert complete control over the operation of the 8250 and, consequently, over the resulting serial communications.

All registers in the 8250 are 8 bits wide. In some cases, however, not all 8 bits may contain significant data. Unless otherwise indicated, undefined bits may assume any value and should be masked off. The definition of some registers is different, depending on whether the register is being read or written. Programmers should be aware that reading and writing registers can also produce side effects, such as the resetting of error flags. These definitions and side effects are noted in the register descriptions that follow. Appendix E contains a summary of all UART registers.

The 8250 produces some signals as complementary outputs. In other words, a logic 1 produces a level 0 output and vice versa. For consistency with UART technical documentation and other references, the actual output signals will be shown and discussed. Bear in mind, however, that in a standard serial port implementation, these signals are inverted by subsequent circuitry, producing outputs that correspond directly to the programmed logic levels. In general, the programmer need never consider the complementary sense of the UART signals.

Transmitter Holding Register (THR)   The process of serial data transmission is initiated when the processor writes a byte of data to the Transmitter Holding Register (THR) of the 8250. Upon completion of the write operation, the 8250 immediately transfers the byte of data directly to its internal Transmitter Shift Register (TSR). There, the byte is serialized, parity and framing bits are added as required, and the resulting bit stream is conveyed to the UART's serial output (SOUT) terminal.

The THR, also known as the Transmitter Buffer Register (TBR), is accessed through UART register 0. The THR is configured as a write-only register. The practical consequence of this is simply that a byte written to the THR is not subsequently readable. If it is necessary to preserve the value of the byte that is written, it must be saved elsewhere by the processor.

The format of the THR is shown in Figure 3.2. The least significant bit of the character to be transmitted is written to bit 0, the least significant bit of the register. Note that, for historical reasons, the least significant bit of the character is the *first* bit to be transmitted over the serial line. The receiving UART understands this, so this convention is transparent to the programmer.

Receiver Buffer Register (RBR)   Serial data received at the 8250's serial in (SIN) terminal is stripped of framing and parity bits, and the data bits are passed to the Receiver Shift Register (RSR). The required number of data bits are then assembled into a character in the RSR. The completed character is next transferred to the Receiver Buffer Register (RBR) where it may be subsequently read by the processor. Note that the number of bits required to form a character are assembled by the RSR even if the transmission contained framing or parity errors.

FIGURE 3.2

The Transmitter Holding Register (THR) and Receiver Buffer Register (RBR)

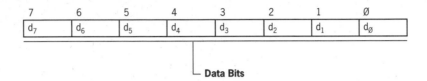

Data bit d_0 is the first bit transmitted and the first bit received.

The 8250 supports character lengths from 5 to 8 bits. When writing a character with fewer than 8 bits to the RBR, the 8250 writes the character into the least significant portion of the 8-bit register. The values of the unused bits are undefined and should be masked off by the processor before using the received value.

The RBR is accessed through UART register 0, the same address as the THR. The RBR, however, is defined as a read-only register. Although they use the same UART register address, the THR and RBR are distinct data spaces. For example, writing a character to the THR while an unread received character is pending in the RBR will not affect the received character. The THR is also used in combination with the Divisor Latch Register (described later in this section) to set the baud of the 8250.

The format of the RBR is shown in Figure 3.2. The data is received from the serial line least significant bit first. The 8250 recognizes this convention and reconstructs the data so that the least significant bit of the character appears in bit 0 of the RBR.

Line Control Register (LCR)   The Line Control Register (LCR) is divided into seven fields. The asynchronous data format used for both receive and transmit operations is selected by the value written to this register. In combination with the Divisor Latch Register (described later in this section), the LCR is also used to set the baud of the 8250.

The LCR is accessed through UART register 3 and may be read or written. Figure 3.3 shows the format of the LCR. Each of the register's fields is explained in the paragraphs that follow.

FIGURE 3.3

The Line Control Register (LCR)

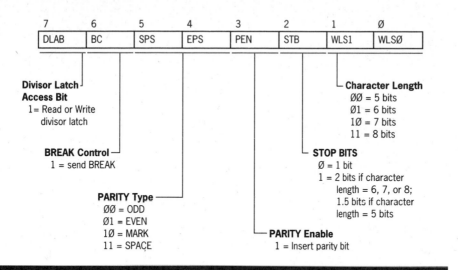

Bits 1-0: Character Length. The contents of this 2-bit field defines the number of data bits that will be considered a single character. The specified number of data bits are then transmitted or received in a single asynchronous frame. Setting this field determines the character length for both transmit and receive operations. Supported character lengths range from 5 to 8 bits and are specified by setting the value of the two bits in this field, as shown here:

Bit 1	Bit 0	Character Length
0	0	5 bits
0	1	6 bits
1	0	7 bits
1	1	8 bits

The data sheet for the 8250 uses the terms *character* and *word* interchangeably when referring to the group of data bits that are transmitted or received by the UART. (This use of these terms has nothing in common with their processor-based definitions of an 8-bit character and a 16-bit word data type.) Because of this, some UART documentation refers to bits 0 and 1 of the LCR as Word Length Select Bit 0 and 1 (WLS0 and WLS1).

Regardless of the character size selected, data is transferred from the processor's data bus to the 8250 8 bits at a time. When characters smaller than 8 bits are selected, the character bits occupy the low-order bits of the byte; the values of the unused bits are ignored during transmitting and undefined during receiving.

Bit 2: Number of STOP Bits (STB). This field specifies the number of STOP bits appended to each frame during transmit. Setting this bit to 0 appends 1 STOP bit to each transmitted character. Setting this field to 1 appends 2 STOP bits to characters with lengths of 6, 7, and 8 bits. If a character length of 5 bits has been selected, setting this field to 1 generates 1.5 STOP bits. (If the concept of half a STOP bit seems strange, recall that a STOP bit isn't really a "bit" at all. Instead, it's simply a period of time during which the communication channel is held at the MARK state. Transmitting 1.5 STOP bits, therefore, simply means holding the channel in the MARK state for 150 percent of the time period occupied by one symbol.)

Note that during receive operations, the 8250 checks only the first STOP bit, regardless of the setting of this field. This action is described incorrectly in some technical reference documentation.

Bits 5-3: Parity. The contents of this field determines whether a parity bit will be generated during transmit operations and checked during receive operations. (If present, a parity bit will appear between the last data bit and the first STOP bit.) Individually, bit 3 is called Parity Enable (PEN), bit 4 is called Even Parity Select (EPS), and bit 5 is called Stick Parity Select (SPS). Together, the settings of these bits specify the rules for parity generation and checking, as shown in Table 3.1.

TABLE 3.1

Parity Selection

Bit 5 (SPS)	Bit 4 (EPS)	Bit 3 (PEN)	Parity
x	x	0	NONE: No parity bit is transmitted or checked
0	0	1	ODD: Taken together, the character bits and parity bit contain an odd number of 1s
0	1	1	EVEN: Taken together, the character bits and parity bit contain an even number of 1s
1	0	1	MARK: The parity bit always has the logical value 1 (MARK)
1	1	1	SPACE: The parity bit always has the logical value 0 (SPACE)

x = any value

The Parity Enable bit is the master on/off switch for parity generation and checking. When bit 3 = 0, parity use is disabled, regardless of the settings of bits 4 and 5. When PEN = 1, the type of parity used is selected by the combination of bits 4 and 5.

When PEN = 1 and Stick Parity Select = 0, either ODD or EVEN parity will be generated, as determined by the setting of the Even Parity Select bit. When EPS = 1 (EVEN parity), the value of the parity bit is chosen such that the character bits and the parity bit, taken together, contain an even number of 1s. Similarly, if EPS = 0 (ODD parity), the value of the parity bit is chosen such that the character bits and the parity bit, taken together, contain an odd number of 1s. For example, if the character 1011011b were transmitted using EVEN parity, the parity bit would have the value 1.

When the Stick Parity bit (bit 5) is set to 1, the type of parity selected by bit 4 is changed. In this case, setting bit 4 = 0 selects MARK parity, meaning that the parity bit is always generated and checked as a logical 1 (MARK). Setting bit 4 = 1, on the other hand, causes the parity bit to be generated and checked as a logical 0 (SPACE). This is called SPACE parity. Because the value of the stick parity bit has no dependence on the data bits in the character, it cannot indicate an error, except in the value of the parity bit itself.

When generating MARK and SPACE parity, the value of the parity bit simply remains at the selected value. For this reason, I find it more evocative to refer to this type of parity as *sticky* parity. In fact, stick parity is referred to as *stuck* parity in the Serial/Parallel Adapter portion of the IBM Technical Reference Options and Adapters manual—an example of a more descriptive, albeit unofficial term.

There are some arcane uses for stick parity. Assume, for example, that you want to ensure that only ASCII characters with values 0 to 127 are transmitted to a system that is using 8-bit characters and no parity. You could, of course, mask each byte with 7Fh before transmitting it—but there is an easier way. Simply program the transmitting UART to use a 7-bit characters and SPACE parity. The high-order bit of each byte will then be forced to a logic 0.

Bit 6: BREAK Control (BC). The setting of this bit directly controls the signal output by the 8250 and is used to generate a BREAK signal. When bit 6 is set to 1, the serial output signal (SOUT) is forced to the SPACE state and remains there, regardless of other transmitter activity. SOUT remains at this state until a 0 is written to the BC bit. The BREAK signal is usually used to get the attention of the connected terminal or system.

Bit 7: Divisor Latch Access Bit (DLAB). The Divisor Latch Access Bit must be cleared to 0 to access the RBR, THR, and IER. Setting DLAB = 1, however, remaps these registers to allow access to the divisor latch. The most significant and least significant byte of the baud divisor may be accessed through UART registers 1 and 0, respectively. The operation of setting the baud divisor is discussed later in this section.

Line Status Register (LSR) The Line Status Register (LSR) is divided into six fields that indicate the status of the data transfer operation. The processor can check the values of these fields by reading the LSR and examining the bits individually. Note that the act of reading this register automatically clears the values of some fields. It is the responsibility of the programmer to preserve the LSR value when it is read.

The LSR is accessed through UART register 5 and is typically treated as a read-only register. Although write operations were not restricted by the original INS8250, writing to the LSR causes problems with some chips from other manufacturers. Before receiving serial data, for example, an extraneous character in the Receiver Buffer register should be purged. This should be done by reading the character from the RBR (clearing the Data Ready bit automatically), not by writing a 0 to the Data Ready bit directly.

Figure 3.4 shows the format of the LSR. Bit 7 of the LSR is permanently set to 0. Each of the register's remaining fields is explained in the paragraphs that follow.

FIGURE 3.4

The Line Status Register (LSR)

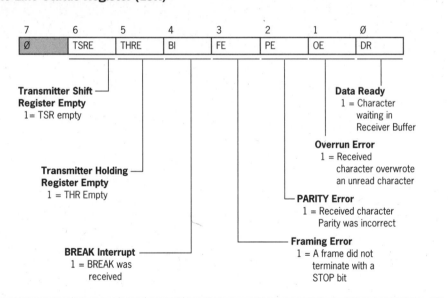

Bit 0: Data Ready (DR). When a complete incoming character has been received by the 8250 and transferred to the Receiver Buffer Register, the Data Ready bit is set to 1. It is not necessary (although it is permissible) to clear this bit manually; reading the character from the RBR automatically clears DR to 0.

Bit 1: Overrun Error (OE). The receiver logic in the 8250 operates continuously. If a character is received, assembled in the RSR, and transferred to the RBR before the previous character has been read by the processor, the previous character is irretrievably destroyed. This condition is called a *receiver overrun error* and, when it is detected, the 8250 sets the Overrun Error bit of the LSR to 1. The OE bit is automatically cleared to 0 when the processor reads the

LSR. Note that no information is available regarding the number of characters that have overrun since the last time the LSR was read.

Bit 2: Parity Error (PE). When a character is received, the parity bit is recalculated according to the parameters set in the LCR. If the parity bit received with the character does not match the recalculated parity bit, the Parity Error bit is set to 1. If a parity error occurs, the PE bit stays set to 1, even if subsequent characters with correct parity are received. The PE bit is cleared to 0 only when the processor reads the LSR.

Note that the documentation provided with the 8250 as well as other technical documentation implies that the PE bit reports parity errors for ODD and EVEN parity only. This is incorrect. Parity errors are detected and reported when ODD, EVEN, MARK, and SPACE parity checking is enabled.

Bit 3: Framing Error (FE). A frame is considered invalid if it does not terminate with at least 1 STOP bit. If the bit following the last data or parity bit is not a STOP bit (that is, is not at the MARK level), the 8250 reports a framing error and sets the Framing Error bit of the LSR to 1. The received character is still transferred to the RBR. The FE bit is automatically cleared to 0 when the processor reads the LSR.

If a framing error occurs, the 8250 automatically attempts to resynchronize by assuming that the incorrect STOP bit was, in fact, the START bit for the next character. A new character is then constructed beginning with this new START bit.

Bit 4: BREAK Interrupt (BI). The 8250 sets this bit to 1 whenever a BREAK condition occurs on its serial data input (SIN) terminal. To initiate a BREAK condition, SIN must be held in the SPACE state for a period of time that exceeds the length of a single frame. (A frame consists of START, data, parity, and STOP bits.) To terminate a break condition, the SIN input must remain at the MARK state for a period of time not less than one-half of one bit length.

Note that if a BREAK occurs, and the BREAK condition on the SIN input is subsequently removed, the BREAK Interrupt bit remains set. The BI bit is cleared to 0 when the processor reads the LSR.

Bit 5: Transmitter Holding Register Empty (THRE). The Transmitter Holding Register Empty bit is set to 1 when the 8250 transfers a character from the THR into the TSR, indicating that the THR is ready to accept the next character to be transmitted. (See the preceding discussion of the THR.) Writing a new character to the THR when this bit is 0 overwrites the untransmitted character presently in the THR, and the original character is lost. This condition is called a *transmitter overrun error,* but is neither detected nor reported by the 8250.

The THRE bit is cleared to 0 when the processor writes a character to the THR. Writing to this bit has no effect on its value. Note that the setting of this bit reflects only the status of the THR. An empty THR does not imply that the TSR is empty or that serial transmission has stopped. See the following description of the TSRE bit.

Bit 6: Transmitter Shift Register Empty (TSRE). When the character in the TSR has been transmitted and no new character is ready to be transferred from the THR, the 8250 sets the Transmitter Shift Register Empty bit to 1. Subsequently, when the 8250 transfers a character from the THR to the TSR, the TSRE bit is cleared to 0. Writing to this bit has no effect on its value.

Some documentation labels this bit as the Transmitter Empty (TEMT) bit, emphasizing the idea that both the THR and TSR must be empty before this bit is set. Serial transmission should not be considered complete until both the THRE and TSRE bits are set to 1.

Modem Control Register (MCR) The Modem Control Register (MCR) controls the output signals sent from the 8250 to a modem (data set) or to a device emulating a modem. The MCR is a read/write register, accessed through UART register 4, and is divided into five fields. Figure 3.5 shows the format of the MCR. Bits 7, 6, and 5 are tied permanently to logical 0. Each of the register's remaining fields is explained the paragraphs that follow.

FIGURE 3.5

The Modem Control Register (MCR)

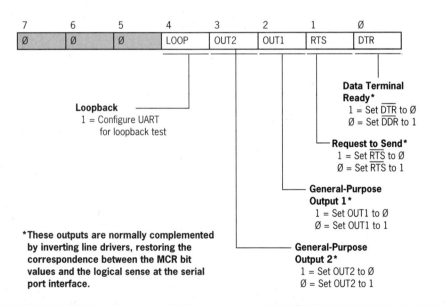

*These outputs are normally complemented by inverting line drivers, restoring the correspondence between the MCR bit values and the logical sense at the serial port interface.

Note that the modem-control signals generated by the 8250 are complements of their EIA RS-232 counterparts—that is, their physical output is inverted from their logical sense. This situation is indicated in the text by a line over the signal name. The complemented signals from the UART are normally applied to an external device through inverting line drivers. This inversion restores the correspondence between the bit value and the logic value of the output. Chapter 4 discusses this situation and explains the application of these control signals.

Bit 0: Data Terminal Ready (DTR). The Data Terminal Ready signal is sent from the 8250 to a connected device. The value written to this field directly controls the output at the 8250's $\overline{\text{DTR}}$ signal output. Setting DTR = 1 forces the $\overline{\text{DTR}}$ output to 0. Similarly, writing a 0 to this field forces the $\overline{\text{DTR}}$ output to 1.

Bit 1: Request To Send (RTS). The Request To Send signal is sent from the 8250 to a connected device. Writing a 0 to this field forces the $\overline{\text{RTS}}$ output to 1. Setting RTS = 1 forces the $\overline{\text{RTS}}$ output to 0.

Bit 2: General-Purpose Output 1 (OUT1). The OUT1 signal is a general-purpose output the use of which is dependent on hardware implementation. Writing a 0 to this field forces the $\overline{\text{OUT1}}$ output to 1. Similarly, setting this field to 1 forces the $\overline{\text{OUT1}}$ output to 0.

Bit 3: General-Purpose Output 2 (OUT2). The Output 2 (OUT2) signal is a general-purpose output the use of which is dependent on hardware implementation. Clearing OUT2 to 0 forces the $\overline{\text{OUT2}}$ output to 1. Similarly, setting this field to 1 forces the $\overline{\text{OUT2}}$ output to 0. On the IBM-PC Asynchronous Communications Adapter, proper programming of OUT2 is required to use interrupt-driven I/O. Details of this implementation are discussed in Chapter 4.

Bit 4: Loopback (LOOP). The Loopback (LOOP) bit activates local loopback, one of the 8250's built-in self-test capabilities. When bit 4 is set to 1, the following changes occur in the operation of the 8250:

- The serial data input (SIN) of the 8250 is disconnected from its normal external connection and connected internally to the serial output (SOUT).

- The output of the Transmitter Shift Register is connected to the input of the Receiver Shift Register.

- The upper 4 bits of the MSR are disconnected from their external connections and connected internally to the lower 4 bits of the MCR as follows:

Modem Control Register	Modem Status Register
$\overline{\text{DCD}}$ (bit 7)	$\overline{\text{OUT2}}$ (bit 3)
$\overline{\text{RI}}$ (bit 6)	$\overline{\text{OUT1}}$ (bit 2)
$\overline{\text{DSR}}$ (bit 5)	$\overline{\text{DTR}}$ (bit 0)
$\overline{\text{CTS}}$ (bit 4)	$\overline{\text{RTS}}$ (bit 1)

When this reconfiguration is completed, any data that is sent to the 8250 for transmission is immediately received. By comparing the data sent to the data received, the processor can verify that the transmit and receive data paths of the 8250 are operational.

The receiver and transmitter interrupt capability of the 8250 also remains fully operational. The interrupt system can be tested by writing into any of the lower four bits of the Modem Status Register and verifying that the correct interrupt occurs. (The interrupt capability of the 8250 is discussed later in this chapter as well as in Chapter 4.)

Modem Status Register (MSR) The Modem Status Register (MSR) is divided into seven fields that indicate not only the current state of the modem status signals, but also whether a change in state has occurred since the last time the MSR was read. In addition, during loopback testing, bits 4 through 7 of the MSR are connected to bits 0 through 3 of the MSR as indicated in the previous section describing the MCR.

The processor can examine the values of these fields by reading the MSR and examining the bits individually. Note, however, that the act of reading this register automatically clears all fields to 0. It is the responsibility of the programmer to preserve the MSR value when it is read.

The MSR is accessed through UART register 6 and is a read/write register. Figure 3.6 shows the format of the MSR, which is also known as the Data Set Status Register (DSSR). Each of the register's fields is explained in the paragraphs that follow.

Bit 0: Delta Clear To Send (DCTS). Any change in the state of the 8250's $\overline{\text{CTS}}$ input (from 0 to 1 or from 1 to 0) sets this bit to 1.

Bit 1: Delta Data Set Ready (DDSR). Any change in the state of the 8250's $\overline{\text{DSR}}$ input sets this bit to 1.

Bit 2: Trailing Edge Ring Indicator (TERI). A change in the state of the 8250's $\overline{\text{RI}}$ input from a low state to a high state sets this bit to 1. Because this is a complementary implemention, this corresponds to the transition of the RI signal from high to low: in other words, the trailing edge of a ring indicator signal.

Bit 3: Delta Data Carrier Detect (DDCD). Any change in the state of the 8250's $\overline{\text{DCD}}$ input sets this bit to 1. In some documentation, this bit is referred to as Delta Receive Line Signal Detect (DRLSD).

Bit 4: Clear To Send (CTS). The value of this bit reflects the complement of the current status of the $\overline{\text{CTS}}$ input. During loopback testing, this bit is connected to the $\overline{\text{RTS}}$ output.

Bit 5: Data Set Ready (DSR). The value of this bit reflects the complement of the current status of the $\overline{\text{DSR}}$ input. During loopback testing, this bit is connected to the $\overline{\text{DTR}}$ output.

Bit 6: Ring Indicator (RI). The value of this bit reflects the complement of the current status of the $\overline{\text{RI}}$ input. During loopback testing, this bit is connected to the $\overline{\text{OUT1}}$ output.

Bit 7: Data Carrier Detect (DCD). This bit reflects the complement of the current status of the $\overline{\text{DCD}}$ input. In some documentation, this bit is referred to as Receive Line Signal Detect (RLSD). During loopback testing, this bit is connected to the $\overline{\text{OUT2}}$ output.

FIGURE 3.6

The Modem Status Register (MSR)

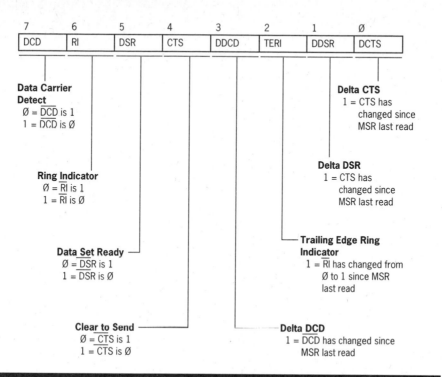

7	6	5	4	3	2	1	Ø
DCD	RI	DSR	CTS	DDCD	TERI	DDSR	DCTS

Data Carrier Detect
Ø = DCD is 1
1 = DCD is Ø

Delta CTS
1 = CTS has changed since MSR last read

Ring Indicator
Ø = RI is 1
1 = RI is Ø

Delta DSR
1 = CTS has changed since MSR last read

Data Set Ready
Ø = DSR is 1
1 = DSR is Ø

Trailing Edge Ring Indicator
1 = RI has changed from Ø to 1 since MSR last read

Clear to Send
Ø = CTS is 1
1 = CTS is Ø

Delta DCD
1 = DCD has changed since MSR last read

Interrupt Enable Register (IER)   The Interrupt Enable Register (IER) individually enables and disables the four types of interrupts that the 8250 can generate. When the situation represented by an enabled interrupt occurs, this fact is reported in the Interrupt Identification Register (IIR). Each interrupt can individually activate the INTR output of the 8250.

Writing a 1 into bit 0, 1, 2, or 3 of the IER enables the corresponding interrupt activity. If any of the conditions required to generate an interrupt exist when an interrupt enable bit is set, the UART immediately issues that interrupt. Interrupt handlers should be in place, therefore, before enabling interrupts.

Similarly, clearing any of the lower 4 bits in the IER to 0 disables the associated interrupt and removes any signalled interrupt from the IIR. A disabled interrupt will not be reported in the IIR, nor will it activate the INTR signal. All other 8250 functions, however, continue to operate in their normal manner, including updating the LSR and MSR. Note that most IBM-PC serial port implementations require additional steps before UART-generated interrupts can be used. This application is discussed in Chapter 4.

The IER is accessed through UART register 1 and is a read/write register. Figure 3.7 shows the format of the IER. Bits 7 through 4 of the IER are permanently set to 0. Each of the register's remaining fields is explained in the paragraphs that follow.

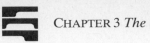

FIGURE 3.7

The Interrupt Enable Register (IER)

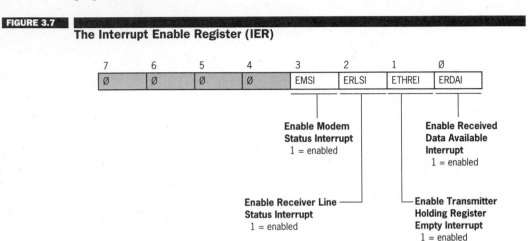

Bit 0: Enable Received Data Available Interrupt (ERDAI). When ERDAI = 0, this interrupt is disabled. Setting this bit to 1 enables the RDA interrupt, and an interrupt will be issued each time a received character is transferred from the RSR to the RBR.

Bit 1: Enable Transmitter Holding Register Empty Interrupt (ETHREI). Setting this bit to 1 enables the THRE interrupt and an interrupt will be issued each time a character is transferred from the THR to the TSR. Clear the ETHREI field to 0 to disable this interrupt.

Bit 2: Enable Receiver Line Status Interrupt (ERLSI). Setting this bit to 1 enables the RLS interrupt, and an interrupt will be issued whenever one or more of the OE, PE, FE, or BI bits (bits 1 through 4 in the LSR) are set to 1. The contents of the LSR can be examined to identify the condition that generated the interrupt. Note that this bit is a global on/off switch for these four conditions. They cannot be enabled or disabled separately.

Bit 3: Enable Modem Status Interrupt (EMSI). Setting this bit to 1 enables the MS interrupt. This field is also known as the Enable Data Set Status Interrupt (EDSSI) bit. When the MS interrupt is enabled, an interrupt will be issued whenever one or more of the DCTS, DDSR, TERI, or DDCD bits (bits 0 through 3 in the MSR) are set to 1. Note that this bit is a global on/off switch for these four conditions. They cannot be enabled or disabled separately. The contents of the MSR must be examined to identify the condition that generated the interrupt.

Interrupt Identification Register (IIR)   The four classes of interrupts described by the IER are prioritized by the 8250. If more than one interrupt type occurs, only the highest priority interrupt is reported in the Interrupt Identification Register (IIR). By generating an interrupt for only the highest priority of the existing conditions, the 8250 helps reduce the amount of processor attention required during data transfers. The four levels of interrupts, shown in descending order of priority, are

- Receiver Line Status (highest priority)

- Received Data Ready

- Transmitter Holding Register Empty

- Modem Status (lowest priority)

Once an interrupt occurs, the processor may read the IIR to determine the condition that caused the interrupt. While the IIR is being read by the processor, interrupt activity continues as usual and is remembered by the 8250, but the IIR is not updated. As soon as the IIR has been read, it is updated to reflect the 8250's new current status. After servicing the activating interrupt, the processor can identify and handle lower priority conditions in a small polling loop.

The IIR is accessed through UART register 2 and is a read-only register. Figure 3.8 shows the format of the IIR. Bits 7 through 3 of the IIR are permanently set to 0. Each of the register's remaining fields is explained in the following paragraphs.

FIGURE 3.8

The Interrupt Identification Register (IIR)

7	6	5	4	3	2	1	Ø
Ø	Ø	Ø	Ø	Ø	IID1	IIDØ	INP

Interrupt Identification
ØØ = Modem Status
Ø1 = THR Empty
1Ø = Received Data Available
11 = Receiver Line Status

Interrupt Not
Pending
Ø = Interrupt is
pending

Bit 0: Interrupt Not Pending (INP). With no interrupts pending, this field will hold the value 1 (true). Any condition that generates an interrupt clears this field to 0. Note that the terminology used to describe these interrupts is from the 8250's point of view, not that of the processor. A pending interrupt, therefore, is simply an indication that the 8250 has some information to report on the status of the serial communication. More than one interrupt may be pending, but only the highest priority interrupt will be reported in the Interrupt ID field.

Bits 2-1: Interrupt ID Field. If the Interrupt Not Pending field (bit 0) is 0, the contents of the Interrupt ID field identify the highest priority interrupt that is pending. The possible interrupts, their priority, type, cause, and the action required to reset them are given in Table 3.2.

TABLE 3.2

8250 Interrupt Identification

Interrupt Identification Register			Interrupt Priority	Interrupt Type	Interrupt Cause	Interrupt Reset Action
Bit 2	Bit 1	Bit 0				
0	0	1	n/a	None	None	n/a
1	1	0	1 (highest)	Line Status	Overrun error, parity error, frame error, or BREAK indicator	Read the Line Status Register
1	0	0	2	Received Data Available	Incoming character available in the Receiver Buffer Register	Read the Receiver Buffer Register
0	1	0	3	Transmitter Holding Register Empty	The Transmitter Holding Register is Empty	Read the IIR; or, write to the Transmitter Holding Register
0	0	0	4 (lowest)	Modem Status	The CTS, DSR, RI, or DCD input signals have changed since the Modem Status Register was last read	Read the Modem Status Register

Divisor Latch Registers   The 8250 contains a programmable baud generator that is capable of dividing an external timing reference by a divisor from 1 to 65535. The result provides the 16x clock that drives the internal transmitter logic. The formula for determining the divisor required to generate a specific baud is

$$\text{divisor} = \frac{f}{16 * \text{baud}}$$

where f is the external timing reference frequency in Hertz. Most PC implementations use a 1.8432 MHz crystal for the external clock reference. IBM manufactures high-speed serial port controllers that use a crystal frequency of 11.0592 MHz and are capable of data speeds up to 345,600 baud.

Table 3.3 gives a list of divisors to produce common communication speeds in systems using a 1.8432 MHz crystal. Divisors for other speeds and crystal frequencies are easily calculated from the previous equation. Note that some early 8250s do not perform reliably at higher rates. National does not recommend using a divisor of 0 in any case.

TABLE 3.3

Common Baud Divisors

Baud	Divisor (for 16x clock)	
	Decimal	**Hexadecimal**
110*	1047	417h
300	384	180h
1200	96	60h
2400	48	30h
9600	12	Ch
19200	6	6
38400	3	3
57600	2	2
115200	1	1

* Actual baud produced is 0.026% faster

The baud divisor is written to the 8250 as two 8-bit bytes: most significant byte and least significant byte. The 16-bit divisor is stored internally in two 8-bit latches. Upon loading a byte to either of these latches, the full 16-bit divisor is loaded. This simply means that the processor may write the bytes making up the divisor to the UART in either order. Figure 3.9 shows the format of the Divisor Latch.

FIGURE 3.9

The Divisor Latch Registers

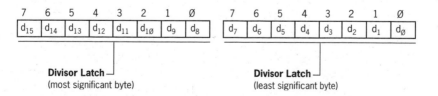

The two 8-bit registers that compose the Divisor Latch 8250 do not have dedicated UART register addresses. Instead, they are addressed through UART registers 0 (least significant byte) and 1 (most significant byte)—the same addresses as the Receiver Buffer and Interrupt Enable registers.

To determine which pair of internal registers receives the data, the UART examines bit 7 of the Line Control Register. Only if this bit, called the Divisor Latch Access bit (DLAB), is 1 does the data written to UART register 0 and 1 go to the Divisor Latch. If DLAB = 0, the data goes to the THR and IER as usual.

The process of loading the Divisor Latch, therefore, requires the following steps:

1. Write a 1 into bit 7 (DLAB) of the LCR.

2. Write the 16-bit divisor latch to UART registers 0 and 1.

3. Write a 0 into bit 7 (DLAB) of the LCR.

Scratch Pad Register (SCR) The 8250 provides one additional 8-bit register, designated the Scratch Pad Register. The SCR is a read/write register accessed through UART register 7. It is unusual in that it has absolutely no influence on the operation of the UART. Instead, this register is designated for use by the programmer as temporary data storage.

If you decide to use the SCR, be aware that others may have made the same decision. A value written by one program is not protected from being overwritten by a different program. This register is not present in early versions of the 8250. Figure 3.10 shows the format of the SCR.

FIGURE 3.10

The Scratch Pad Register (SCR)

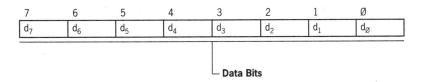

Data Bits

The 16550 UART

The 8250 greatly simplified the programming of serial communications. Operated at speeds of up to 9600 baud, it performed admirably—even on the retrospectively slow speed of the IBM-PC. But despite its past success and near-universal popularity, today's combination of extremely high communication speeds and multitasking operating systems have conspired to make the 8250 appear somewhat threadbare.

In response to this situation, National introduced the PC16550C/NS16550AF, an improved version of the original 8250-type UART.

By default, the 16550 emulates an 8250 and in most cases can act as a pin-for-pin equivalent. Operating in compatibility mode, the 16550 is functionally equivalent to an 8250 or 16450 UART. Any study of the 16550, therefore, should include a review of the data presented for the 8250 earlier in this chapter. Only the new capabilities and modes of operation of the 16550 are described in detail here.

Unlike the 8250, the 16550 has a second mode of operation that is designed to reduce the amount of CPU intervention required for serial data transfer. In this mode, the internal receiver and transmitter buffers are expanded from 1 byte to 16 bytes and are managed using first-in-first-out (FIFO) logic. The receiver FIFO buffer also stores three bits of error data per character. Parity errors, framing errors, and BREAK signals are buffered in correspondence to the character with which they are associated.

Features and Capabilities

The 16550 is upwardly compatible with the 8250 and 16450. As such, it expands on their list of features and capabilities. These features include

- Easily interfaced between the PC's address/data bus and a modem or other external device

- Automatic addition, removal, and checking of framing bits

- Generation and checking of parity bits under software control

- Separate indicators for the status of transmit and receive operations as well as reporting the line and data set status

- Built-in hold and shift registers for both transmit and receive operations also eliminate the need for precise synchronization between the processor and the serial data

- A programmable baud generator based on an external timing reference of up to 24 MHz

- Modem-control signal handling logic that is tied into its interrupt system

- A built-in self-test capability

- Capable of running all 8250/16450 software

- Internal buffers that allow up to 16 characters (and relevant errors) to be stored for both transmit and receive operations

Block Diagram

The 16550 is basically an enhanced 8250. As such, the internal configuration of the 16550 is quite similar to that of the 8250 and can be visualized as a collection of timing circuits, control and selection logic, buffers, and 12 accessible registers. Figure 3.11 shows a simplified block diagram of the internal structure of the 16550 UART. The relationships between subunits and some of the signals that typically pass back and forth are shown as well.

The 16550 uses the same packaging as the 8250. Two pins have been redefined, however, to allow signalling of DMA transfers. On the 8250, the CSOUT output pin provides feedback to the system that the chip has been selected and is ready for data transfer. On the 16550, this pin now provides the $\overline{\text{TXRDY}}$ signal. When there are no characters in the transmitter buffer, this signal is driven low. The signal remains low until the transmitter buffer is full. The impact of this change is minimal, as standard 8250-based IBM-PC serial port implementations make no connection to this pin.

The 16550 defines an additional output signal to indicate the status of the receiver buffer. The $\overline{\text{RXRDY}}$ signal is driven low when there is at least one character in the receiver buffer. It remains low until there are no more characters in the receiver buffer. The impact of this change is also minimal, as on the 8250 this pin is defined as NC (no connection).

Register Descriptions

For the most part, the bit-field definitions of the 16550's registers are identical to their 8250 counterparts in both 8250-emulation mode and FIFO mode. For the following registers, no description is given; details can be found in the 8250 register description section presented earlier in the chapter.

- Transmitter Holding Register (THR)
- Receiver Buffer Register (RBR)
- Line Control Register (LCR)
- Divisor Latch Registers
- Scratch Pad Register (SCR)
- Modem Control Register (MCR)
- Modem Status Register (MSR)

To support the new FIFO capabilities of the UART, the 16550 defines one new register, and the scope of some existing registers has been expanded. These changes are described here.

FIFO Control Register (FCR)   The FIFO Control Register is divided into six fields. By writing to this register, the transmitter and receiver FIFO buffers can be enabled, disabled, and cleared. This register also controls the DMA signals produced by the chip and the trigger level for the receiver FIFO interrupt.

FIGURE 3.11

16550 UART block diagram

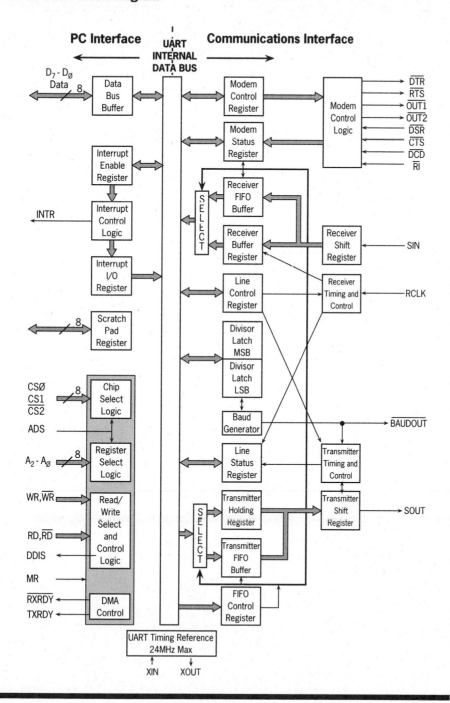

The FCR is a write-only register that is accessed through UART register 2, an address it shares with the IIR. Bit 0 of FCR must be 1 before any fields can be programmed. Figure 3.12 shows the format of the FCR. Each of the register's fields is explained in the following paragraphs.

FIGURE 3.12

The 16550 FIFO Control Register (FCR)

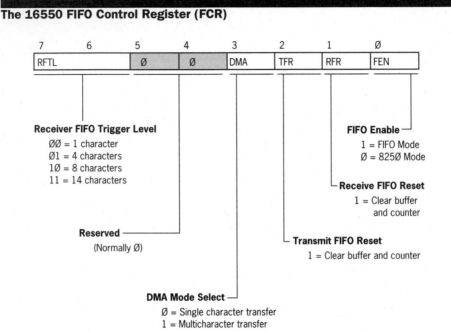

Bit 0: Enable FIFO Mode (FEN). Setting this field to 1 enables both the transmitter and receiver FIFO buffers. Clearing this field to 0 terminates FIFO mode and returns the 16550 to 8250 emulation mode. Changing the state of this bit effectively clears the receiver and transmitter FIFO buffers, the RBR, and the THR. The RSR and TSR registers, however, are not affected. This field also acts as an access latch for the remainder of the register. This bit must be 1 when attempting to write the other fields of the FCR or the data will not reach the register.

Bit 1: Receiver FIFO Reset (RFR). This field is valid only in FIFO mode. Writing a 1 to this field clears all bytes in the receiver FIFO buffer and resets the character counter for the FIFO to 0. Note, however, that any unfinished character that is being assembled in the RSR is not affected by this operation. It is not necessary to clear this bit manually; this bit clears itself when the operation is complete.

Bit 2: Transmitter FIFO Reset (TFR). This field is valid only in FIFO mode. Writing a 1 to this field clears all bytes in the transmitter FIFO buffer and resets the character counter for the FIFO to 0. Note, however, that any character currently being transmitted from the TSR is not affected by this operation. It is not necessary to clear this bit manually; this bit clears itself when the operation is complete.

Bit 3: DMA Mode Select (DMA). The setting of this field determines the logic that controls the signals available at the $\overline{\text{RXRDY}}$ and $\overline{\text{TXRDY}}$ pins. Writing a 0 to this field selects DMA mode 0 and enables support for single-character transfer DMA. This DMA mode is available in both 8250-emulation mode and FIFO mode.

In DMA mode 0, if a character is present in the RBR (8250 emulation mode) or in the receiver FIFO buffer (FIFO mode), the $\overline{\text{RXRDY}}$ pin is driven active (low). Once the $\overline{\text{RXRDY}}$ pin is activated, it remains active until the RBR or receiver FIFO buffer is empty.

In DMA mode 0, if no characters are present in the THR (8250 emulation mode) or in the transmitter FIFO buffer (FIFO mode), the $\overline{\text{TXRDY}}$ pin is driven active (low). Once the $\overline{\text{TXRDY}}$ pin is activated, it is deactivated after the first character is loaded into the THR or transmitter FIFO buffer.

Setting the DMA Mode Select field to 1 enables DMA mode 1 and is available only when the 16550 is in FIFO mode. DMA mode 1 supports multiple-character transfers, where characters are transferred until the receiver FIFO buffer has been emptied or the transmitter FIFO buffer has been filled.

In DMA mode 1, the $\overline{\text{RXRDY}}$ pin is driven active (low) when the number of characters in the receiver FIFO reaches the trigger level or characters have been present in the FIFO longer than the timeout value. Once activated, the $\overline{\text{RXRDY}}$ pin remains active until the receiver FIFO is empty.

In DMA mode 1, if no characters are present in the transmitter FIFO buffer (FIFO mode), the $\overline{\text{TXRDY}}$ pin is driven active (low). Once the $\overline{\text{TXRDY}}$ pin is activated, it remains activate until the transmitter FIFO is completely full.

Bits 5-4: Reserved. These two bits are marked as reserved for future use. As on the 8250, both bits are normally cleared to logic 0.

Bits 7-6: Receiver FIFO Trigger Level (RFTL). The contents of this 2-bit field defines the number of characters that must be present in the receiver FIFO buffer before the receiver FIFO interrupt will be generated. The supported buffer trigger values and the bit settings required to select them are shown here:

Bit 7	Bit 6	Trigger Level
0	0	1 character
0	1	4 characters
1	0	8 characters
1	1	14 characters

Line Status Register (LSR)   The individual fields of the Line Status Register (LSR) indicate the status of the data transfer operation. Figure 3.13 shows the format of the LSR as implemented by the 16550. The new definitions for the fields in bits 1 and 7 of the LSR are explained in the following paragraphs. The remainder of the register's fields function as described for the 8250.

 FIGURE 3.13

The 16550 Line Status Register (LSR)

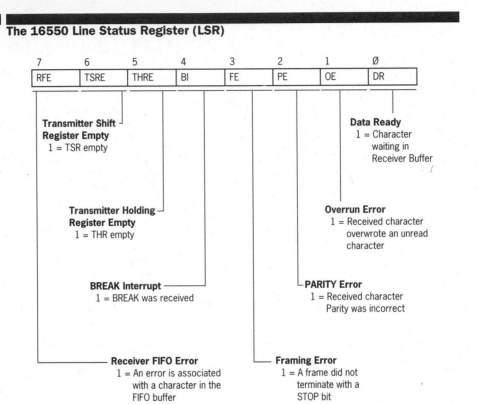

Bit 1: Overrun Error (OE). The receiver logic in the 16550 operates continuously. Characters are received, assembled in the RSR, and transferred to the RBR or FIFO buffer, depending on the chip's mode. In 8250 mode, a character that is completely received will overwrite an unread character in the RBR, destroying the character.

In FIFO mode, the chip behaves somewhat differently. If the FIFO fills beyond the trigger level, an overrun error occurs when the FIFO is completely full and the next character has been completely received in the RSR. The overrun error is not queued, but is written to the LSR when it occurs. The character in the RSR is not written to the FIFO. Subsequent characters will overwrite the character in the RSR, not the FIFO. The OE bit is automatically cleared to 0 when the processor reads the LSR.

Bit 7: Receiver FIFO Error (RFE). In 8250-emulation mode, this bit is always 0. In FIFO mode, this bit is set to 1 when a parity error, framing error, or BREAK indication is associated with one or more of the characters in the receiver FIFO buffer. The error is reported in the other fields of the LSR when the appropriate character is next to be read from the FIFO buffer.

Note that write operations to the FCR are restricted when the 16550 is operating in FIFO mode. To load a data byte into the receiver FIFO, the character must be written using the chip's loopback. Bits 0 and 7 of the LSR can't be written in any case while FIFO mode is enabled.

Interrupt Enable Register (IER)   The Interrupt Enable Register individually enables and disables the four types of interrupts that can be generated by the 8250. When the situation represented by an enabled interrupt occurs, this fact is reported in the Interrupt Identification Register.

The format of this register in the 16550 is, for the most part, identical to that of the 8250, as shown in Figure 3.7. In FIFO mode, the definition of bit 0, however, has been expanded as follows.

Bit 0: Enable Receiver FIFO Timeout Interrupt. In FIFO mode, setting this bit to 1 enables the receiver FIFO timeout interrupt. When enabled, an interrupt will be issued when the following conditions exist simultaneously:

- At least one character is present in the receiver FIFO

- A serial character has not been received for longer than four continuous character times

- The receiver FIFO has not been read by the CPU for longer than four continuous character times

A character time is derived from the baud generator clock, making the delay threshold baud-independent. If no interrupt has occurred, the timeout timer is reset each time a character is received or read from the receiver FIFO buffer.

Interrupt Identification Register (IIR)   Like the 8250, the 16550 generates and prioritizes four classes of interrupts. If more than one interrupt type occurs, only the highest priority interrupt is reported in the IIR. In 8250-emulation mode, the description of this register is identical to that given for the 8250 earlier in this chapter. When operating in FIFO mode, the 16550 additionally defines two new fields in the IIR and one new interrupt condition that is reported.

The four levels of interrupts, shown in descending order of priority, are

- Receiver Line Status (highest priority)

- Received Data Ready or Receiver FIFO Buffer Timeout

- Transmitter Holding Register Empty

- Modem Status (lowest priority)

The IIR is accessed through UART register 2 and is a read-only register. Figure 3.14 shows the format of the IIR on the 16550. The new fields in bits 3, 6, and 7 of the LSR are explained in the following paragraphs. The remainder of the register's fields function as described for the 8250.

The 16550 Interrupt Identification Register (IIR)

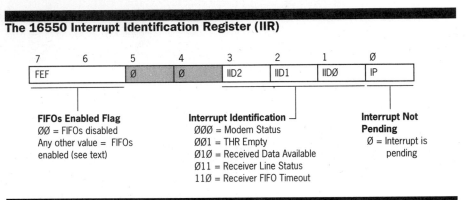

Bits 3-1: Interrupt ID Field. If the Interrupt Not Pending field (bit 0) is 0, the contents of the Interrupt ID field identify the highest priority interrupt that is pending. The possible interrupts, their priority, type, cause, and the action required to reset them are given in Table 3.4.

Bit 7-6: FIFO Mode Enabled Flag. When FIFO mode is enabled by writing a 1 to bit 0 of the FIFO Control Register, the 16550 sets this field to 11b. These bits are defined as 0 on the 8250 and 16450. When the 16550 is operating in 8250-emulation mode, this field is cleared to 00 for compatibility.

The serial port controllers on IBM PS/2 system boards use these two bits to identify themselves, as shown in Table 3.5. A type 1 controller is equivalent to an 8250-based asynchronous adapter. A type 2 controller uses the equivalent of a 16550 and supports FIFO operations. A type 3 controller supports both the FIFO and DMA operations available with the 16550.

Note that a bug in some type 2 controllers on PS/2 Modem 55 system boards causes them to not set bit 6 of the IIR when FIFO mode is enabled. An application using the FIFO mode flags to identify this controller will not detect FIFO capabilities. Regardless of the controller type, FIFO operations are not supported on PS/2 Model 50 systems.

Identifying UARTs

Fortunately for programmers, the UART provides one of the most consistent programming interfaces available on the PC. For example, from a programmer's point of view, the 8250 and 16450 UARTs are indistinguishable. The appearance of the 16550 on the scene, however, has changed this situation. It's true that the 16550 provides an 8250-emulation mode that is indistinguishable from that earlier chip. But an application has no guarantee that the chip is operating in that mode when it gets control.

TABLE 3.4

16550 Interrupt Identification

Interrupt Identification Register				Interrupt Priority	Interrupt Type	Interrupt Cause	Interrupt Reset Action
Bit 3	Bit 2	Bit 1	Bit 0				
0	0	0	1	n/a	None	None	n/a
0	1	1	0	1 (highest)	Receiver Line Status	Overrun error, parity error, frame error, or BREAK indicator	Read the Line Status Register
0	1	0	0	2	Received Data Available	Incoming character available in the Receiver Buffer Register	Read the Receiver Buffer Register
1	1	0	0	2	Receiver FIFO Timeout	Receiver FIFO buffer contains at least one character and has had no input or output activity for at least four continuous character times	
0	0	1	0	3	Transmitter Holding Register Empty	The Transmitter Holding Register is Empty	Read the IIR; or, write to the Transmitter Holding Register
0	0	0	0	4 (lowest)	Modem Status	The CTS, DSR, RI, or DCD input signals have changed since the Modem Status Register was last read	Read the Modem Status Register

TABLE 3.5

16550 Interrupt Identification

FIFO Mode Flags		IBM Serial Controller Type
Bit 7	Bit 6	
0	0	Type 1
0	1	Type 3
1	0	Unused
1	1	Type 2

PC hardware being what it is, it would not be surprising to find a combination of 8250/16450 and 16550 UARTs installed in the same computer. Before a program takes advantage of the advanced features of the 16550 or assumes that the underlying chip is an 8250, it must determine the type of UART that is installed. The utility UARTID, the assembly language listing for which is given in Listing 3.1, will identify the type of UARTs installed.

LISTING 3.1

UARTID.ASM

```
;==============================================================================
; UARTID.ASM - Identify the installed UARTs
;
; From: PC Magazine Programmer's Technical Reference
;       Data and Fax Communications
;       Robert L. Hummel
;
; To create an executable version of this program, use the following
; commands:
;       MASM UARTID;
;       LINK UARTID;
;       EXE2BIN UARTID.EXE UARTID.COM
;       DEL UARTID.EXE
;------------------------------------------------------------------------------
; This demonstration program examines only those ports identified by
; the BIOS. The BIOS in some systems won't locate the ports at COM3 and
; COM4. If you prefer, you can hard-code the search for the following
; standard addresses:
;       COM1    3F8H
;       COM2    2F8H
;       COM3    3E8H
;       COM4    2E8H
;------------------------------------------------------------------------------
CSEG            SEGMENT PARA    PUBLIC  'CODE'
        ASSUME  CS:CSEG, DS:CSEG, ES:CSEG, SS:CSEG
                ORG     100H                    ;COM file format

;==============================================================================
; This routine determines the type of the UARTs located by the BIOS.
```

LISTING 3.1

UARTID.ASM (Continued)

```
; An explanation is then displayed on the console.
;------------------------------------------------------------------------
MAIN        PROC    NEAR
        ASSUME  CS:CSEG, DS:CSEG, ES:CSEG, SS:CSEG

            CLD                             ;All str ops forward

            MOV     DX,OFFSET PROGID$        ;Display program info
            CALL    PRINT$
;------------------------------------------------------------------------
; Retrieve the base addresses of the installed UARTs from the BIOS
; data area.
;------------------------------------------------------------------------
            SUB     AX,AX                   ;Clear AX
            MOV     ES,AX                   ;Point to low memory
        ASSUME  ES:NOTHING
            MOV     SI,400H                 ;Point to data area

            MOV     CX,4                    ;Examine 4 addresses
;------------------------------------------------------------------------
; Loop through the 4 possible base addresses and display the installed
; devices.
;------------------------------------------------------------------------
MAIN_1:
            MOV     DX,OFFSET UARTIS$       ;Start message
            CALL    PRINT$

            LODS    WORD PTR ES:[SI]        ;Get base address
            OR      AX,AX                   ;0 = not installed
            JNZ     MAIN_2
;------------------------------------------------------------------------
; If the base address is 0, no UART is present.
;------------------------------------------------------------------------
            MOV     DX,OFFSET NONE$         ;Say not there
            JMP     SHORT MAIN_3
;------------------------------------------------------------------------
; Test the UART at the base address by attempting to turn on FIFO mode.
; If the FIFO mode flags are not set, the chip is an 8250/16450.
; Some IBM PS/2 Model 55 systems don't set bit 6 of the IIR correctly
; when switched to FIFO mode. These serial ports won't be identified as
; having FIFO capability.
;------------------------------------------------------------------------
MAIN_2:
            MOV     DX,AX                   ;Put base adr in DX
            ADD     DX,2                    ;DX -> IIR/FCR

            MOV     AL,1                    ;Enable FIFOs
            OUT     DX,AL                   ;Write to FCR

            IN      AL,DX                   ;Read IIR
            AND     AL,0C0H                 ;Mask FIFO enabled bits
            MOV     DX,OFFSET U8250$        ;Assume an 8250
            JZ      MAIN_3                  ; ZR = no bits set

            MOV     DX,OFFSET U16550$       ;Upgrade to 16550
MAIN_3:
            CALL    PRINT$
```

LISTING 3.1

UARTID.ASM (Continued)

```
;-----------------------------------------------------------------------
; Increment the UART # in the string and loop for remaining ports.
;-----------------------------------------------------------------------
                INC     BYTE PTR [UARTNUM]      ;Change ASCII char
                LOOP    MAIN_1

                MOV     AX,4CØØH                ;Terminate program
                INT     21H                     ; thru DOS

MAIN            ENDP


;=======================================================================
; All program data appears here.
;-----------------------------------------------------------------------
PROGID$         DB      "UARTID 1.Ø ",254," Robert L. Hummel",13,1Ø
                DB      "PC Magazine Programmer's Technical Reference"
                DB      13,1Ø,"Data and Fax Communications",13,1Ø
                DB      1Ø,"$"

UARTIS$         DB      "UART #"
UARTNUM         DB      "1 is $"

U825Ø$          DB      "an 825Ø/1645Ø.",13,1Ø,"$"
U1655Ø$         DB      "a 1655Ø.",13,1Ø,"$"
NONE$           DB      "not present.",13,1Ø,"$"


;=======================================================================
; This routine simply uses the DOS "Print String" function to display a
; message on the console and is included only to clarify the appearance
; of the MAIN proc. It is assumed that the string offset is passed in
; the DX register relative to the DS segment.
;-----------------------------------------------------------------------
PRINT$          PROC    NEAR
        ASSUME  CS:CSEG, DS:NOTHING, ES:NOTHING, SS:NOTHING

                MOV     AH,9
                INT     21H
                RET

PRINT$          ENDP

CSEG            ENDS
                END     MAIN
```

The UARTID program uses the FIFO Control Register and the Interrupt Identification Register to determine the type of UART present. If the UART is a 16550, writing a 1 to the FCR enables the FIFO buffers and sets one or both of bits 7 and 6 of the IIR to 1. If not, the bits will both be 0. UARTID tests the UART's reaction to this operation and displays the UART type.

RS-232 AND THE SERIAL PORT

CHAPTER 3 DOCUMENTED THE CAPABILITY OF THE UART TO MANAGE SERIAL communications. Through a simple I/O interface, the UART can be configured and data exchanged with the processor. Once programmed with a choice of signaling rate (baud), parity, character size, and framing protocols, the UART automatically manages the communication process.

This chapter will present an overview of the next phase in the communication process: data exchange between the UART and the outside world. I'll begin with a review of the RS-232/V.24 interface, the de facto asynchronous communication standard among PCs. Included are descriptions of the electrical and mechanical characteristics of the interface as well as signal descriptions and applications.

The chapter examines the translation of the RS-232 ideal into reality in the form of a generic implementation of an asynchronous communications adapter for the IBM-PC. Following that are some examples of real-world interface situations and the cabling required for effective communication. Finally, this chapter concludes with a summary of the programming techniques required to implement interrupt-driven serial communications on the IBM PC.

Note that this chapter is not a replacement for the RS-232 or V.24 standards. Nor is it a complete design guide to the IBM-PC serial port adapter. Additional documentation on these topics is available from the sources listed in the bibliography in Appendix D of this book.

The RS-232 Standard

If the signal characteristics of two serial devices are known, it's a relatively straightforward procedure to construct an interface that will connect them. Creating a general interface that can accommodate different signal characteristics and work with disparate standards is correspondingly more difficult. For generalized communication, a small group of common interface standards is a clear and present requirement.

In 1969, an industry-constituted body released a standard for interconnection of equipment. The Electronics Industries Association (EIA) released version C of its Recommended Standard (RS) number 232. This standard was entitled, "Interface Between Data Terminal Equipment and Data Circuit-Terminating Equipment Employing Serial Binary Data Interchange" and known simply as RS-232-C. The CCITT released its own version of the standard as the V.24 and V.28 standards. Similarly, the U.S. Department of Defense has issued a nearly identical standard under the designation Mil-Std-188C.

Although the RS-232-C standard was popular, the serial connection it defines is not particularly robust. When constructed to specification, an RS-232-C connection (transmitter, receiver, and interconnecting cable) is guaranteed to support a maximum signaling rate of only 20 kbit/s. The EIA has issued recommended standards for circuits operating at greater rates, but the RS-232-C standard continues to be the connection of choice for IBM-compatible personal computers.

Revision D of the standard was released in 1987, defining some additional test circuits and also fixing what many considered to be an oversight in RS-232-C. Strictly speaking, the goal of RS-232-C was to standardize the signals, not to ensure that everyone used a plug-and-play standard. Nonetheless, revision D of the standard specified the familiar DB-25 as the preferred connector choice.

The latest revision of the RS-232 standard, issued in July 1991, is available as EIA/TIA-232-E. Revision E incorporates no technical changes that will create compatibility problems with equipment conforming to previous versions of the standard. The material in this chapter is based on the specifications put forth by EIA/TIA-232-E. Except where a particular revision of the standard is being discussed, however, the term RS-232 will be used to encompass revisions C through E.

Scope

Devices that represent the origin or destination of data over a communications system are formally classified as *data terminal equipment* (*DTE*). Examples of DTEs range from the simplest terminals (such as might be connected to a mainframe) to personal computers to the mainframes themselves.

Interposed between the DTE and the communications system are additional devices collectively known as *data circuit-terminating equipment* (*DCE*). (More often than not, DCE is incorrectly cited as an acronym for data communications equipment.) A DCE converts the output from a DTE into a form that is appropriate for transmission over the communications system. The most common example of a DCE is the modem (called a *data set* by the telephone company), which converts the output of a PC's serial port, for example, into signals that can be transmitted over the telephone network.

The EIA/TIA-232-E standard applies specifically to the interconnection between DTE and DCE when the data interchange is performed using binary serial communications. Specifically, the standard defines the characteristics of the signals, characterizes the mechanical interface, and provides functional descriptions of the data, timing, and control circuits. The interface described is appropriate for both synchronous and asynchronous communications. The standard also includes example wiring plans for representative communication system configurations. This section provides a summary of the standard.

Electrical Characteristics

The RS-232 standard defines the electrical characteristics of the individual interchange signals and associated circuitry. Signals are assumed to be originated by a *generator* and detected by a *receiver*. The circuit voltage is measured at the point where the two devices connect, which is known as the *interface point*.

Unlike the logic circuits commonly found in computers (where 0V is defined as the OFF state and 5V as the ON state), the RS-232 interface uses bipolar logic. The use of both positive and negative voltages in the interface increases the noise immunity of the system. All voltage levels in the interface are measured with respect to a common connection called the *signal ground*.

A number of restrictions are imposed on the interface circuit by EIA/TIA-232-E. These restrictions protect both sides of the interface from damage. Leaving a generator unconnected (an open circuit condition), for example, must not harm the generator nor result in a voltage greater than 25V in magnitude appearing on the circuit. In addition, the generator must be able to withstand a short circuit between itself and any other interchange circuit in the interface without causing damage to itself or to the other circuit. Similarly, a receiver must be able to withstand any input signal that falls within the range -25V to +25V without damage.

Normal signal voltages on an RS-232 interchange circuit represent one of two states. The signal is in the first state when the voltage is between -15V and -3V. The second state is defined as a voltage between +3V and +15V. The region from -3V to +3V is defined as the *transition region,* and the state of the circuit is undefined when the voltage is within this region. Table 4.1 summarizes the correspondence between the circuit states and definitions for data transmission and timing and control functions.

TABLE 4.1

RS-232 Signal Definitions

Application	Voltage Level	
	$-15 \leq V \leq -3$	$3 \leq V \leq 15$
Data (Signal State)	MARK	SPACE
Data (Binary Value)	1	0
Timing and Control Functions	OFF	ON

Signal Descriptions

The interchange circuits defined by RS-232 are functional descriptions. It is perfectly acceptable (and quite common) to have more than one circuit function assigned to the same physical connection in the interface. Similarly, functions that are not required need not be present in the physical interface. Examples of this are presented later in this chapter.

All RS-232 defined interchange circuits between DTEs and DCEs are divided into four general categories: signal common, data, control, and timing. Table 4.2 lists the interchange circuits present in the DTE/DCE interface. For each circuit, the table provides the signal's category, designation, and name. Additionally, it shows the direction of the signal flow between DTE and DCE. For each RS-232 designation, the corresponding CCITT V.24 circuit designation is also given. (The V.24 circuit definitions are described in more detail in the next section.) All of the circuits are defined in the following paragraphs.

TABLE 4.2

RS-232 DTE/DCE Interchange Circuits

Circuit Category	RS-232 Circuit Designation (CCITT Equivalent)	Circuit Name	Signal Direction
Common	AB (102)	Signal Common	n/a
Data	BA (103)	Transmitted Data	DTE → DCE
	BB (104)	Received Data	DTE ← DCE
Control	CA (105)	Request to Send	DTE → DCE
	CB (106)	Clear to Send	DTE ← DCE
	CC (107)	DCE Ready	DTE ← DCE
	CD (108/1,/2)	DTE Ready	DTE → DCE
	CE (125)	Ring Indicator	DTE ← DCE
	CF (109)	Received Line Signal Detector	DTE ← DCE
	CG (110)	Signal Quality Detector	DTE ← DCE
	CH (111)	DTE-Source Data Signal Rate Selector	DTE → DCE
	CI (112)	DCE-Source Data Signal Rate Selector	DTE ← DCE
	CJ (133)	Ready for Receiving	DTE → DCE
	RL (140)	Remote Loopback	DTE → DCE

TABLE 4.2

RS-232 DTE/DCE Interchange Circuits (Continued)

Circuit Category	RS-232 Circuit Designation (CCITT Equivalent)	Circuit Name	Signal Direction
Control	LL (141)	Local Loopback	DTE → DCE
	TM (142)	Test Mode	DTE ← DCE
Timing	DA (113)	DTE-Source Transmitter Signal Element Timing	DTE → DCE
	DB (114)	DCE-Source Transmitter Signal Element Timing	DTE ← DCE
	DC (115)	DCE-Source Receiver Signal Element Timing	DTE ← DCE
Secondary Data	SBA (118)	Secondary Transmitted Data	DTE → DCE
	SBB (119)	Secondary Received Data	DTE ← DCE
Secondary Control	SCA (120)	Secondary Request to Send	DTE → DCE
	SCB (121)	Secondary Clear to Send	DTE ← DCE
	SCF (122)	Secondary Received Line Signal Detector	DTE ← DCE

Signal Common (Circuit AB)   This circuit provides the common electrical ground path for all of the circuits in the interface. The standard recommends that this signal be connected to a protective (chassis) ground by way of an internal connection inside the DCE. The implication is that the DCE chassis is subsequently connected to the earth ground provided by the electrical outlet.

Most modems used with PCs draw their power from low-voltage external transformers. These transformers often provide no connection to the ground of the electrical system. On most systems, therefore, this signal will not be connected to a protective ground unless the connection is made within the DTE.

Transmitted Data (Circuit BA)   The signals that appear on the Transmitted Data circuit are originated by the local DTE for transfer to the local DCE. The signals sent may be command codes to control the operation of the local DCE (modem commands) or they may be data destined for transmission by the local DCE to a remote DCE.

When a DTE is not transmitting data, it holds this circuit in the MARK state. This property can be used to distinguish a DTE from a DCE. According to the standard, a DTE will not transmit data unless the Request to Send, Clear to Send, DCE Ready, and DTE Ready control circuits are simultaneously in the ON state.

Regardless of whether the device is a DTE or a DCE, this circuit is always called Transmitted Data, corresponding to the perspective of the DTE. It is therefore an output at the DTE and an input at the DCE.

Received Data (BB)   The signals that appear on this circuit are originated by the local DCE for transfer to the local DTE. The signals sent may be responses to commands sent by the local DTE, or they may be data received from a remote DCE.

When not acknowledging commands, a standard DCE holds this circuit in the MARK state when the Received Line Signal Detect (Carrier Detect) circuit is in the OFF condition. This property can be used to distinguish a DTE from a DCE.

During half-duplex operation, this circuit is held in the MARK state as long as the Request to Send circuit is ON and for a brief interval following the ON to OFF transition, to allow for the completion of transmission.

Regardless of whether the device is a DTE or a DCE, this circuit is always called Received Data, corresponding to the perspective of the DTE. It is therefore an output at the DTE and an input at the DCE.

Request to Send (CA)   The signals on this circuit are originated by the DTE. In simplex or duplex connections, setting this circuit to ON maintains the DCE in the transmit mode. Placing an OFF condition on this circuit inhibits the DCE from transmitting. The receive operation of the DCE is not affected in either case.

In half-duplex connections, placing an ON condition on this circuit causes the DCE to enter its transmit mode and inhibits its receive function. When the DTE turns this circuit OFF, the DCE enters its receive mode.

Once the DTE has turned Request to Send OFF, it must not turn Request to Send ON again until the DCE acknowledges by turning the Clear to Send circuit OFF.

A transition of the Request to Send circuit from OFF to ON instructs the DCE to enter its transmit mode. The DCE may then perform any actions it requires to prepare for transmission. When complete, the DCE sets the Clear to Send circuit ON, indicating that the DTE may transmit data.

A transition of Request to Send from ON to OFF instructs the DCE to complete processing of any data that it has already received from the DTE. The DCE then assumes a non-transmit or receive mode. The DCE signals when the transition is complete by turning the Clear to Send circuit OFF.

Clear to Send (CB)   The signals on this circuit are originated by the DCE and indicate whether the DCE is ready to accept data from the DTE. When Clear to Send is OFF, the DTE should not transmit data. When the DCE turns Clear to Send ON, it is ready to accept data. Note that the data may be commands for the DCE or data to be transmitted across the communications channel.

Normally, the Clear to Send signal is a response to the Request to Send signal. The DCE may turn Clear to Send OFF independent of the condition of Request to Send, however, to signal the DTE to interrupt the transfer of data for a finite period of time. Any data transmitted after the DCE turns Clear to Send off may be ignored by the DCE. The DCE may turn Clear to Send on at any time, provided that Request to Send is also ON. This operation is commonly known as *hardware flow control*. See also the definition of the Ready for Receiving circuit.

If the Request to Send circuit is not implemented, the DCE should operate all other circuits as if Request to Send were in the ON state at all times.

DCE Ready (CC)   The DCE uses this circuit to indicate to the DTE whether it is ready to operate. (This signal is more commonly known as Data Set Ready or Modem Ready.) An ON condition indicates that the DCE is prepared to exchange information with the DTE and to initiate the transfer of data.

In some implementations, this signal, in combination with the Test Mode circuit, is used to control the exchange of signals used for testing and maintenance of the DCE. In other cases, this signal is used in combination with the Clear to Send signal to control and program DCEs that support serial automatic dialing.

DTE Ready (CD)   The signals on this circuit are originated by the DTE. Turning DTE Ready ON instructs the DCE to prepare to connect to the communications channel. If the DCE is able to automatically answer incoming calls, it will do so only if DTE Ready is ON. (The condition of DTE Ready does not affect the signals present on the Ring Indicator circuit, however.)

If a connection is currently established, holding DTE Ready in the ON condition instructs the DCE to maintain the connection. If DTE Ready is subsequently turned OFF, the DCE will disconnect from the communications channel following the completion of any in process transmission. If DTE Ready is turned OFF, it should not be turned ON again until the DCE has responded by turning the DCE Ready circuit OFF.

Ring Indicator (CE)   The DCE uses this circuit to indicate that a ringing signal is being received on the communications channel. The Ring Indicator circuit approximates the state of the ringing signal: ON during the presence of a ringing signal and OFF during the absence of a ringing signal. This circuit is always active. The DTE, however, may choose to ignore this signal at its discretion.

Received Line Signal Detector (CF)   The DCE turns this circuit ON when it receives via the communications channel a signal that it takes as an indication that a suitable connection can be established. When this circuit is OFF, it indicates that no signal or no appropriate signal is being received. The determination of suitability is solely at the discretion of the DCE. (This circuit is more commonly known as Carrier Detect.)

If circumstances during data transfer require the DCE to set the Received Line Signal Detector circuit to OFF (indicating a loss of carrier), the DCE will also set the Received Data output to the MARK state.

For half-duplex connections, Received Line Signal Detector is held in the OFF condition whenever Request to Send is in the ON condition and for a brief interval of time following the ON to OFF transition of Request to Send.

Signal Quality Detector (CG)   The use of this circuit is no longer recommended.

DTE-Source Data Signal Rate Selector (CH)   The DTE places signals on this circuit to command the DCE to select between two data signaling rates or ranges of rates. An ON condition selects the higher rate.

DCE-Source Data Signal Rate Selector (CI)   The DCE places signals on this circuit to report which of two data signaling rates or ranges of rates has been selected. An ON condition indicates that the higher rate is in effect.

Ready for Receiving (CJ)   To provide a documented method for implementing hardware flow control, the standard defines the Ready for Receiving circuit. To indicate to the DCE that it is capable of accepting data, the DTE turns Ready for Receiving ON.

Conversely, an OFF condition indicates that the DTE cannot receive data from the DCE. In that case, the DCE must retain the untransmitted data. The DCE may, optionally, signal the remote DCE to suspend transmission of data on the communications channel.

Note that in systems that use the Ready for Receiving circuit, other DTE and DCE circuits behave as if the Request to Send circuit is present and permanently in the ON condition. Effectively, this circuit simply redefines an existing circuit.

Local Loopback (LL)   The DTE uses this circuit to place the local DCE into a loopback mode for testing. When the DTE sets the Local Loopback circuit to ON, the DCE disconnects its signal output from the communications channel and reconnects it to its own input circuits. The DCE then sets the Test Mode circuit to ON. The effect is that any data transmitted by the DTE to the DCE is immediately received by the DCE and sent back to the DTE. When the Local Loopback circuit reverts to the OFF condition, the DCE reconfigures itself for normal operation.

The setting of the Local Loopback Circuit does not affect the operation of the Ring Indicator circuit.

Remote Loopback (RL)   The DTE uses this circuit to place the remote DCE into a loopback mode for testing. When the local DTE sets the Remote Loopback circuit to ON, the local DCE requests the remote DCE to establish a remote loopback configuration. When the configuration is complete, the local DCE will turn the Test Mode circuit ON.

During remote loopback testing, data transmitted by the local DTE passes through the local DCE and over the communications channel. At the remote DCE, the data is received and then immediately retransmitted back to the local DCE over the communications channel and subsequently to the local DTE. When the local DTE sets the Remote Loopback circuit to OFF, the local DCE signals the remote DCE to terminate the test.

During the remote loopback test, the remote DCE sets its DCE Ready circuit to OFF and its Test Mode circuit to ON, indicating that it is not able to communicate with the remote DTE.

Test Mode (TM)   The DCE sets the Test Mode circuit ON to indicate to the DTE that the DCE has placed itself in test mode. The DCE takes this action in response to receiving an ON condition over the Local Loopback or Remote Loopback circuits. The Test Mode circuit is also set to ON when the DCE responds to a remote request to enter remote loopback mode. When the Test Mode circuit is in the OFF condition, it indicates that the DCE is ready for normal operation.

If the DCE has been placed in test mode through the DTE/DCE interface, the DCE Ready circuit operates normally. Otherwise, the DCE Ready circuit is held in the OFF condition.

DTE-Source Transmitter Signal Element Timing (DA)   The DTE places signals on this circuit to provide the DCE with signal element timing during synchronous transmission. The ON to OFF transitions of this circuit nominally indicate the center of each signal element (symbol) the DTE is placing on the Transmitted Data circuit. If implemented, timing information is normally provided on this circuit whenever the DTE is in a power-on mode.

DCE-Source Transmitter Signal Element Timing (DB)   The DCE places signals on this circuit to provide the DTE with signal element timing during synchronous transmission. The DTE should place signal elements (symbols) on the Transmitted Data circuit so that the transitions between signal elements nominally occur at the time of the transition of this circuit from OFF to ON. If implemented, timing information is normally provided on this circuit whenever the DCE is able to generate it.

DCE-Source Receiver Signal Element Timing (DD)   The DCE places signals on this circuit to provide the DTE with signal element timing during synchronous transmission. The ON to OFF transitions of this circuit nominally indicate the center of each signal element (symbol) the DCE is placing on the

Received Data circuit. If implemented, timing information is normally provided on this circuit whenever the DCE is able to generate it.

Secondary Transmitted Data (SBA)   This circuit is equivalent to the Transmitted Data circuit except that the DTE uses it to send data to the DCE for transmission on the secondary channel.

Secondary Received Data (SBB)   This circuit is equivalent to the Received Data circuit except that the DCE uses it to pass data received on the secondary channel to the DTE.

Secondary Request to Send (SCA)   This circuit is equivalent to the Request to Send circuit except that the DTE uses it to request the DCE to establish a secondary channel.

Secondary Clear to Send (SCB)   This circuit is equivalent to the Clear to Send circuit except that the DCE uses it to indicate the availability of the secondary channel to the DTE.

Secondary Received Line Signal Detector (SCF)   This circuit is equivalent to the Received Line Signal Detector except that the DCE uses it to inform the DTE of activity on the secondary channel.

Mechanical Interface

The RS-232-C standard simply defined 25 interchange circuits and stated that a female connector should be used for DCE and that a male connector should be used for DTE. Beyond that, no requirements were set for the mechanical interface. This oversight has been remedied, however, and EIA/TIA-232-E specify the familiar 25-pin D-shell (DB-25) connectors.

NOTE   The use of an alternate 26-pin connector, designated Alt A, is also specified by EIA/TIA-232-E. Although it contains an additional pin, the connector is physically smaller, being only about half the size of a DB-25 in its widest dimension. This connector is not commonly seen on PCs.

Table 4.3 shows the pin assignments required to configure a DB-25 connector for an RS-232 interface. Note that some pins are assigned to more than one circuit. This was required to put EIA/TIA-232-E in agreement with similar international standards. Of course, not all circuits are required for every interface. The timing circuits, for example, provide support solely for synchronous communication. And circuits not specifically defined in the preceding section may be assigned to the connector interface by mutual agreement of the DTE and the DCE.

TABLE 4.3

RS-232 Pin Assignments

Connector Pin Number	Circuit Designation	Circuit Name
1	n/a	Shield
2	BA	Transmitted Data
3	BB	Received Data
4[1]	CA	Request to Send
	CJ	Ready for Receiving
5	CB	Clear to Send
6	CC	DCE Ready
7	AB	Signal Common
8	CF	Received Line Signal Detector
9	n/a	(Reserved for Testing)
10	n/a	(Reserved for Testing)
11[2]	n/a	(Unassigned)
12[3]	SCF	Secondary Received Line Signal Detector
	CI	DCE-Source Data Signal Rate Selector
13	SCB	Secondary Clear to Send
14	SBA	Secondary Transmitted Data
15	DB	DCE-Source Transmitter Signal Element Timing
16	SBB	Secondary Received Data
17	DD	DCE-Source Receiver Signal Element Timing
18	LL	Local Loopback
19	SCA	Secondary Request to Send
20	CD	DTE Ready
21	RL	Remote Loopback
	CG	Signal Quality Detector
22	CE	Ring Indicator
23[3]	CH	DTE-Source Data Signal Rate Selector

TABLE 4.3

RS-232 Pin Assignments (Continued)

Connector Pin Number	Circuit Designation	Circuit Name
	CI	DCE-Source Data Signal Rate Selector
24	DA	DTE-Source Transmit Signal Element Timing
25	TM	Test Mode

1 When hardware flow control is required, circuit CA may take on the functionality of circuit CJ.

2 This pin is unassigned and will not be assigned in future versions of RS-232. It is defined in international standard ISO 2110, however.

3 In designs that use circuit SCF, circuits CH and CI are assigned to pin 23. If SCF is not used, this pin is defined as circuit CI.

The CCITT V.24 Standard

The CCITT V.24 standard is entitled "List of Definitions for Interchange Circuits Between Data Terminal Equipment (DTE) and Data Circuit-Terminating Equipment (DCE)" and deals solely with the functional signal definitions for a DTE/DCE interface. The CCITT V.28 standard, "Electrical Characteristics for Unbalanced Double-Current Interchange Circuits," provides the electrical characteristics of the interface. Together, the two standards provide the same information as the EIA/TIA-232-E standard.

Table 4.4 lists the interchange circuits specified by the V.24 standard. The category and direction of signal flow for each circuit are also indicated. Table 4.2 cross-references the RS-232 circuit names to the V.24 designations. Definitions for the circuits present in both standards are given in the "Signal Descriptions" section earlier in this chapter.

TABLE 4.4

V.24 DTE/DCE Interchange Circuits

Circuit Category	Circuit Number	Circuit Name	Signal Direction
Ground	102	Signal Ground or Common Return	n/a
	102a	DTE Common Return	n/a
	102b	DCE Common Return	n/a
	102c	Common Return	n/a

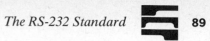

TABLE 4.4

V.24 DTE/DCE Interchange Circuits (Continued)

Circuit Category	Circuit Number	Circuit Name	Signal Direction
Data	103	Transmitted Data	DTE → DCE
	104	Received Data	DTE ← DCE
Control	105	Request to Send	DTE → DCE
	106	Ready for Sending	DTE ← DCE
	107	Data Set Ready	DTE ← DCE
	108/1	Connect Data Set to Line	DTE → DCE
	108/2	Data Terminal Ready	DTE → DCE
	109	Data Channel Received Line Signal Detector	DTE ← DCE
	110	Data Signal Quality Detector	DTE ← DCE
	111	DTE-Source Data Signal Rate Selector	DTE → DCE
	112	DCE-Source Data Signal Rate Selector	DTE ← DCE
Timing	113	DTE-Source Transmitter Signal Element Timing	DTE → DCE
	114	DCE-Source Transmitter Signal Element Timing	DTE ← DCE
	115	DCE-Source Receiver Signal Element Timing	DTE ← DCE
Control	116/1	Back-up Switching in Direct Mode	DTE → DCE
	116/2	Back-up Switching in Authorized Mode	DTE → DCE
	117	Standby Indicator	DTE ← DCE
Data	118	Transmitted Backward Channel Data	DTE → DCE
	119	Received Backward Channel Data	DTE ← DCE
Control	120	Transmit Backward Channel Line Signal	DTE → DCE
	121	Backward Channel Ready	DTE ← DCE
	122	Backward Channel Received Line Signal Detector	DTE ← DCE
	123	Backward Channel Signal Quality Detector	DTE ← DCE
	124	Select Frequency Groups	DTE → DCE

TABLE 4.4

V.24 DTE/DCE Interchange Circuits (Continued)

Circuit Category	Circuit Number	Circuit Name	Signal Direction
Control	125	Calling Indicator	DTE ← DCE
	126	Select Transmit Frequency	DTE → DCE
	127	Select Receive Frequency	DTE → DCE
Timing	128	DTE-Source Receiver Signal Element Timing	DTE → DCE
Control	129	Request to Receive	DTE → DCE
	130	Transmit Backward Tone	DTE → DCE
Timing	131	Received Character Timing	DTE ← DCE
Control	132	Return to Non-Data Mode	DTE → DCE
	133	Ready for Receiving	DTE → DCE
	134	Received Data Present	DTE ← DCE
	136	New Signal	DTE → DCE
	140	Loopback/Maintenance Test	DTE → DCE
	141	Local Loopback	DTE → DCE
	142	Test Indicator	DTE ← DCE
	191	Transmitted Voice Answer	DTE → DCE
	192	Received Voice Answer	DTE ← DCE

The Asynchronous Communications Adapter

When IBM introduced its Personal Computer, the system board provided no circuitry to support serial communications. As an option, however, IBM offered its Asynchronous Communications Adapter. This plug-in adapter provided an interface between the PC's microprocessor (via the expansion bus) and a programmable RS-232-like interface. The adapter could be configured for either of two I/O address and hardware interrupt pairs. The adapter even supported a current-loop teletype interface required to drive some older IBM printers.

IBM followed its original Asynchronous Communications Adapter with the PC AT Serial/Parallel Adapter card. This card provided a parallel port in addition to a serial port. Of course, IBM wasn't the only one making serial adapters. Over the years, a literally uncountable number of adapters from nearly as many manufacturers have been sold and installed.

From a programming perspective, it's fortunate that serial adapters fall into three general categories. In the first category are adapters that contain or emulate the simple 8250 or 16450 UART. These adapters are by far the most common. And because more advanced adapters are usually backward compatible, this category represents the lowest common communications denominator.

The second category of adapters are similar to the first in most respects, but contain or emulate the 16550 and its FIFO buffering capability. Because the 16550 UART is relatively new and marginally more costly, these adapters are not nearly as widespread as non-FIFO types. Driven by the popularization of high-speed modems and multitasking environments, however, the installed base of these adapters can be expected to increase.

The third category comprises special adapters such as the IBM Type 3 Serial Port Controller and the Hayes Enhanced Serial Interface (ESI). The Type 3 controller, for example, supports DMA transfers on both transmit and receive, performs character matching on the incoming data stream, and provides its own flow control. The Hayes ESI is a complete communications coprocessor, using its own microprocessor to manage communications almost independently of the PC.

Software development for special adapters is highly dependent on the support provided by the manufacturer. The requirement for custom device drivers and programming libraries, sometimes-daily firmware revisions, and evolving manufacturer goals render these devices moving targets. For current programming information, it's best to contact the manufacturer directly; refer to the bibliography for information sources.

This section presents a description of a generic serial adapter. We'll review the adapter's architecture, addressing requirements, and the pin-outs of the serial port connectors.

Serial Port Architecture

Most serial adapters are more remarkable for their commonalties than for their differences. The reason is not a lack of creativity on the part of the manufacturers, but the necessity of meeting a simple and rigidly defined standard. The requirements to interface to the PC's expansion bus, to provide the programmability expected by applications, and to present a serial port interface to the outside world leave little room for originality. A block diagram of a representative serial adapter is shown in Figure 4.1 and explained below.

FIGURE 4.1

Generic serial port adapter

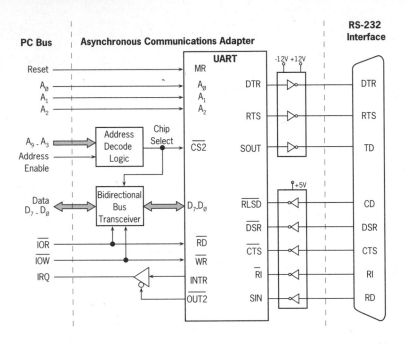

I/O Address   When IBM introduced its serial adapter, it established two I/O address ranges for use by the card. When configured as first serial port (COM1), the adapter was allocated eight consecutive I/O addresses beginning at a base address of 3F8h. The base address for the second serial port (COM2) was established at I/O address 2F8h. For both serial ports, the lower three bits of the PC I/O address specify the number of the UART register being addressed. UART register 4 of COM2, for example, is addressed at PC I/O address 2F8h + 4 = 2FCh.

NOTE   Actually, the COM1 and COM2 are the names of the devices assigned by MS-DOS to the first two serial ports in the system. Because most programs access the hardware directly, these device names have become universally understood to refer to their corresponding hardware adapters.

As devices with serial interfaces became more popular, many users found themselves wanting more than two serial ports. IBM, however, made no provision for addressing more than two serial ports in the PC, XT, or AT. To fill this void, other manufacturers produced adapters that were configurable for base addresses other than 3F8h and 2F8h. Eventually, the industry standardized on addresses of 3E8h for the third serial port (COM3) and 2E8h for the fourth serial port (COM4). A summary of serial port numbers and their corresponding I/O addresses is shown in Table 4.5.

TABLE 4.5

Standard Serial Port Assignments

Serial Port Number	UART I/O Base Address	Default IRQ
1	3F8h - 3FFh	4
2	2F8h - 2FFh	3
3	3E8h - 3EFh	4
4	2E8h - 2EFh	3

PC Bus Interface   To read or write one of the UART's registers, the I/O address of the register is placed on the PC's address bus. The PC then strobes either its $\overline{\text{IOR}}$ (I/O read) or $\overline{\text{IOW}}$ (I/O write) line, as appropriate for the desired operation. When the address decoding logic on the serial card (typically an AND gate) determines that its address has been placed on the bus, it asserts the UART's chip select ($\overline{\text{CS2}}$) line. This action accesses the UART register specified by the PC's A_2-A_0 address lines—the lower three bits of the I/O address.

The chip select line also connects the data lines of the UART to the PC's data bus through a bidirectional bus transceiver. The direction of data flow through the transceiver is derived by examining the PC's $\overline{\text{IOR}}$ and $\overline{\text{IOW}}$ lines. These lines are also connected to the UART's $\overline{\text{RD}}$ and $\overline{\text{WR}}$ inputs, respectively.

Interrupt Interface   For each of the two standard serial ports, one interrupt connection is provided from the UART's INTR line to the PC bus. IBM assigned IRQ 4 for use by COM1 and IRQ 3 for use by COM2. Later, when the I/O addresses for COM3 and COM4 were standardized, these serial cards simply reused the IRQs assigned to the first two ports. The IRQ assignments for each port are summarized in Table 4.5.

Most applications written to perform interrupt-driven serial communications expect exclusive use of an IRQ line. The operation of some devices, such as a serial mouse, is so interrupt-intensive as to make interrupt sharing impractical. In general, therefore, two serial ports cannot use the same IRQ line *at the same time*.

This problem has been somewhat ameliorated by the general availability of serial cards that can be configured to use interrupt lines other than IRQ 3 or 4. To avoid conflicts with existing serial ports or other options (such as network cards), these cards may allow the UART's INTR line to be tied to IRQ 2, 3, 4,

5, or 7. An application must be configurable to take advantage of nonstandard IRQ lines.

As you can see in the block diagram, the UART's INTR line is not connected directly to an IRQ line at the PC's bus. Instead, a logic gate, controlled by the UART's OUT2 signal, is used as a switch to turn the connection on or off. In this way, the OUT2 bit in the UART's modem control register performs service as a master interrupt enable switch for the serial card.

PC-XT Device Select The design of the IBM PC-XT required that any card installed in slot 8 (closest to the power supply) was to activate the CARD SLCTD line on the PC bus when it was selected. The CARD SLCTD line was then to be used by the system board to direct the appropriate drivers to read from or write to the device in slot 8. To meet this requirement, IBM's Asynchronous Communications Adapter card included both the logic and a jumper to activate the CARD SLCTD line when selected.

The RS-232 Interface The DTR, RTS, and SOUT pins of the UART are connected to the RS-232 interface through line drivers. These drivers convert the 0V/+5V levels of the UART to the -12V/+12V levels specified by the RS-232 standard. Similarly, the RS-232 CD, DSR, CTS, RI, and RD input signals are connected to their corresponding UART pins through line receivers that perform the inverse operation.

For design reasons, RS-232 line drivers are usually implemented as *inverting* drivers. In other words, the drivers reverse the logic sense of signals passing through them at the same time as they perform the required level conversion. Because the UART input and output signals are already inverted, this double inversion restores the correspondence between the UART function names and the signals appearing on the RS-232 interface.

Note that PC serial cards do not implement the full RS-232 interface. It's important to understand that RS-232 is a *recommended* standard that is designed to accommodate a variety of interfacing situations. When a particular application (such as connecting a PC serial port to a modem) doesn't require the generality provided by the full RS-232, it's common for only a subset to be implemented.

Serial Connector Pin-Outs

Although 25-pin D-shell (DB-25) connectors were not specified by the RS-232-C standard, time (and revision D) have linked them inextricably with serial port connections. Figure 4.2 shows the connector and pin assignments that are provided by IBM-compatible DB-25 male connectors.

FIGURE 4.2

The DB-25 serial connector

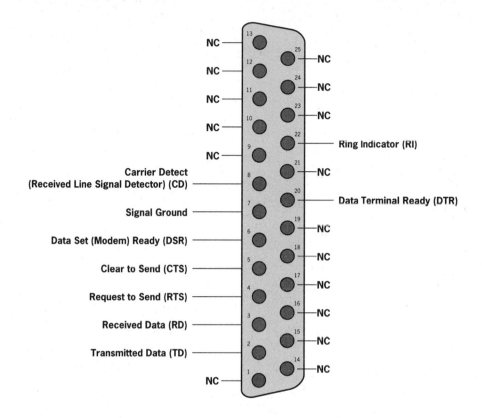

Of the 25 pins available in the DB-25 connector, only 9 are used to implement the PC serial port interface. When IBM created its Serial/Parallel Adapter for the PC AT, it chose to save space on the card end bracket by replacing the male DB-25 connector serial port connector with a male DB-9 connector. Note that the pin assignments in the DB-9, shown in Figure 4.3, bear no relationship by design to those of the DB-25.

PS/2 Serial Controllers

IBM classifies its PS/2 serial port controllers as type 1, 2, or 3. The type 1 controller is essentially equivalent to an 8250-based asynchronous adapter, as described previously. The type 1 controller may be configured only as COM1 or COM2 tied to IRQ 4 or 3, respectively.

FIGURE 4.3

The DB-9 serial connector

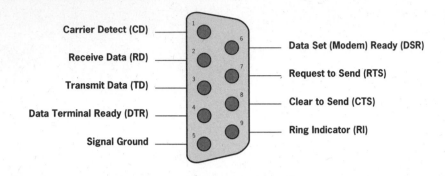

The type 2 controller is also limited to the addresses for COM1 or COM2, but uses the equivalent of a 16550 and supports FIFO operations. Note that in the original versions of this controller provided with the PS/2 models 50, 60, and 80, the UART contained a bug that disabled FIFO operation. This problem was fixed in the release of the PS/2 model 60 and subsequent versions of models 50, 60, and 80.

Note that the PS/2 model 50 does not support FIFO mode operations—even if a nondefective type 2 serial controller is installed. An application that activates FIFO mode in this scenario is subject to undetectable data loss. The model 50 model/submodel byte identification is FCh/04h.

Some type 2 controllers on PS/2 model 55 and 65SX system boards do not respond as documented. If FIFO mode is enabled, bit 6 of the interrupt identification register (IIR) is erroneously cleared to 0. An application using the FIFO mode flags to identify this controller will not detect FIFO capabilities. Note that the model 55 ABIOS ignores these flags. Applications that perform serial operations through the ABIOS, therefore, can use the FIFO mode.

The Type 3 Controller   The type 3 controller supports both the FIFO and DMA operations available with the 16550 and can be configured to respond as any one of eight serial ports. Each type 3 controller installed in a system may be configured to use either IRQ 3 or IRQ 4. More than one serial port may be assigned to the same IRQ line without conflict.

Table 4.6 shows the base I/O addresses for 8250-type registers and extended register sets for each port. Note that the base addresses used by IBM for COM3 and COM4 do not conform to the industry-wide standard for those ports.

TABLE 4.6

PS/2 Type 3 Controller I/O Addresses

Serial Port Number	8250-Type Registers Base Address	Enhanced Registers Base Address
1	3F8h	83F8h
2	2F8h	82F8h
3	3220h	B220h
4	3228h	B228h
5	4220h	C220h
6	4228h	C228h
7	5220h	E220h
8	5228h	E228h

The enhanced register base addresses shown in the table are generated simply by adding 8000h to the compatible register address. These additional I/O addresses give access to the type 3-specific control and identification registers listed in Table 4.7.

TABLE 4.7

Type 3 Controller Enhanced Registers

Enhanced Register Number	Register Name
0	Enhanced Command Register
1	Reserved
2	Enhanced Interrupt Identification Register
3	Enhanced Function Register 1
4	Enhanced Function Register 2
5	Enhanced Function Register 3
6	Character Compare Data Register
7	Receive Character Count Register

Cable Configurations

In theory, connecting a standard DTE to a standard DCE is as simple as connecting each pin in the DTE connector to its corresponding pin in the DCE connector. In most cases, however, you can omit many of the connecting wires without affecting the cable's functionality. As shown earlier in this chapter, for example, the PC serial port requires a maximum of nine wires to function with all standard serial peripherals. In some cases, you can connect a PC to a modem using only three wires.

Another common circumstance arises when a 9-pin DTE (such as the serial port on the IBM AT) must be connected to a 25-pin DCE, such as a modem. To connect these devices, an adapter or custom cable must be used. (Fortunately, these adapters are commonplace.) Finally, connecting two DTEs together—as is the case when two PCs are connected without an intervening modem—requires that a special cable be constructed to "fool" the RS-232 interface. This section presents special cable configurations for several of those situations.

DTE to DCE

The simplest cables to create are those that connect a DTE, such as the PC serial port, to a DCE, such as a modem using the same size connector. For the DB-25 connector, pins 2 through 8, 20, and 22 should be connected. For cables where DB-9 connectors are required on each end, simply connect each pair of pins. If one device uses a DB-9 connector and the other a DB-25 connector, use the wiring diagram shown in Figure 4.4.

Some of the signal lines supported by the serial port were designed to control primitive modems (the RTS/CTS signal pair, for example). As intelligent modems became more popular, many cable manufacturers omitted these lines to reduce cabling costs. Commercial communications programs have also become less rigidly dependent on the hard-wired modem status lines such as DSR and CD.

Each side of the DB-25 cable shown in Figure 4.5 causes the output signals generated by a device to satisfy its own input requirements. Note that this cable will not support a number of features, such as hardware flow control, now used by many high-speed modems and communications software.

DTE to DTE (Null Modem)

Connecting the serial ports of two PCs together presents some problems for the RS-232 interface. Assuming that DB-25 connectors are in use, each PC expects to transmit data on pin 2 and receive data on pin 3. Consequently, both PCs transmit on the same pin and neither can hear the other. The handshaking signals of the interface are similarly mismatched input to input and output to output. To solve this problem, you must use a *null-modem* cable.

FIGURE 4.4

DB-25 to DB-9 conversion cable

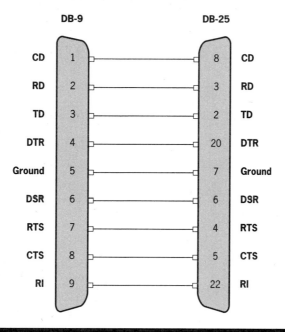

FIGURE 4.5

Abbreviated DTE/DCE DB-25 cable

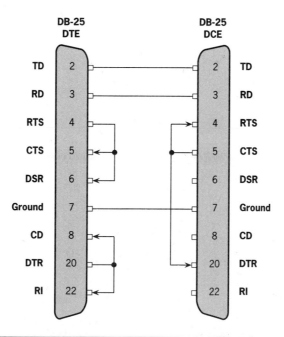

One common configuration for a DB-25 to DB-25 null-modem cable is shown in Figure 4.6. The most important thing to notice about this diagram is the crossing of wires connecting pins 2 and 3. This connection aligns the output of one PC to the input of the other, permitting communication to take place. Some null-modem applications require only the connection of pins 2, 3, and 7. Optional connections that allow hardware handshaking to take place are shown as dashed lines in the figure. In some applications, the RI signal (pin 22) and CD signal (pin 8) in a connector may also be wired together.

FIGURE 4.6

DTE/DTE DB-25 null-modem cable

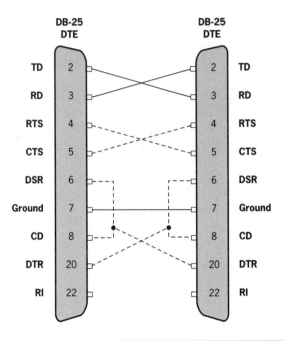

DTE to Serial Printer

Attempting to connect a PC to a serial printer remains a frequent source of frustration. This is simply because the RS-232 interface contains no explicit support for a printer. There's no circuit labeled "paper out," for example. Thus each serial printer manufacturer has been free to assign signals to pins seemingly at random.

Members of the HP LaserJet family of printers, for example, are equipped with female DB-25 connectors to support a serial interface. But the LaserJet printer is configured as DTE, not DCE as its connector would imply. Thus although the cable that works with your modem cable will plug into a LaserJet, it won't work.

The cable in Figure 4.7 will interface the DB-25 serial port of a PC to a Laser-Jet printer serial interface. Note the crossing of pins 2 and 3 as in the null-modem cable. Details on cabling other printers to a serial port are best obtained from the printer's manufacturer.

FIGURE 4.7

DTE/DTE DB-25 LaserJet printer cable

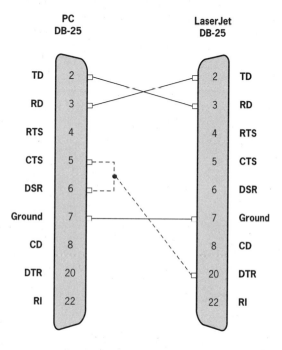

Interrupt-Driven Communications

The advantage of interrupt-driven communications is that the CPU is no longer required to monitor the state of the data transfer constantly. Instead, an interrupt can be generated each time the CPU's attention is required. This arrangement is typically referred to as *interrupt-driven serial communications*.

Before an application attempts to use interrupt-driven communications on the PC, however, several steps must be taken to accommodate the implementation-specific nature of the PC's serial port and interrupt hardware. These requirements are described in this section.

Enabling the UART Interrupt

As described in Chapter 3, the 8250 UART can be programmed to individually enable or disable interrupts corresponding to these four different communication conditions:

- An unread character is in the RBR.

- The THR is empty.

- A line status error (parity error, framing error, overrun error, or BREAK) occurs.

- The UART detects a change in the status of the CTS, DSR, or DCD lines or detects the trailing edge of a ring.

When the bit in the UART Interrupt Enable Register that corresponds to one of these conditions is set, the occurrence of the condition will cause the UART to assert its INTR line.

The UART's INTR line is not connected directly to an IRQ (interrupt request) line at the PC's bus, however. Instead, a logic gate, controlled by the UART's $\overline{\text{OUT2}}$ signal, is used as a switch to turn the connection on or off, serving as a master interrupt enable. Before the interrupt request can reach the bus, therefore, bit 3 of the UART's modem control register (MCR) must be set to 1.

The Programmable Interrupt Controller

The UART can prioritize its own interrupts. Members of the 80x86 CPU family, however, have no such built-in circuitry. Instead, these functions are performed by an external support chip, the 8259A programmable interrupt controller (PIC). A single 8259A PIC, located at I/O address 20h in the PC and XT, accepts up to eight external user-defined interrupts and routes them to the CPU's INTR input signal.

In the design of the PC AT and compatible 386 and 486 computers, more than eight peripheral interrupts were required. By cascading two PICs, 15 unique interrupts can be supported. The primary PIC remains at I/O address 20h and handles IRQ 0, 1, and 3 through 7. The secondary PIC, located at I/O address A0h, accepts as inputs IRQs 8 through 15 and has its output tied into the IRQ 2 input of the primary PIC. The bus line that was connected to the PIC's IRQ 2 input in the PC is now sent to the secondary PIC's IRQ 9 input. The PC's BIOS then redirects this interrupt to the original IRQ 2 handler to maintain backward compatibility.

By default, an interrupt request generated by COM1 is signaled on the IRQ 4 line of the PC's bus. This line is subsequently connected to the PIC. But whether the interrupt signaled on this line is passed to the CPU depends on the setting of the PIC's interrupt mask register (IMR).

The IMR is an 8-bit read/write register that contains one bit for each of the interrupt input lines it controls in a pleasant correspondence. For the primary PIC, bit 3 in the IMR controls IRQ 3, and bit 4 of the IMR controls IRQ 4.

When an IMR bit is set to 1, the corresponding IRQ line is disabled (masked). To allow the interrupts from COM1 to pass to the CPU, the corresponding bit in the primary PIC's IMR must be unmasked (cleared to 0). IMR bit values not specifically being altered should be preserved.

The 8088-based PC and XT contain only one PIC. On these machines, the only IMR that must be manipulated is located at I/O address 21h. On AT and higher class machines, IRQ 2 is impersonated by IRQ 9. Unmasking this IRQ requires that both bit 2 of the primary PIC (IRQ 2 cascade input) and bit 1 of the secondary PIC (IRQ 9 input) be cleared to 0.

As interrupts are received by the PIC, it prioritizes them and passes them on to the CPU. IRQ 0 has the highest priority and IRQ 7 the lowest. A higher priority interrupt that arrives while a lower priority interrupt is being serviced will interrupt the lower priority interrupt. A lower priority interrupt that arrives while a higher priority interrupt is being serviced will not be acknowledged until the higher priority interrupt handler clears the interrupt. To do this, the handler must send a *nonspecific end-of-interrupt* (EOI) command to the PIC by writing the value 20h to I/O address 20h (or to A0h for the secondary PIC).

The Interrupt Service Routine

Fortunately, once enabled, this IRQ processing takes place automatically. An application program is free to perform other tasks until control is transferred to it by a CPU-generated interrupt instruction. The application must have an interrupt handler in place prior to enabling the PC's interrupt mechanism. Table 4.8 shows the CPU interrupt numbers generated for the hardware IRQs typically used in serial communications.

TABLE 4.8

IRQ-Generated Processor Interrupts

IRQ Number	CPU Interrupt
2	Int Ah[1]
3	Int Bh
4	Int Ch
5	Int Dh
7	Int Fh

1 May be redirected by BIOS from Int 71h for compatibility.

On AT and later computers, IRQ 9 (masquerading as IRQ 2) actually generates an Int 71h. This interrupt points to the BIOS, which issues an EOI to the secondary controller, and then executes an Int Ah instruction. This makes IRQ 2 appear to operate as it did on the PC and XT.

5 *D*ATA MODEMS

PCS AND OTHER DTE DEVICES ARE FUNDAMENTALLY DIGITAL, AND THE INformation that they generate and receive is expected to be in digital format. The serial communications adapter described in Chapter 4 changes the voltage levels of the PC's signals, but it doesn't change their digital nature. In contrast, the general switched telephone network (GSTN) is theoretically an analog network. Information is transferred over the network using principles that have changed little since the days of Alexander Graham Bell.

At its simplest, a modem is simply a device that interfaces between the digital world of the DTE and the analog world of the GSTN, as shown in Figure 5.1. The modem receives digital information from the PC and converts it to an analog signal in the form of audio tones. These audio tones are transmitted over the telephone lines to another modem and reconverted back to digital form. It is from this process of *mo*dulating and subsequently *dem*odulating a signal that we derive the acronym mo-dem.

This chapter begins with a general overview of modem characteristics and then explains the basic principles that support modem operation. It summarizes the primary modulation methods used in modems. Finally, a review of some of the more advanced techniques used in modems, including the MNP 5 and V.42bis compression standards, is presented.

Classifying Modems

All modems are not created equal. In fact, there are nearly as many different types of modems available today as there are communication problems to overcome—in other words, a truly bewildering number. Characterizing a modem requires examining the modem's intended use, its physical configuration and connection requirements, and its ability to respond to changing conditions. The primary reason for classifying modems is to ensure compatibility between the two ends of a communications link.

FIGURE 5.1

A typical long-distance communication path

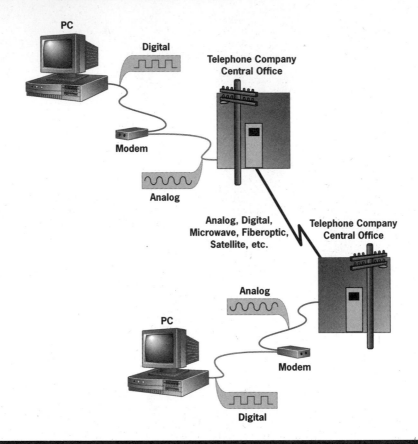

Modems fall into two broad categories, as determined by the type of communications channel to which they are designed to be connected. The first type of modem operates over a telephone line that has been leased from a common carrier. (These are also called private lines.) A *leased-line modem* may operate synchronously or asynchronously using half-duplex or full-duplex communication. It is common for a leased line to provide two two-wire pairs, with each pair carrying data exclusively in one direction.

The situation implied by the use of a private line is that the modems on each end are generally required to talk only to each other. It is common, therefore, for manufacturers to use proprietary modulation techniques and command sets in an effort to improve performance and distinguish their products. The result is that broad compatibility among leased line modems is less critical and consequently less common.

The second type of modem is designed for use over the GSTN. These modems, commonly known as *dial-up modems,* face a situation opposite that of the leased-line modems. Because the GSTN is designed to connect any two points in the system, theoretically a modem can never be sure of what type of equipment is on the other end of the connection. It's of more importance, therefore, for dial-up modems to conform to nonproprietary standards. Operating characteristics and standards for modems are discussed here.

Physical Characteristics

At one time, the American Telephone and Telegraph company (AT&T) held a near-monopoly on the local and long-distance telephone network in the United States. As a result, it typically specified, created, and owned any piece of equipment that connected to the network. In the recent past, establishing a data connection required the user to manually dial the phone, wait for a tone from the answering modem, and then plunge the handset into an acoustic coupler or toggle a voice/data switch. When the session was completed, the user simply hung up the phone.

Fortunately, modems based on these techniques have all but disappeared. Today, even low-cost modems are designed for direct connection to the telephone network via a standard modular connector. Most modems provide an extra jack, usually under modem control, to which you can reconnect your telephone, allowing digital and voice communications to share a single line.

Internal modems are designed to plug into one of the PC's expansion slots and are popular among both desktop and laptop users. These modems are typically fabricated on a half-length adapter and draw their power directly from the PC itself. An on-board UART interface exchanges data directly with the PC, eliminating the need for an RS-232 interface.

Functionally, an external modem is identical to its internal counterpart. But because an external modem requires a case, power supply, display unit, RS-232 interface, and other hardware not required by an internal unit, it tends to be more expensive.

Data Handling

The data handling capabilities of a modem are described by the modulation, error control, and data compression techniques it supports. Modulation methods, for example, range from the simple 300 bps scheme described by the Bell 103 standard to the 28.8 kbps V.FAST standard currently under development by the CCITT. For many applications, transfer speed has become *the* critical modem characteristic.

Hand-in-hand with an increase in modem transfer speeds is an increase in the modem's susceptibility to line noise and other interference. A burst of noise that occurs for the duration of one bit at a 300 bps transfer rate will destroy 32 bits in the same time at 9600 bps! To compensate for this, all 9600 bps and faster modems (and many lower speed modems) incorporate some form of error control. Of course, for the error control to be effective, the modems on both ends of the connection must be using the same method.

Increasing the modem speed is one way to increase data throughput. Another method, however, is to compress the data so that the same information can be sent in less time. This is exactly the function that data compression modems perform. The concept of data compression isn't new. But the increased demand for higher transfer speeds and the availability of standardized compression algorithms has brought the use of this technique to the forefront of modem discussions. More information on modulation, error control, and data compression techniques is presented later in this chapter.

Intelligence

Early modems were most often used to connect dumb terminals to a mainframe computer. Typically, a user would dial the phone manually and then throw a switch (or use an acoustic coupler) to connect the modem to the phone line. There wasn't any requirement for the modem to dial the telephone or negotiate protocols. In retrospect, these modems are generally referred to as *dumb modems*.

Conversely, nearly all PC modems today are known as smart modems. The term *Smartmodem* was coined (and trademarked) by Hayes Microcomputer Products Inc. to describe its then-revolutionary 300 baud modem. The Smartmodem differed from the majority of earlier modems in that it operated in two distinct modes. In *command* mode, the characters sent to the modem by the DTE (a PC, for example) were interpreted as commands for the modem itself, not data to be transmitted. The modem was also able to reply, reporting its status to the DTE. All modems of this type are now referred to as smart or intelligent modems.

Smartmodem commands always begin with the two-character sequence AT (nominally, for *at*tention). These characters were required to be both uppercase or both lowercase, and, because they were expected by the modem, were used to determine the speed and data format in use by the DCE. This system was widely copied by other manufacturers, making it a de facto standard. Typical AT commands include those to dial a number, turn the built-in speaker on or off, and answer an incoming call.

Another property of the Smartmodem that is widely emulated is the use of internal modem registers. The values written to these registers are used to customize the operation of the modem. Examples of programmable modem options included the number of rings to wait before answering an incoming call and how long to try to establish a link before giving up.

The original AT command set was very modest, as befitted the capabilities of the original Smartmodem. As modem capabilities increased, the AT command set was expanded to provide additional control functions. To make their modems "Hayes compatible," other manufactures copied the basic AT command set, and then defined proprietary command extensions of their own. So, although most modems share the basic AT commands, it's all too rare to find two modems that use the same commands or syntax to implement advanced features.

The AT command set is discussed in more detail in Chapter 6. A reference guide to the common and proprietary AT commands is also given in Appendix A. Further extensions to the AT command set to support fax operations are described in Chapter 9.

Modem Operation

In a typical connection between a PC and a modem, the data signal is in the form of digital data values impressed as voltage changes directly onto the interconnecting transmission line. The modem then converts the digital data into a series of audio signals and subsequently transmits them over the telephone line. The procedure the modem uses to convert the digital data to audio tones is called *modulation*.

Fundamental Modulation Types

To represent the digital values 0 and 1, the modem may modulate the amplitude, frequency, or phase of an audio signal. Figure 5.2 shows a representation of a digital signal and the resulting audio tones produced by amplitude, frequency, and phase modulation.

Figure 5.2a shows the original digital data consisting of the binary sequence 1011001. This signal is called the *baseband signal*. Figure 5.2b shows the signal that results when the binary signal is used to modulate the amplitude of the audio signal. When the digital input signal is 1, the amplitude of the output tone is high (loud). Conversely, when the digital input is 0, the amplitude of the output tone is low. This technique is called *amplitude modulation (AM)*.

Figure 5.2c shows an example of frequency modulation. When the value of the digital modulating signal is 1, a high-frequency audio tone is transmitted. Conversely, a low audio tone is used to represent a 0. This modulation is often referred to as *frequency shift keying (FSK)*.

Note that both of the audio tones used in FSK have the same amplitude. If an FSK demodulator is designed to respond to frequency changes but be insensitive to amplitude changes, it will discriminate against most forms of noise that would corrupt an amplitude modulated signal.

In phase modulation, a single audio tone at a constant amplitude is transmitted. The characteristic of the audio tone that is modulated by the digital input signal is the phase of the tone. This situation is shown in Figure 5.2d. At the receiver, the phase of the tone is measured with respect to some reference value. This modulation is known as *phase-shift keying (PSK)*.

FIGURE 5.2

Baseband and modulated signals

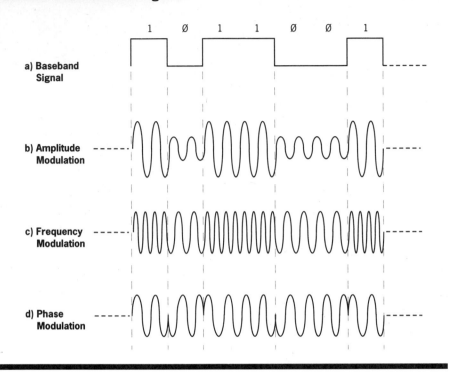

When the phase of the tone shifts, there is an instantaneous frequency change. This frequency change is detected as a corresponding phase change at the receiver. Frequency and phase modulation are not completely independent, since the frequency cannot be varied without also varying the phase, and vice versa.

Amplitude modulation is rarely used by itself because of its susceptibility to errors caused by noise bursts and signal fading. Frequency modulation is inexpensive to implement and is typically seen in modems that operate at speeds of 1200 bps or slower. To achieve speeds greater than 1200 bps reliably, modems often combine phase and amplitude modulation, as described later in this section.

Differential Phase-Shift Keying

In a PSK system, the receiver's demodulator must provide some method of determining phase shifts. Because there is no ready source of absolute phase reference at the receiver, the demodulator must derive a phase reference. In basic PSK systems, the received signal is compared with a fixed phase source. Some systems also periodically transmit phase-reference information.

The requirement for an absolute phase reference can be eliminated, however, by measuring the relative phase of the current signal element with respect to the previous signal element. Thus the demodulator detects the *difference* in phase between the two signal elements. This technique is called *differential phase-shift keying* (*DPSK*).

DPSK systems may be identified by the number of phase states they provide for signal encoding. A binary DPSK system, for example, would provide two phase states and be referred to as DSPK-2. In this case, each bit of the modulating baseband signal would correspond to one phase change in the transmitted signal. A 0 digit might be encoded as a +90° phase change and a 1 digit as a +270° phase change relative to the previous signal element.

Recall, however, that a signal element (or, equivalently, a symbol) is defined as a *change in state* of the circuit. In other words, regardless of the number of independent states that the circuit can assume, a signal element is the transition between any two of those states. To increase the data transfer rates without increasing the signaling rate it's necessary to define sufficient states to encode more than 1 bit per signal element.

It's quite common for DPSK systems to encode more than 1 bit per signal element, with a resultant increase in the number of defined phase change states. A DPSK-4 system encodes two binary digits (a dibit) per signal element. The four states might be defined as shown in Table 5.1.

TABLE 5.1

Phase Changes Encoded by a DPSK-4 System

Dibit Value	Phase Change
00	+270°
01	+180°
10	+90°
11	0°

Other systems use DPSK-8 modulation to encode three binary digits (a tribit) per signal element. In this case, adjacent phase states would be separated by a 45° phase shift. The use of higher levels of DPSK encoding is limited both by the ability of the system to generate and detect smaller phase changes and by the increased susceptibility of the system to small errors (jitter) in phase or frequency during transmission.

Quadrature Amplitude Modulation

Another encoding system that uses phase changes to carry information is *quadrature amplitude modulation* (*QAM*). Unlike the one-dimensional DPSK encoding system, where only one component of the signal (phase) carries information, QAM is a two-dimensional signal system, varying both phase and amplitude.

In the transmitter, the incoming data stream is split into two streams a(*t*) and b(*t*). The a(*t*) bit stream is modulated by the signal cos(ωt) and the b(*t*) bit stream is modulated by the signal sin(ωt), where ω is related to the carrier frequency by the relationship f=ω/2π. The modulation results are summed to give the transmitted signal x(*t*), as shown here:

```
x(t)=a(t)*cos(ωt)+b(t)*sin(ωt)
```

Portions of the modulating data streams are used to modulate the amplitude of each signal. The sin(ωt) and cos(ωt) signals represent carrier tones that are always 90° out of phase—that is, in *quadrature*. Hence the term quadrature amplitude modulation.

The CCITT V.29 standard contains three examples of QAM encoding schemes. The simplest scheme is used to encode data for transmission at 4800 bps. The bit stream to be transmitted is divided into groups of two bits (dibits). The value of each dibit determines the phase change relative to the previous signal element, as shown in Table 5.2.

TABLE 5.2

Phase Change Encoding Used in 4800 bps V.29 Operation

Bit 1	Bit 2	Phase Change
0	0	0°
0	1	90°
1	0	270°
1	1	180°

To visualize the resulting signal, the set of all phase and amplitude points is usually plotted on a two-dimensional graph called a signal space diagram or a *constellation*. On this graph, each of the possible phase/amplitude combinations is shown as a point. The point is simply the tip of the vector with the specified amplitude rotated to the appropriate absolute phase angle. Phase is measured from the 0° axis, with rotation in the counterclockwise direction representing increasingly positive phase.

In the V.29 encoding scheme described, the amplitude of the signal elements at 4800 bps is, in all cases, 3. The resulting constellation is shown in Figure 5.3. Of course, as the scheme shown here illustrates, a QAM system that uses only a single amplitude degenerates to a DPSK system.

FIGURE 5.3

Constellation for V.29 4800 bps QAM encoding

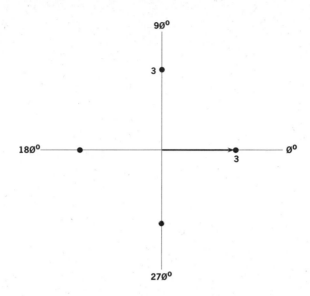

At 7200 bps, the encoding system used by V.29 becomes more intriguing. The bits to be transmitted are divided into groups of three consecutive bits (tribits). The value of each tribit determines the phase change relative to the previous signal element, as shown in Table 5.3.

TABLE 5.3

Phase Change Encoding Used in 7200 bps V.29 Operation

Bit 1	Bit 2	Bit 3	Phase Change
0	0	0	45°
0	0	1	0°
0	1	0	90°
0	1	1	135°
1	0	0	270°
1	0	1	315°
1	1	0	225°
1	1	1	180°

CHAPTER 5 *Data Modems*

If each of the signal elements was transmitted with the same amplitude, this would again degenerate into simply a DPSK system. But in this case, the amplitude of each signal element is determined by its absolute phase. If the phase of the element to be transmitted is 0°, 90°, 180°, or 270°, its amplitude is set to 3. If the phase is 45°, 135°, 225°, or 315°, the amplitude is set to √2. The resulting constellation is shown in Figure 5.4.

FIGURE 5.4

Constellation for V.29 7200 bps QAM encoding

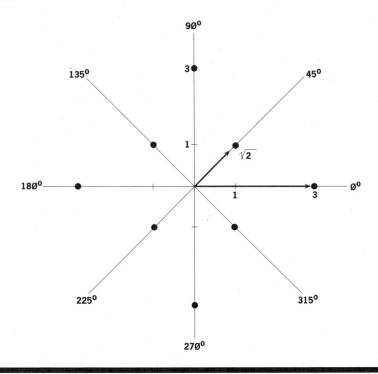

It is precisely this combination of two independent forms of modulation that makes QAM such a powerful form of modulation. To understand why, convert the 7200 bps transfer system just described into a DPSK-8 system by transmitting all signal elements with the same amplitude. Now imagine that a signal element, transmitted at 45°, is corrupted during transmission and arrives at the receiving modem with a phase of 22.5°. Because the signal element is equally close to the valid 0° and 45° signal states, the modem is unable to determine the intended value.

In the QAM implementation, however, the modem need not rely solely on the phase information. Instead, it can attempt to select the closest valid signal state with the correct amplitude. The same phase error that crippled the DPSK system in the previous example is easily handled by the QAM system. The correct phase value for the signal element that arrives with a phase of 22.5° and an amplitude of √2 is 45°.

The final QAM scheme used in V.29 implements a 9600 bps transfer rate. By defining two possible amplitude values for each of eight possible phase values, one of 16 possible states can be encoded in each signal element. The data stream to be transmitted is grouped 4 bits (a quadbit) at a time. Three of the bits are used to determine the differential phase exactly as in the 7200 bps scheme. The fourth bit is used to determine the amplitude, as shown in Table 5.4. The resulting constellation is shown in Figure 5.5.

FIGURE 5.5

Constellation for V.29 9600 bps QAM encoding

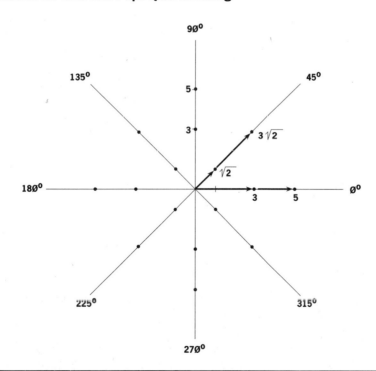

TABLE 5.4

Signal Element Amplitude Determination in V.29 9600 bps Encoding

Bit 4	Absolute Phase	Relative Amplitude
0	0°, 90°, 180°, or 270°	3
	45°, 135°, 225°, or 315°	$\sqrt{2}$
1	0°, 90°, 180°, or 270°	5
	45°, 135°, 225°, or 315°	$3\sqrt{2}$

QAM Demodulation   The goal of a QAM receiver is to recover the original a(*t*) and b(*t*) bit streams that were used to modulate the carrier. To do so, the incoming signal x(*t*) is fed through a Hilbert transformer that splits the input signal into two components that are 90 degrees out of phase with respect to each other. (This affects only the phase, not the amplitude.) The two resulting signals are multiplied by the two quadrature components of the carrier and applied to low pass filters to recover the baseband components. Figure 5.6 shows a block diagram of the demodulation process. The demodulation equations are shown here.

$$a(t)=x(t)*\cos(\omega t)-x(t+90°)*\sin(\omega t)$$
$$b(t)=-x(t)*\sin(\omega t)-x(t+90°)*\cos(\omega t)$$

FIGURE 5.6

Block diagram of a QAM demodulator

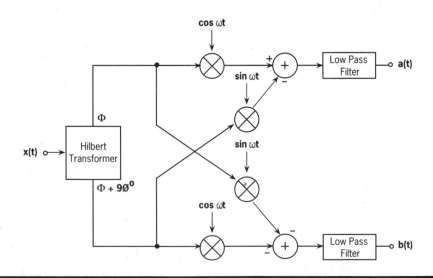

Trellis Coding

The number of phase/amplitude points that can be defined in a practical QAM constellation is limited by a number of physical factors. As the distinct states move closer together in phase and amplitude, there's an increasing chance that a small change in phase or amplitude will result in an error. To improve the reliability of a QAM system, a forward error correction scheme known as *trellis coding* may be employed.

Simply put, a trellis coding algorithm accepts m data bits as input and produces $m+1$ bits as output. The extra bit is generated by a convolution algorithm and represents redundant information. The $m+1$ bits are then fed into a normal QAM system with 2^{m+1} states.

Because only m bits are really being encoded, only 2^m states are required to represent the data. Thus, only a subset of the possible signal points in the constellation are defined as valid. If a line error causes a signal element to resolve to an invalid signal point, the receiver selects the most likely valid signal point. Trellis coding thus reduces the system's susceptibility to signal errors.

A practical example of trellis coding is found in the V.32 standard for transmission at 9600 bps. In this case, the data bits to be transmitted are selected four at a time. The first and second bits of the group, designated $Q1_n$ and $Q2_n$, are differentially encoded with the previous encoder outputs, $Y1_{n-1}$ and $Y2_{n-1}$, to produce the bits $Y1_n$ and $Y2_n$. Here, the n subscript represents the sequence number of the quadbit in time.

This encoding process is shown as a state diagram in Figure 5.7. The dibit values in the large circles represent the encoder outputs. To find the encoder output that results from a new dibit input, start from the circle that contains the previous value of the encoder output. Then follow the arrow marked with the dibit value corresponding to Q1 and Q2 to the next encoder state. The relationship between the input and output states of the encoder is also tabulated in Table 5.5.

TABLE 5.5

V.32 9600 bps Differential Encoding Table

Data Bits (Input)		Previous Output		Encoder Output	
$Q1_n$	$Q2_n$	$Y1_{n-1}$	$Y2_{n-1}$	$Y1_n$	$Y2_n$
0	0	0	0	0	0
0	0	0	1	0	1
0	0	1	0	1	0
0	0	1	1	1	1
0	1	0	0	0	1
0	1	0	1	0	0
0	1	1	0	1	1
0	1	1	1	1	0

TABLE 5.5

V.32 9600 bps Differential Encoding Table (Continued)

Data Bits (Input)		Previous Output		Encoder Output	
1	0	0	0	1	0
1	0	0	1	1	1
1	0	1	0	0	1
1	0	1	1	0	0
1	1	0	0	1	1
1	1	0	1	1	0
1	1	1	0	0	0
1	1	1	1	0	1

FIGURE 5.7

V.32 9600 bps differential encoding state diagram

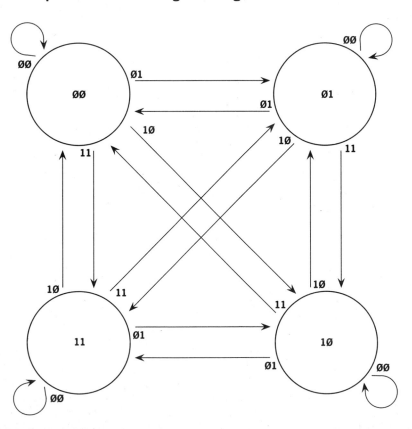

Once encoded, the bits Y1 and Y2 are fed to a convolutional encoder that generates the redundant bit Y0. Figure 5.8 shows a logic diagram of the convolutional encoder defined by the V.32 standard.

FIGURE 5.8

V.32 9600 bps convolutional encoder circuit

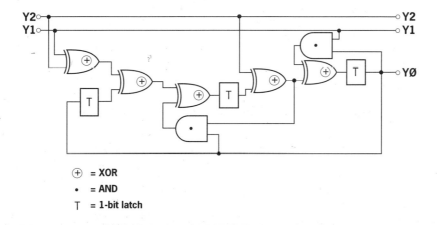

$\oplus$ = XOR

$\cdot$ = AND

T = 1-bit latch

Finally, the five bits Q4, Q3, Y2, Y1, and Y0 are used to generate the points of the QAM constellation, as listed in Table 5.6. The signal point locations are given in cartesian coordinates on the real (x) and imaginary (y) axes. (This is simply for convenience, and the coordinates can be easily expressed in radial coordinates, as in the previous section.) The resulting constellation is shown in Figure 5.9.

Packetized Ensemble Protocol

Not all noteworthy modulation techniques are embodied in international standards. The Telebit Corporation uses a proprietary form of QAM in many of its modems, and it allows data transfer speeds of up to 23 kbps before data compression. This modulation management system has been dubbed *dynamically adaptive multicarrier QAM (DAMQAM)*. More often, it's known by the more common term, *packetized ensemble protocol (PEP)*.

The PEP modulation scheme works by dividing a telephone voice channel into 511 subbands. When two PEP modems attempt a connection, they transmit calibration signals to each other over each of these subbands. After evaluating the signals received, the modems negotiate how to adapt themselves to the usable frequencies and thus exchange the maximum amount of data permitted by the current connection conditions.

TABLE 5.6

V.32 9600 bps Trellis Coded Signal Points

Encoded Input Bits					Trellis Code Output	
Y0	Y1	Y2	Q3	Q4	Real (x)	Imaginary (y)
0	0	0	0	0	-4	1
0	0	0	0	1	0	-3
0	0	0	1	0	0	1
0	0	0	1	1	4	1
0	0	1	0	0	4	-1
0	0	1	0	1	0	3
0	0	1	1	0	0	-1
0	0	1	1	1	-4	-1
0	1	0	0	0	-2	3
0	1	0	0	1	-2	-1
0	1	0	1	0	2	3
0	1	0	1	1	2	-1
0	1	1	0	0	2	-3
0	1	1	0	1	2	1
0	1	1	1	0	-2	-3
0	1	1	1	1	-2	1
1	0	0	0	0	-3	-2
1	0	0	0	1	1	-2
1	0	0	1	0	-3	2
1	0	0	1	1	1	2
1	0	1	0	0	3	2
1	0	1	0	1	-1	2
1	0	1	1	0	3	-2
1	0	1	1	1	-1	-2
1	1	0	0	0	1	4
1	1	0	0	1	-3	0
1	1	0	1	0	1	0
1	1	0	1	1	1	-4
1	1	1	0	0	-1	-4
1	1	1	0	1	3	0
1	1	1	1	0	-1	0
1	1	1	1	1	-1	4

FIGURE 5.9

Constellation for V.29 9600 bps QAM encoding

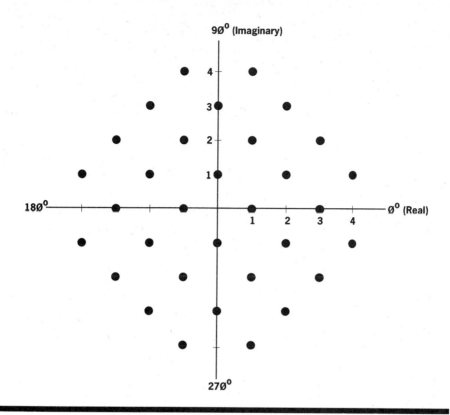

Compared to other high-speed modems, PEP modems are more readily able to adjust themselves to work with imperfect line conditions. Faced with adverse conditions, PEP modems will typically reduce their transmission speeds in steps as small as 100 bps. Of course, both modems must support the PEP encoding system to take advantage of increased transfer rates.

Data Scrambling

Most high-speed data transmission standards perform synchronous data transmission over the GSTN. Recall that in synchronous transmission, a clock signal is required to identify the signal elements in the data stream. Most synchronous modems derive the clock signal from the data itself. To do so, however, requires that the incoming data stream contains a sufficient number of state changes to provide synchronization.

To ensure that the receiving modem doesn't receive a long stream of unchanging data, modern standards specify the use of a data *scrambler*. The scrambler randomizes the data so that all bit patterns have a near-equal chance of occurring. This action also ensures that the energy of the modulated carrier is spread over the band of interest.

In the V.22 standard, the scrambler's operation is represented using polynomial operations. The transmitting modem contains a scrambler based on the generator polynomial $1+x^{-14}+x^{-17}$. The incoming data stream is divided by the generator polynomial. The coefficients of the quotients of the division form the bit sequence that appears at the output of the scrambler. Optional circuitry may be included to detect and modify input strings that—even after scrambling— would result in loss of synchronization.

In a practical circuit, this scrambler is typically implemented a 17-bit shift register. Bit outputs from the 14th and 17th stages are XORed, and then the result is further XORed with the input bit. The resulting bit is then transmitted by the modem. At the receiving modem, the demodulated data stream is fed through a descrambler that performs the complementary operation. Note that in some standards, different generator polynomials are used for scrambling, depending on the direction of data flow.

Channel Separation Techniques

The GSTN is designed to facilitate the transfer of analog voice signals. To modems attempting to exchange digital data, however, the GSTN can be a hostile environment. Transformers, carrier systems, and loaded lines attenuate all signals below 300 Hz and above 3400 Hz. This signal bandwidth restriction ultimately limits the signaling rate that can be used in modulation schemes.

Other problems result because signals from either end of the connection must travel over the same two-wire circuit path. A modem listening on the same circuit on which it transmits will hear only itself. This problem is compounded by the presence of echoes of the original signal caused by mismatched electrical connections in the transmission line.

To keep the transmitted and received data separate under these conditions, modems must implement some form of channel separation. Channel separation techniques commonly found in modems are discussed in this section.

Time Multiplexing The simplest method of channel separation isolates the data in time. In a half-duplex system, data can flow in either direction—but in only one direction at a time. After establishing a connection, the two modems must implement a protocol that includes a method for alternating roles as transmitter and receiver (turning the line around).

Because half-duplex systems can be implemented quite simply, they often represent a savings in hardware cost. In other cases—fax transmissions for example—the flow of data is typically one way. The inability of the receiver to interrupt the transmitter, however, pits high throughput against fast-response error control.

Frequency Multiplexing   Full-duplex data transmission—simultaneous transmission and reception—is possible using a technique called *frequency multiplexing*. In this system, the GSTN voice channel is divided into two bands of frequencies. To separate the transmit and receive signals, the *originating* modem transmits in the low band and receives in the high band, while the *answering* modem transmits in the high band and receives in the low band. (The terms originate and answer serve only to identify the frequencies used and bear no relation to which modem initiated the connection.)

The Bell 103 standard describes a 300 baud full-duplex FSK system using frequency multiplexing. In this case, the center frequencies of each band are established by carriers of nominally 1170 Hz and 2125 Hz. A frequency shift of ±100 Hz about the carrier frequency is used to generate the MARK and SPACE tones within each band. Figure 5.10 shows an idealized representation of the frequency allocation for this system. The success of any frequency multiplexed system relies on the ability to accurately generate and discriminate the frequency of audio signals.

FIGURE 5.10

Channel separation by frequency multiplexing

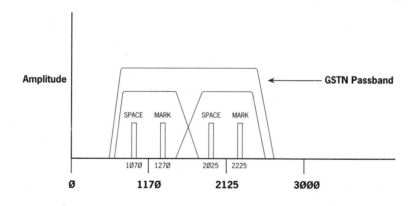

The total information carrying capacity of a frequency multiplexed full-duplex system and a half-duplex system over the same channel is identical. In the full-duplex system, however, the total capacity is split, each direction having somewhat less than half of the total system capacity. In many cases, the benefits of full-duplex transmission may outweigh the reduced transfer speed.

Some systems divide the frequency spectrum asymmetrically. A majority of the data carrying capacity is dedicated to transmission in one direction. This direction is called the *primary channel*. The remainder of the spectrum is used for lower-speed transmission and is called the *back channel*. Typically, the back channel is used to transmit control messages, acknowledgments, and other commands.

Echo Cancellation Although frequency multiplexing provides full-duplex data transfer on the GSTN, it does so at the expense of information-carrying capacity. Modems with higher signaling rates require more bandwidth than can be provided in a split channel. A new technique, called *echo cancellation*, was developed to overcome these limitations.

In a system equipped with echo cancellation, the transmitters in both modems can transmit using approximately the same analog tones at the same time. In this way, each modem is able to use the entire available bandwidth of the channel to transmit information. Each modem's transmitted signal, however, appears at the input of its receiver. This unwanted signal is called the *near-end echo* and masks the signal from the remote modem.

To allow each modem's receiver to hear an incoming signal, the local transmitter signal is subtracted from the composite signal on the transmission line. By canceling its own transmitted signal, each modem is able to hear the signal being sent by the other modem. Figure 5.11 shows a block diagram of an echo cancellation system.

FIGURE 5.11

Channel separation using echo cancellation

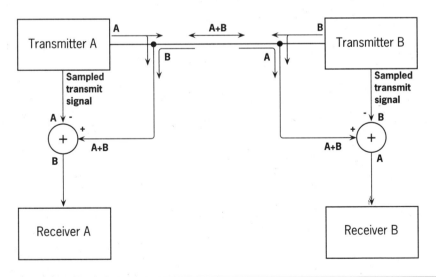

Error Control

As a modem's data transfer rate increases, so does its susceptibility to line noise and other interference. Software-based error control protocols—XMODEM for example—have been developed to ensure error-free data transfer. These protocols, however, depend on the intelligence in the receiving DTE to determine whether an error has occurred. If an examination of the received data reveals an error, the receiving DTE requests a retransmission of the data from the remote DTE. In keeping with the trend toward increased intelligence in modems, error control functions are being relocated into the modems themselves.

Several proprietary methods of error control have been developed. The Hayes V-series modems, for example, use the LAP-B (Link Access Procedure-Balanced) protocol to implement error control. (LAP-B is the link layer portion of the X.25 standard that specifies packet mode operation on a public data network.) And USRobotics, Inc., uses a proprietary error control standard developed for their HST line of high-speed modems.

Proprietary methods aside, however, most manufacturers implement one of two error control protocols. The first is based on the family of Microcom Networking Protocol (MNP) standards. The second error control protocol is called Link Access Procedure for Modems (LAPM). Both error control methods are specified by the CCITT as part of the V.42 standard. The LAPM protocol is the primary method, while MNP 4 is specified as the alternative method.

Note that alternative doesn't mean optional. For a modem to be termed V.42 *compliant*, it must implement both the LAPM and MNP 2 through 4 protocols. A modem that implements only the LAPM protocol is considered V.42 *compatible*. Unless specified by user options, however, two V.42 modems must first attempt a LAPM connection. If one or both of the modems support only MNP, they will communicate using that protocol.

Microcom Networking Protocol   As with other modem enhancements, a few pioneers blazed the paths for the standards that followed. Microcom, Inc., developed a series of protocols for error control that became the de facto standards in high-performance modems. The Microcom Networking Protocol standards are divided into a series of classes. The first four classes, MNP 1 through 4, have been placed in the public domain. Use of the remaining classes requires a license agreement from Microcom. The MNP classes applicable to error control are described here.

MNP class 1 is applicable to asynchronous byte-oriented half-duplex data exchange. It was developed to allow devices with minimal hardware resources to implement error control. Since the development of MNP 1, modems have become dramatically more powerful. As a result, MNP 1 capability is not included in current modems.

MNP class 2 represents an upgrade to full-duplex communication and requires a microprocessor-based modem. Data is still exchanged using standard asynchronous framing techniques. Because the protocol overhead must be transmitted in addition to the original data, the actual throughput of the modem is less than its transfer rate.

MNP class 3 establishes a synchronous connection between modems. The bytes of data received from the DTE are arranged in groups called *packets*. Each packet is sent as a synchronous frame. This technique eliminates the

START and STOP bits normally sent with each byte, decreasing the transmission overhead.

MNP class 4 introduces two new data management techniques. The first technique enables the modem to change the size of the data packets in response to the condition of the connection. Possible packet sizes include 32, 64, 128, 192, and 256 bytes. On noisy lines, for example, the size of the packets is reduced, increasing the chance that a packet will be transferred without error and thus not need to be retransmitted. On high-quality lines, the size of the packets is increased, reducing the overhead and increasing throughput.

The second technique embodied in MNP 4 allows repetitive control information to be eliminated from the data stream. The result is that overhead is reduced and more of the information capacity of the channel is used to carry data. These two techniques, combined with MNP 3, can produce a throughput of 120 percent of the modem's data rate.

The MNP error control protocol is implemented as an alternative procedure in V.42. Two modes of operation are available based on the format of the data. For byte-oriented data streams (where each byte is sent with its own START and STOP bits), four special values are used as flags to identify the beginning and end of a data packet. A byte-oriented packet consists of the following fields:

- Start flags

- Header

- Information

- Stop flags

- 16-bit Frame Check Sequence (FCS)

The start flags occupy three bytes and the stop flags occupy two bytes. The flag values are chosen to ensure that data values are not misread as flags and vice versa. The header field contains both fixed-length and variable-length parameters and carries commands, responses, and packet sequence numbers. The information field contains the data being transferred.

Note that the frame check sequence (a 16-bit CRC value) is appended to the packet following the stop flags. The CRC polynomial used in this mode is not the same as that used by the LAPM protocol.

The second MNP mode operates on the data as if it were a continuous bit stream. In this case, the packets have the following fields:

- Start flag

- Header

- Information

- 16-bit Frame Check Sequence (FCS)

■ Stop flag

In this mode, the start and stop flags are identical and occupy 8 bits. The 16-bit FCS is identical to that used in the LAPM procedure. All other fields are the same as for the byte-oriented packet.

During high-speed data transfer, the transmitting modem sends a stream of packets. It does not wait for each packet to be acknowledged individually before sending the subsequent one. As a result, when an error is reported, the modem may have to back up several packets before beginning the retransmission. All packets after the corrupted one are retransmitted—even if they were received without error. MNP class 9 improves the efficiency of this operation by allowing retransmission of only the corrupted packets.

MNP class 10 is relatively new, and is designed to allow data transfer under adverse or varying line conditions, such as those found in cellular telephone connections. Key features of MNP 10 include allowing multiple connection attempts, dynamically adjusting the modem's transmit level, and a greater ability to adjust packet size. An additional enhancement provided by MNP 10 is the ability to change the connection speed not only down (fallback), but also up if line conditions improve.

V.42 Link Access Procedure for Modems   The CCITT V.42 standard specifies Link Access Procedure for Modems (LAPM) as its primary error control protocol. LAPM is a protocol based on High-level Data Link Control (HDLC) formats and procedures. LAPM provides some advantages over MNP 4, including improved handshaking during connection establishment, better performance over poor lines, and compatibility with emerging OSI communications standards for ISDN.

Under LAPM, all data is transmitted in packets (frames) that are bracketed by an 8-bit flag value. Each packet contains the following fields:

■ Opening flag

■ Address

■ Control

■ Information (optional)

■ Frame Check Sequence (FCS)

■ Closing flag

The address field identifies the packet's sequence number. If required by the error control protocol, the sequence number can be used to specify the packet to be retransmitted. The control field is used to distinguish between the two different frame types: command and response. Depending on the type of the frame, the information field may be present. The frame check sequence is a 16-bit or 32-bit CRC value used to check the integrity of the packet. Packets are

exchanged by the two modems as required to transfer the data and implement error control.

Data Compression

The technique of data compression is hardly a modern invention. Its integration into high-speed modems, however, has made it a popular topic. Data compression works by watching the data stream for repeated sequences of characters and converting them into a shorthand notation. At the receiving modem, this shorthand is expanded into a duplicate of the original data. In effect, more information has been moved in the same period of time, giving an apparent increase in the modem's throughput.

The more sophisticated compression algorithms used in data modems must typically undergo a learning period. If the composition of the data stream changes radically, the effective transfer speed will suffer until sufficient data has been transferred to allow the algorithm to relearn. Many types of files cannot be compressed during transmission. Executable files, for example, and files that have been compressed before transmission are poor candidates for compression in the modem.

Two data compression standards are in common use. The first is defined in the CCITT V.42bis standard and is designed to be used in conjunction with the V.42 error control technique. The second compression standard is defined in Microcom's MNP protocols as MNP 5 and MNP 7 and is designed to be used with MNP 2-4 error control. Both the MNP and V.42bis forms of data compression are explained here.

MNP 5   The MNP 5 protocol uses a combination of adaptive Huffman encoding and run length encoding (RLE) to reduce highly compressible data to approximately 50 percent of its uncompressed size. The result is an effective transfer rate of twice the modem's data rate.

The first stage of MNP 5 compression uses run length encoding to avoid sending large sequences of repetitive characters. This technique converts runs of between 3 and 253 identical contiguous characters to the form *character* × *count*. Because run length encoding is non-computationally intensive, it is particularly suited to on-line transmission of data.

In operation, a run length encoding system examines the outgoing stream of data. The algorithm remains passive until it detects that three identical contiguous characters have been transmitted. When this occurs, the algorithm then counts and removes up to 250 subsequent identical contiguous characters from the data stream. The count byte is transmitted following the three original characters and transmission resumes. Figure 5.12 shows an example of run length encoding on a data stream.

The ability of run length encoding to compress long strings of identical characters is beyond dispute. Yet, Figure 5.12 also identifies one of the algorithm's weaknesses. Encoding a run of exactly 3 characters actually *expands* the data stream.

FIGURE 5.12

MNP 5 run length encoding

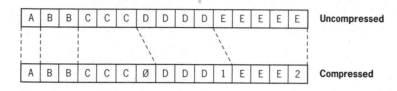

The second stage of MNP 5 compression employs adaptive Huffman encoding, also known as *adaptive frequency encoding*. Huffman encoding operates on the assumption that some characters will appear more frequently in the data stream than others. Characters that appear more often are recoded using fewer bits. Less frequently appearing characters are sent using longer bit sequences.

When the format of the data being transmitted is relatively well known and consistent, the encoding of the bit sequences, or tokens, can be established ahead of time. An adaptive algorithm, however, is able to learn from the data and change its tokens to suit the data.

In MNP 5, 256 tokens are defined for each possible 8-bit value (octet). A token consists of a 3-bit prefix (header) and a suffix (body) that varies from 1 to 8 bits in length. Both transmitter and receiver initialize their character-to-token tables to the state shown in Table 5.7. The first and last entries in the table represent the most and least frequently occurring octet, respectively.

TABLE 5.7

The Character-to-Token Map as It Would Appear at the Start of Compression

Octet Value (Decimal)	Token Header	Token Body
0	000	0
1	000	1
2	001	0
3	001	1
4	010	00
5	010	01
6	010	10
7	010	11
8	011	000
⋮	⋮	⋮

TABLE 5.7

The Character-to-Token Map as It Would Appear at the Start of Compression (Continued)

Octet Value (Decimal)	Token Header	Token Body
15	011	111
16	100	0000
⋮	⋮	⋮
31	100	1111
32	101	00000
⋮	⋮	⋮
63	101	11111
64	110	000000
⋮	⋮	⋮
127	110	111111
128	111	0000000
⋮	⋮	⋮
254	111	1111110
255	111	11111110

As each octet is processed, the table is re-sorted based on the frequency of occurrence of each character. Thus octets that appear most frequently become assigned to the shortest tokens. At the receiving end, the token is re-translated into a character. The frequency of that character is then incremented and the receiving table is re-sorted. Thus the encoding and decoding tables are self-synchronizing.

MNP 7 MNP 7 compression implements a more efficient algorithm than MNP 5 and is able to achieve compression ratios of 3:1. MNP 7 uses an improved form of Huffman encoding in combination with a predictive Markhov algorithm to create the shortest possible Huffman code sequences.

The Markhov algorithm attempts to predict the occurrence of a second character based on the appearance of the first. For each octet, a table of all 256 possible following octets, sorted by their frequency of appearance, is created. An octet is encoded by selecting the column headed by the value of the previous octet, and then searching for the value of the current octet in that column. The row in which the octet is found gives the token in the same way as for Huffman coding described previously. After each octet is coded, the order of entries in the selected column is re-sorted as required to reflect the new octet frequencies.

Figure 5.13 shows an example of how the string of octets 3 1 2 0 would be encoded, assuming that the most recent octet transmitted was 0. As shown, the previous octet column headed by 0 is searched for the 3 entry. The Huffman code for that position in the table is then transmitted. The previous octet column headed by 3 is then searched for the entry that matches the next octet—1 in this case. The resulting Huffman code is then transmitted. Of course, in this example, the adaptive portion of the algorithm that changes the order of entries in each column isn't illustrated.

FIGURE 5.13

Huffman coding using the Markhov Predictive Algorithm

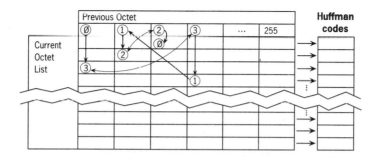

V.42bis The compression techniques embodied in the MNP 5 and MNP 7 protocols are being superseded by designs using the dictionary-based Lempel-Ziv-Welch (LZW) algorithm. The LZW algorithm has two major advantages over MNP. First, LZW compression can produce up to 4:1 compression ratios on cooperative files. Secondly, and perhaps more importantly, the LZW technique has been sanctioned by the CCITT in its V.42bis standard.

V.42bis compression is based on the creation of a tree-based dictionary of strings, each corresponding to a unique codeword. Incoming data is compared against the strings in the dictionary one character at a time. As matches are found, the corresponding codeword for the string is then transmitted. The dictionary of strings is created and updated dynamically by the algorithm.

For example, consider the strings A, BAG, BAR, BIG, CAT, and CE. Figure 5.14 shows how these strings would be represented as trees in the V.42bis dictionary. Each path from a root node to a leaf node represents a string that can be encoded with a single codeword. Existing strings can be expanded until a maximum length is reached. New strings can be added as required, limited only by the size of the dictionary in use.

FIGURE 5.14

V.42bis string dictionary entries

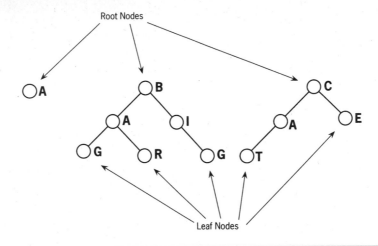

The V.42bis algorithm is flexible. Parameters that can be negotiated between modems include the maximum codeword size, total number of codewords, character size, number of characters in the alphabet, and maximum string length. In addition, the algorithm monitors the input and output data streams to determine its effectiveness. If compression is not occurring (due to the nature of the data), the algorithm disables its operation. This property provides better performance when transferring files that are already compressed or that appear to be compressed.

Modem Standards

The two organizations that have authored most of the modem standards are AT&T and the CCITT. Table 5.8 provides a summary of these standards. For each standard, the data rate, duplex type, modulation method, baud, and connection type are given.

TABLE 5.8

Common Modem Standards

Standard	Data Rate (bps)	Duplex Capability	Modulation	Baud	Sync/ Async
Bell 103/113[1]	0-300	Full	FSK	0-300	Async
Bell 201	2400	Full[2]	DPSK-4	1200	Sync

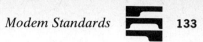

TABLE 5.8

Common Modem Standards (Continued)

Standard	Data Rate (bps)	Duplex Capability	Modulation	Baud	Sync/Async
Bell 202	1200	Half	FSK	1200	Async
	5 (reverse)	Half	On/Off Keying	5	n/a
Bell 208	4800	Full[2]	DPSK-8	1200	Sync
Bell 209A	9600	Full	QAM-16	2400	Sync
Bell 212A	1200	Full	DPSK-4	600	Sync
	300	Full	FSK	300	Async
V.17 fax	14400	Half	Trellis-128	2400	Sync
	12000	Half	Trellis-64	2400	Sync
	9600	Half	Trellis-32	2400	Sync
	7200	Half	Trellis-16	2400	Sync
V.21	0-300	Full	FSK	0-300	Async
V.22	1200	Full	DPSK-4	600	Both
	600	Full	DPSK-2	600	Both
	0-300	Full	FSK	0-300	Async
V.22bis	2400	Full	QAM-16	600	Both
	1200	Full	DPSK-4	600	Both
V.23	1200	Half	FSK	1200	Both
	600	Half	FSK	600	Both
	75 (reverse)	Half	FSK	75	Async
V.26	2400	Full	DPSK-4	1200	Sync
	75 (reverse)	Full	FSK	75	Async
V.26bis	2400	Half	DPSK-4	1200	Sync
	1200	Half	DPSK-2	1200	Sync
	75 (reverse)	Half	FSK	75	Async
V.26ter	2400	Full	DPSK-4	1200	Both
	1200	Full	DPSK-2	1200	Both
V.27	4800	Full	DPSK-8	1600	Sync
	75 (reverse)	Full	FSK	75	Async
V.27bis	4800	Full[2]	DPSK-8	1600	Sync

TABLE 5.8

Common Modem Standards (Continued)

Standard	Data Rate (bps)	Duplex Capability	Modulation	Baud	Sync/ Async
	2400	Full[2]	DPSK-4	1200	Sync
	75 (reverse)	Full[2]	FSK	75	Async
V.27ter	4800	Half	DPSK-8	1600	Sync
	2400	Half	DPSK-4	1200	Sync
	75 (reverse)	Half	FSK	75	Async
V.29	9600	Full	QAM-16	2400	Sync
	7200	Full	QAM-8	2400	Sync
	4800	Full	QAM-4	2400	Sync
V.32	9600	Full	Trellis-32	2400	Sync
	9600	Full	QAM-16	2400	Sync
	4800	Full	QAM-4	2400	Sync
V.32bis	14400	Full	Trellis-128	2400	Sync
	12000	Full	Trellis-64	2400	Sync
	9600	Full	Trellis-32	2400	Sync
	7200	Full	Trellis-16	2400	Sync
	4800	Full	QAM-4	2400	Sync
V.33	14400	Full	Trellis-128	2400	Sync
	12000	Full	Trellis-64	2400	Sync
V.FAST[3]	28800	Full	TBD	TBD	Sync

1 This standard represents an entire family of modems. Not all models possess all operation features.
2 Full duplex operation only on four-wire lines. Half-duplex operation on two-wire lines.
3 Unofficial designation. Standard is being developed by the CCITT.

In many cases, a standard may provide support for more than one mode of operation. Backward compatibility with earlier standards, for example, may be optional. Other standards may provide full-duplex operation on four-wire leased lines, but only half-duplex operation on the GSTN. The table lists all possibilities, and does not necessarily indicate that a modem following that standard meets all possible permutations.

6 THE AT COMMAND SET

IN CHAPTER 5, WE CLASSIFIED MODEMS AS EITHER DUMB OR INTELLIGENT, DE-
pending on their ability to accept command information in the data stream. The
so-called dumb modem acted as a simple modulation/demodulation device, interfacing a DTE to a communications channel. Outside its restricted scope, the
dumb modem took no active part in the communications process. Specifically,
a dumb modem could not be programmed or controlled interactively.

The intelligent modem, in contrast, is characterized by its programmability.
Unlike the dumb modem, an intelligent modem operates in two distinct modes.
In *data mode,* it operates identically to the dumb modem, interfacing the DTE
and the communications channel. In *command mode,* the modem can carry on
a private conversation with the DTE, accepting programming commands and
returning responses. This exchange over the data connection between modem
and DTE is known as *in-band communications* and is characteristic of an intelligent modem. (Other control signals, such as DTR and RTS, are known as *out-
of-band communications.*)

The concept of the intelligent modem didn't originate with Hayes Microcomputer Products, Inc. Before Hayes' introduced its Smartmodem 300, other
manufacturers had included intelligence and programmability in their modems.
Hayes' contribution was not the development of yet another proprietary command set, but—by virtue of capturing the majority of market share—the establishment of that command set as a standard across the industry.

The command set for the Smartmodem 300 was very modest, as befitted
the capabilities of the modem. As modem capabilities increased, Hayes expanded the command set to provide additional control functions. To make their
modems "Hayes compatible," other manufacturers copied the basic command
set, and then defined proprietary command extensions to support their modem's unique features. So, although most modems share the basic commands,
it's all too rare to find two modems that use the same commands or syntax to
implement advanced features.

This chapter introduces the system of modem control commands commonly known as the *AT command set.* The basic commands and modem responses that are shared nearly universally by all modems are discussed in detail.
Additionally, the common set of internal modem registers that support modem
programmability is also discussed. Finally, the command set defined in the

CCITT V.25bis standard is also presented. Detailed descriptions of advanced and proprietary commands and registers for a wide variety of modems and manufacturers may be found in Appendices A and B.

The Command Line

The system of commands and registers that Hayes developed for its Smartmodem is known collectively as the AT command set because a command sent to the modem must begin with the two-character sequence AT. The modem must be in command mode for the AT characters to be recognized as the start of a command.

The original Smartmodem required that the AT characters be entered in uppercase. Later modems generally accept these characters as either both uppercase or both lowercase. In no case is a mixed case attention command (At or aT) recognized by the modem. Because these characters must precede any command, the modem can use them to derive the speed and data format in use by the DCE.

The string of characters that is sent to the modem is called a *command line*. A command line can contain none, one, or more than one command. A command line must begin with the attention characters AT or at. Following this, any number of valid commands may appear. The command line ends with a carriage return character. All modems support a minimum command-line length of 40 characters, excluding the AT and the terminating carriage return character. Depending on the manufacturer, the buffer may be as large as 255 characters. The syntax of a command line is shown here:

```
AT[[command[argument]]...]<CR>
```

Spaces can be included in the command line to improve readability. These spaces, however, are ignored by the modem and are not counted as part of the character line length limit. The backspace character may be used to edit the command line before the terminating carriage return is entered.

Command Syntax

The original AT command set was quite small and used single-character alphabetic commands that, for the most part, were mnemonically reminiscent of their actions. The D command, for example, dialed a telephone number. And the L command controlled the loudness of the speaker. These commands are known as the *basic commands*.

As modems grew more complex, a corresponding increase in the number of commands was required. To accommodate this, a second type of command, called an *extended command,* was introduced. An extended command is formed by combining a nonalphabetic prefix character with an alphabetic character. For its extended command set, Hayes chose the prefix character & (ampersand).

Examples include &D to control the modem's response to the DTR signal and &F to recall configuration information from nonvolatile memory.

Other manufacturers followed suit and copied these extended commands. In addition, they defined—and redefined—additional proprietary commands using the \, #, %, $, :, @, *, -, +, and) characters as prefixes. In all cases, the command characters can be either uppercase or lowercase.

Because of the proliferation of command sets, the term *Hayes-compatible* has come to mean little more than "my commands begin with an AT." Even Hayes modems are no longer literally Hayes-compatible, since the same command may not work the same on all modems.

The A/ Command The A/ command represents an exception to the standard command format. It must be entered as the only command on a line. It is neither preceded by AT nor followed by a carriage return. The modem responds to this command by reexecuting the entire last command line it received.

Each command line sent to the modem remains in the command buffer until the next AT command is processed or power is removed from the modem. If the modem receives new commands, loses power, or is reset, the commands in the buffer are discarded and the A/ command has no effect.

The S Command The S command sets or examines the contents of the modem's internal registers and has three distinct forms. The first form is Sr?, where r represents the number of the register and is specified as a one- to three-digit decimal number in the range 0 to 255. The modem responds by displaying the current value of register r. The second form, S$r=n$, sets register number r to the value n. The third form, Sr, designates a default register for subsequent commands. S registers are explained in detail later in this chapter.

Arguments

Some AT commands require an argument, for some an argument is optional, and others accept no arguments at all. If present, an argument must follow the command on the command line with no intervening characters except spaces. A command and its arguments must appear in the same command line and cannot be separated by a terminating carriage return.

In general, AT commands accept numeric arguments. The dial command and some command extensions that support fax modems, however, also accept nonnumeric data. Numeric arguments are always specified in decimal, and leading zeros are not required. If no argument is specified, commands that accept an argument will assume a 0. In other words, the modem interprets ATC as ATC0.

Modem Responses

Just as important as sending commands to the modem is receiving responses. As the modem processes commands, it may respond to indicate success, failure, or to return a requested value or status. At the very least, a modem response indicates that a modem is, indeed, connected to the DTE.

Each time the modem receives a command line (initiated by the AT sequence) it sends an in-band response to the DTE. The modem may be programmed to respond either in English words or numeric characters. Word responses are preceded and followed by a carriage return and line feed character pair. Numeric character responses are issued with only a following carriage return.

For the most part, the modem's response depends on the command, returning the information requested or the status of the modem. Two standard responses, however, are OK and ERROR. The OK response (0 if numeric) generally means that the command has been accepted and the modem is ready for the next command.

If the modem detects the use of an invalid argument or an improperly formatted command, it will issue the ERROR response (4 if numeric). Unrecognized and unimplemented commands may also produce this response. In other cases, such as obsolete commands, an OK will be issued to preserve compatibility with communications software, but no change is made in the modem's state.

Different modems handle command-line errors differently. Traditionally, any error in the command line causes the entire command line to be discarded without affecting the modem's state. Depending on the manufacturer, however, some modems may process valid commands until they encounter an error, at which time processing of the command line ceases. Applications receiving an ERROR response should assume that the entire command sequence will have to be repeated.

Command Types

A modern intelligent modem is basically a communications processor, providing services to a DTE client. Getting the modem to perform the required tasks is simply a matter of sending it the proper instructions. Given the complexity of some modems, however, this is more easily said than done. Microcom's QX/4232bis+ modem, for example, defines over 130 separate AT commands! Multiply this by dozens of different manufacturers—all varying their command definitions slightly—and programming a modem becomes a daunting task.

Fortunately, most modems set the majority of their options to default values appropriate to basic serial communications. This reduces the number of required commands to only a handful. These few commands are all that you need to establish communications in most circumstances. This core subset of commands also lends itself naturally to division into three categories: configuration, action, and dial commands.

This section examines the three groups that make up the core subset of AT commands required for basic configuration and operation of most modems. Advanced and proprietary commands are covered in detail in Appendix A. A comprehensive listing of S registers is given in Appendix B.

Configuration

Commands that change the modem's user interface or specify how the modem is to operate are known as *configuration commands*. These commands do not directly cause the modem to take any action, but may influence whether an action will occur. The commands listed here are used for basic modem configuration. Note that the P and T commands are discussed in the Dial Modifiers section and the S command is explained in the section on S registers.

E   Modem Command Echo   When the modem is in command mode, the E command (echo) determines whether the commands received by the modem are echoed (retransmitted) to the DTE. The command ATE0 disables command echo and is usually the default. To enable command echo, use the command ATE1.

0   Command echo disabled

1   Command echo enabled

L   Speaker Volume   Some modems support the L (loudness) command to provide software control of the speaker volume. On modems with a manual volume control or without a speaker, this command is ignored, but does not produce an error. The L command changes between three different volume levels. To disable the speaker entirely, use the M command.

0   Low volume

1   Low volume

2   Medium volume

3   High volume

M   Monitor (Speaker) Control   The M (monitor) command enables or disables the speaker according to specific requirements. Most modems use ATM1 as the default, allowing the user to monitor the call from dial through negotiation. In this way, the user can hear telephone company voice announcements, busy signals, or a person answering the phone. During troubleshooting, it's often necessary to monitor the negotiation process that takes place between the modems. Some modems support an ATM3 command that turns the speaker off during dialing, and then on until the call is established.

0   Always off

1   On until call established

2   Always on

Q Enable or Disable Modem Responses   The Q (quiet) command controls whether the result codes acknowledging commands and reporting call status will be send by the modem to the DTE. The ATQ0 command enables responses and is normally the factory default. The ATQ1 command disables the OK and ERROR responses to commands as well as the OK, BUSY, and RING commands sent by the modem to indicate call status. Disabling modem responses will cause most communications software to fail.

0   Modem responses enabled

1   Modem responses disabled

V   Result Code Format   The setting of the V (verbose) command determines whether the modem will issue responses as numeric characters or as word responses.

0   Use numeric character responses

1   Use word responses

By default, most modems are set to give word responses. Consequently, most communications software depends on receiving responses in this form. Alternately, the ATV0 command configures the modem to use numeric responses. The eight basic modem responses are shown here.

Numeric	Word
0	OK
1	CONNECT
2	RING
3	NO CARRIER
4	ERROR
6	NO DIALTONE
7	BUSY
8	NO ANSWER

Note that, in some cases, a word response is preferable to a numeric response. A modem establishing a high-speed connection, for example, might issue a message such as CONNECT 57600. A general-purpose communications program looking for the CONNECT string would most likely detect that a connection had been established. The corresponding numeric command for the message (18, in the case of the Practical Peripherals 14400FXSA modem) would probably not be recognized.

X Select Result Code Set   In a general sense, the setting of the X command establishes compatibility with older modems. The messages that will be sent to the DTE by the modem and the conditions they report are controlled by this command.

0   CONNECT

1   CONNECT *bps*

2   CONNECT *bps*, NO DIALTONE

3   CONNECT *bps*, BUSY

4   CONNECT *bps*, NO DIALTONE, BUSY

When configured with the ATX0 command, for example, the modem behaves like the original Smartmodem 300. The modem dials blindly—dial tones and busy signals are ignored—and the CONNECT message is returned if a connection is established. This command set is typically enabled for a short-haul modem-to-modem direct connection.

The ATX1 command causes the modem to send a connect code reflecting the bps rate of the connection. The numeric value replaces the *bps* in the preceding examples.

If the modem has received the ATX2 configuration command, it will attempt to detect a dial tone before dialing. If a dial tone is not detected within five seconds, the NO DIALTONE message is returned.

The ATX3 command ignores the dial tone, but detects a BUSY signal and terminates the call. The ATX4 command enables all detection and messaging capabilities. Note that these result codes may be further modified by other command settings that determine connect rate, error control, and data compression options.

&V View Stored Configuration Profiles   The AT&V command instructs the modem to display the current values of selected configuration parameters and S registers. On modems equipped with nonvolatile memory, profiles (stored with the &W command) that are stored in nonvolatile memory will also be displayed. The &V command takes no arguments. The format and contents of the information displayed varies, depending on the modem manufacturer. A representative display produced by this command is shown in Figure 6.1. Stored profiles may be loaded using the Z and &F commands described in the next section.

FIGURE 6.1

The AT&V command produces a listing of the modem's stored configuration profiles.

```
AT&V
ACTIVE PROFILE:
B1 E1 L2 M1 N1 Q0 T V1 W0 X4 Y0 %G1 &C1 &D2 &G0 &J0 &K3 &Q5 &R0 &S0 &T4 &X0 &Y0
S00:000 S01:000 S02:043 S03:013 S04:010 S05:008 S0
S10:014 S11:095 S12:050 S18:000 S25:005 S26:001 S36:007 S37:000
S46:138 S48:007 S49:008 S50:255

STORED PROFILE 0:
B1 E1 L2 M1 N1 Q0 T V1 W0 X4 Y0 %G1 &C1 &D2 &G0 &J0 &K3 &Q5 &R0 &S0 &T4 &X0
S00:000 S02:043 S06:002 S07:050 S08:002 S09:006 S10
S25:005 S26:001 S36:007 S37:000 S38:020 S44:003 S46:138 S48:007 S49

STORED PROFILE 1:
B1 E1 L2 M0 N1 Q0 T V1 W1 X4 Y0 %G1 &C1 &D2 &G0 &J0 &K3 &Q5 &R0 &S0 &T4 &X0
S00:000 S02:043 S06:002 S07:050 S08:002 S09:006 S10
S25:005 S26:001 S36:007 S37:000 S38:020 S44:003 S46:138 S48:007 S49

TELEPHONE NUMBERS:
0=                                      1=
2=                                      3=

OK
```

&W*n*   **Save Profile in Memory**   (*n* = number of configuration profile) On modems that provide nonvolatile memory for the storage of configuration profiles, this command is used to save the current modem settings to memory. The &W command takes as an argument the number of the memory profile in which the current modem state is to be saved. The command AT&W0, for example, saves the current configuration as profile 0. Legal values for profile numbers are determined by each modem individually. Stored profiles may be loaded using the Z and &F commands described in the next section.

Action Commands

Unlike configuration commands, action commands have an immediate effect on the status of the local modem or its connection to the remote modem. Typical action commands include those to answer a call, hang up the phone, and reset the modem. Note that the D (dial a telephone number) command is discussed under "Dial Commands."

A   **Answer an Incoming Call**   The A (answer) command forces the modem to immediately go off-hook (on-line) and issue its answer tone. The command takes no arguments. Normally, the modem's response to an incoming call is determined by the setting of register S0, as described in the section on S registers later in this chapter. Use of this command, however, overrides the setting of S0.

If a connection is established successfully, the modem will issue the appropriate CONNECT result code. Before the connection is established, the attempt may be aborted and the modem returned to the command mode by sending any character to the modem. In this case, or if a connection is not established before the time specified in the S7 register expires, a NO CARRIER message is issued.

H   Switch Hook Control   The H (hook control) command simulates the actions of lifting and replacing the handset of a standard telephone. The ATH0 command is typically used to force the modem to terminate an established connection and hang up the line immediately.

0   Go on-hook (hang up)

1   Go off-hook (on-line)

O   Return to On-Line State   The ATO command switches the modem from the command mode to the on-line (data) mode. It takes no arguments. Normally, the modem is in the data mode after a connection has been established. The modem can be returned to the command mode, however, using an escape sequence, as explained later in this chapter. You use this command when you wish to return the modem to the data mode.

Zn   Soft Reset   (n = number of configuration profile) The Z command is used to recall a selected configuration profile. Any nonstorable parameters are reset to their factory default settings. The Z commands causes the modem to go on-hook, terminating any existing connection immediately. Commands that appear on the command line following the Z command are ignored.

&Fn   Load Factory Configuration   (n = number of configuration profile) The &F command sets selected configuration parameters and S register values to a factory-specified default condition. The current values and option settings are lost when this command is executed. Unlike the Z command, the &F command does not cause the modem to go on-hook.

Dial Commands

The command ATDs instructs the modem to dial the telephone according to the information in the dial string s. A single dial string can contain any number of characters, and is limited only by the space remaining in the command buffer. The dial string can contain hyphens, spaces, or parentheses for clarity; they are ignored by the modem.

The string ATD555-1212, for example, causes the modem to go off-hook, wait for the period specified in the S6 register, and then dial the telephone number 555-1212. The modem then attempts to establish a connection for the period of time specified in register S7.

P   Pulse Dialing   The P (pulse) command instructs the modem to use the make/break system of dialing used by rotary dial telephones. Most modems use this dialing method by default.

T   Tone Dialing   Most telephone systems today accept the faster and more versatile tone dialing system. The T (tone) command instructs the modem to use this method when dialing. Tones are also used during call establishment to enter credit card and calling card numbers and to maneuver through telephone systems and long distance service providers.

Used by themselves, the T and P commands set the dialing mode for subsequent executions of the D command. They can also be issued as part of the dialing command and alternated as desired. For example, the string

```
ATDP555-9999T2978
```

instructs the modem to go off-hook, pulse dial the number 555-9999, and then tone dial the four digits 2978.

Dial Modifiers   Sometimes a telephone number can be quite simple, such as the seven-digit number used in the preceding example. At other times—such as when accessing an alternate long-distance service or negotiating the maze of an internal phone system—the process can be extremely complex, especially for a modem. For this reason, special commands known as *dial modifiers* were created. The dial modifiers described here, valid only within a dial string, modify and control how the modem dials a telephone number. Note that not all modifiers are available on all modems.

0-9 A B C D # *   **Digits/Characters for Dialing**   These digits and characters represent the individual elements that make up a telephone number. The digits 0 through 9 are valid on all systems. The characters A B C D # and * represent specific tone pairs—not the characters on the numeric keys—and are valid only on tone dialing systems; they are ignored if pulse dialing is selected.

,   (Comma) Pause   When the modem encounters the comma (,) dial modifier in a dial string, it pauses for the amount of time specified in the S8 register (the typical default setting is 2 seconds) before processing the next character. A comma is frequently inserted to give an internal phone system time to connect to an outside line or to wait for a dial tone. If a longer delay is required, more than one comma may be used.

@   Wait for Silence   The @ modifier instructs the modem to listen for 5 seconds of silence (a quiet answer) before continuing. The amount of time the modem will wait for the silent period to begin is specified by register S7. If the silence is not detected, the modem hangs up and returns the NO ANSWER result code. If the silence is detected, the modem continues execution of the dial string. The modem does not listen for silence until it first detects a nonsilence such as a dial tone, ring signal, and so on.

!   Hook Flash   When the modem processes the ! modifier, it goes on-hook for a brief period of time (typically about a half-second), and then goes off-hook again. This feature is often used to access some phone system features such as call transfer.

;   Return to Command Mode   The semicolon (;) modifier is used only as the last character in a command line. It instructs the modem to return to command mode after dialing, but not to break the connection. The semicolon is useful if a very long dial string has to be continued across more than one command line. Also, with this feature, the modem can be used as a telephone dialer without generating a carrier signal.

L   Redial Last Number   The L command causes the modem to redial the last dial string it has received. Unlike the A/ command, the L command reexecutes only the dial string and not the entire command buffer. On some modems, the command ATDL? will display the last number dialed.

R   Originate Call in Answer Mode   When calling an originate-only modem, the R command instructs the local modem to attempt to establish the call using the answer carrier tones instead of the originate carrier tones. (Recall from Chapter 5 that originate and answer refer only to the carrier tones used by the modems and bear no relationship to call placement.)

S=*n*   Dial Stored Number   Some modems support the storing of telephone numbers in nonvolatile RAM. On these modems, the ATDS=*n* command will dial the stored telephone number indicated by *n*.

W   Wait for Dial Tone   The W command instructs the modem to wait for a dial tone. This is useful when accessing an external line from a PBX system. When the dial tone is detected, processing of the dial string continues.

S Registers

S registers are memory storage locations within the modem that are used to hold information about its operating parameters. These registers affect various operating characteristics, let you obtain information about the modem, and permit you to test the modem. Each register has a factory-set default value that can be read or changed to suit a particular situation.

Individual S registers are identified by a decimal number from 0 to 255. Most modems define uses for only a small number of the 256 possible registers. For any particular modem, many S registers will be marked as reserved. These registers are used as local storage by the modem's microprocessor to hold compressed (bitmapped) parameter tables. Occasionally, an application program will attempt to increase efficiency by reading, interpreting, and setting these bitmaps directly. Generally, deciphering these bitmaps is not necessary for manual control of a modem, since explicit commands exist to control the same parameters.

Register Manipulation Commands

The AT command set contains two commands designed to examine and manipulate S registers. The command to examine the current value of a register has the form Sr?, where r is the register number. The modem responds with the value of the register expressed as a three-digit decimal number.

The value of an S register is set using the command Sr=n, where r is the register number and n is the value to which the register is to be set. Note that n is expressed as a decimal number with a value in the range between 0 and 255. Leading zeros may be omitted. To put the value 30 into register S7, for example, use the command ATS7=30.

If a register is to be accessed repeatedly, the Sr command can be used to make register r the implied register. Subsequent commands of the form AT? and AT=n will read and write that register implicitly. Register r remains the implied register until the S command is used to read or write a different register. The last explicitly referenced register always becomes the implied register.

S Register Definitions

As with AT commands, some level of congruence exists for S register definitions between modem manufacturers. Beyond a certain point, however, the S registers are considered fair game for whatever scheme each manufacturer wants to implement for that modem model. Any comprehensive manipulation of S registers will, by its nature, have to be modem-specific. The 13 registers listed below can be generally assumed to be present and consistent across manufacturers.

S0   Ring to Answer On   Assigning a nonzero value to the S0 register places the modem in auto-answer mode. The value in this register specifies how many rings (1 to 255) must occur before the modem goes off-hook to answer the incoming call. Setting this register to 0 turns off the auto-answer feature.

S1   Number of Rings Counter   As incoming rings are counted, the S1 register is updated to reflect the count value. When the value in this register equals the (nonzero) value in S0, the modem automatically answers the telephone. Approximately 8 seconds after the last ring occurs, this register resets itself to 0.

S2   Escape Character Value   The S2 register holds the ASCII value of the character used in the escape sequence that switches the modem from data mode to command mode. Values from 0 to 127 are valid values for this register. A value greater than 127 disables this feature. Industry-wide, this register defaults to ASCII 43, the plus (+) character. Use of this character in implementing the escape sequence is discussed later in this chapter.

S3   Carriage Return Character   The modem uses the value in the S3 register to define its carriage return character. This is the character it expects will be used to terminate a modem command line. The modem also uses this character when it generates a response. Valid values for this character are 0 through 127. By default, this register is set to ASCII 13.

S4   Line Feed Character   The value in register S4 defines the character used by the modem when generating word responses. Valid values for this character are 0 through 127. By default, this register is set to ASCII 10.

S5   Backspace Character   The S5 register contains the ASCII value of the character used to implement the destructive backspace function. When received by the modem, this character is echoed to the DTE to implement the backspace editing function. Valid values for this character are the nonprinting ASCII characters 0 through 31 and 127. The default value is ASCII 8.

S6   Blind Dialing Wait Time   If the modem executes a dial command with the X0, X1, or X3 response set in effect (dial tone detection disabled), the value in the S6 register specifies how many seconds it will wait after going off-hook before it dials the first digit in the dial string. This procedure is known as *blind dialing*. Most modems set this register to 2 seconds by default, but allow a value of up to 255 seconds to be set.

S7   Carrier Wait Time   The value in the S7 register tells the modem how many seconds to wait after dialing to establish a connection. If the modem does not detect a carrier after the specified time has elapsed (between 1 and 60 seconds), it hangs up and returns the NO CARRIER message. On most modems, this time is set to 30 (seconds) by default. Due to the complex negotiation of speed, error correction protocol, and compression protocol that occurs between modern high-speed modems, this default value may not give the modems sufficient time to establish a connection.

S8   Comma Modifier Pause Time   The pause time generated by the comma dialing modifier (in seconds) is specified by the value in the S8 register. By default, most modems initialize this value to 2 seconds. Values between 1 and 255 seconds are valid.

S9   Carrier Detect Response Time   The S9 register specifies the time that the carrier signal from the remote modem must be present (in tenths of a second) before the local modem issues a carrier detect. Typically, the default setting for this register is 6, which is equivalent to 0.6 seconds. Valid values range from 1 (0.1 seconds) to 255 (25.5 seconds).

S10   Time Between Carrier Loss and On-Hook   The S10 register sets the time (in tenths of a second) that a remote modem's carrier may disappear from the telephone line without causing the local modem to assume that it has been disconnected. This feature provides some compensation for noisy telephone lines. A typical default value for this register is about 15 (1.5 seconds). Setting this register to 255 makes the modem ignore the data carrier detect signal and behave as if the remote modem's carrier is always present.

S11   Touch Tone Duration and Spacing   The S11 register sets the duration of each tone used during dialing and the spacing between adjacent tones. The time is specified in milliseconds. Default times vary, but 50 milliseconds is considered the minimum value that is properly recognized by phone systems. This command has no effect on the pulse dialing speed, which is nominally 10 pulses per second.

S12   Escape Sequence Guard Time   The S12 register sets the duration of the guard time that must occur before and after the escape code sequence used to switch the modem from data mode to command mode without disconnecting. The time is specified in fiftieths of a second. When a guard time is used, the industry-standard default time is 1 second (S12=50).

Indirectly, this register also specifies the maximum time that can elapse between the individual characters of the escape code without resetting the escape code detection sequence. If S12 is set to 0, guard time detection is disabled. The next section contains more information on the escape sequence.

Escape Sequences

The modems used on personal computers are capable of operating in two distinct modes: command mode and data mode. In command mode, the characters from the DTE are interpreted as commands for the modem. In data mode, the modem receives characters from the DTE and transmits them over the communication channel.

Normally, switching between command and data modes is handled automatically by the modem's internal logic. After processing a dial command and negotiating a connection, for example, the modem will switch automatically from command mode to data mode. Similarly, when the connect terminates, the modem reverts to command mode.

Modem designers recognized that there may be times when you need to switch modes after a connection is established without terminating the current connection. The mechanism that allows this to take place is called an *escape*. The two categories of escape methods are in-band and out-of-band.

Out-of-Band Escape

An *out-of-band escape* is simply a command sent to the modem over a signal path that is independent of the data path. For the command to be effective, the modem must be designed to expect and react properly to the signal. By its nature, a modem that uses an out-of-band escape sequence is independent of the data stream. As such, the chance of an inadvertent escape taking place is negligible.

The out-of-band escape's inherent weakness is the same as its strength: the use of an independent signal path for the escape command. In many environments (local area networks, for example), there is no direct connection between the modem and the PC. In these cases, use of an out-of-band escape is not possible and an in-band escape must be used instead.

In-Band Escape

When operating in data mode, the modem accepts data from the DTE and transmits it over the communication channel. In theory, the modem ignores the data, passing it transparently to the channel. In fact, the modem is constantly monitoring the data stream for an identifiable sequence of characters known as an *in-band escape*. An in-band escape is simply an identifiable sequence of characters sent from the DTE to the modem that, when received, causes the modem to switch from data mode to command mode.

The obvious problem with an in-band escape is defining a sequence of characters that do not normally occur in the data stream to be used to switch the mode of the modem. Regardless of the length or complexity of the escape string, you can never be completely assured that the string will not occur accidentally in some portion of a data transmission. Two approaches to reducing accidental escape have been developed: the guard time system and the TIES system.

Guard Time Escape Sequence

In the early 1980s, Dale Heatherington, an employee at Hayes, developed a technique that improved the reliability of modems using an in-band escape. His technique required that the escape be surrounded by periods of no data transmission known as *guard times*. For a string to be recognized as a valid escape, it has to be immediately preceded and followed by a guard time.

The guard time system virtually eliminated the problems associated with the in-band escape, by removing the dependence of the system on the probability of character occurrence in the data stream. Heatherington was issued United States patent number 4,549,302 (referred to as the '302 patent) for this development.

The character used in the escape is specified by register S2. By default, this is the plus (+) character. Similarly, the minimum length of silent time that will be recognized as a guard time is specified by the setting of register S12. To switch a modem from data mode to command mode requires that the DTE transmit three copies of the escape character, bracketed by guard times, as shown here:

```
<guard time>+++<guard time>
```

The escape sequence is not followed by a carriage return or any other character. When the modem has switched to command modem and is ready to accept commands, it issues the OK response. The ATO command returns the modem to data mode.

Note that the setting of the S12 register also establishes the maximum amount of time that can elapse between the characters of the escape sequence. If the characters are entered too slowly, the guard time detection circuitry will reset. The default guard time is 1 second, which is adequate for most operations. You can disable the guard time detection by setting S12 to 0. In this case, any occurrence of +++ in the data stream will cause the modem to escape. You can disable the escape mechanism by setting register S2 to a value greater than 127.

As robust as the guard time escape sequence is, it is not without its limitations. The escape sequence is not recognized by the local modem until *after* the second guard time. Meanwhile, the escape string has been transmitted to the remote modem. If the remote modem is set to recognize the same escape character as the local modem, the remote modem may inadvertently escape. Although the ATO command will return the local modem to the data mode, the remote modem will remain in command mode.

Another weakness of the '302 system is its dependence on absolute timing between the DTE and modem. In many environments—network operations or packet transmission, for example—the timing between elements of the data stream is not preserved. This raises the likelihood that the guard time system will not detect an otherwise valid escape.

Time Independent Escape Sequence (TIES)

Hayes possession of the '302 patent has allowed it to demand royalties and license agreements from other modem manufacturers that wish to include a guard time escape sequence in their modems. In 1991, a group of modem manufacturers (including Ven-Tel, Everex, and Multi-tech) introduced an escape sequence that is not covered by the Hayes patent. This mechanism has been dubbed the *time independent escape sequence* (TIES).

Essentially, TIES retains the three-character escape string, but eliminates the requirement of surrounding guard times. Further, TIES requires that the appearance of the escape string be followed by a valid AT command. In other words, the complete TIES escape sequence has the following format:

```
+++AT[[command[argument]]...]<CR>
```

where "+++" represents three repetitions of the escape character specified in register S2. The AT characters may be upper- or lowercase. The time that elapses between characters of this sequence is inconsequential. The terminating carriage return is mandatory and is part of the sequence.

No small amount of controversy has surfaced regarding the immunity of TIES to inadvertent escapes. Opponents argue that because no guard times are required, the appearance of a TIES escape string in data during a normal transfer will cause the local modem to escape. While proponents acknowledge this, they also present theoretical and practical studies alleging that the chance of this occurring is minimal.

The problem of identifying whether a data transmission contains an inadvertent TIES sequence is not straightforward. Assume, for example, that the string "+++ATH<cr>" is entered into a communications program for transmission as data. The actual bytes sent to the modem may bear little resemblance to this string after the effects of compression or file transfer protocols are taken into account. Similarly, an escape sequence could be created from innocuous data by a chance application of these techniques.

V.25bis Command Set

The AT command set is not the only choice for control of modems. The CCITT V.25bis standard defines a set of commands to control a class of DCEs known as automatic calling or automatic answering equipment (that is, intelligent modems). The DTE issues commands and the DCE responds. Some advanced modems are able to support both AT and V.25bis command sets. The commands and responses detailed in the V.25bis standard are described in this section.

Commands

The command set specified in V.25bis is considerably smaller than the AT command set. The commands are applicable for the most part to dialing and answering calls. These commands are described here.

CIC   Connect Incoming Call   The CIC command instructs the modem to immediately answer an incoming call. If there is no incoming call when this command is entered, the modem returns the INV (invalid) response.

CRN*s*   Call Requested Number   Entering the CRN command followed by a dial string *s* instructs the modem to go off-hook and dial the telephone. The dial string may contain spaces or hyphens for clarity; the modem ignores them. If the string contains more than 50 characters, the modem returns the INV response.

CRS*a*   Call Request with Address   The CRS command instructs the modem to dial a telephone number from one of its internal memories. The *a* argument specifies the memory address to be used.

DIC   Disregard Incoming Call   An incoming call will be ignored if the DIC command is entered. If the modem is configured to automatically answer, this command will override that setting for the current call only. If there is no incoming call when this command is entered, the modem returns the INV response.

PRN*a;s*   Program Number   The PRN command is used to store a telephone dial string *s* in the modem's internal memory location, specified by the *a* argument. The dial string can contain up to 50 characters, including any hyphens or

spaces. You can also use this command to erase memory entry *a* by entering PRN*a* with no dial string.

RLD   Request List of Delayed Numbers   The RLD command instructs the modem to send a list of delayed numbers to the DTE. A country's telephone authority may require that the modem place a number on the delayed list if a call to that number fails. The modem is proscribed from placing a call to that number until a specified time has elapsed or until the modem is reset by a power on/off cycle.

   If there are no numbers on the delayed list, it returns the LSD (list of delayed numbers) response. A RLD command response with one number on the list would appear as follows:

```
RLD
LSD;12035551212;30
```

In this case, the modem cannot call this number again for 30 minutes. If delayed numbers are not implemented, the modem responds to the RLD command with the INV response. The delayed number list is usually implemented to prevent the use of modems for rapid repetitive dialing (attack dialing).

RLF   Request List of Forbidden Numbers   When the RLF command is received by the modem, a list of forbidden numbers is sent to the DTE. A country's telephone authority may require that the modem place a number on the forbidden list if a call placed to that number fails. The modem is subsequently unable to dial that number until the modem is reset by a power on/off cycle. If no numbers are on the forbidden list or if the forbidden list function is not implemented, the modem returns the INV response.

RLI   Request Listed Numbers   The RLI command causes the modem to display a list of stored numbers. If all addresses are empty, the modem returns the LSN (list of stored numbers) response.

Modem Responses

As part of the V.25bis standard, the modem is able to respond to the DTE. The responses may be a direct result of a command or as part of call progress reporting. V.25bis modem responses are described here.

CFI*ff*   Call Failure Indicator   If a connect attempt that is made with the CRN and SRS commands fails, the modem reports using the CFI*ff* response, where *ff* indicates one of the following failure types:

AB   Abort. The modem aborted a call because no dial tone was detected or a character was received from the DTE.

CB   DCE Busy. The local modem detected an incoming call after a dialing command was entered. According to V.25bis, the incoming call has priority. This response is also issued if a command is entered at the DTE during manual answering or dialing.

ET   Engaged Tone. The local modem detected a busy signal when it dialed the indicated number.

FC   Forbidden Call. The number specified was on the forbidden list and cannot be dialed.

NS   Number Not Stored. The memory address indicated with the CRS command did not contain a number.

NT   No Tone. No responding tone was detected from the remote modem.

RT   Ring Tone. A ringback was detected, but the call was not completed due to a timeout.

CNX   Connection   The local modem issues the CNX response to the DTE when a connection has been successfully negotiated with the remote modem.

DLC*t*   Delayed Call   The telephone number specified was on the delayed call list. The modem cannot dial the number until the time specified by *t* has expired.

INC   Incoming Call   The modem sends the INC response to the modem whenever it detects an incoming call.

INV   Invalid   When a command is entered incorrectly or the modem is unable to execute a command, it returns the INV response.

LSD   List of Stored Delayed Numbers   The LSD response is issued by the modem when it receives a RLD command. If numbers are present on the delayed list, each is displayed, preceded by the LSD response.

LSF   List of Forbidden Numbers   The LSF response is issued by the modem when it receives a RLF command. If numbers are present on the forbidden list, each is displayed, preceded by the LSF response.

VAL   Valid   The modem responds to CIC, DIC, and PRN*a;n* commands with the VAL response if the requested command can be executed. The VAL response is also used during call progress reporting.

FACSIMILE

INDISPUTABLY, THE ALCHEMICAL MIX OF FACSIMILE AND PERSONAL COMPUT-
ers has created and widened markets for both devices. Because the growth of
PC-based facsimile technology has been so explosive, it's easy to be lulled into
thinking of facsimile technology as a relatively recent development. In reality,
facsimile is virtually primeval.

Facsimile (fax) technology, comprising the ability to transmit images, was
invented in 1843, predating the invention of the typewriter by sixty years and
the introduction of the IBM PC by 138 years! For many years, practical applications of fax technology were limited by the lack of an effective communications infrastructure. In the 1920s, fax saw increasing use by news organizations
to transmit photographs (wirephotos). Fax is still the preferred method for
transmitting weather maps to remote locations and ships at sea. The fax technology used in these applications today remains virtually unchanged.

Older fax machines were inconvenient to use and quite expensive to operate.
Over the past decade, reductions in cost and improvements in the underlying
technology helped bring fax into the mainstream of business communications.
Over the past few years, further simplifications have made the fax machine a com-
modity item found in nearly every office and in many homes. Today, fax capability is nearly universal, being found even in PC modems that sell for less than $50.

For all its complexity, data communications technology is simply the transmission of numbers. To transmit a page of text, for example, the characters of
the text are encoded into a series of numeric values, transmitted over the communications channel, and then decoded back into numbers for processing at the
receiver.

Using fax technology, however, the transmission of information proceeds
somewhat differently. The individual characters of a message are not separately
encoded. Instead, the entire page is treated as a single image. The signal that is
transmitted across the channel represents the pattern of black and white areas
that describe the image. At the receiver, a facsimile of the original page is produced by redrawing the image according to the received signal.

Transmitting a page of text using fax is slower than transmitting the same text
as data. A page of text that contains 60 lines of 80 characters takes approximately
5 seconds to transmit at 9600 bps. The same page would take approximately 60
seconds to transfer using modern fax equipment. But fax transmission has advantages over simple data transmission that compensate for the increased transfer

155

time. Foremost is its ability to transmit graphic images. Fax also allows printed text to be transmitted without rekeying.

In this chapter, we'll review the basic principles of facsimile theory. First, a brief survey of the primary technologies involved in converting a graphic image to an electrical signal and back again is presented. Following that, the fax group structure and the standards that define the electrical parameters of fax transmission and reception are discussed in detail.

Imaging Techniques

The components that make up a traditional fax system can be divided into three major categories according to their role in the facsimile process. Components in the first category deal with image reduction, the conversion of a graphic image to an electronic signal. The second category handles information transmission, including any required modulation and demodulation. Third-category components implement the functions required for image replication. Examples of the physical systems required to implement fax imaging systems are described in this section.

Scanning

Scanning is the process of reducing a continuous graphic image to an electrical signal suitable for processing by a transmission system. The two major factors that distinguish scanning systems are their mechanical operation and the type of electrical signal they produce.

Early fax machines relied heavily on mechanical systems for scanning. A typical system consisted of a heavy rotating drum, a light source, and a photo-electric detector used to reduce the image to an analog signal. Figure 7.1 shows a simplified diagram of such a system. Although these early systems are mostly obsolete, their influence on fax operation and terminology is still felt in the most modern machinery.

A drum system is driven by a synchronous motor, with timing derived from a crystal or tuning-fork frequency standard. The image to be transmitted is attached to the drum, which turns at a constant speed. A spot light source is focused onto the image, and the reflected light is subsequently detected by a photoelectric detector (a photocell, photomultiplier tube, or phototransistor).

In operation, the rotation of the drum produces the horizontal scanning of the image. The light source and detector, typically mounted on a carriage, are driven across the image to provide the vertical scanning. The carriage is usually propelled by a threaded rod or similar mechanism driven by a separate synchronous motor. The speed of the horizontal and vertical scans determines the resolution of the scanned image. The reflected light received by the detector is converted into a voltage that is representative of the brightness of the portion of the image being scanned. This voltage is then fed to the portion of the fax apparatus responsible for signal modulation.

FIGURE 7.1

A mechanical-drum scanning system

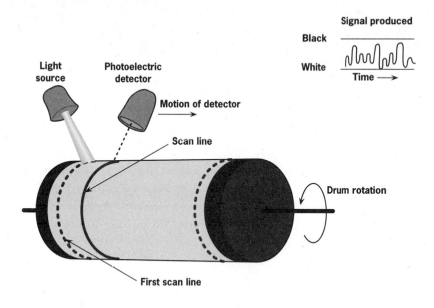

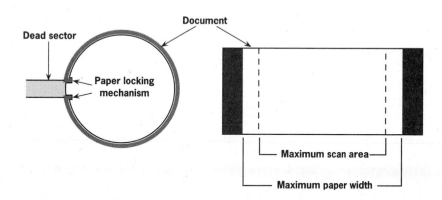

The most important factors for a mechanical drum scanning system are the drum size and the scanning speeds. The scanning density of the facsimile system (expressed in lines per inch or per millimeter) and the bandwidth required for transmission are determined both by the rotation speed of the drum and the scanning speed of the detector carriage. With slow drum speeds and a very fine light beam, the quality of scanned images can approach photographic resolutions.

The drum size directly defines the maximum image size that can be scanned and subsequently transmitted. The drum on a Western Union Telefax machine, for example, accepted a sheet of paper measuring only 4 $^1/_2$ x 6 $^1/_2$ inches. Facsimile machines used for business communications used drums that typically accommodated a standard 8 $^1/_2$-by-11-inch or A4 (210mm by 297mm) size image.

A typical scanning drum is shown in Figure 7.1. The physical size of the drum determines the maximum paper size that can be accommodated. The vertical scanning system defines the maximum usable scan area of an image. The maximum useful horizontal scanning size is determined by the circumference of the drum less the area occupied by the paper locking mechanism. The portion of the drum circumference that cannot be used to hold the image is known as the *dead sector*.

By its physical nature, a drum fax system scans an image using a single spot. This signal is transmitted as a continuous signal that must be received and decoded synchronously. Synchronization of the transmitter and receiver takes place before the image is sent and must hold throughout the entire transmission. Except for specialized applications, the use of drums has been supplanted by other mechanical systems.

Most modern business fax machines use a line-oriented scanning system such as that shown in Figure 7.2. In this example, pinch rollers move the paper past the scanning mechanism, providing the vertical scanning. Rather than using a horizontal scanning mechanism, these machines use an array of photodetectors to simultaneously encode an entire line of the image. The detector array produces a series of signals representing the reflected light received by each individual detector. The signals are then fed to the portion of the apparatus responsible for signal modulation. The maximum horizontal resolution of the system is determined by the spacing of the detectors in the array.

Replication

Replication is the complementary process of scanning. The electrical signals resulting from the demodulation process are used to duplicate the original scanned image. A variety of replication systems employing differing technologies is available.

Analog fax machines generally use printing techniques that produce an image using an electric current that passes through a treated paper. The coating on electrosensitive paper burns off in proportion to the current passing through it. A similar process uses electrolytic paper that changes color proportional to the printing current. In both systems, a mechanism positions the stylus on the paper to duplicate the raster generated by the scanning system.

Modern business fax systems generally use one of two printing methods. The first uses a treated paper that changes color in response to applied heat. The image is transferred to the paper when it passes across an array of elements, one element per dot of resolution. Although inexpensive, the images produced by this system lack permanence and fade over time.

FIGURE 7.2

A line-oriented scanning system

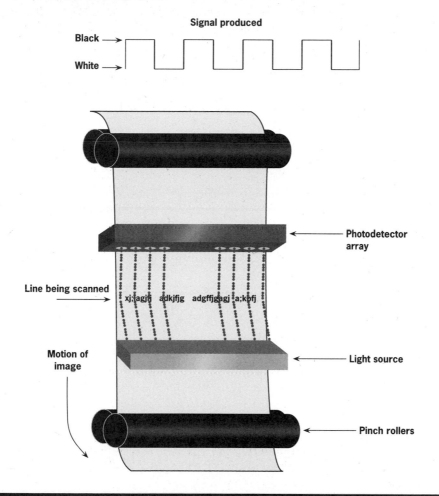

The second system uses the same techniques employed in copy machines and laser printers. The incoming signal controls the transfer of an electrostatic charge to an imaging drum. Toner is applied to the drum, and is then heat-fused to untreated paper. In dielectric systems, the static charge is applied directly to the paper, but the effect is the same.

Modulation

The signal produced by the scanning system is an electrical representation of the image. Depending on the design of the fax apparatus, the signals produced may be analog or digital. This signal is subsequently transmitted to the receiver by the modulation system. The CCITT classifies standard fax apparatus into four *groups,* depending on the scanned signal type, modulation method, and communication capabilities. Each of the four groups is described in this section.

Group 1 and 2 Analog

The specifications for group 1 (G1) fax machines are described in the 1968 CCITT standard T.2. Group 1 machines encode and transmit analog signals. The scanning line frequency is specified as 180 lines per minute, although the standard mentions that other speeds (240 lines per minute, for example) may be selected manually as dictated by characteristics of the communications channel. Group 1 machines operate at a resolution of approximately 100 lines per inch (3.85 lines per millimeter) and take approximately 6 minutes to transmit an A4 size document.

On leased circuits only, group 1 machines may use amplitude modulation. The carrier frequency must be within the range 1300 Hz to 1900 Hz. During transmission, the highest signal level corresponds to black and the lowest to white.

On both leased and switched circuits, group 1 machines may use frequency modulation. The carrier frequency, f_O, is specified as 1700 Hz for switched circuits. For leased circuits, the carrier frequency must fall within the range 1300 Hz to 1900 Hz. The frequency f_O + 400 Hz corresponds to black and the frequency f_O - 400 Hz corresponds to white. U.S. conventions specify a 1900 Hz carrier, 1500 Hz as white, and 2300 Hz as black.

Prior to the transmission of an image, a 15-second *phasing signal* is transmitted. During phasing, the transmitter sends a series of lines that are approximately 95 percent black and 5 percent white. The receiver is adjusted so that the center of the white area (phasing pulse) is approximately centered within the dead sector.

In 1976, the CCITT approved standard T.3, describing the requirements for a group 2 (G2) fax machine. Group 2 machines encode and transmit analog signals, as do group 1 machines, but use a modulation technique that is more efficient. This allows a standard scanning rate of 360 lines per minute. (300 lines per minute is specified as an alternative rate.) Group 2 machines operate at the same 100 lines per inch (3.85 lines per millimeter) as group 1 machines but take only 2 to 3 minutes to transmit the same image.

Whenever a carrier is modulated, frequency bands, called *sidebands,* are produced on both sides of the carrier. The modulation produces two sidebands that are mirror images of each other and carry identical information. Group 2 machines are designed to operate over telephone-type circuits using vestigial sideband amplitude modulation. This modulation system suppresses one of the redundant sidebands, resulting in a smaller overall signal bandwidth and correspondingly greater information bandwidth. Group 2 machines use a carrier frequency of 2100 Hz. A white signal is represented by maximum signal amplitude. Conversely, black is represented by a minimum (at least 26 Db below white) or no signal level.

Prior to transmission of an image, group 2 machines send a phasing signal, as shown in Figure 7.3. The signal consists of a series of scan lines transmitted as 94–96 percent white, with the remainder transmitted as black. The phasing signal is sent for 6 ± 0.5 seconds, the equivalent of 36 ± 3 scan lines. The phase of the carrier may be reversed in alternate lines. An optional line conditioning signal (LCS) may precede the phasing signal.

FIGURE 7.3

The CCITT group 2 phasing signal

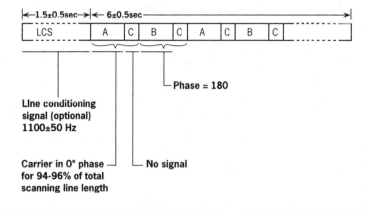

Group 3 Digital

The 1980 release of the CCITT T.4 standard brought group 3 (G3) machines into being. T.4 has been reissued twice, once in 1984 and subsequently in 1988. A minor revision, dated 1990, endorsed both the encoding schemes developed for group 4 fax transmission as well as the higher transmission speeds specified by V.17, V.29, and V.33. A new release of T.4 awaits the approval of the recommendations of a 1992 study group. Drafts of this document detail higher optional resolutions and binary file transfer capability.

The group 3 fax machines mark the transition from analog to digital techniques and differ considerably from those in groups 1 or 2. Digital fax apparatus views an image as a series of discrete dots (pixels). Each pixel may assume a value of black (1) or white (0)—no intermediate shades are possible. The series of binary digits produced by the digitization of the image can then be compressed, transmitted, and error-controlled using any of the techniques applied to data modems.

All group 3 machines must support a standard vertical resolution of 3.85 lines per millimeter. An optional higher resolution of 7.7 lines per millimeter may also be available. For both these vertical resolutions, the horizontal resolution is fixed at 1728 pixels for a standard scan line length of 215 millimeters, equivalent to 8 pixels per millimeter. The 1992 revision of T.4 adds a new higher resolution mode that encodes 15.4 lines per millimeter vertically and 16 pixels per millimeter horizontally.

The 1992 revision of T.4 also recognizes that inch-based measurements may be used when determining resolution. Table 7.1 shows the inch-based measurements endorsed. According to the standard, the English and metric measurements shown in Table 7.1 are to be considered functionally equivalent. Despite their slight numeric discrepancies, therefore, no conversion is required. Communication between these resolutions, however, will cause some distortion and a reduction in the reproducible area.

TABLE 7.1

English and Metric Resolution Equivalents

English (Lines per inch)		Metric (Lines per millimeter)	
Vertical	Horizontal	Vertical	Horizontal
100	200	3.85	8
200	200	7.7	8
300	300	No equivalent	
400	400	15.4	16

Group 3 fax may operate at speeds of 2400 bps and 4800 bps using the modulation methods specified in CCITT V.27ter. Alternately, the 7200 bps and 9600 bps rates specified in CCITT V.29 may be used. The 1990 revision adds the half-duplex 7200, 9600, 12000, and 14400 bps modes of V.17 (formerly titled V.FAX) and the V.33 full-duplex speeds of 12000 bps and 14400 bps. Transmission time is greater for a more detailed image, but an A4 size image at standard resolution requires between 30 seconds and 1 minute.

The digital encoding used by group 3 machines is not tied to the motion of a rotating drum. Furthermore, the digitized data making up each scan line is compressed before transmission. As such, the amount of time required to transmit a single scan line can vary within an arbitrarily specified range. The T.4 specification recommends a 20-millisecond minimum transmission time per coded scan line, but recognizes options ranging from 0 to 40 milliseconds. The maximum transmission time for any coded scan line must be less than 5 seconds.

One-Dimensional Encoding The T.4 standard describes a one-dimensional run-length encoding scheme used to compress the data making up a scan line. Each scan line is encoded as a series of variable-length codewords, where each codeword represents a run of either all black or all white pixels. A total of 1728 pixels are encoded for one 8.5 inch (215 mm) scan line.

Within a single scan line, runs of white and black pixels alternate. To ensure that the colors produced by the receiving system remain in synchronization with the transmitter, all data lines must begin with a run of white pixels. If the actual line begins with a black pixel, a white run length of zero is transmitted.

Codewords are classified as one of two types: *terminating codewords* and *makeup codewords*. Runs of 0 to 63 pixels are represented by the terminating codeword indicated in Table 7.2. Runs from 64 to 1728 pixels are encoded by a combination of a makeup codeword followed by a terminating codeword. The makeup codeword representing the largest number of pixels less than or equal to the run codeword is selected from Table 7.3. The terminating codeword representing the difference between the run length and the number of pixels represented by the makeup codeword is then selected from Table 7.3.

TABLE 7.2

Terminating Codewords for Group 3 One-Dimensional Run Length Encoding

Run Length	White Code Word	Black Code Word
0	00110101	0000110111
1	000111	010
2	0111	11
3	1000	10
4	1011	011
5	1100	0011
6	1110	0010
7	1111	00011
8	10011	000101
9	10100	000100
10	00111	0000100
11	01000	0000101
12	001000	0000111
13	000011	00000100
14	110100	00000111
15	110101	000011000
16	101010	0000010111
17	101011	0000011000
18	0100111	0000001000
19	0001100	00001100111

TABLE 7.2

Terminating Codewords for Group 3 One-Dimensional Run Length Encoding (Continued)

Run Length	White Code Word	Black Code Word
20	0001000	00001101000
21	0010111	00001101100
22	0000011	00000110111
23	0000100	00000101000
24	0101000	00000010111
25	0101011	00000011000
26	0010011	000011001010
27	0100100	000011001011
28	0011000	000011001100
29	00000010	000011001101
30	00000011	000001101000
31	00011010	000001101001
32	00011011	000001101010
33	00010010	000001101011
34	00010011	000011010010
35	00010100	000011010011
36	00010101	000011010100
37	00010110	000011010101
38	00010111	000011010110
39	00101000	000011010111
40	00101001	000001101100
41	00101010	000001101101
42	00101011	000011011010
43	00101100	000011011011
44	00101101	000001010100
45	00000100	000001010101
46	00000101	000001010110
47	00001010	000001010111
48	00001011	000001100100
49	01010010	000001100101

TABLE 7.2

Terminating Codewords for Group 3 One-Dimensional Run Length Encoding (Continued)

Run Length	White Code Word	Black Code Word
50	01010011	000001010010
51	01010100	000001010011
52	01010101	000000100100
53	00100100	000000110111
54	00100101	000000111000
55	01011000	000000100111
56	01011001	000000101000
57	01011010	000001011000
58	01011011	000001011001
59	01001010	000000101011
60	01001011	000000101100
61	00110010	000001011010
62	00110011	000001100110
63	00110100	000001100111

TABLE 7.3

Makeup Codewords for Group 3 One-Dimensional Run Length Encoding

Run Length	White Code Word	Black Code Word
64	11011	0000001111
128	10010	000011001000
192	010111	000011001001
256	0110111	000001011011
320	00110110	000000110011
384	00110111	000000110100
448	01100100	000000110101
512	01100101	0000001101100
576	01101000	0000001101101
640	01100111	0000001001010
704	011001100	0000001001011

TABLE 7.3

Makeup Codewords for Group 3 One-Dimensional Run Length Encoding (Continued)

Run Length	White Code Word	Black Code Word
768	011001101	0000001001100
832	011010010	0000001001101
896	011010011	0000001110010
960	011010100	0000001110011
1024	011010101	0000001110100
1088	011010110	0000001110101
1152	011010111	0000001110110
1216	011011000	0000001110111
1280	011011001	0000001010010
1344	011011010	0000001010011
1408	011011011	0000001010100
1472	010011000	0000001010101
1536	010011001	0000001011010
1600	010011010	0000001011011
1664	011000	0000001100100
1728	010011011	0000001100101
1792	00000001000	00000001000
1856	00000001100	00000001100
1920	00000001101	00000001101
1984	000000010010	000000010010
2048	000000010011	000000010011
2112	000000010100	000000010100
2176	000000010101	000000010101
2240	000000010110	000000010110
2304	000000010111	000000010111
2368	000000011100	000000011100
2432	000000011101	000000011101
2496	000000011110	000000011110
2560	000000011111	000000011111
EOL	000000000001	000000000001

An examination of the codewords in the two tables will show that this run length encoding system produces its maximum reduction for very short runs of black, short to medium runs of white, and large expanses of either color. This mix is a fair graphical description of a typical typewritten document. The codewords actually expand the number of bits required to transmit images that contain gray-shaded areas (encoded as alternating black and white pixels)—explaining why those images require an extended time for transmission. An example of this encoding is shown in Figure 7.4.

FIGURE 7.4

Group 3 one-dimensional encoding

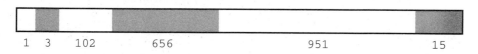

```
1   3    102        656              951              15
```

Color	Run Length	Makeup Codeword	Terminating Codeword
white	1	–	00 0111
black	3	–	10
white	102	1 1011	0001 0111
black	656	0 0000 0100 1010	00 0000 0111
white	951	0 1101 0011	0101 1000
black	15	–	0 0001 1000

The end-of-line (EOL) codeword is transmitted following each line of data. The 12 bits of the EOL, 000000000001, can never occur within a valid line of data. This property can be used to recover synchronization after a transmission error. The EOL codeword is also transmitted prior to the first data line of a page.

Occasionally, it may be necessary to insert a period of no data into the transmission stream. For example, if the combination of encoded data and the EOL line character is less than the minimum specified transmission time for a coded scan line, fill must be inserted to pad the transmission time. Fill, consisting simply of a variable-length sequence of 0s, can be inserted only between the end of the encoded data and the EOL codeword. Fill can never appear within a line of data.

Finally, to indicate that the transmission of a document has completed, six consecutive EOLs are sent. This sequence is known simply as the *return-to-control* (RTC) sequence. Additional handshaking will normally take place after the RTC sequence has been sent.

Two-Dimensional Encoding   In addition to the one-dimensional encoding scheme described in the preceding section, the T.4 standard describes an optional two-dimensional encoding scheme. In this scheme, a scan line is encoded one-dimensionally, as described previously. Subsequent lines, however, are encoded relative to that line. Consecutive scan lines that contain only minor differences can be encoded more efficiently using this method.

Of course, the two-dimensional encoding scheme's increased dependence on data relationships makes it likely that a single error will propagate through multiple lines. To limit the disturbed area in case of an error, an arbitrary limit of K related lines is set. In other words, after a one-dimensionally encoded line is transmitted, at most K-1 successive two-dimensionally encoded lines will be transmitted. The recommended maximum value of K is 2 for standard vertical resolution (3.85 lines per millimeter), and 4 for higher resolution (7.7 lines per millimeter).

Two-dimensional encoding starts with the one-dimensional encoding of the first line in a related group. This line is referred to as the *reference line*. The next line to be transmitted is called the *encoding line*. The reference line and encoding line are compared and several key pixels are identified.

The key pixels are known as *transition pixels* and are simply pixels whose color is different than the preceding pixel in the same line. All encoding lines are assumed to begin on an imaginary white pixel positioned prior to the first real pixel in the line. Figure 7.5 shows the juxtaposition of a portion of a reference line and the corresponding portion of a encoding line and defines the five categories of transition pixels.

a_0 The anchor pixel of the encoding line. Initially, a_0 represents the imaginary white pixel that begins each encoding line. As the encoding proceeds in sections, the position of a_0 is redefined by the algorithm.

a_1 The first transition pixel on the encoding line to the right of a_0.

a_2 The first transition pixel on the encoding line to the right of a_1.

b_1 The first transition pixel on the reference line that is both to the right of a_0 and of the opposite color.

b_2 The first transition pixel on the reference line to the right of b_1.

The next step is to determine the encoding mode, based on the relative positions of the identified transition pixels. When b_2 appears to the left of a_1, this situation is defined as *pass mode*. In this case, the codeword 0001 is transmitted. The receiver interprets this as an instruction to fill pixels of the current a_0 color from position a_0 to the encoding pixel just before b_2. The anchor pixel a_0 is then redefined to be the pixel in the encoding line directly below b_2 in preparation for the continuation of the algorithm. Figure 7.6a illustrates this situation.

FIGURE 7.5

Definition of transition pixels for two-dimensional encoding

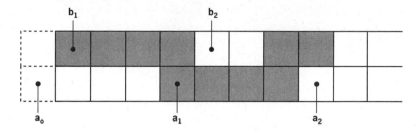

a_0 = Anchor pixel on the encoding line

a_1 = First pixel on the encoding line after a_0 of opposite color to a_0

a_2 = First pixel on the encoding line after a_1 of opposite color to a_1

b_1 = First pixel on the reference line after a_0 of opposite color to a_0

b_2 = First pixel on the reference line after b_1 of opposite color to b_1

If pass mode is not detected, the position of pixel a_1 relative to pixel b_1 is determined. If a_1 appears within 3 pixels to the left or right of b_1, this situation is defined as *vertical mode* and is illustrated in Figure 7.6b. The relative distance is encoded using the codewords shown in Table 7.4. The anchor pixel a_0 is then redefined to be at position a_1 in preparation for the continuation of the algorithm. At the receiver, pixels of the current a_0 color are written from the current a_0 position to the encoding pixel at the position relative to b_2 as given by the codeword.

TABLE 7.4

Codewords for Vertical Mode Encoding

Position	Number of Pixels	Codeword
a_1 under b_1	0	1
a_1 appears to the right of b_1	1	011
	2	000011
	3	0000011
a_1 appears to the right of b_1	1	010
	2	000010
	3	0000010

FIGURE 7.6

Two-dimensional encoding mode examples

(a) Pass mode

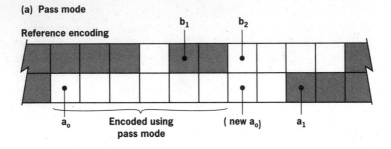

(b) Vertical mode

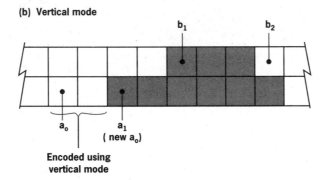

(c) Horizontal mode

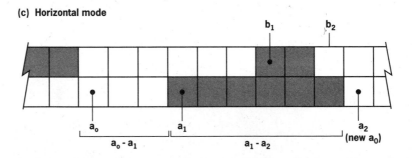

If pass mode is not detected, and a_1 is positioned farther than 3 pixels from b_1, this situation is defined as *horizontal mode* and is illustrated in Figure 7.6c. In this case, the codeword 001 and the one-dimensional codewords for the runs a_0-a_1 and a_1-a_2 are transmitted. The anchor pixel a_0 is then redefined to be at position a_2 in preparation for the continuation of the algorithm. At the receiver, pixel runs of the appropriate colors and lengths are written as encoded.

Options   The T.4 standard contains five annexes that detail enhancements that may be included in group 3 fax apparatus. (An annex is differentiated from an appendix in that the annex forms an integral part of the standard. An appendix simply contains supplementary information.) Each of the annexes contains an optional procedure that may be used between compatible apparatus. A brief description of each annex is presented here.

Annex A: Optional Error Correction Mode   Annex A specifies the format of the packets required to implement error control during fax transmission. The High-level Data Link Control (HDLC) packet format with its 16-bit frame check sequence is used to encode the binary pixel data.

Annex B: Optional Error Limiting Mode   Annex B describes the process by which the effect of transmission on the replicated image errors can be limited. Scan lines are divided into smaller parts, with each part being separately encoded. At the receiver, the encoding of each part is examined and, if found to be corrupted, is replaced with the corresponding part from the previous scan line.

Annex C: Optional File Transfer   Annex C outlines a method by which the high transfer rates and error control properties of fax apparatus can be put to use transferring data files. As a prerequisite for file transfer, the error correction mode described in annex A must be in effect. Annex C describes these four transfer modes:

- Basic Transfer Mode (BTM): Files of any type are exchanged with no additional information appended.

- Document Transfer Mode (DTM): Files of any type are exchanged as in BTM, but are preceded by an information header. The header may contain details about the file such as name, type, and so on.

- Binary File Transfer (BFT): Files of any type are exchanged preceded by an information header as in DTM. In this case, however, the information in the header is used to implement automatic processing of the file at the receiving side. More information on BFT is contained in T.434 and T.30.

- Edifact Transfer: Provides a means for users of group 3 equipment to exchange Edifact files encoded according to ISO/IEC 9735 rules.

Annex D: Optional Character Mode for Group 3   Annex D specifies the technical requirements of a mode available to group 3 apparatus that allows characters to be transferred by means of the T.30 protocol. Use of the error correction mode described in annex A is a prerequisite for character mode operation.

Annex E: Optional Mixed Mode for Group 3   Annex E specifies the technical requirements of a mode available to group 3 apparatus that allows pages containing both character data and facsimile data to be exchanged. Use of the error correction mode described in annex A is a prerequisite for character mode operation. In mixed mode, a page is divided into zones horizontally. Each zone contains either data (characters) or image (facsimile) information, but not both.

Group 4 Digital

The enhancements that distinguish group 4 (G4) facsimile apparatus from group 3 are incremental rather than radical. Furthermore, the co-option of the G4 higher resolution modes into the G3 specification has further blurred the distinction between these two groups. For the most part, application of G4 service concentrates on the integration of facsimile service with other electronic messaging and communications services. Describing G4 requires references to an inconvenient number of standards, as listed here:

T.6   Facsimile Coding Schemes and Coding Control Functions for Group 4 Facsimile Apparatus

T.60   Terminal Equipment for use in the Teletex Service

T.61   Character Repertoire and Coded Character Sets for the International Teletex Service

T.62   Control Procedures for Teletex and Group 4 Facsimile Services

T.62bis   Control Procedures for Teletex and Group 4 Facsimile Services Based on Recommendations X.215/X.225

T.70   Network-independent Basic Transport Service for Telematic Services

T.72   Terminal Capabilities for Mixed Mode of Operation

T.73   Document Interchange Protocol for the Telematic Services

T.503   A document application profile for the interchange of group 4 facsimile documents

T.521   Communication Application Profile for Document Bulk Transfer Based on the Session Service

T.563   Terminal Characteristics for Group 4 Facsimile Apparatus

F.161   International Group 4 Facsimile Service

Group 4 service adds some desirable improvements to facsimile transmission while retaining the concept of raster-based graphics. Basic document resolutions of 200, 300, and 400 dots per inch have been defined, for example. An uncompressed mode has been added to allow images to be transmitted without being subject to the usual compression algorithms. A new mode, termed *mixed mode,* provides a standard for sending text as data and graphics in raster form. Optional encoding schemes for grey scale and color images are also mentioned by the T.6 standard, but only as subjects for further study.

G4 standards create three classes of facsimile terminals according to their operational characteristics. Terminals that simply send and receive facsimiles are defined as class 1. A class 2 terminal adds the ability to receive both Teletex (machine-to-machine transfers of data) and mixed mode transmissions. A terminal belonging to class 3 adds the ability to create, transmit, and receive these services.

Document Transmission

A facsimile machine is the manifestation of mechanical, electrical, and modulation systems. Just as important, albeit less tangible, is the protocol under which facsimile information transmission is managed. The keystone that holds fax protocols together is the CCITT standard T.30, "Procedures for Document Facsimile Transmission in the General Switched Telephone Network."

The T.30 standard is a fluid document, and the 1988 version that appears in the CCITT Blue Book Volume 7.3 is out of date. Before writing an application to direct facsimile transmission, be certain to obtain the latest copy of the standard. This section presents an overview of the protocols described in T.30. It is not intended to be a substitute for this 100-page standard.

The Facsimile Session

The T.30 standard divides a fax session into the five distinct phases shown here:

Phase A: Call establishment

Phase B: Pre-message procedure

Phase C: Message transmission

Phase D: Post-message procedure

Phase E: Call release

The period from phase A to phase E, inclusive, is known as the *facsimile session*. The period that includes phases B, C, and D, is known as the *facsimile procedure*. The facsimile session is shown graphically in Figure 7.7 and explained in the following paragraphs.

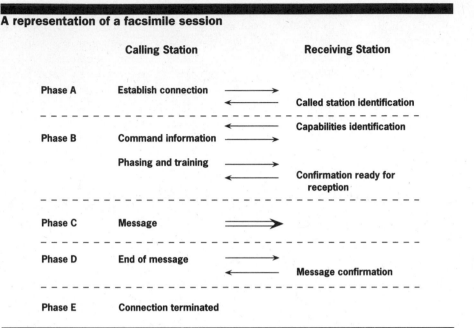

FIGURE 7.7

A representation of a facsimile session

The first phase of a connection is *call establishment.* This simply means that a person (manually operated station) or the machine itself (automatic station) originates a call to the receiving station. At the receiving station, the fax machine answers (automatic station) or a person answers (manually operated station). At manually operated stations, a procedure is performed to connect the fax equipment to the communications channel. Call establishment is complete when the two fax machines end up connected to each other.

During the pre-message procedure (phase B), the two fax terminals negotiate, select, and confirm the parameters of the connection. These parameters include the terminals' group and supported options. After confirmation, the terminals will exchange phasing and training signals, establish synchronization, and perform other functions required to ensure a stable communications connection.

Phase C comprises both message transmission and in-message procedures. The message transmission is simply the formatting and transmission of the image data. The in-message procedure occurs at the same time as message transmission and involves commands and responses that control synchronization, error detection, error correction, and line supervision.

The post-message procedure portion of the communication may include the exchange of a variety of messages. Typical messages report or request the transmission of additional pages, confirm or indicate an end-of-message, or initiate end-of-transmission activity.

The final period during any successful fax transmission is represented by phase E, call release. During this phase, both stations simply hang up the phone—manually, automatically, or a combination of both.

The Facsimile Procedure

All receiving facsimile terminals identify their capabilities by transmitting a sequence of tonal and binary coded messages. Figure 7.8 shows a diagram of a typical identification signal sent by the receiving facsimile terminal to the transmitter.

FIGURE 7.8

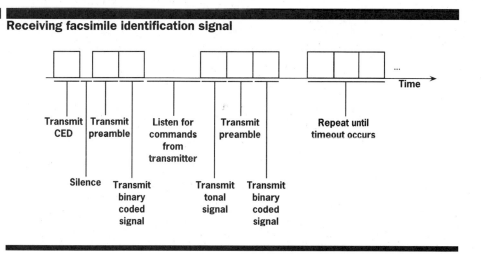

Receiving facsimile identification signal

The first signal sent is CED. Approximately 1.8 to 2.5 seconds after the called station is connected to the line, it sends a continuous 2100 Hz tone. The tone must last not less than 2.6 seconds and not more than 4.0 seconds. The called station then pauses for approximately 75 milliseconds before transmitting further signals.

The transmit preamble precedes all binary coded signaling whenever a new transmission of information begins in any direction (a line turnaround). The preamble ensures that all elements of the communication channel (echo suppressers, for example) are conditioned so that the subsequent data may pass unimpaired. For group 3 machines, the standard data signaling rate for the preamble is 300 bps, with 2400 bps being a recognized option.

The binary coded signal is sent following the preamble. The binary information is transmitted using an HDLC frame structure. The basic HDLC structure consists of a number of frames, each of which is further divided into fields. During phase B, this signal carries information on the basic and extended capabilities of the receiving fax station. The transmitting station ignores information describing capabilities it doesn't understand.

After sending the binary coded signal, the receiving station listens for a response for approximately 3 seconds. If no response is forthcoming, the receiving station transmits a tonal signal that is compatible with group 1 and 2 facsimile apparatus, as described in T.2 and T.3. (Implementation of this will, of course, depend on the receiving station's ability to implement group 1 and 2 communications.)

For approximately 1.5 seconds, the receiving station will transmit a continuous 1650 Hz (group 1) or 1850 Hz (group 2) tone. If both group 1 and group 2 are supported, a 1650 Hz tone is transmitted for 1.5 seconds, followed immediately by a 1850 Hz tone for 0.75 seconds. As shown in Figure 7.8, the sequence of preamble, binary signal, pause, and tonal signal is repeated until the calling machine responds or a timeout occurs.

The in-message procedure formats and specific signals for phase C are described in standards T.2, T.3, and T.4 for group 1, 2, and 3 fax stations, respectively. These signals control the transmission of data as well as the implementation of error control procedures.

In phase D, post-message commands are sent from the transmitter to the receiver. Depending on the capabilities of the receiver and the specifics of the transmission, the transmitter may send one or more messages. The end-of-message command, for example, indicates that the end of a complete page has been sent and that the transmitter is returning to phase B. The multipage command indicates that the transmitter will return to phase C upon receipt of a confirmation signal. And the end-of-procedure command indicates that the current fax transmission has completed and that no further documents are forthcoming.

8 *F*AX MODEMS

AS THE EVOLUTION OF FACSIMILE LEFT ROTATING DRUMS AND ANALOG MOD-
ulation behind, it was inevitable that it would merge with data modem technology. At the physical level, fax modems and data modems are virtually
indistinguishable. The data pumps, modulation schemes, and error detection
methods used in data modems are equally applicable to fax modems. A discussion of these physical systems was presented in Chapter 5.

A commonality between data and fax modems may also be seen in the information that is exchanged. The transfer of a digitized facsimile image is, after
all, simply a transfer of binary numbers. The culmination of a fax transmission
differs little from the exchange of a bitmapped graphics image between two cooperative software applications using ordinary data modems.

The principle difference between a modem designed for generalized data
transfer and a fax modem lies in the protocols that direct the communications
session. The fax modem must support the protocols described in CCITT specifications T.4, T.6, and T.30. In addition, the fax modem must provide new commands and responses to allow software to initiate and conduct a fax session.

This chapter begins with a description of the Electronic Industries Association (EIA) fax modem class structure. The division of responsibility for the fax
protocols between the DCE (modem) and DTE (PC) for each modem class is
explained. An overview of the EIA extensions to the AT command set used for
fax modem control is then presented.

This chapter also includes two short examples of PC-driven fax sessions
using the EIA command sets. In addition to the EIA commands, a brief summary of several other fax control systems is presented. Detailed descriptions of
advanced and proprietary commands and registers for a wide variety of modems and manufacturers may be found in Appendices A and B.

EIA Class Structure

The addition of fax capability to PC modems created the need for a new command interface. But no single manufacturer has controlled a majority of this
emerging market. As a result, fax modem development has had all the organi-
zation of a gold rush. Each manufacturer, blazing new trails, developed a proprietary—and incompatible—interface.

Although the origin of this surfeit of interfaces is understandable, it has created problems. End users, accustomed to widespread compatibility, discovered a general lack of interoperability among fax modem control programs. Using a particular fax modem required using the custom software bundled with the modem by the manufacturer. Independent software developers, attempting to develop a generalized fax control program, were overwhelmed by the task of distinguishing and subsequently supporting a large number of widely differing modems and command sets.

To address these problems, the EIA has developed a series of standards that define the protocols and commands for use between a DTE and fax DCE. The goal is to separate modems into three classes, as determined by the ability of the modems to conduct a fax session independent of the DTE. This section describes the three classes of fax modems.

Class Definitions

A stand-alone fax machine implements all phases of the session, from image preparation through the exchange of data over the communications channel through image reconstruction. When the session is conducted using a PC and a fax modem, however, the responsibilities for session management are partitioned between the two devices. The EIA specifications for fax modems both define where this separation occurs and establish the details of the interface. Figure 8.1 shows a representation of the interface layers in a fax session as well as their division by class.

FIGURE 8.1

EIA fax modem class interface partitioning

User Level	T.4/T.6	T.30	Physical Level
Image reduction and reproduction	Image encoding and decoding	FAX session protocols	Modem V-protocols, data pump HDLC

DTE / DCE — Class 1

DTE / DCE — Class 2.0

DTE / DCE — Class 3

The EIA defines a Class 1 fax modem in specification EIA/TIA-578. Class 1 means simply that the fax modem provides the minimum services necessary to implement a Group 3 fax session. As Figure 8.1 shows, the PC is responsible for encoding the image (per T.4) and managing the document transmission (per T.30). A Class 1 fax modem provides the following services, as required:

- GSTN interface
- Autodialing
- V series signal conversion (modulation)
- Data transmission and reception
- HDLC data framing, transparency, and error detection
- Control commands and responses

A fax session conducted using a Class 1 modem must always be managed under control of a software application. Unlike a typical data modem session, the timing, decoding, and sequencing requirements of T.30 make it impractical to control a fax session using manually issued commands.

A Class 2.0 fax modem contains a good deal more intelligence than a Class 1 modem. The partitioning is changed, as shown in Figure 8.1, so that the tedium of implementing a fax session using T.30 is offloaded from the PC to the modem. A Class 2.0 modem is expected to provide the following services:

- GSTN interface
- Autodialing
- V series signal conversion
- T.30 protocol implementation
- Session status reporting
- Phase C data transfer
- Padding for minimum scan line time
- Quality check on receive data
- Packet protocol for DTE/DCE interface

The designation Class 2.0 (with the ".0" revision level) applies only to fax modems that are compliant with the final version of specification TIA/EIA-592. During development, draft versions of this standard have been issued under the designation SP-2388. The final version, however, differs significantly from early drafts. Modems that were manufactured based on SP-2388-A return simply "2" as their class number. (Command sets for both drafts appear in Appendix A.)

A Class 2.0 modem makes and terminates calls, manages the communication session, transports the image data, and may optionally convert between T.4 (Group 3) and T.6 (Group 4) image formats. The PC retains the responsibility for preparing and compressing the image data for transmission and interpreting the compressed data on receive. The PC transfers the image data as prompted by the modem. The command interface of a Class 2.0 modem is not necessarily upwardly compatible with a Class 1 modem; implementation of the Class 1 commands is optional.

The Class 3 fax modem specification is currently under study. It is planned that it will continue the trend of offloading fax processing responsibility from the PC to the modem, as shown in Figure 8.1. In addition to implementing T.30 and the physical modem functions, a Class 3 modem will convert a file of image data into a T.4 or T.6 compressed image for transmission. The modem may optionally expand an image on reception. (This expansion might not be needed or desired for a fax store-and-forward system, for example.)

It is likely that Class 3 modems will accept some form of TIFF (Tagged Image File Format) graphics files as well as ASCII text files for conversion. This file-based support will allow fax interchange capability to be integrated into most types of applications software. Additionally, a Class 3 interface will enhance the usability of fax equipment over a network or other sharing environment where the timing of messages between the DTE and DCE is not controllable. The Class 3 specification is currently under development by the EIA.

EIA Fax Commands

The EIA commands for control of Class 1 and Class 2.0 fax modems have been designed as syntactical extensions to the AT command set. As with data modem commands, the string of characters sent to the modem is called a command line and must begin with the attention characters *AT* or *at*. The command line contains only printable ASCII characters and ends with a carriage return character.

Only the low-order 7 bits of each character are examined when the modem interprets a command; uppercase command characters are equivalent to lowercase characters. (All 8 bits are required for data transmission, however.) Spaces and control characters other than ASCII 13 (carriage return) and ASCII 8 (backspace) that appear in the command line are ignored. If a command accepts a numeric argument, an omitted argument defaults to a value of 0. By default, all fax modems must accommodate XON/OFF (in band) flow control; other types of flow control may be optionally included.

Class 1 Syntax

Each EIA fax command begins with the fax extension characters +F. Three general forms of command syntax are available, depending on the particular command. The three forms are *capabilities, status,* and *set.* Note that not all forms are appropriate for every command.

To determine the capabilities of the modem, the *capabilities* command syntax is used. This has the form

```
+Fcommand=?
```

where *command* represents a valid fax command. The modem will respond by listing the value or range of values that it supports. A Class 1 modem's response to the command line AT+FCLASS=? (tell me what class of fax communication you support), for example, might be as follows:

```
0,1
```

This response indicates that the modem can be configured as a Class 1 fax as well as an ordinary data modem (Class 0).

The second command syntax requests that the modem report the current value of a parameter or configuration option. This command uses the following form:

```
+Fcommand?
```

To determine the current operation mode, for example, you would issue the command AT+FCLASS?. A modem configured to operate as a Class 1 fax modem would respond with the following message:

```
1
```

The final command syntax is used to set the value of a parameter or pass a parameter that controls modem operation. The set syntax appears as

```
+Fcommand=val
```

where *command* represents the parameter to be set and *val* represents the desired parameter value. Depending on the command, *val* may be numeric or alphabetic. Numeric arguments to both the standard data modem AT commands and Class 1 fax commands are expressed as decimal numbers.

The default command-line terminator is the carriage return character. Alternately, the command line may be terminated by a semicolon (;). With the exception of the +FTS and +FRS command, a Class 1 command must be the last command in the line. (Although this is clearly specified in EIA/TIA-578, many Class 1 fax modems will accept multiple fax commands in a single line without intervening separators.)

The fax modem may be programmed to respond either in alphabetic (verbose) or numeric (nonverbose) characters. Alphabetic responses are preceded and followed by a carriage return and line feed character pair. Numeric character responses are issued with only a following carriage return. The result codes OK (0), CONNECT (1), NO CARRIER (3), and ERROR (4) are mandatory.

Class 2 Syntax

EIA Class 2.0 commands have essentially the same syntax as defined for Class 1 and all begin with the extension characters +F. The three general forms of command syntax (capabilities, status, and set) are also available when appropriate.

For Class 2.0, the command syntax used to set the value of a parameter or pass a parameter that controls modem operation may support numeric or string values. Unlike Class 1 commands, however, *Class 2.0 numeric constants must be specified in hexadecimal*. A numeric constant may be made up of the characters "0" through "9" (ASCII 30h through 39h) and "A" through "F" (ASCII 41h through 46h) only. The decimal constant 255, equivalent to the hexadecimal constant FFh, would be sent as the two characters "FF". (Note that although the *h* suffix is used to designate hexadecimal numbers in this text, the *h* character is not sent to the modem.)

String constants consist of a string of printable ASCII characters surrounded by the double-quote character ("). A null string is designated by two consecutive double-quote characters ("").

In addition to single values, ranges of values may be passed as arguments or returned by a Class 2.0 fax modem. The syntax differs from that of a Class 1 modem. In response to a capabilities query, the modem returns its range of values as an ordered list. The list begins with a left parentheses character "(" and ends with a right parentheses character ")". The list may contain a single value, multiple values, or a range of values. To provide compatibility with Class 1 modems, the Class 2.0 response to the AT+FCLASS=? command doesn't follow this convention.

In an ordered list that contains multiple values, the values are separated by the comma (,) character. An example of such a response is (0,2,4,8). A value range is expressed as two values separated by a hyphen character (-). A range of 0 to 255 decimal, for example, would be expressed as (0-FF). Class 2 commands may also accept compound values consisting of a series of values, each enclosed within parentheses, separated by commas. Embedded spaces should be ignored. The following string represents a typical compound value:

```
(Ø,1,2),(Ø),(Ø-3)
```

Class 2 commands are executed from left to right within a command line. Each command is executed individually, regardless of what follows on the command line. If all commands execute correctly, a single result code is issued to indicate the status of the final command on the line. If a command produces an error, or if an invalid command is found, execution of the command line ceases and any unprocessed commands on the command line are ignored. A Class 2 fax modem supports the following result codes:

0   OK

1   CONNECT

2   RING

3   NO CARRIER

4   ERROR

6   NO DIALTONE

7   BUSY

8   NO ANSWER

Compatibility   The development of the Class 2.0 fax modem specification is being conducted by the TR-29.2 subcommittee on Facsimile Digital Interfaces. In August, 1990, this subcommittee issued SP-2388-A, the first draft of what is ultimately to become TIA/EIA-592, the Class 2.0 fax standard. A host of chip manufacturers, including Sierra, Rockwell, and Exar, designed and produced over a million units that implemented the Class 2 standard described by the August, 1990 draft.

Based on the comments received on SP-2388-A, and despite the large installed base of hardware based on that standard, the subcommittee felt it necessary to revise the document extensively. (The fax connect message, for example, was changed from +FCON to +FCO.) SP-2388-A was declared obsolete, and SP-2388-B was issued. In a partial acknowledgment of the installed base of August 1990 Class 2 modems, the CLASS command has been redefined to return the following values:

0   data modem

1   EIA/TIA-578

2   SP-2388-A (marked as reserved for manufacturers)

2.0 TIA/EIA-592

Example Fax Sessions

This section presents some examples of Class 1 and 2.0 fax sessions that demonstrate the major steps required to send and receive fax data. The examples are purposely kept simple; they assume that no errors occur during transmission, for instance. Even so, these examples should help you analyze and understand the basis of data exchange during a fax connection.

Be aware that the EIA/TIA-578 and TIA/EIA-592 (SP-2388B) specifications simply establish a set of commands necessary to conduct a fax session using a compliant fax modem. They do not explain the theory or operation of the T.30 protocols or T.4 and T.6 image preparation. They are, in fact, extremely obtuse documents. To program a successful fax session, the programmer must have a solid knowledge of the techniques and protocols expressed in the T.30 and T.4 standards.

Class 1 Operation

A Class 1 fax session requires a good deal of attention from the PC (DTE). Control and data information must be formatted by the PC and then transmitted to the modem. Likewise, data received by the modem is passed to the PC to be decoded and interpreted. Figure 8.2 shows the chronology of a fax session where a Class 1 modem originates a call and sends one page of image data without errors.

FIGURE 8.2

A sample Class 1 fax session sending a single page to a remote fax terminal

PC (DTE)	Local Modem (Originating)	Remote Fax Terminal (Printing)
AT+FCLASS=1 ->		
	<- "OK"	
ATDs ->	Dial number	
		Answer
	CNG ->	
		<- CED
		<- V.21 carrier
		<- HDLC flags
	<- "CONNECT"	
		<- NSF frame
	<- NSF data	
	<- <DLE><ETX>	
	<- "OK"	
AT+FRH=3 ->		
	<- "CONNECT"	
		<- CSI frame
	<- CSI data	
	<- <DLE><ETX>	
	<- "OK"	
AT+FRH=3 ->		
	<- "CONNECT"	
		<- DIS frame
		drop carrier
	<- DIS data	
	<- <DLE><ETX>	
	<- "OK"	
AT+FRH=3 ->		
	<- "NO CARRIER"	
AT+FTS=20 ->	(200 ms of silence)	

FIGURE 8.2

A sample Class 1 fax session sending a single page to a remote fax terminal (Continued)

PC (DTE)	Local Modem (Originating)	Remote Fax Terminal (Printing)
AT+FTH=3 ->	V.21 carrier -> <- "CONNECT"	
TSI data -> <DLE><ETX> ->	TSI frame -> <- "CONNECT"	
DCS data -> <DLE><ETX> ->	DCS frame -> drop carrier <- "OK"	
AT+FTS=8 ->	wait 80 ms	
AT+FTM=96 ->	V.29 carrier -> <- "CONNECT"	
TCF data -> <DLE><ETX> ->	TCF frame -> drop carrier <- "OK"	
AT+FRH=3 ->	<- "CONNECT" <- CFR data <- <DLE><ETX> <- "OK"	<- V.21 carrier <- CFR frame drop carrier
AT+FRH=3 -> AT+FTS=20 ->	<- "NO CARRIER" (200 ms of silence)	
AT+FTM=96 ->	V.29 carrier -> <- "CONNECT"	
<image data> -> <DLE><ETX> ->	<image data> -> drop carrier <- "OK"	
AT+FTS=8 ->	wait 80 ms	
AT+FTH=3 ->	V.21 carrier -> <- "CONNECT"	
EOP data -> <DLE><ETX> ->	EOP frame -> drop carrier <- "OK"	

FIGURE 8.2

A sample Class 1 fax session sending a single page to a remote fax terminal (Continued)

PC (DTE)	Local Modem (Originating)	Remote Fax Terminal (Printing)
		<- V.21 carrier
AT+FRH=3 ->		
	<- "CONNECT"	
		<- MCF frame
		drop carrier
	<- MCF data	
	<- \<DLE>\<ETX>	
	<- "OK"	
AT+FRH=3 ->		
	<- "NO CARRIER"	
AT+FTS=20 ->	(200 ms of silence)	
AT+FTH=3 ->	V.21 carrier ->	
	<- "CONNECT"	
DCN data ->	DCN frame ->	
	drop carrier	
	<- "OK"	
ATH0 ->	hang up	

The session begins when the PC sets the local modem to fax mode and dials the number of the remote fax terminal. The local modem generates the CNG (calling) signal, an 1100 Hz tone held on for 0.5 second and off for 3 seconds. The remote fax answers with the CED (called station identification) signal, a continuous 2100 Hz tone lasting 2.6 to 4 seconds.

The remote fax then establishes the carrier specified for 300 bps V.21 channel 2 modulation and sends the HDLC flags. (The local modem is configured to use this modulation implicitly when it receives the AT+FCLASS=1 command.) When the HDLC flags are received, the local modem returns the CONNECT message to the PC.

The local modem next receives an HDLC frame from the remote site and sends the data shown in Figure 8.3 to the PC. The first byte of this frame is the HDLC address field, which is always FFh for communications on the GSTN.

The address field is followed immediately by the HDLC control field that can assume one of two values. If the value is C0h, this frame is *not* the final frame in this procedure. A value of C8h indicates that this is the final frame. Note, however, that this byte is delivered to the PC with the *bit order reversed* with respect to the descriptions published in T.30. Thus the 03h (00000011b) shown in Figure 8.3 becomes C0h (11000000b).

The next byte received is the facsimile control field (FCF) and identifies the type of information being exchanged. As before, the bit order of the received

FIGURE 8.3

An example of an optional nonstandard facilities (NSF) frame

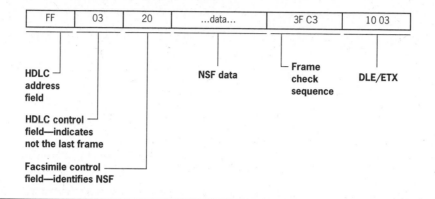

| FF | 03 | 20 | ...data... | 3F C3 | 10 03 |

HDLC address field

HDLC control field—indicates not the last frame

Facsimile control field—identifies NSF

NSF data

Frame check sequence

DLE/ETX

byte must be reversed to decode this field according to T.30. The 20h becomes 04h, a unique code identifying this data as the optional NSF (nonstandard facilities) frame. The format of the data in this frame is set by each individual manufacturer and may be used to indicate specific requirements or capabilities that are not called out in T.30. In Figure 8.3, the data is omitted because the PC is simply going to ignore this frame.

Following the frame data, the 16-bit CRC frame check sequence (FCS) is passed to the PC. The FCS is sent as two bytes. The high byte is transmitted first, followed by the low byte, although the order of the bits within each byte is reversed. The FCS is for information only. The PC needn't examine the FCS, since the modem has already recalculated the FCS of the frame and compared it to the FCS that was received with the frame. Finally, the frame is closed with the two-byte end-of-frame sequence 10h (DLE) 03h (ETX).

In the example session, the optional CSI (called subscriber identification) frame arrives next. The PC reads this with an explicit AT+FRH=3 (read an HDLC frame using 300 bps V.21 channel 2 modulation) command. This frame follows the same general format as the NSI frame. The CSI frame is identified by a fax control field of 02h (transmitted as 40h to the PC).

In most cases, this field contains ASCII characters representing the telephone number of the answering fax machine. The characters of the ASCII string are sent last character first, but the bits in each byte are not reversed. Thus if the identification of the called fax was set to "800-555-1212", the PC would receive the string "2121-555-008" (and possibly some trailing space characters) followed by the FCS and the DLE/ETX pair.

The PC then issues another AT+FRH=3 command to read the next frame sent by the remote fax. Figure 8.4 shows this frame. In this case, the FFh HDLC address byte is followed by a control field of C8h (13h as received by the PC). This indicates to the PC that this is the last frame the remote site intends to send in this procedure.

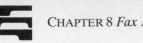

FIGURE 8.4

An example of the mandatory digital identification signal (DIS) frame

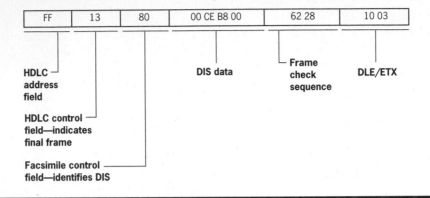

| FF | 13 | 80 | 00 CE B8 00 | 62 28 | 10 03 |

HDLC address field

HDLC control field—indicates final frame

Facsimile control field—identifies DIS

DIS data

Frame check sequence

DLE/ETX

The next byte, the FCF, is 01h (sent reversed as 80h to the PC), indicating that the DIS (digital identification signal) frame follows. The DIS contains a minimum of 24 bits (3 bytes) of flags that indicate the capabilities of the receiving fax. This information is used by the sending fax to determine the optimum settings for the session.

The first byte of the DIS contains information that pertains only to Group 1 and 2 fax operations and can be safely ignored by equipment that supports only Group 3. The next 3 bytes of the DCS (CEh B8h 00h) must then be expanded and bit reversed. These flags are then interpreted according to the information in the T.30 specification, as shown in Figure 8.5.

When the PC receives NO CARRIER in response to another AT+FRH=3 command, the modems are ready to turn the line around. Strictly speaking, the PC need not issue this command. The last HDLC address field indicated that it was the final frame. If, despite the address value, data is received, it would indicate that the preceding frame was invalid.

Although not specified in EIA/TIA-578, T.30 states that a fax DCE should allow no less than 200 ms to elapse before it begins transmitting after turning the line around. This is accomplished using the AT+FTS=20 command. The AT+FTH=3 command then tells the local modem to condition itself to transmit using V.21 channel 2 modulation (300 bps).

After receiving a CONNECT message, the PC sends its TSI (transmitting subscriber identification) data to the modem. This, and other frames, are terminated by the two-character pair DLE (10h) and ETX (03h). The PC does not have to calculate and transmit an FCS for the frame, since this service is performed by the modem.

The TSI frame usually contains the telephone number of the calling station and may be used by the receiving modem to implement additional security (giving your station the ability to refuse unsolicited faxes, for example). Next, the

FIGURE 8.5

Interpretation of the sample DIS bit flags describing the capabilities of the receiving fax

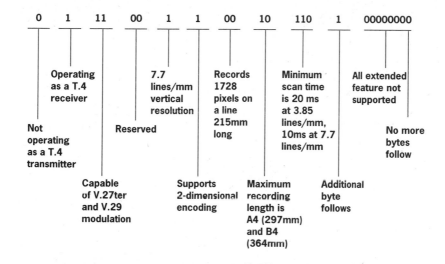

PC sends the DCS (digital command signal) data to select its choice of session capabilities identified by the DIS frame.

Negotiation complete, the PC switches the local modem to 9600 bps (V.29 modulation). Before doing so, the PC instructs the modem to pause for 80 ms to allow the receiving modem to reconfigure itself. (Again, this requirement of T.30 is not addressed specifically by EIA/TIA-578.)

After the V.29 connection is established, the local modem returns the CONNECT message. The PC then sends the TCF (training check) frame. This digital signal verifies synchronization and provides an opportunity for the modems to determine the suitability of the line for transmission. The PC then turns the line around and listens for the CFR (confirmation to receive) frame from the receiving modem at 300 bps. The reception of this frame implies that the entire pre-message procedure has been completed and image data transmissions may begin. Alternately, the remote modem may indicate a problem and propose a renegotiation, such as lowering the data transmission rate.

After a high-speed link is successfully negotiated, the PC sends the fax image data to the local modem in a single continuous stream, as directed by the flow control established between the PC and the local modem. The encoding method specified in T.4 gives the receiver some ability to resynchronize after an error, but specific data error detection and control procedures are optional. After sending the image data for a single page, the PC sends the EOP (end of procedures) frame. EOP indicates the end of a complete page of image data and also indicates that no further documents are forthcoming.

The PC next listens for confirmation from the remote fax. In this example, the modem confirms successful receipt of the image by sending the MCF (message confirmation) frame. It then returns control to the calling modem. Finally, the PC issues the AT+FTH=3 command, connects to the receiving modem, and sends the DCN (disconnect) frame. A hang up command completes the session.

Class 2 Operation

As illustrated in the preceding section, a Class 1 fax session requires constant attention from the controlling DTE. The Class 2.0 modem, in contrast, handles all T.30 and some T.4 protocols internally. As shown in Figure 8.6, the equivalent session is greatly simplified when conducted using a Class 2.0 modem.

FIGURE 8.6

A sample Class 2.0 fax session

PC (DTE)	Local Modem	Remote Fax Terminal
AT+FCLASS=2.0 ->		
	<- "OK"	
ATDs ->	dial number	
		answer
	CNG ->	
		<- CED
	<- "+FCO"	<- HDLC flags
	<- "+FNF:*nsf*"	<- NSF frame
	<- "+FCI:*csi*"	<- CSI frame
	<- "+FIS:*dis*"	<- DIS frame
	<- "OK"	
AT+FDT ->	TSI frame ->	
	DCS frame ->	
	TCF frame ->	
	<- "+FCS:*cfr*"	<- CFR frame
	<- "CONNECT"	
<image data> ->	<image data> ->	
<DLE><2Eh> ->	EOP frame ->	
	DCN frame ->	<- MCF frame
	<- "OK"	
ATH0 ->	hang up	hang up

After configuring the modem for Class 2.0 operation, the PC issues the ATD command to dial the number of the remote fax terminal. When a connection is established, the local modem sends a +FCO message to the PC. The two modems then exchange the NSF, CSI, and DSI frames. (This information may have been programmed into the modem by the DTE at an earlier time—during setup, for example.) At each stage, the frame is interpreted by the local modem, and an ASCII string is sent to the PC indicating the results. The individual flags of the DIS frame, for example, are parsed and sent to the PC as a series of character flags separated by commas. (These character flags are represented by *dis* in the table.)

The PC then issues the AT+FDT command. This instructs the local modem to negotiate compatible parameters, including a reliable speed for data transfer. After the modems have completed a successful negotiation, the local modem sends the CONNECT message to the PC. The PC then sends the image data to the local modem as a single stream, as directed by flow control.

Following the image data, the PC sends <DLE><2Eh> to tell the modem that this is the final page of the transmission. Based on this flag, the local modem will append the EOP (end of page) frame after it has transferred the image data to the remote modem. Further, the modem sends the DCN (disconnect) frame to the remote modem and returns the OK response to the PC. The PC then terminates the call by hanging up the phone with the ATH0 command.

Alternate Fax Interfaces

The EIA fax modem Class system and associated commands represent the result of industry collaboration. Other standards, however, have been—and still are—being developed throughout the industry. These standards are often developed to provide services not implemented by industry standards. More often, they are developed when the wheels of standardization grind too slowly for the rapid development of the market.

This section briefly reviews four alternate interface specifications for fax or fax-related services. Some of these specifications are designed to apply to products from more than one manufacturer. Others are product specific. To obtain more information about these specifications, consult the list of vendors in Appendix D.

DCA/Intel Communicating Applications Specification

The communicating applications specification (CAS) is a joint development of Digital Communications Associates (DCA) and Intel. It has been released into the public domain and is not confidential or proprietary.

Briefly, CAS is a high-level programming interface for data communications applications. Software developers make calls to this interface to add communications functions to their products. The CAS interface seen by the programmer is independent of the hardware and software used to implement the digital communications. CAS was developed mainly to support Intel's Communications Coprocessor, a microprocessor-driven fax card equipped with an 80188 CPU and 256K of RAM.

CAS depends on the presence of a Resident Manager to translate the application's requests into actions. This manager is simply implemented as a memory-resident runtime library on the PC. Application requests are passed to the manager, which then administers the data transmission without further interaction with the application. CAS is implemented as a set of function calls accessed through the PC multiplex interrupt, 2Fh.

This hardware-specific resident manager must be furnished either as part of the system software or by the manufacturer of the fax device. Before using CAS, the application developer must establish that a resident manager, compatible with each modem, is available for all platforms on which the application is to be implemented. Although it provides other services beside hardware independence, the CAS system doesn't so much eliminate as redistribute the problem of programming fax hardware.

FaxBios

The FaxBios system was developed by a consortium of companies—chiefly WordPerfect, Hewlett Packard, and Everex. Unlike CAS, FaxBios is designed to run in client/server environments. The goal of FaxBios is to relieve programmers from having to implement system-specific code and allow "fax-naive" applications access to fax services.

On PC platforms, FaxBios is designed to be implemented as a memory-resident program. FaxBios functions are accessible through the PC multiplex interrupt, 2Fh. A Windows API that supports dynamic data exchange (DDE) has also been defined.

Like CAS, FaxBios provides many high-level fax services such as scheduling and file transfer. Unfortunately, it also suffers from the requirement that *someone* must write the needed hardware interface. Without the crucial back-end, FaxBios application are unable to access the communications hardware.

Sierra Sendfax

Sierra Semiconductor manufactures a staggering array of single-chip modems, modem controllers, data pumps, and digital signal processors. To support fax operations, Sierra developed a set of extensions to the AT command set called *Sendfax*. All Sendfax commands start with the # prefix. A multipage fax can be sent with only one AT command line.

The Sendfax AT# fax commands were developed and used in Sierra modem chips prior to the adoption of the EIA-578 Class 1 standard and the release of the SP-2388-A proposal. In the past few years, a tremendous number of modems based on the Sierra chips have been sold. Although Sierra continually revises the firmware in its modems to implement Class 1 fax commands and keep up with the changing Class 2 proposal, the large installed base of Sendfax modems means that most serious fax control programs will have to accommodate this interface.

USRobotics High Level Fax Interface

The High Level Fax (HLF) application software interface was developed by USRobotics to provide programming access to their line of WorldPort fax products. The HLF commands are implemented as proprietary extensions to the standard AT command set. Using HLF commands, sending or receiving a fax can be accomplished with the single AT command line AT\V2+F2Ds.

The WorldPort makes and terminates fax calls, manages the scan time and communications session, and transmits fax data according to the T.30 protocols. Outgoing fax data must be compressed in accordance with T.4. The WorldPort also receives incoming fax data, processes it, and makes it available to the DTE. The *high-level* in HLF refers to the level of fax management provided by the WorldPort modem, not necessarily to the level of the programming interface.

APPENDIX A

AT COMMAND SET REFERENCE

The AT command sets representative of a variety of modem manufacturers are presented alphabetically in this appendix. The entry for each command includes a description of the operation and use of the command, notes on inconsistencies, and a list of modem types on which the command is applicable.

Where one mnemonic is used to implement different instructions (from different manufacturers, for example), a separate entry appears for each application. The B instruction, for example, selects the communication protocol on Hayes modems and enables trellis coding on Black Box modems.

Example Reference Listing

Each entry in this reference follows the same basic format, an example of which is shown in Figure A.1. An explanation of each element in a reference entry is given below.

1. *Title*. Instruction mnemonic and a short description.

2. *Description*. The full syntax of the command is given, including the AT prefix where applicable. Replaceable parameters are shown in italics. Following that, the various forms of the command are listed, accompanied by a description of the action of that command form. If the command arguments accept a range of values, the range and units are given. The default value for the command (if any) appears at the end of the description.

   Not all command forms are supported by all modem manufacturers, or the same form may have a different function. To indicate manufacturer-specific forms, the application follows the command enclosed in square brackets, as shown here.

   J0   Dial using tone.

   J1   Dial using pulse.

         Dial using European tones. [Bmodem]

   J2   Dial using both tones and pulse. [Bmodem]

Reference listing example

N

Handshake Negotiation Options

Description ATN*n*

N0   When originating or answering, handshake using only the protocol specified by S37 and B*n*.

N1   Originating: Initiate handshake using the protocol specified by S37 and B*n* and fallback to a slower speed as required. Answering: Attempt handshake using the fastest protocol supported and fallback to a slower speed as required.

N2   Originating: Initiate handshake using the protocol specified by S37 and B*n* and fallback to a slower speed as required. Answering: Attempt handshake using the fastest protocol supported and fallback to a slower speed as required. [Hayes]

N3   Originating: Handshake using only the protocol specified by S37 and B*n*. Answering: Attempt handshake using the fastest protocol supported and fallback to a slower speed as required. [Hayes, Practical]

N4   Originating: Handshake using only the protocol specified by S37 and B*n*. Answering: Attempt handshake using the fastest protocol supported and fallback to a slower speed as required. [Hayes]

N5   Originating: Initiate handshake using the protocol specified by S37 and B*n* and fallback to a slower speed as required. Answering: Handshake using only the protocol specified by S37 and B*n*. [Hayes, Practical]

Default

N1

The N command directs the protocol negotiation that the modem may perform when originating or answering a call.

Application   Dallas, Hayes, Practical, Prometheus, Rockwell, Telebit, Twincom

Related To   B, %G, S37

In this example, the J0 command explanation applies to all modems listed in the Application block. The J1 command is defined to mean "dial using pulse" for all modems in the application block *except* Bmodem. The Bmodem definition for J1 is shown explicitly. The J2 command applies *only* to the modems listed following the command, Bmodem in this example.

3. *Application.* This section lists the modem types that support this command. A modem appears in this listing if at least one modem corresponding to that type supports the command. In other words, not all commands are supported by all modems made by a single manufacturer.

4. *Related To.* Where other commands or the setting of registers affects the behavior or effectiveness of a command, they will appear in this listing. Not all cross-referenced commands are supported by all manufacturers.

5. Additional information that is applicable to the command including limitations, interactions, and so on.

+++

Escape Sequence

Description   +++

The escape sequence is an in-band escape mechanism used to switch the modem from data mode to command mode.

In a guard-time (Hayes) escape, the character used is specified by register S2. By default, this is the plus (+) character. Similarly, the minimum length of silent time that will be recognized as a guard time is specified by the setting of register S12. To command a modem to switch from data mode to command mode requires the DTE to transmit three copies of the escape character bracketed by guard times, as shown here:

```
<guard time>+++<guard time>
```

The escape sequence is not followed by a carriage return or any other character. When the modem has switched to command mode and is ready to accept commands, it issues the OK response. The ATO command returns the modem to data mode. The setting of the S12 register also establishes the maximum amount of time that can elapse between the characters of the escape sequence.

The TIES (time-independent escape sequence) retains the three-character escape string, but eliminates the requirement of surrounding guard times. Further, TIES requires that the appearance of the escape string be followed by a valid AT command. In other words, the complete TIES escape sequence has the following format:

```
+++AT[[command[argument]]...]<CR>
```

where "+++" represents three repetitions of the escape character specified in register S2. The AT characters may be uppercase or lowercase. The time that elapses between characters of this sequence is inconsequential. The terminating carriage return is mandatory and is part of the sequence.

Related To   S2, S12

?

Address Last S Register

Description   AT?

This command displays the value of the last explicitly referenced S register.

Related To   S

/

Short Pause

Description AT/

This command causes the modem to pause for 125 milliseconds while process-ing the command line. More than one / may be used for a longer pause. Unlike the comma (,), this command does not have to appear within a dial string.

Application USRobotics

$

Description   AT*c*$

        c = specific help category indicator (shown below) or omitted

        $ Help on basic commands.

        &$ Help on extended commands.

        D$ Help on dial commands.

        S$ Help on S registers.

        This command displays a command summary on the requested topic.

Application   USRobotics

%

%

Remote Modem Access Character

Description   %

This command allows you to send commands to a remote modem as if the commands had been entered at the remote DTE. Remote access must be enabled on the remote modem. All commands in a command line that follow the percent sign (%) are directed to the remote modem.

Application   Telebit

Related To   S45

A/

Reexecute Last Command Line

Description   A/

When it receives the A/ command, the modem immediately reexecutes the last command line it executed.

The A/ command is neither preceded with AT nor followed with a carriage return. It must be entered as the only command on a line. The modem responds to this command by reexecuting the entire last command line it received.

Each command line sent to the modem remains in the command buffer until the next AT command is processed or power is removed from the modem. If the modem receives new commands, loses power, or is reset, the commands in the buffer are discarded and the A/ command has no effect.

Application   AT&T, Black Box, Dallas, Hayes, Infotel, Practical, Prometheus, Rockwell, Sierra, Telebit, Twincom, USRobotics, Zoom

Related To   A>

A>

Reexecute Last Command Line Continuously

Description   A>

When it receives the A> command, the modem begins to reexecute continuously the last command line it processed. The execution may be cancelled by sending any character to the modem. Dial strings are executed a maximum of ten times.

The A> command is neither preceded with AT nor followed with a carriage return. It must be entered as the only command on a line.

Each command line sent to the modem remains in the command buffer until the next AT command is processed or power is removed from the modem. If the modem receives new commands, loses power, or is reset, the commands in the buffer are discarded and the A> command has no effect.

Application   USRobotics

Related To   A\

A

Answer an Incoming Call

Description   ATA

This command forces the modem to immediately go off-hook (on-line) and issue its answer handshake tone. When operating in fax mode, the modem will issue the CED tone.

Typically, the A command is used to manually answer an incoming call. The modem's default response to an incoming call is determined by the setting of register S0. Use of this command, however, overrides the setting of S0. This command may have no effect in some communications configurations.

If a connection is established successfully, the modem will issue the appropriate CONNECT result code. Before the connection is established, the attempt may be aborted and the modem returned to the command mode by sending any character to the modem. In this case, or if a connection is not established before the time specified in the S7 register expires, a NO CARRIER message is issued.

Application   AT&T, Black Box, Dallas, Hayes, Infotel, Microcom, Practical, Prometheus, Rockwell, Sierra, Telebit, Twincom, USRobotics, Zoom

Related To   &A, S0, S7

Notes   **1.** Using the &A command, the modem can be forced to answer in the originate mode. [Hayes]

B

Select Communications Protocol

Description   ATB*n*

B0   Use CCITT V.21 protocol during 300 bps operation and CCITT V.22/V.22bis protocol during 1200 bps operation.

B1   Use Bell 103 protocol during 300 bps operation and Bell 212A protocol during 1200 bps operation.

B2   Use CCITT V.23 protocol to transmit at 75 bps and receive at 1200 bps. [AT&T, Dallas, Sierra]

B3   Use CCITT V.23 protocol to transmit at 75 bps and receive at 1200 bps. [AT&T]

Default

B1

Application   Dallas, Infotel, Microcom, Practical, Prometheus, Rockwell, Sierra, Telebit, Twincom, USRobotics, Zoom

Notes

1. Default is 1 for U.S. and 0 for Japan. [Rockwell]

2. USRobotics must be configured with B0 to answer using V.32bis. B1 (the default) enables HST modulation. [USRobotics]

3. When B2 is selected, commands must be entered at 1200 bps. [Sierra]

B

Select Communications Protocol

ATB*n*

n = protocol parameter

Group 1 Protocols

B0   Use V.22 at 1200 bps.

B1   Use Bell 212A at 1200 bps.

B2   Use V.23 R1200/T75 bps with ASB when link is at R1200/T1200 bps. [Dallas, Hayes]

B3   Use V.23 R75/T1200 bps with ASB when link is at R1200/T1200 bps. [Dallas, Hayes]

B4   Use V.23 R75/T1200 bps when link is at R75/T1200 bps. [Hayes]

B5   Use V.23 1200 bps half-duplex when link is at R1200/T1200 bps. [Hayes]

Group 2 Protocols

B10   Use V.23 R1200/T75 bps when link is at R1200/T75 bps. [Hayes]

B11   Use V.23 R600/T75 bps when link is at R600/T75 bps. [Hayes]

Group 3 Protocols

B15   Use V.21 when line speed is 110 or 300 bps. [Dallas, Hayes, Practical]

B16   Use Bell 103 when line speed is 110 or 300 bps. [Dallas, Hayes, Practical]

Group 4 Protocols

B20   Use V.23 R600/T75 bps with ASB when link is at R600/T600 bps. [Hayes]

B21   Use V.23 R75/T600 bps with ASB when link is at R600/T600 bps. [Hayes]

B22   Use V.23 R75/T600 bps split speed when link is at R75/T600 bps. [Hayes]

B23   Use V.23 600 bps half-duplex when link is at 600 bps. [Hayes]

Group 5 Protocols

B30   Use V.22bis when link is at 2400 bps. [Dallas, Hayes]

Group 6 Protocols

B41   Use V.32 full-duplex when link is at 4800 bps. [Dallas, Hayes]

B42   Use Express96 when link is at 4800 bps. [Hayes]

Group 7 Protocols

B50   Use V.29 half-duplex when link is at 7200 bps. [Hayes]

B52   Use V.32 full-duplex when link is at 7200 bps with error control. [Dallas]

Group 8 Protocols

B60   Use V.32 full-duplex when link is at 9600 bps. [Dallas, Hayes]

B61   Use Express96 when link is at 9600 bps. [Hayes]

B63   Use V.29 half-duplex when link is at 9600 bps. [Hayes]

B70   Use V.32bis full-duplex when the link is at 12000 bps. [Dallas]

B75   Use V.32bis full-duplex when the link is at 14400 bps. [Dallas]

Default

B1, B41, B60

This command selects the communications protocol for a specific data link speed. One speed from each protocol group may be selected and set as the default independent of other group settings.

ASB (automatic speed buffering) is Hayes's term for operating the serial port at a different speed than the data link with flow-control. Express96 is a Hayes proprietary protocol that simulates full duplex 9600 bps operation and was previously known as Hayes's fast-turnaround Ping-Pong protocol.

Application   Dallas, Hayes, Practical

B

Enable Trellis Coding

Description ATB*n*

B2   Enable trellis coding.

B3   Disable trellis coding.

Default

B2

This command enables or disables the use of trellis coding (forward error correction) for V.32 9600 bps connections.

Application Black Box

Related To % U

C

Select Modem Transmit Carrier Operation

Description   ATC*n*

C0   Transmit carrier is always off.

C1   Modem manages transmit carrier switching.

Default

C1

When configured with the C1 command, the modem's internal logic manages carrier operation automatically. The modem will assert its carrier when attempting to establish a connection and drop it when the connection is terminated. In response to the C0 command, the transmit carrier is unconditionally inhibited until a C1 command is subsequently issued.

Application   Dallas, Hayes, Rockwell, Sierra, Twincom, Zoom

Notes

1. This command is supported on early Hayes modems and some compatibles. More modern high-speed modems will return ERROR in response to the C0 command and retain carrier-switching control. In most cases, the C1 command, although having no effect on the operation of these modems, may be accepted for compatibility with older communications software.

D

Dial a Number

ATD*s*

s = dial string

This command places the modem in originate mode, dials a number, and attempts to establish a connection. To cancel the dial attempt, the DTE may send any character to the modem. (Unless &D0 is set, lowering DTR will also cancel the dial.) The D command must be the last command on a command line.

The dial string may consist of the digits 0–9, other dialing characters (* and #), and dial modifiers. Dial modifiers are special commands that, for the most part, are valid only within a dial string. They modify and control how the modem dials a telephone number. Not all dial modifiers are available on all modems.

0-9 A B C D # *   Digits/Characters for dialing

These digits and characters represent the individual elements that make up a telephone number. The digits 0–9 are valid on all systems. The characters A B C D # and * represent specific tone pairs—not the characters on the PC keyboard—and are valid only on tone-dialing systems; they are ignored if pulse dialing is selected.

,   (Comma) Pause

When the modem encounters the comma (,) dial modifier in a dial string, it pauses for the amount of time specified in the S8 register (the typical default setting is 2 seconds) before processing the next character. A comma is frequently inserted to give an internal phone system time to connect to an outside line or to wait for a dial tone. If a longer delay is required, more than one comma may be used.

@   Wait for silence (Quiet Answer)

The @ modifier instructs the modem to listen for at least one ring followed by 5 seconds of silence (a quiet answer) before continuing. The amount of time the modem waits for the silent period is specified by register S7. If the silence is not detected, the modem hangs up and returns the NO ANSWER result code. If the silence is detected, the modem continues execution of the dial string. The modem does not listen for silence until it first detects a nonsilence.

! Hook Flash

When the modem processes the ! modifier, it goes on-hook for a brief period of time (typically about a half-second), then goes off-hook again. This feature is often used to access some phone system features such as call-transfer.

^ Turn on Calling Tone

Turns on the periodic 1300 Hz calling tone if originating the call. The calling tone must be enabled on a call-by-call basis. [Rockwell, Twincom]

; Return To Command Mode

The semicolon (;) modifier is used only as the last character in a command line. It instructs the modem to return to command mode after dialing, but not to break the connection. The semicolon is useful if a very long telephone number has to be continued across more than one command line. Also, using this feature, the modem can be used as a telephone dialer without generating a carrier signal.

" Translate Letters

Alphabetic characters that are enclosed within double quotes are converted to their numerical equivalents. This allows so-called vanity numbers to be entered directly, as in the example ATDT1-800-"MCIMAIL". [Practical, USRobotics]

$ Wait for Bong

Tells the modem to wait for the calling-card prompt tone (bong) before continuing to process the dial string. The modem will wait for the time specified in the S7 register. [Practical]

/n Dial a Stored Telephone Number

Dials one of the stored telephone numbers placed in memory by the &Z or \P commands. [Microcom, Sierra]

\n Dial a Stored Telephone Number

Dials one of the stored telephone numbers placed in memory by the &Z or \P commands. [Prometheus]

+n Force Log-On Sequence

Dial, connect, and perform logon sequence n, where n=1–9. [Microcom]

J Link Negotiation

Perform link negotiation at 1200 bps. This is equivalent to the *H1 command. [Microcom]

K   Cellular Connection

Sets the)M1 command for this connection only. [Microcom]

L   Redial last number

This command causes the modem to redial the last dial string it has received. Unlike the A/ command, only the dial string and not the entire command buffer are reexecuted. On some modems, the command ATDL? will display the last number dialed.

M   Dial in V.42 Mode

Placed anywhere in the dial string, this dial modifier overrides the current operating mode and forces the modem to attempt to establish a V.42 RELIABLE link. This modifier affects the current dial attempt only. [Microcom]

N*n*   Dial An Alternate Stored Number

This dial modifier must appear following the last character in the dial string. If the modem fails to make a connection with the number specified by the dial string, it will dial the alternate telephone number. Values for *n* range from 01 to 20 (default is 01) and represent numbers stored with the &Z or \P commands.

If the N dial modifier is included in a stored number that is dialed and the connection attempt fails, the modem will dial the specified number (N*n*) or the next number in sequence (N). Up to ten numbers can be dialed in sequence. [Microcom]

P   Pulse dialing

The P command instructs the modem to use the make/break system of dialing used by rotary dial telephones. It remains the default until changed.

Q   Dial in V.42 Mode with Fallback to NORMAL

Placed anywhere in the dial string, this dial modifier overrides the current operating mode and forces the modem to attempt to establish first a V.42 RELIABLE link, then fall back to a NORMAL link. This modifier affects the current dial attempt only. [Microcom]

R   Originate Call in Answer Mode

When calling an originate-only modem, this command instructs the local modem to attempt to establish the call using the answer carrier tones instead of the originate carrier tones. (Recall from Chapter 5 that originate and answer refer only to the carrier tones used by the modems and bear no relationship to call placement.)

S=*n* Dial Stored Number

Some modems support the storing of telephone numbers in nonvolatile RAM. On these modems, the ATDS=*n* command will dial the stored telephone number indicated by *n*, where *n* may range from 0 to 3. [Infotel, Prometheus, Rockwell, Sierra, Twincom]

S*n* Dial Stored Number

Some modems support the storing of telephone numbers in non-volatile RAM. On these modems, the ATDS*n* command will dial the stored telephone number indicated by *n*, where *n* may range from 0 to 3. [Prometheus]

S Dial First Stored Number

This modifier causes the modem to dial the first stored telephone number. It cannot appear as part of the first dial string. [Microcom]

T Tone Dialing

The T command instructs the modem to use the tone system of dialing used by DTMF telephones. It remains the default until changed.

U Dial in DIRECT Mode

Placed anywhere in the dial string, this dial modifier overrides the current operating mode and forces the modem to attempt to establish a DIRECT link. This modifier affects the current dial attempt only. [Microcom]

V Dial in V.42 Mode with Fallback to MNP

Placed anywhere in the dial string, this dial modifier overrides the current operating mode and forces the modem to attempt to establish first a V.42 RELIABLE link, then fall back to an MNP RELIABLE link. This modifier affects the current dial attempt only. [Microcom]

W Wait for dial tone

This command instructs the modem to wait for a dial tone up to the time specified by register S7. This is useful when accessing an external line from a PBX system. If the dial tone is detected before the S7 time delay expires, processing of the dial string continues. If no dialtone is received, the modem returns NO DIALTONE and hangs up. [Prometheus]

X Dial in AUTO RELIABLE Mode

Placed anywhere in the dial string, this dial modifier overrides the current operating mode and forces the modem to attempt to establish an AUTO RELIABLE link. This modifier affects the current dial attempt only. [Microcom]

Y   Dial in MNP RELIABLE Mode

Placed anywhere in the dial string, this dial modifier overrides the current operating mode and forces the modem to attempt to establish an MNP RELIABLE link. This modifier affects the current dial attempt only. [Microcom]

Z   Dial in NORMAL Mode

Placed anywhere in the dial string, this dial modifier overrides the current operating mode and forces the modem to attempt to establish a NORMAL link. This modifier affects the current dial attempt only. [Microcom]

Application   Hayes, Infotel, Microcom, Practical, Prometheus, Rockwell, Sierra, Telebit, Twincom, USRobotics, Zoom

Notes   1. After disconnecting, there may be up to a 5-second delay before the modem goes off-hook in the originate mode in response to this command.

E

Select Modem Command Character Echo

Description

ATE*n*

E0   Characters sent by the DTE to the modem in command mode are not echoed.

E1   Characters sent by the DTE to the modem in command mode are echoed.

Default

E1

When the modem is in command mode, the E command determines whether characters received by the modem are echoed (retransmitted) to the DTE. When echo is enabled (E1), all characters, regardless of their validity as commands, are echoed.

Application   AT&T, Black Box, Dallas, Hayes, Infotel, Microcom, Practical, Prometheus, Rockwell, Sierra, Telebit, Twincom, USRobotics, Zoom

Related To   \E, F

F

Select Modem Data Character Echoplex

Description ATF*n*

F0   Characters sent by the DTE to the modem in data mode are echoed. Returns ERROR if not supported.

F1   Characters sent by the DTE to the modem in data mode are not echoed.

Default

F1

When the modem is in data mode, the F command determines whether characters received by the modem are echoed (retransmitted) to the DTE. This is known as echoplex mode. When echoplex is enabled (F1), all characters, regardless of their validity as commands, are echoed.

Application Dallas, Hayes, Infotel, Rockwell, Telebit, Twincom, USRobotics, Zoom

Related To \E

Notes

1. This command is supported on early Hayes modems and some compatibles. More modern modems will not echo data and return ERROR in response to the F0 command. In most cases, the F1 command, although having no effect on the operation of these modems, is accepted without error for compatibility with older communications software.

G

Switch to Voice Mode

Description   ATG

This command instructs the modem to cease data transmission and free the telephone handset for voice use. The handset must be off-hook before this command is entered.

Application   Telebit

H

Switch Hook Control

Description ATH*n*

    H0   Go on-hook (hang up).

    H1   Go off-hook (on-line).

    H2   Operate line relay only. [Hayes]

Default

    H0

This command simulates the actions of lifting and replacing the handset of a standard telephone. The ATH0 forces the modem to go on-hook, hanging up the phone. This command is typically used to force the modem to terminate an established connection and hang up the line immediately.

When it receives the H1 command, the modem will go off-hook, access the phone line, issue the OK response, and await further commands. This command does not initiate the handshaking process (that function is performed by the A command). It is not necessary to use the H1 command when dialing, as the D command will cause the modem to go off-hook automatically.

Application AT&T, Black Box, Dallas, Hayes, Infotel, Microcom, Practical, Prometheus, Rockwell, Sierra, Telebit, Twincom, USRobotics, Zoom

Related To %D, S29

Notes
1. This command may take several seconds to execute when the modem is severing a V.32 connection. [Sierra]
2. Ring signals and DTR transitions are ignored for 5 seconds after disconnect. [Microcom]
3. The H2 command is available only on certain Smartmodem 1200 products. [Hayes]

H

Select Hang-Up Type

Description   ATH*n*

H2   Enable CCITT V.32 hang up.

H3   Enable fast hang up.

Default

H2

This command determines the type of hang-up protocol that will be used when the H0 command is received during a connection.

Application   Black Box

I

Identify Modem

Description ATI*n*

I0	Display product code.
I1	Display ROM checksum as a 3-digit decimal number. This may be a dummy value or an error diagnostic value.
I2	Calculate ROM checksum and return OK or ERROR status.
	Display result of RAM test. [USRobotics]
	Return OK or report the CONNECT status. [Telebit]
I3	Display firmware (ROM) revision level. [Dallas, Infotel, Prometheus, Rockwell, Sierra, Telebit, Twincom]
	Display call duration or current time. [USRobotics]
	Display modem serial number. [AT&T]
I3=*hh:mm:ss*	Set real-time clock. [USRobotics]
I4	Display configuration settings. [Dallas, Sierra, USRobotics]
	Display modem capabilities and ID as a bitmapped string encoded for communications software. [Dallas, Hayes, Practical, Prometheus, Zoom]
	Display negotiated parameters for the current or most recent connection. [Telebit]
	Display modem model designation. [AT&T]
I5	Display 4-digit modem chip set number. [Dallas, Sierra]
	Display stored configurations. [USRobotics]
	Display most recently dialed number. [Telebit]
	Display hardware configuration. [Practical]
	Display part number of the modem's circuit card. [AT&T]
I6	Display link diagnostics. [Practical, USRobotics]
	Display hardware platform determination. [Telebit]

	Display software part number. [AT&T]
I7	Display product configuration. [USRobotics]
I9	Display modem's serial number and product code. [Prometheus]
	Display firmware revision number. [AT&T]
I11	Display hexadecimal checksum of ROM. [AT&T]
I11	Display firmware revision number in alphanumeric form. [AT&T]
I33	Display 4-digit internal code revision identification. [Dallas, Sierra]

Default

I0

Application Black Box, Hayes, Infotel, Microcom, Prometheus, Rockwell, Sierra, Twincom, USRobotics, Zoom

Related To K, %V

Notes

1. Although Hayes has established a bitmapped standard for the I4 response, correspondence to this format should not be expected from other modem manufacturers.

2. The information returned by I3 command is controlled by the K command. [USRobotics]

K

Program Modem Clock

Description ATK*n*

K0   The I3 command displays the duration of the current call if
connected or of the previous call if disconnected.

K1   The I3 command displays the current time.

Default

K0

This command determines the information that will be displayed by the I3
command. The real-time clock is initialized with the command I3=*hh:mm:ss*.

Application USRobotics

Related To I

L

Select Speaker Volume Level

Description   ATL*n*

L0   Low speaker volume

L1   Low speaker volume

L2   Medium speaker volume

L3   High speaker volume

Default

L2

This command sets the volume level of the modem's speaker under software control. On modems with a manual volume control or without a speaker, this command may be ignored, and does not produce an error.

The L command selects from three different volume levels. To disable the speaker entirely, use the M command.

Application   AT&T, Black Box, Dallas, Hayes, Infotel, Microcom, Practical, Prometheus, Rockwell, Sierra, Telebit, Twincom, Zoom

Related To   M

M

Select Monitor (Speaker) Function

Description ATM*n*

M0   Speaker is always off.

M1   Speaker is on until remote carrier is detected.

M2   Speaker is always on.

M3   Speaker is off during dialing, then on until carrier is detected. [Black Box, Dallas, Hayes, Infotel, Microcom, Practical, Prometheus, Rockwell, Sierra, Telebit, Twincom, USRobotics, Zoom]

Default

M1

The M command controls whether audio from the phone line is relayed to the modem's speaker during the dialing, handshaking, and connection phases of a session.

Most modems default to ATM1, allowing the user to monitor the call from dial through negotiation. In this way, the user can hear telephone company voice announcements, busy signals, or another user answering the phone. During troubleshooting, it's often necessary to monitor the negotiation process that takes place between the modems.

Application AT&T, Black Box, Dallas, Hayes, Infotel, Microcom, Practical, Prometheus, Rockwell, Sierra, Telebit, Twincom, USRobotics, Zoom

Related To L

N

Handshake Negotiation Options

Description   ATN*n*

N0   When originating or answering, handshake using only the protocol specified by S37 and B*n*.

N1   Originating: Initiate handshake using the protocol specified by S37 and B*n* and fallback to a slower speed as required. Answering: Attempt handshake using the fastest protocol supported and fallback to a slower speed as required.

N2   Originating: Initiate handshake using the protocol specified by S37 and B*n* and fallback to a slower speed as required. Answering: Attempt handshake using the fastest protocol supported and fallback to a slower speed as required. [Hayes]

N3   Originating: Handshake using only the protocol specified by S37 and B*n*. Answering: Attempt handshake using the fastest protocol supported and fallback to a slower speed as required. [Hayes, Practical]

N4   Originating: Handshake using only the protocol specified by S37 and B*n*. Answering: Attempt handshake using the fastest protocol supported and fallback to a slower speed as required. [Hayes]

N5   Originating: Initiate handshake using the protocol specified by S37 and B*n* and fallback to a slower speed as required. Answering: Handshake using only the protocol specified by S37 and B*n*. [Hayes, Practical]

Default

N1

The N command directs the protocol negotiation that the modem may perform when originating or answering a call.

Application   Dallas, Hayes, Practical, Prometheus, Rockwell, Telebit, Twincom

Related To   B, %G, S37

N

Save Telephone Directory Entry

Description   ATN*n*=*s* \ *i* \

   n = 0–9, telephone number to store

   s = telephone dial string

   i = identification string

This command stores telephone numbers and optional identification strings in the modem's telephone directory. The total length of the dial and identification strings cannot exceed 50 characters.

When callback security is enabled, the identification string serves as the password.

Application   Telebit

Related To   N?

N?

Display Telephone Directory

Description ATN?

This command displays the entire telephone directory, the current settings of selected S registers, and the firmware version number.

Application Telebit

Related To N, &V

O

Return to On-Line State

Description $\text{ATO}n$

O0   Switch to the on-line (data) mode.

O1   Retrain adaptive equalizer, if present, when operating at 2400 bps or higher, then switch to the data mode.

O3   Issue rate-renegotiation sequence then return to data mode. [Prometheus]

Initiate a 2400 bps speed shift and fallback to 1200 bps. Applies only to calls at 2400 bps. [USRobotics]

The O command forces the modem to go immediately into the on-line (data) mode. Typically, this command is used to return the modem to data mode and to reduce errors due to loss of equalization.

Application   AT&T, Black Box, Dallas, Hayes, Infotel, Microcom, Practical, Prometheus, Rockwell, Sierra, Telebit, Twincom, USRobotics, Zoom

Related To   \O

P

Pulse Dialing

Description ATP

Used outside of a dial string, this command sets the default dialing mode to pulse dialing. Until subsequently changed, the modem will use the make/break system of dialing used by rotary dial telephones.

Related To D, T

Q

Select Result Code Responses

ATQ*n*

> Q0   Modem returns all result codes to the DTE.
>
> Q1   All modem responses are disabled.
>
> Q2   Modem will return result codes to the DTE only when originating a call. The answer mode result codes are disabled: RING, CONNECT, and NO CARRIER. [AT&T, Hayes, Microcom, Practical, Rockwell, Telebit, Twincom, USRobotics]

> **Default**
>
> > Q0

The Q (quiet) command controls whether the result codes acknowledging commands and reporting call status will be send by the modem to the DTE.

The ATQ0 command enables responses and is normally the factory default. The ATQ1 command disables the OK and ERROR responses to commands as well as the OK, BUSY, and RING commands sent by the modem to indicate call status. Disabling modem responses will cause most communications software to fail. The ATQ2 command is typically used on UNIX systems to prevent the answering system from interpreting result codes as login attempts.

Application   AT&T, Black Box, Dallas, Hayes, Infotel, Microcom, Practical, Prometheus, Rockwell, Sierra, Telebit, Twincom, USRobotics, Zoom

Related To   V, W, X, \V, S59

Notes

> **1.** Some modem firmware treats values of *n* greater than 1 as 1. This can give unexpected results when all modem responses are disabled.

Q

Select Alternate Return Codes

Description   ATQ*n*

Q3   Return numeric result codes 32 and 30 for CONNECT 9600 and CONNECT 4800, respectively.

Q4   Return numeric result codes 12 and 11 for CONNECT 9600 and CONNECT 4800, respectively.

Default

Q3

This command selects between two alternate sets of numeric return codes for the indicated CONNECT messages. It is provided to allow the modem to be configured for compatibility with existing communications software.

Application   Black Box

S

Access S Registers

Description ATSn (Make S*n* the default register operand)

ATS*n*=*v*	Set register S*n* to the value *v*.
ATS*n*=*v*^	Set register S*n* to the hex value *v*. [Black Box]
ATS*n*?	Read and display the value of register S*n*.
ATS*n*?^	Read and display the value of register S*n* in hex. [Black Box]

The ATS commands are used to read and write the values of the S registers that report on and control the modem's operation. Register values are specified and displayed in decimal unless specifically noted otherwise. See Appendix B for details on the S registers themselves.

T

Tone Dialing

Description   ATT

Used outside of a dial string, this command sets the default dialing mode to tone dialing. Until subsequently changed, the modem will use the DTMF system of dialing used by push-button telephones.

Related To   D, T

u

Update System Password

Description ATU

This command is used to change the system callback security password. The modem will prompt for and confirm the current password before accepting the new password.

Application Telebit

V

Select Result Code Format

Description ATV*n*

V0   Result codes are displayed in numeric (short) form.

V1   Result codes are displayed in text (long) form.

V2   Select alternate numeric code set for short form responses. [AT&T]

Default

V1

The V command configures the modem to issue responses as numeric characters or as text (verbose) responses. By default, most modems are set to give word responses. Consequently, most communications software depends on receiving responses in this form.

Text responses are issued using the following format:

`<CR><LF>text_response<CR><LF>`

Numeric responses are issued in the following form:

`numeric_response<CR>`

Here, <CR> and <LF> represent the carriage-return and line-feed characters specified in the S3 and S4 registers, respectively.

In some cases, a word response is preferable to a numeric response. A modem establishing a high-speed connection with extended result codes, for example, might issue a message such as CONNECT 57600. A general-purpose communications program looking for the CONNECT string would most likely detect that a connection has been established.

Application AT&T, Black Box, Dallas, Hayes, Infotel, Microcom, Practical, Prometheus, Rockwell, Sierra, Telebit, Twincom, USRobotics, Zoom

Related To Q, W, X, \V, -M, S3, S4, S14, S59

Notes **1.** See the X command entry for a list of CONNECT codes.

W

Negotiation Progress Reporting

Description ATW*n*

W0   Disable error-control call progress.

W1   Enable error-control call progress.

W2   Disable error-control call progress. CONNECT *bps* message reports modem speed. [Hayes, Practical, Prometheus, Rockwell, Twincom, Zoom]

Default

W0 [Dallas, Practical, Sierra, Telebit, Zoom]

W1 [Prometheus]

W2 [Rockwell, Twincom]

This command enables an additional set of result codes that report the progress of the negotiation phase of an error-control link. These codes report the modem speed and the error-control protocol.

Application Dallas, Hayes, Practical, Prometheus, Rockwell, Sierra, Telebit, Twincom, Zoom

Related To Q, V, X, \V, S95

Notes   **1.** See the X command entry for a list of CONNECT codes.

W

Connection Speed Reporting

Description

W0   Displays CONNECT message with serial port connection speed.

W1   Displays CONNECT message with serial port connection speed. (Same as W0)

W2   Displays CONNECT message with data link speed.

Default

     W2

When W0 or W1 is set, the speed reported in the CONNECT message is the serial port speed. When W2 is selected, the speed reported is the modem-to-modem data link speed. If X0 is selected, CONNECT displays, regardless of the W setting.

Application   Microcom

Related To   Q, V, X, \V

Notes   **1.** See the X command entry for a list of CONNECT codes.

X

Select Call Progress Result Code Set

Description   ATX*n*

X0   Enable result codes 0–4. Blind dial. Do not return connection speed. (Smartmodem 300-compatible.)

X1   Enable result codes 0–5 and 10. Blind dial. Return connection speed.

Enable result codes 0–52. [Telebit]

X2   Enable result codes 0–6 and 10. Enable dial tone detection. Return connection speed.

Enable MNP extended result codes. [Telebit]

X3   Enable result codes 0–5, 7, and 10. Enable busy signal detection. Return connection speed.

Enable MNP and PEP extended result codes. [Telebit]

X4   Enable result codes 0–7 and 10. Enable dial tone and busy signal detection. Return connection speed.

X5   Enable result codes 0–5 and 7–43. [USRobotics]

Append /REL suffix to the CONNECT message if a RELIABLE connection is established. [AT&T]

X6   Enable result codes 0–43. [USRobotics]

Append /V42 or /MNP suffix to the CONNECT message if a V.42bis or MNP5 connection is established. [AT&T]

X7   Enable result codes 0–11 and 13–43. [USRobotics]

Display the serial port speed instead of the data link speed in the CONNECT message. [AT&T]

X10 Enable result codes 0–4. [Telebit]

X11 Enable result codes 0–5, 10–12, and 14. [Telebit]

X12 Enable result codes 0–6, 10–12, and 14. [Telebit]

X13 Enable result codes 0–5, 7, 10–12, and 14. [Telebit]

X14 Enable result codes 0–7, 10–12, and 14. [Telebit]

Default

   X4

In a general sense, the setting of the X command establishes compatibility with older modems. The messages that will be sent to the DTE by the modem and the conditions they report are controlled by this command.

When configured with the ATX0 command, for example, the modem behaves like the original Smartmodem 300. The modem dials blindly—dial tones and busy signals are ignored—and the CONNECT message is returned if a connection is established. This command set is typically enabled for a short-haul modem-to-modem direct connection.

The ATX1 command causes the modem to send a connect code reflecting the bps rate of the connection. The format is CONNECT *bps*, where a numeric value replaces the *bps*. If the modem has received the ATX2 configuration command, it attempts to detect a dial tone before dialing. If a dial tone is not detected within five seconds, the NO DIALTONE message is returned.

The ATX3 command ignores the dial tone, but detects a busy signal and terminates the call. The ATX4 command enables all detection and messaging capabilities. Note that these result codes may be further modified by other command settings that determine connect rate, error control, and data compression options. The following table shows the common responses that are enabled for the X0–X4 commands.

Result Code		X0	X1	X2	X3	X4
0	OK	*	*	*	*	*
1	CONNECT	*	*	*	*	*
2	RING	*	*	*	*	*
3	NO CARRIER	*	*	*	*	*
4	ERROR	*	*	*	*	*
5	CONNECT 1200		*	*	*	*
6	NO DIALTONE			*		*
7	BUSY				*	*
8	NO ANSWER					*
10	CONNECT 2400		*	*	*	*

The following list shows the more prevalent result codes issued by many popular modems. Not all modems support (or have a need to use) all codes. Where specific modems differ from the prevailing responses, they have been noted.

Numeric	Verbose
0	OK
1	CONNECT
2	RING
3	NO CARRIER
4	ERROR
5	CONNECT 1200
6	NO DIALTONE
7	BUSY
8	NO ANSWER
9	CONNECT 0600 [Rockwell, Twincom]
10	CONNECT 2400
11	CONNECT 4800
	RINGING [USRobotics]
12	CONNECT 9600
	VOICE [USRobotics]
13	CONNECT 9600 [USRobotics]
	CONNECT 14400 [Practical, Prometheus]
14	CONNECT/ARQ [USRobotics]
	CONNECT 19200 [Practical, Prometheus, Telebit]
15	CONNECT 1200/ARQ [USRobotics]
	CONNECT 38400 [Telebit]
16	CONNECT 19200 [Rockwell, Twincom]
	CONNECT 2400/ARQ [USRobotics]
17	CONNECT 38400 [Rockwell, Twincom]
	CONNECT 1200/REL [Practical, Prometheus]
	CONNECT 9600/ARQ [USRobotics]

Numeric	Verbose
17	CONNECT 76800 [Telebit]
18	CONNECT 57600
	CONNECT 2400/REL [Practical, Prometheus]
	CONNECT 4800 [USRobotics]
	CONNECT 115200 [Telebit]
19	CONNECT 4800/REL [Practical, Prometheus]
	CONNECT 4800/ARQ [USRobotics]
20	CONNECT 9600/REL [Practical, Prometheus]
	CONNECT 7200 [USRobotics]
21	CONNECT 12000 [USRobotics]
22	CONNECT 12000/ARQ [USRobotics]
24	CONNECT 7200 [Practical, Prometheus]
	CONNECT 7200/ARQ [USRobotics]
25	CONNECT 12000 [Practical, Prometheus]
26	CONNECT 1200/75 [Prometheus]
	CONNECT 14400/ARQ [USRobotics]
27	CONNECT 75/1200 [Prometheus]
28	CONNECT 38400 [Practical, Prometheus]
31	CONNECT 115200 [Prometheus]
33	FAX [Dallas]
34	FCERROR [Dallas]
35	DATA [Dallas]
40	CARRIER 300
42	CARRIER 75/1200 [Prometheus]
43	CARRIER 1200/75 [Prometheus]
	CONNECT 16800 [USRobotics]
44	CARRIER 1200/75 [Prometheus]
45	CARRIER 75/1200 [Prometheus]
46	CARRIER 1200

Numeric	Verbose
47	CARRIER 2400
	CONNECT 16800/ARQ [USRobotics]
48	CARRIER 4800 [Practical, Prometheus]
49	CARRIER 7200 [Practical, Prometheus]
50	CARRIER 9600
51	CARRIER 12000
52	CARRIER 14400
66	COMPRESSION:CLASS 5
67	COMPRESSION:V.42BIS
69	COMPRESSION:NONE
70	PROTOCOL:NONE
77	PROTOCOL:LAPM
80	PROTOCOL:ALT
81	PROTOCOL:MNP2 [Prometheus]
82	PROTOCOL:MNP3 [Prometheus]
83	PROTOCOL:MNP4 [Prometheus]

Application Black Box, Dallas, Hayes, Infotel, Microcom, Practical, Prometheus, Rockwell, Sierra, Telebit, Twincom, USRobotics, Zoom

Related To &A, D (@ dial modifier), Q, V, W, -M, S22, S95

Notes

1. When dialtone detection is disabled, the modem waits for the S6 time delay to expire, then dials blindly.

2. X0, X1, and X2 may not be used for fax operations. [Rockwell, Twincom]

Y

Select Long Space Disconnect

Description ATY*n*

Y0   Disable long space disconnect.

Y1   Enable long space disconnect.

Default

Y0 [Black Box, Dallas, Hayes, Infotel, Microcom, Practical, Prometheus, Rockwell, Sierra, Telebit, Twincom, Zoom]

Y1 [AT&T]

The Y1 command instructs the local modem to terminate a session upon receiving a long space (1.6 seconds of BREAK) signal from the remote modem. When the Y0 command is issued, the local modem will ignore long space disconnect signals received from the remote modem.

When enabled, this option also controls the modem's response to an H0 command or to a DTR transition if the &D2 and &M0 options have been selected. Before going on-hook in these situations, the local modem will send a 4-second BREAK signal (long space disconnect) to the remote modem.

Application AT&T, Black Box, Dallas, Hayes, Infotel, Microcom, Practical, Prometheus, Rockwell, Sierra, Telebit, Twincom, Zoom

Related To H, &D, &M, S21, S82

Y

Select Line Current Disconnect

Description ATY*n*

    Y2   Disable line-current detection.

    Y3   Go on-hook after 90 milliseconds without line current.

    Y4   Go on-hook after 8 milliseconds without line current.

Default

    Y3

After a remote site severs a connection, the GSTN will normally remove line current from the channel. This command controls the modem's reaction to the loss of line current.

Application Black Box

Related To S32

Z

Perform a Soft Reset

Description   A T Z

Z   Reset modem to default settings. [USRobotics]

ATZ*n*

Zn   Reset modem to stored profile *n*.

n = 0–1, profile number. [AT&T, Black Box, Dallas, Hayes, Infotel, Practical, Prometheus, Rockwell, Sierra, Telebit, Twincom, Zoom]

n = 0–3, profile number. [Microcom]

Z0   Reset modem to stored profile number contained in register S255. [Telebit]

Z1   Reset modem to stored profile 0. [Telebit]

Z2   Reset modem to stored profile 1. [Telebit]

Reset modem to the profile specified by the &Y command. [AT&T]

The Z command causes the modem to go immediately on-hook and reset its parameters according to the selected stored profile.

During reset, any parameters not explicitly saved in the stored profile are reset to their factory default settings. Any commands that appear on the command line following the Z command are ignored.

Application   Black Box, Dallas, Hayes, Infotel, Microcom, Practical, Prometheus, Rockwell, Sierra, Telebit, Twincom, USRobotics, Zoom

Related To   &F, &V, &W, &Y, &Z, \S

&A

Select Auto-Answer Mode

Description AT&A*n*

&A0 Use answer tones when auto-answering.

&A1 Use originate tones when auto-answering.

Default

&A0

This command determines whether the modem will use the answer or originate tones when answering a call in auto-answer mode.

Application Hayes, Practical

&A

Enable Extended Result Codes

Description AT&A*n*

&A0   Disable ARQ result codes.

&A1   Enable ARQ result codes.

&A2   Append HST or V32 modulation indicator to result code.

&A3   Append error-control type (LAPM, HST, MNP, SYNC, or NONE) and data-compression type (V42BIS or MNP5) indicators to result code.

Default

&A1

This command enables expanded result code messages indicating error-control and compression type.

Application USRobotics

Related To X

&B

Select V.32 Auto-Retrain

Description AT&B*n*

&B0   Do not retrain; hang up.

&B1   Retrain if line quality is poor. If unable to retrain with time specified by S7, hang up.

&B2   Do not retrain, do not hang up. [Prometheus]

Default

&B1

This command selects the action to be taken by the modem if the line quality
deteriorates during a V.32 or V.32bis connection.

Application Dallas, Hayes, Practical, Prometheus

Related To %E, *Q, S7

&B

Serial Port Speed Conversion

Description AT&B*n*

&B0   The serial port speed is adjusted to match the data link speed.

&B1   The serial port speed remains constant, regardless of the data link speed. Allowable rates are 300, 1200, 2400, 4800, 9600, 19200, and 38400 bps.

&B2   The serial port speed shifts to a user-defined fixed rate for ARQ calls following the connection rate for non-ARQ calls. Effective in answer mode only.

Default

&B0

Application   USRobotics

&B

Enable Blind Mode

Description AT&B

This command disables the command processor within the modem, causing the modem to ignore any local commands. Result codes are still returned according to the setting of the Q command. Blind mode is cleared when power is removed from the modem.

Application Telebit

&C

Select Data Carrier Detect (DCD) Option

Description   AT&C*n*

&C0   DCD is always ON, regardless of the state of the remote carrier.

&C1   DCD indicates the true state of the remote carrier.

&C2   DCD is always ON except momentarily at disconnect. (This is known as "wink when disconnect".) [AT&T, Black Box, Hayes, Microcom, Telebit]

&C3   DCD is the inverse of the clear-to-send (CTS) signal. [Telebit]

DCD follows DTR. [AT&T]

&C4   Synchronous operation only. The DCD signal indicates the true state of the received carrier. When the modem detects a V.13 pattern from the remote modem, it drops DCD. [Telebit]

DCD follows the remote modem's RTS line via V.13 simulated remote-control carrier signaling. [AT&T]

&C5   DCD is ON only when received data is being sent to the DTE. [Telebit]

DCD follows DTR. Upon a disconnect, DCD always goes OFF. DTR must then transition from OFF to ON to turn DCD ON. [AT&T]

&C6   DCD follows DTR when the modem is on-hook. DCD goes ON after the CONNECT message is sent to the DTE and stays ON for the duration of the connection. [Telebit]

Default

&C0 [AT&T, Black Box, Dallas, Infotel, Practical, Prometheus, Sierra, Rockwell, Telebit, Twincom, Zoom]

&C1 [Hayes, Prometheus, Rockwell, Microcom, Telebit, Twincom, USRobotics]

Application   AT&T, Black Box, Dallas, Hayes, Infotel, Microcom, Practical, Prometheus, Rockwell, Sierra, Telebit, Twincom, USRobotics, Zoom

Related To   &D, \D, &R, &S, \Q, S47, :T15

Notes

1. This signal is known variously as data carrier detect (DCD), carrier detect (CD), and received line signal detected (RLSD).

2. The default setting for this command is specified by the OEM regardless of the default specified for the chip set, and it will vary.

3. The default setting for this command is &C0, but is set to &C1 by hardware configuration switches. Hardware flow control overrides the &C setting for CTS operation. The &C setting is ignored during V.23 half-duplex direct mode (%F3) or CCITT V.13 (&R2). [Microcom]

&D

Select Data Terminal Ready (DTR) Option

Description   AT&D*n*

n = 0–3, [Hayes, Infotel, Microcom, Prometheus, Rockwell, Sierra, Twincom, Zoom]

n = 0–2, [USRobotics]

Default

&D0 [AT&T, Black Box, Dallas, Infotel, Microcom, Practical, Prometheus, Sierra, Telebit, Zoom]

&D2 [Rockwell, Twincom, Prometheus, USRobotics]

The &D command interacts with the &Q command to determine the action taken by the modem following an ON-to-OFF DTR transition according to the following table:

	&D0	**&D1**	**&D2**	**&D3**
&Q0, &Q5, &Q6, &Q8, &Q9	None	Action 2	Action 3	Action 4
&Q1, &Q4	Action 1	Action 2	Action 3	Action 4
&Q2, &Q3	Action 3	Action 3	Action 3	Action 3

Action 1: Modem disconnects and returns OK to the DTE.

Action 2: Modem switches to command mode (if in data mode) and returns OK to the DTE.

Action 3: Modem disconnects, returns OK to the DTE, and disables auto-answer while DTR is OFF.

Action 4: Modem performs a soft reset (ATZ).

The minimum OFF time following an ON-to-OFF transition of DTR is specified by the S25 register. OFF-to-ON transitions that occur within 5 seconds of disconnect are ignored.

Application Dallas, Hayes, Infotel, Microcom, Practical, Prometheus, Rockwell, Sierra, Telebit, Twincom, USRobotics, Zoom

Related To &C, &Q, &R, &S, S25

Notes

1. The default setting for this command is typically established independently of the chip set.

2. The default setting for this command is &D0, but is set to &D2 by hardware configuration switches. If &D2 or &D3 is set, DTR is required for auto-answer operation. [Microcom]

3. The profile indicated by register S255 is loaded after a soft reset. [Telebit]

4. &D1 and &D3 are identical to &D2. [AT&T]

&E

Recall Stored Profiles

Description AT&E*n*

&E0   Retrieve user profile specified by register S255.

&E1   Retrieve user profile 0.

&E2   Retrieve user profile 1.

This command loads the specified profile from nonvolatile memory into the current profile.

Application Telebit

&F

Load Factory Configuration Profile

Description AT&F

&F Restore factory default settings. [AT&T, Black Box, Dallas, Hayes, Infotel, Microcom, Practical, Prometheus, Rockwell, Telebit, Twincom, USRobotics, Zoom]

  AT&F*n*

  n = number of configuration profile.

&F0 Load Hayes factory default profile. [Dallas, Practical, Prometheus, Sierra]

  Load enhanced command mode profile. [Telebit]

  Load TTY mode profile according to the S254 register. [Telebit]

  Load asynchronous dial profile. [AT&T]

&F1 Load Microcom factory default profile. [Dallas, Prometheus, Sierra]

  Load IBM-compatible mode profile. [Practical]

  Load conventional command mode profile. [Telebit]

  Load unattended answer mode profile. [Telebit]

  Load synchronous dial profile. [AT&T]

&F2 Load Sierra factory default profile for AUTO RELIABLE MNP operation. [Dallas, Prometheus, Sierra]

  Load Macintosh software flow control-compatible factory default profile. [Practical]

  Load enhanced command mode and SDLC defaults. [Telebit]

  Load intelligent answer mode profile. [Telebit]

  Load leased-line asynchronous answer mode profile. [AT&T]

&F3 Load Sierra factory default profile for V.42bis operation. [Dallas, Prometheus, Sierra]

  Load Macintosh hardware flow control-compatible factory default profile. [Practical]

  Load V.32 synchronous mode with full-duplex operation on GSTN lines profile. [Telebit]

  Load System V (HDB) UUCP mode profile. [Telebit]

  Load Unix dial mode profile. [AT&T]

&F4 Load Ver 2 (BSD) UUCP 4.2-4.3 and SCO Xenix mode profile. [Telebit]

  Load leased-line asynchronous originate mode profile. [AT&T]

&F5 Load transparent synchronous mode profile. [Telebit]

&F6 Load half-duplex transparent synchronous mode with LPDA dialing profile. [Telebit]

&F8 Load IBM-PC/Macintosh software flow control mode profile. [Telebit]

&F9 Load IBM-PC/Macintosh hardware flow control mode profile. [Telebit]

&F10 Load leased-line asynchronous originate mode profile. [Telebit]

&F11 Reset modem to leased-line asynchronous answer mode defaults. [Telebit]

&F12 Reset modem to leased-line synchronous originate mode defaults. [Telebit]

&F13 Reset modem to leased-line synchronous answer mode defaults. [Telebit]

&F14 Reset modem to half-duplex PEP SDLC mode with no command set selection defaults. [Telebit]

&F15 Reset modem to half-duplex PEP SDLC mode with LPDA dialing defaults. [Telebit]

&F32 Reset modem to defaults for synchronous mode 1 (&Q1). [Telebit]

&F33 Reset modem to HP 3000 host mode defaults. [Telebit]

&F34   Reset modem to HP 3000 terminal mode defaults. [Telebit]

Default

&F [AT&T, Black Box, Hayes, Infotel, Microcom, Prometheus, Rockwell, Telebit, Twincom, USRobotics]

&F0 [AT&T, Sierra]

&F3 [Prometheus]

The &F command instructs the modem to reset selected configuration parameters and S register values to a factory-specified default condition. The current S register values and option settings are lost when this command is executed. Stored telephone numbers are preserved. Unlike the Z command, the &F command does not cause the modem to go on-hook.

Application   AT&T, Black Box, Dallas, Hayes, Infotel, Microcom, Prometheus, Rockwell, Sierra, Telebit, Twincom, Zoom

Related To   Z, &V, &W, &Y, &Z, S254, S255

&G

Select Guard Tone Option

Description AT&G*n*

    &G0   Disable guard tone.

    &G1   Enable 550 Hz guard tone. (Required in some European countries.)

    &G2   Enable 1800 Hz guard tone. (Required in the United Kingdom and some Commonwealth countries.)

Default

    &G0

The &G command determines whether the modem will transmit guard tones when transmitting in the high band (answer mode) during CCITT operation.

If enabled, guard tones are issued by the modem when transmitting in the answer mode and during the answer handshake. Guard tones are used only during CCITT V.22 and V.22bis connections.

Application AT&T, Black Box, Dallas, Hayes, Infotel, Microcom, Practical, Prometheus, Rockwell, Sierra, Telebit, Twincom, USRobotics, Zoom

Related To B

Notes

1. Implementation of this command is manufacturer-specific, but most modems will accept this command for compatibility.

&H

Transmit Data Flow Control

Description   AT&H*n*

&H0   Disable all flow control.

&H1   CTS flow control. The modem uses the CTS line to control data
transfer from the DTE.

&H2   XON/XOFF flow control. The modem uses the XOFF character to
suspend and the XON character to resume data transfer from the
DTE.

&H3   CTS and XON/XOFF flow control. The modem uses the CTS line
and XON/XOFF characters to control data transfer from the DTE.

Default

&H0

This command selects the type of flow control, if any, that will be used for data
transmission from the DTE to the modem.

Application   USRobotics

Related To   &I

&I

Received Data Flow Control

Description AT&I*n*

&I0 Disable flow control.

&I1 Transparent XON/XOFF flow control. The local modem honors XON/XOFF flow control characters received from the local DTE, and passes them to the remote modem.

&I2 XON/XOFF flow control. The modem suspends data transfer when it receives the XOFF character and resumes when it receives the XON character.

&I3 Enable HP ENQ/ACK protocol; the modem emulates a host.

&I4 Enable HP ENQ/ACK protocol; the modem emulates a terminal.

&I5 XON/XOFF flow control (same as I2) in ARQ mode. Transparent XON/XOFF flow control (same as I1) in non-ARQ mode.

Default

&I0

Application USRobotics

Related To &H

&I

Set Transmit Level

Description AT&I*n*

n = 10–25, set power to -*n* dBm, default=10

This command sets the power level the modem will use to transmit data over GSTN lines. The power level can range from –10 dBm to –25 dBm.

Application AT&T

Related To &J

&J

Telephone Jack Selection

Description AT&J*n*

&J0   Never close the auxiliary relay.

&J1   Close the auxiliary relay when the modem is off-hook.

           Connect A/A1 telephone leads. [Telebit]

&J2   Connect MI/MIC telephone leads. [Telebit]

Default

     &J0

The setting of the &J command selects the type of telephone jack by determining how the modem will control the operation of the auxiliary relay.

The &J0 command should be used for RJ-11, RJ-41S, and RJ-45S telephone jacks. The &J1 command should be used for RJ-12 and RJ-13 phone jacks.

Application   Black Box, Dallas, Hayes, Infotel, Practical, Rockwell, Sierra, Telebit, Zoom

Notes   **1.** Not all modems contain the hardware necessary to support this option.

&J

Set GSTN Mode

Description   AT&J

&J   Fix transmit level for permissive lines (-9 dBm).

AT&J*n*

&J0   Fix transmit level for permissive lines (-9 dBm).

&J1   Transmit level is programmable.

This command configures the modem to operate with permissive or programmable telephone lines. When used after an &I command, it overrides the &I command settings.

Application   AT&T

Related To   &I

&K

Select Serial Port Flow Control

Description AT&K*n*

&K0   Disable serial port flow control.

&K1   Returns ERROR. [Dallas, Rockwell, Sierra, Telebit, Twincom, Zoom]

Bidirectional local RTS/CTS flow control. The modem uses the CTS line to control data transfer from the DTE. The DTE uses the RTS line to control data transfer from the modem. [Practical, Prometheus]

&K2   Returns ERROR. [Dallas, Rockwell, Sierra, Telebit, Twincom, Zoom]

Bidirectional local XON/XOFF flow control. Both the modem and the DTE suspend data transfer when they receive the XOFF character and resume when they receive the XON character. [Practical, Prometheus]

&K3   Bidirectional local RTS/CTS flow control. The modem uses the CTS line to control data transfer from the DTE. The DTE uses the RTS line to control data transfer from the modem.

&K4   Bidirectional local XON/XOFF flow control. Both the modem and the DTE suspend data transfer when they receive the XOFF character and resume when they receive the XON character.

&K5   Transparent XON/XOFF flow control. The local modem ignores XON/XOFF flow control characters received from the local DTE, but passes them to the remote modem.

&K6   Local and remote XON/XOFF flow control. The local modem honors XON/XOFF flow control characters received from the local DTE, and also pass them to the remote modem. [Practical]

&K7   Bidirectional local RTS/CTS flow control with remote XON/XOFF flow control. The modem uses the CTS line to control data transfer from the DTE. The DTE uses the RTS line to control data transfer from the modem. XON/XOFF flow control characters received from the local DTE are passed to the remote modem. [Practical]

Default

    &K0 [Dallas, Sierra]

    &K3 [Dallas, Practical, Prometheus, Rockwell, Telebit, Twincom, Zoom]

    &K4 [Prometheus]

This command selects the type of flow control, if any, that will be used between the DTE and the modem.

If the serial port data-transfer speed is faster than the effective speed of the data link between modems, the modem will buffer data from the DTE and request that it stop sending data. This situation is common during RELIABLE connections when retransmissions reduce the effective data link transfer rate.

The following equivalences are typically in effect:

Command	Equivalent
&K0	\Q0\X0
&K1	\Q1\X0
&K2	\Q3\X0
&K3	\Q1\X0
&K4	\Q3\X0
&K5	\Q1\X1

Application   Dallas, Hayes, Practical, Prometheus, Rockwell, Sierra, Telebit, Twincom, Zoom

Related To   \Q, *F

Notes   **1.** This command is linked to the \Q and *F commands. [Prometheus]

&K

Select Data Compression

Description   AT&K*n*

&K0   Disable data compression.

&K1   Enable data compression unless &B0 is selected and the serial port speed changes to match the data link speed.

&K2   Enable data compression regardless of &B setting.

&K3   Enable selective data compression; disable MNP 5.

Default

&K1

Application   USRobotics

&L

Select Dial-Up/Leased-Line Option

Description   AT&L*n*

&L0   Select dial-up line operation.

&L1   Select leased-line operation.

            Select two-wire originate leased line. [AT&T, Microcom]

&L2   Select four-wire originate leased line. [AT&T, Microcom]

            Select programmable dial-up line operation. [Black Box]

&L3   Select two-wire answer leased line. Modem goes off-hook automatically in 6 seconds in either originate or answer mode depending on the hardware switch setting. [AT&T, Microcom]

&L4   Select four-wire answer leased line. Modem goes off-hook automatically in 6 seconds in either originate or answer mode depending on the hardware switch setting. [AT&T, Microcom]

Default

        &L0

The &L command configures the modem's internal logic as appropriate for the type of operation desired. The &L0 command configures the modem for operation on the GSTN.

Application   AT&T, Black Box, Dallas, Hayes, Infotel, Microcom, Practical, Rockwell, Sierra, Telebit, Twincom, USRobotics, Zoom

Related To   A, D, &M, &Q, S91, S100, S104

Notes   **1.** This command is not implemented on internal modems. External modems have only a single line connection, but the power level is changed when selecting leased-line operation. [Twincom]

&M

Select Communications Mode

Description   AT&M*n*

&M0   Asynchronous mode.

&M1   Synchronous mode 1: asynchronous dialing using AT commands, switch to synchronous mode after dialing.

Synchronous mode. Error control disabled. [USRobotics]

&M2   Synchronous mode 2: synchronous terminal support. Dial the first stored telephone number after an OFF-to-ON DTR transition.

Reserved. [USRobotics]

&M3   Synchronous mode 3: manually originate call. Enter synchronous mode after an OFF-to-ON DTR transition.

Reserved. [USRobotics]

Same as &M1. [AT&T]

&M4   AUTO RELIABLE asynchronous mode. The modem will attempt to negotiate an ARQ link. If an ARQ link cannot be established, the modem will attempt to fallback to a NORMAL connection. [USRobotics]

&M5   RELIABLE asynchronous mode. The modem will attempt to negotiate an ARQ link. If an ARQ link cannot be established, the modem will disconnect. [USRobotics]

Default

&M0 [AT&T, Black Box, Dallas, Infotel, Microcom, Prometheus, Rockwell, Sierra, Telebit, Twincom, Zoom]

&M4 [USRobotics]

The &M command selects the communications mode to be used by the modem. In many modems, this command has been replaced by the &Q command. Most modems continue to support this command for compatibility with older communications software.

Application AT&T, Black Box, Dallas, Infotel, Microcom, Practical, Prometheus, Rockwell, Sierra, Telebit, Twincom, USRobotics, Zoom

Related To &D, &Q, &X, S25

Notes

1. Internal modems generally accept only &M0.

2. External modems respond with ERROR if operating at less than 1200 bps. In synchronous mode, the &D setting is ignored. The &M command must be sent when the modem is not on-line. The CTS signal is always on during asynchronous command and data modes and can be controlled using the &R command during synchronous data mode. [Sierra]

&N

Set Data-Link Speed

Description   AT&N*n*

&N0   Modem negotiates the highest possible data-link speed with the remote modem.

&N1   Set data link to 300 bps.

&N2   Set data link to 1200 bps.

&N3   Set data link to 2400 bps.

&N4   Set data link to 4800 bps.

&N5   Set data link to 7200 bps.

&N6   Set data link to 9600 bps.

&N7   Set data link to 12000 bps.

&N8   Set data link to 14400 bps.

&N9   Set data link to 16800 bps. (HST-to-HST only.)

Default

&N0

This command sets the data-link speed. By default, the modem will attempt to negotiate the highest possible data-link speed. If the data-link speed is set to a fixed rate and the remote modem cannot communicate at that speed, the local modem will hang up.

Application   USRobotics

&N

Display Stored Profiles

Description AT&N*n*

&N0   Retrieve user profile specified by register S255.

&N1   Retrieve user profile 0.

&N2   Retrieve user profile 1.

This command displays the specified profile stored in nonvolatile memory.

Application Telebit

&O

Connect to PAD

Description   AT&0*n*

&O0   Go to PAD command mode for the last selected channel. If no previous channel, selects channel 1.

&O1   Go to PAD command mode for channel 1.

&O2   Go to PAD command mode for channel 2.

&O3   Go to PAD command mode for channel 3.

&O4   Go to PAD command mode for channel 4.

Default

&O0

The &O command moves from the AT command mode to a PAD (packet assembler/disassembler) waiting state. The modem is then ready to receive X.25 PAD commands. A reset operation is performed on the selected channel.

Application   Hayes

&P

Set Pulse Dial Make/Break Ratio

Description AT&P*n*

    &P0   Select a make/break ratio of 39%/61% at 10 pulses per second (USA and Canada).

    &P1   Select a make/break ratio of 33%/67% at 10 pulses per second (United Kingdom, Europe, and Hong Kong).

    &P2   Select a make/break ratio of 33%/67% at 20 pulses per second (Japan). [Dallas, Rockwell, Twincom, Zoom]

Default

    &P0

This command controls the ratio of the make (off-hook) to break (on-hook) interval used when pulse dialing. This command has no effect on tone dialing.

Application Black Box, Dallas, Infotel, Microcom, Practical, Prometheus, Rockwell, Sierra, Telebit, Twincom, USRobotics, Zoom

Related To D (P dial modifier)

Notes

    1. Modems made for Japan support &P1 and &P2 only. [Rockwell, Twincom]

&Q

Select Communications Mode Option

Description AT&Q*n*

&Q0 Select asynchronous mode. A direct connection is established; the serial port speed must match the modem speed.

&Q1 Select synchronous mode 1. Supports terminals that communicate in both asynchronous and synchronous modes. The modem uses the dial command to place a call in asynchronous mode, then switches to synchronous mode after a connection is established. The modem goes on-hook and switches back to asynchronous mode after detecting either an ON-to-OFF DTR transition or a carrier loss exceeding the time specified in the S10 register.

&Q2 Select synchronous mode 2. Supports synchronous terminals with stored-number dialing. The modem automatically dials the first number in the dialing directory when it detects an OFF-to-ON DTR transition. The modem goes on-hook and switches back to asynchronous mode after detecting either an ON-to-OFF DTR transition or a carrier loss exceeding the time specified in the S10 register.

&Q3 Select synchronous mode 3. The DTR signal functions as a talk/data switch. The operator manually places the call with DTR OFF. The operator then switches the modem to data mode by turning DTR ON. The modem goes on-hook and switches back to asynchronous mode after detecting either an ON-to-OFF DTR transition or a carrier loss exceeding the time specified in the S10 register.

Same as &Q1. [AT&T]

&Q4 Select Hayes AutoSync mode. DTR must be ON after the connection is established. The serial port speed is 9600 bps, which is not the same as the speed at which the modem's responses are sent or the data link speed. [Hayes]

Accepted but not supported. [Dallas, Rockwell, Twincom, Zoom]

Returns ERROR. [Sierra]

&Q5 Select error control mode. The modem will attempt to negotiate a RELIABLE link. If a RELIABLE link cannot be established, the modem will either disconnect or fallback to a NORMAL connection, depending on the setting of S36. [Dallas, Practical, Rockwell, Sierra Telebit, Twincom, Zoom]

   Select error control mode. For V-series products, it may select LAPB, LAPM, X.25, or MNP, according to the settings of registers S36, S46, and S48. [Hayes]

&Q6 Select NORMAL buffered mode. [Dallas, Hayes, Practical, Rockwell, Sierra, Twincom, Zoom]

   Select transparent synchronous mode. [Telebit]

&Q7 Accepted but not supported. [Dallas, Rockwell, Twincom, Zoom]

&Q8 Force the modem to behave as if S48=128 and fallback to MNP. If bit 1 of S36=1, then the modem acts as if S36=7. Otherwise, it acts as if S36=5. [Dallas, Hayes, Practical, Rockwell, Twincom, Zoom]

&Q9 This command behaves like &Q5 with S48=7 and S46=138. The modem will attempt V.42bis, fallback to LAPM, then fallback to NORMAL. [Dallas, Hayes, Practical, Rockwell, Twincom, Zoom]

Default

   &Q0 [AT&T, Dallas, Infotel, Practical, Rockwell, Sierra, Twincom]

   &Q5 [Dallas, Practical, Rockwell, Telebit, Twincom, Zoom]

The &Q command selects the communications mode to be used by the modem and replaces the &M command.

Application AT&T, Dallas, Hayes, Infotel, Practical, Prometheus, Rockwell, Sierra, Telebit, Twincom

Related To &C, &M, &S, \N, S10, S36, S46, S48

Notes

  1. Internal modems generally do not accept &Q1, &Q2, or &Q3.

  2. External modems respond with ERROR if operating at less than 1200 bps. In synchronous mode, the &D setting is ignored. The &Q command must be sent when the modem is not on-line. The CTS signal is always on during asynchronous command and data modes and can be controlled using the &R command during synchronous data mode. [Sierra]

3. Synchronous operation is supported only by the SC11091 modem controller. [Sierra]

4. To disable V.42bis operation, use &Q0, &Q3, or &Q6 or modify S36, S46, and S48. [Sierra]

&R

Select RTS/CTS Synchronous Options

Description   AT&R*n*

&R0   The RTS signal is ignored in command mode. CTS follows RTS when the modem is in data mode.

&R1   The RTS signal is always ignored. CTS is always ON when the modem is in data mode.

&R2   CCITT V.13 emulates half-duplex over a full-duplex line. [Microcom]

Received data is sent to the DTE only when RTS is high. [USRobotics]

When connected, CTS follows RTS with a fixed 200-millisecond delay, and RTS/CTS flow control is honored. When not connected, CTS is OFF. [Telebit]

Allows the local RTS signal to control the remote modem's DCD signal. [AT&T]

&R3   CTS is always ON if RTS/CTS flow control is disabled. [Telebit]

Control carrier mode. [AT&T]

&R4   While connected, CTS follows RTS with a delay specified by S26. When not connected, CTS follows DTR. CTS is OFF at the end of dialing when call-progress monitoring begins or when the modem goes off-hook to answer a call. [Telebit]

&R5   Same as &R0, plus the modem transmits the V.13 pattern when RTS is OFF. Valid for synchronous operation only. [Telebit]

&R6   Same as &R4, plus the modem transmits the V.13 pattern when RTS is OFF. Valid for synchronous operation only. [Telebit]

&R7   CTS follows RTS when the modem is in data mode. [Telebit]

&R8   SDLC CTS control. The modem sends the SDLC packet to the DTE following an ON to OFF transition of RTS, then turns on CTS. When RTS goes OFF, the modem restarts the SDLC accelerator. [Telebit]

Default

&R0 [Dallas, Infotel, Microcom, Practical, Rockwell, Sierra, Twincom, Zoom]

&R1 [AT&T, Black Box, Rockwell, Telebit, Twincom, USRobotics]

&R3 [Telebit]

The &R command is used for synchronous operation only. It is ignored during asynchronous operation. When &R0 is selected, the clear-to-send (CTS) signal follows the request-to-send (RTS) signal using the delay specified by S26.

Application AT&T, Black Box, Dallas, Hayes, Infotel, Microcom, Prometheus, Rockwell, Sierra, Telebit, Twincom, USRobotics, Zoom

Related To &C, &D, &M, &Q, &S, S26, S28, :T15

Notes

1. Internal modems do not generally support synchronous connections and will return ERROR in response to this command.

&R

Force Retrain or Renegotiation

Description AT&R*n*

&R0   Force a retrain.

&R1   Renegotiate data compression and protocol support in PEP
mode.

The &R0 command forces the modem to reevaluate the condition of the connection and adjust its data rate accordingly. The &R1 causes the modem to renegotiate the connection and data compression protocols in use based on the settings of the S110 and S111 registers. Data stored in the serial buffers during renegotiation is discarded.

Application Telebit

Related To S110, S111

&S

DSR Control

AT&S*n*

&S0   DSR is always ON.

&S1   DSR is turned ON at the start of handshaking and remains on during the connection. DSR is turned OFF when the modem is in a test mode, idle, or when the carrier is lost.

&S2   DSR is turned ON at the end of handshaking before the CONNECT message is issued and remains on during the connection. DSR is turned OFF when the modem is in a test mode, idle, or when the carrier is lost. [Hayes, Practical]

DSR is always ON except momentarily for the period defined by register S47 when disconnecting a call. This is known as "wink when disconnect". [AT&T, Telebit, USRobotics]

Same as &S0. [Telebit]

&S3   If the carrier is lost, the modem sends the DTE a pulsed DSR signal. clear-to-send (CTS) does not follow carrier detect (CD). [USRobotics]

DSR follows DTR. [AT&T, Telebit]

&S4   DSR is turned ON at the end of handshaking after the CONNECT message is issued and remains on during the connection. DSR is turned OFF when the modem is in a test mode, idle, or when the carrier is lost. [Telebit]

DSR is OFF when the modem is idle. DSR goes ON immediately upon a command to enter data mode. [AT&T]

DSR follows CD. [Practical]

&S5   DSR is turned ON at the end of handshaking after the CONNECT message is issued and remains on during the connection. DSR is turned OFF when the modem is in a test mode, idle, or when the carrier is lost. [AT&T]

Default

&S0 [AT&T, Black Box, Dallas, Infotel, Microcom, Practical, Prometheus, Rockwell, Sierra, Telebit, Twincom, USRobotics, Zoom]

&S1 [Hayes]

This command determines whether the data set ready (DSR) signal generated by the modem operates in accordance with the EIA-232-D and later specification.

Application   AT&T, Black Box, Dallas, Hayes, Infotel, Microcom, Practical, Prometheus, Rockwell, Sierra, Telebit, Twincom, USRobotics, Zoom

Related To   &C, &D, &R, \D

Notes

1. &S0 is equivalent to \D0. &S1 is equivalent to \D3. [Microcom]

2. The QBlazer treats &S2 and &S1 the same as &S0. [Telebit]

&T

Self-Test Options

AT&T*n*

&T0   End test in progress. Ends a test in progress without terminating a connection and returns the local and remote modems to normal operation. If a self-test is in progress, &T0 causes any errors to be reported. The escape sequence must precede this command and it must be the last command on the command line.

&T1   Start local analog loopback test. This test verifies the path between the local DTE and the local modem. The modem should echo the same characters it receives. The modem must be in NORMAL or DIRECT mode and set to 1200 bps or higher.

&T3   Start local digital loopback test. This test verifies the condition of the path from a remote modem, through the local mode, and back to the remote modem. Allows a remote modem that does not support the CCITT V.54 standard to perform a remote digital loopback test with the local modem. The local modem must be connected in NORMAL or DIRECT mode and set to 1200 bps or higher.

&T4   Grant remote request for remote digital loopback test. Allows the local modem to respond to a remote caller's request to enter remote digital loopback mode.

&T5   Deny remote request for remote digital loopback test. Prevents the modem from responding to a remote digital loopback request.

&T6   Start remote digital loopback test. This test verifies the path between the local DTE and the remote modem. Instructs the remote modem to initiate a remote digital loopback test. The local modem must be connected in NORMAL or DIRECT mode and set to 1200 bps or higher.

&T7   Start remote digital loopback test with self-test. This test is similar to &T6 except the local modem sends the CCITT V.54 test pattern to the remote modem and examines the validity of the returned data. Upon completion of the test, the local modem returns a 3-digit error count to the local device. The local modem must be connected in NORMAL or DIRECT mode and set to 1200 bps or higher.

&T8   Start local analog loopback test with self-test. The local modem sends itself the CCITT V.54 test pattern and verifies that it is received correctly. Upon completion of the test, the local modem returns a 3-digit error count to the local DTE.

&T9   Disconnects the telephone line and runs the power-on self test. Results of the test can be displayed using the I1 command. [AT&T, Telebit]

&T19   Perform RTS/CTS cable test. The modem works with the DTE to determine the proper operation of the RTS and CTS signals. [Hayes, Practical]

Default

     &T0 [Dallas, Prometheus, Sierra, Infotel, USRobotics]

     &T4 [Microcom, Rockwell, Telebit, Twincom, Zoom]

This command performs local and remote diagnostics according to the scenarios described above.

Application   AT&T, Black Box, Dallas, Hayes, Infotel, Microcom, Practical, Prometheus, Rockwell, Sierra, Telebit, Twincom, USRobotics, Zoom

Related To   S18

Notes   **1.** The &T command is not supported for Bell 103, V.13, V.21, V.23 modes. [Microcom]

&U

Enable Trellis Coding

Description   AT&U*n*

&U0   Enable trellis coding.

&U1   Disable trellis coding.

Default

&U0

This command enables or disables the use of trellis coding (forward error correction) for V.32 9600 bps connections.

Application   Dallas, Hayes, Practical, Prometheus

&V

View Configuration Profiles

Description AT&V

&V   Display all stored profiles. [Dallas, Hayes, Infotel, Practical, Prometheus, Rockwell, Sierra, Telebit, Twincom, Zoom]

AT&V*n*

&V0   Display profile 0. [Prometheus]

Display all stored profiles. [AT&T, Black Box]

&V1   Display profile 1. [Prometheus]

Display modem status. [Black Box]

Display profile specified by &Y command. [AT&T]

&V2   Display profile 0. [AT&T]

&V3   Display profile 1. [AT&T]

&V4   Display stored telephone number 0 and 1. [AT&T]

&V6   View blacklisted entries. [Hayes]

This command instructs the modem to return the values of selected configuration parameters and S registers in the current and stored profiles. Stored telephone numbers are also displayed.

After receiving this command, the modem will return the current profile parameters. Modems equipped with nonvolatile memory will additionally return stored profiles. The format and contents of the information displayed vary, depending on the modem manufacturer.

Application AT&T, Black Box, Dallas, Hayes, Infotel, Practical, Prometheus, Rockwell, Sierra, Telebit, Twincom, Zoom

Related To Z, &F, &W, &Y, &Z

&V

Set Leased-Line Timer

Description AT&V*n*

n = 0–90 minutes, default = 5 minutes

This command sets the amount of time in minutes that the originate modem waits for a connection. If no connection is established within the specified time, the dial-backup modem is enabled and the modem dials the telephone number stored in the first memory position. If no connection results, the modem switches back to leased-line mode.

Application Microcom

Related To D (N dial modifier)

&W

Store Active Profile in Memory

Description   AT&W

&W   Save current profile in memory. [USRobotics]

   AT&W*n*

&W0   Save current profile to memory profile 0.

          Save current profile to the memory profile specified by the S255 register. [Telebit]

          Save current profile to the memory profile specified by the &Y command. [AT&T]

&W1   Save current profile to memory profile 1.

          Save current profile to memory profile 0. [Telebit]

&W2   Save current profile to memory profile 2. [AT&T, Microcom]

          Save current profile to memory profile 1. [Telebit]

&W3   Save current profile to memory profile 3. [Microcom]

This command saves a manufacturer-selected subset of modem command settings and S register values to memory.

For this command to be effective, the modem must contain nonvolatile memory for the storage of configuration profiles. Legal values for profile numbers are determined by each modem individually.

Application   AT&T, Black Box, Dallas, Hayes, Infotel, Practical, Prometheus, Microcom, Rockwell, Sierra, Telebit, Twincom, USRobotics, Zoom

Related To   Z, &F, &V, &Y, &Z, *W

Notes   **1.** The QBlazer saves the current profile to memory profile 0 or 1 as indicated by register S255. [Telebit]

&X

Select Synchronous Transmit Clock Source

Description AT&X*n*

&X0   Internal timing. The modem generates the synchronous clock signal and provides it on EIA-232 pin 15.

&X1   External timing. The local DTE generates the synchronous clock signal and provides it to the modem on EIA-232 pin 24. The modem subsequently provides this signal on EIA-232 pin 15.

&X2   Slave receive timing. The modem derives the synchronous clock signal from the incoming data stream and provides it on EIA-232 pin 15.

Default

    &X0

Application AT&T, Black Box, Dallas, Hayes, Infotel, Microcom, Practical, Prometheus, Rockwell, Sierra, Telebit, Twincom, USRobotics, Zoom

Related To &M, &Q

Notes   **1.** Internal modems generally do not support synchronous operation and return ERROR in response to the &X command.

&Y

Select Default Configuration Profile

Description   AT&Y*n*

n = profile number

&Y*n*   Use memory profile *n* after reset or power-up.

n = 0–1, default = 0 [AT&T, Black Box, Dallas, Hayes, Infotel, Practical, Prometheus, Rockwell, Sierra, Telebit, Twincom, Zoom]

n = 0–3, default = 0 [Microcom]

This command designates the stored profile that is to become the active profile when the modem is turned on or hard reset.

For this command to be effective, the modem must contain nonvolatile memory for the storage of configuration profiles. Legal values for profile numbers are determined by each modem individually. This command is saved immediately; you do not need to issue &W to save it, and it is not affected by the &F command.

Application   AT&T, Black Box, Dallas, Hayes, Infotel, Microcom, Practical, Prometheus, Rockwell, Sierra, Telebit, Twincom, Zoom

Related To   Z, &F, &V, &W, &Z

&Y

Select Break Handling

Description   AT&Y*n*

&Y0   Empty transmit buffers. Do not send BREAK to remote modem.

&Y1   Empty transmit buffers. Immediately send BREAK to remote modem.

&Y2   Do not empty transmit buffers. Immediately send BREAK to remote modem.

&Y3   Do not empty transmit buffers. Send BREAK to remote modem in sequence with transmitted data.

Default

&Y1

This command determines how a break signal received from the DTE is handled. If data compression is in use, &Y0 and &Y1 causes both modems to reset their compression dictionaries.

Application   USRobotics

&Z

Store Telephone Number

Description   AT&Z*n*=*s*

n = telephone number memory location to use

s = dial string to be saved

&Z*n*=*s* (Write string to telephone number memory *n*.)

n = 0–1, *s*≤40 characters [AT&T]

n = 0–3, *s*≤36 characters [Black Box, Dallas, Hayes, Infotel, Practical, Prometheus, Rockwell, Sierra, Twincom, USRobotics, Zoom]

n = 0–3, *s*≤50 characters [Telebit]

n=0–10, *s*≤40 characters [AT&T]

n = 01–20, *s*≤39 characters [Microcom]

This command stores a telephone dial string in nonvolatile memory. The string may contain any character that is valid in a normal dial string. It must be the last command on the command line. Nondial characters are removed before the string is stored.

The commands &Z*s* and &Z=*s* are equivalent to &Z0=*s*.

Application   Dallas, Hayes, Infotel, Microcom, Practical, Prometheus, Rockwell, Sierra, Telebit, Twincom, USRobotics, Zoom

Related To   DS (dial command)

Notes
1. Four telephone memory locations, 0–3, are supported. When operating in Class 2 fax mode, however, memory location 3 is unavailable. [Sierra]

2. The total number of characters stored in all dial strings cannot exceed 114. [Rockwell, Twincom]

3. The total number of characters stored in both dial strings cannot exceed 40 for modems with only two number memories. [AT&T]

4. The command &Z*n*? will display the telephone number specified by *n*. [USRobotics]

\A

Set MNP Block Size

Description　AT\An

\A0　　Set maximum block size to 64 characters.

\A1　　Set maximum block size to 128 characters.

\A2　　Set maximum block size to 192 characters.

\A3　　Set maximum block size to 256 characters.

\A4　　Set maximum block size to 32 characters. [AT&T]

\A5　　Set maximum block size to 16 characters. [AT&T]

Default

\A2 [Rockwell, Twincom]

\A3 [AT&T, Black Box, Dallas, Microcom, Practical, Prometheus, Sierra, Zoom]

This command sets the maximum size of the data blocks transmitted by the modem during MNP stream link operations. This command affects only MNP 4 and MNP 5 operations. MNP 3 and lower protocols fix the block size at 64 characters.

When transferring data over a poor telephone connection, this command can be used to force the modem to use smaller blocks. This will avoid the retransmission of large blocks of data and increase throughput.

Application　AT&T, Black Box, Dallas, Microcom, Practical, Prometheus, Rockwell, Sierra, Twincom, Zoom

Notes　　**1.** A block size of 128 characters is used during V.42 operation.

\B

Transmit BREAK

Description   AT\B*n*

\B*n*   Send BREAK of *n* * 100 milliseconds during non-MNP operation.

n = 0–9, default = 3

Send BREAK of 300 milliseconds during MNP operation. (*n* is ignored.)

\B   Send a BREAK of 700 milliseconds. [Black Box]

Executing this command transmits a BREAK to the remote system and is equivalent to pressing the BREAK key on a host keyboard.

No argument is required for MNP operation for which the BREAK length is always 300 ms. For non-MNP connections, a number from 1 to 9 must be included as an argument to this command. Specifying 0 is equivalent to specifying 3. This number specifies the duration of the BREAK signal in units of 100 ms.

Application   Black Box, Dallas, Microcom, Practical, Prometheus, Rockwell, Sierra, Twincom, Zoom

Related To   \K

\C

Set MNP AUTO RELIABLE Buffering Method

Description AT\C*n*

\C0   Data is not buffered when establishing an MNP RELIABLE connection. Modem switches to NORMAL or DIRECT mode if a SYN character is not detected within 3 seconds.

\C1   Buffer data on the answering modem until 200 non-SYN characters are received or a SYN character is detected within 3 seconds. (This delay is longer for speeds of 300 bps and lower.) If 200 non-SYN characters are received, the local modem switches to NORMAL mode and passes the data through to the DTE. If the modem detects a SYN character within 3 seconds, it attempts to establish an MNP RELIABLE connection. Otherwise, it switches to NORMAL mode.

\C2   Data is not buffered when establishing an MNP RELIABLE connection. Modem switches to normal buffered operation when auto fallback character defined by the %A command is detected.

Default

\C0

This command selects the buffering method, if any, that will be used during the 3-second interval in which the modem attempts to establish an MNP RELIABLE connection when it is set to MNP AUTO RELIABLE mode and auto-answer.

Application AT&T, Black Box, Dallas, Microcom, Practical, Prometheus, Sierra

Related To \N, %A

\D

Serial Port DSR/CTS Control

Description   AT\D$n$

     \D0   DSR and CTS are always ON.

     \D1   DSR and CTS follow DCD. If &C1 is also set, DSR follows off-hook.

     \D2   DSR and CTS follow DCD. CTS turns OFF momentarily during disconnect. [AT&T, Microcom]

     \D3   DSR operates per CCITT recommendations. CTS is always ON. [Microcom]

             CTS follows DTR. [AT&T]

     \D4   DSR and CTS operate per CCITT recommendations. [Microcom]

Default

     \D0

The setting of this command determines how the DSR and CTS signals on the serial port connection will be controlled.

Application   AT&T, Black Box, Microcom

Related To   &C, &D

\E

Select Modem Data Character Echo

Description   AT\E*n*

\E0   Characters sent by the DTE to the modem in data mode are not echoed.

\E1   Characters sent by the DTE to the modem in NORMAL mode are echoed.

Default

\E0

When the modem is in data mode, the \E command determines whether characters sent to the modem from the DTE are echoed (retransmitted) to the DTE.

When echo is enabled (\E1), all characters, regardless of their validity as commands, are echoed. The \E1 command is valid only during NORMAL connections.

Application   Dallas, Microcom, Practical, Prometheus, Sierra

Related To   E, F

Notes   **1.** This command is supported by the Sierra 11061 controller only. [Sierra]

\E

Optimize Echo Cancellation

Description   AT\E

This is a one-shot command that can be used to optimize the local echo cancellation. If issued when the modem is not connected, the modem will attempt to optimize its electrical match to the GSTN network impedance. The match parameters are then saved in nonvolatile memory.

Application   Dallas, Zoom

\F

Display Stored Telephone Numbers

Description   AT\F

This command displays the telephone dial strings currently stored in the modem's directory.

Application   Dallas, Microcom, Practical, Prometheus, Sierra

Related To   D, \P, &Z

\G

Select Data Link Flow Control

Description AT\G*n*

\G0 Disable flow control.

\G1 Enable bidirectional XON/XOFF flow control.

\G2 Enable local XON/XOFF flow control. [Microcom]

Default

\G0.

This command determines the flow-control method that will be used between modems during a NORMAL connection.

When \G2 is set, the local modem sends XOFF and XON characters to the remote modem, but ignores XON and XOFF characters received from the remote modem.

A RELIABLE link uses its own flow-control protocol and ignores the setting of the \G command. However, the \Q command setting remains active during a RELIABLE link.

Application AT&T, Black Box, Dallas, Microcom, Practical, Prometheus, Rockwell, Sierra, Twincom, Zoom

Related To \J, &K, \Q, \X, :T9, :T10

Notes **1.** Both modems must use the same primarily flow-control characters. [Microcom]

\H

Hewlett Packard ENQ/ACK

Description AT\H*n*

\H0   Disable HP ENQ/ACK protocol.

\H1   Enable HP ENQ/ACK protocol during an MNP RELIABLE link; modem emulates a terminal.

\H2   Enable HP ENQ/ACK protocol during an MNP RELIABLE link; modem emulates a host.

Default

\H0

This command allows the modem to emulate the ENQ/ACK protocol when an MNP RELIABLE link is established. Flow control may be used in addition to the ENQ/ACK protocol if the host or terminal supports it. Each data block should not exceed 250 characters.

This protocol is not supported during V.42 RELIABLE connections.

Application Microcom

\J

Serial Port Speed Conversion

Description AT\J*n*

\J0   The serial port speed remains constant, regardless of the data link speed.

\J1   The serial port speed is adjusted to match the data link speed.

Default

\J0 [Black Box, Dallas, Practical, Prometheus, Sierra]

\J1 [Microcom]

When the \J0 command is in effect, the serial port connection speed is independent of the rate of the communications channel connection. If \J1 is selected, the serial port speed of the modem is changed to match the bps rate of the communications channel connection.

When \J0 is selected and the serial port and data-link rates differ, flow control should be used on the serial port connection.

Application Black Box, Dallas, Microcom, Practical, Prometheus, Sierra

Related To &K, \Q, *S

Notes **1.** The default setting for this command is \J1, but is set to \J0 by hardware configuration switches. [Microcom]

\K

Description AT\K*n*

$n = 0–5$, default = 5

This command selects the modem's response when it receives either a BREAK from the DTE or the remote modem or the transmit BREAK (\B) command from the DTE, as shown in the table. Note that during a RELIABLE connection, the remote modem's \K setting determines how the local modem responds to a BREAK.

	DTE sends BREAK to local modem		DTE sends \B command to local modem	Remote modem sends BREAK to local modem
	DIRECT connection	NORMAL or RELIABLE connection	NORMAL or RELIABLE connection	NORMAL connection
\K0	No action	Enter command mode. Do not send BREAK to remote modem.	Empty transmit buffers. Immediately send BREAK to remote modem.	Empty receive buffers. Immediately send BREAK to local DTE.
\K1	No action	Empty transmit buffers. Immediately send BREAK to remote modem.	Empty transmit buffers. Immediately send BREAK to remote modem.	Empty receive buffers. Immediately send BREAK to local DTE.
\K2	No action	Enter command mode. Do not send BREAK to remote modem.	Immediately send BREAK to remote modem.	Immediately send BREAK to local DTE.
\K3	No action	Immediately send BREAK to remote modem.	Immediately send BREAK to remote modem.	Immediately send BREAK to local DTE.

\K4	No action	Enter command mode. Do not send BREAK to remote modem.	Send BREAK to remote modem in sequence with transmitted data.	Send BREAK to local DTE in sequence with received data.
\K5	No action	Send BREAK to remote modem in sequence with transmitted data.	Send BREAK to remote modem in sequence with transmitted data.	Send BREAK to local DTE in sequence with received data.

During a LAPM RELIABLE link, BREAKs are timed, meaning that the modem attempts to preserve the duration of the BREAK when transmitting it to the remote modem. During an MNP RELIABLE link, BREAKs are not timed, as MNP 4 has no facility for maintaining the duration of the signal; a short BREAK is the same as a long BREAK.

Application AT&T, Black Box, Dallas, Practical, Prometheus, Rockwell, Sierra, Twincom, Zoom

Related To \B, &Y, S82

\L

Select MNP Link Type

Description   AT\L*n*

\L0   MNP connections will use stream mode.

\L1   MNP connections will use block mode.

Default

\L0

This command selects the mode that will be used for data transfer during an MNP RELIABLE link.

Application   Dallas, Prometheus, Rockwell, Twincom, Zoom

Related To   \A

\M

Select Error-Control Detection Phase

Description AT\M*n*

\M0   Disable error-control detection phase.

\M1   Enable error-control detection phase.

Default

M1

This command determines whether the originating modem will send the V.42 control sequence to the answering modem to determine the type of error correction it supports. If disabled, both modems must be set to use identical protocols before attempting a connection.

Application Black Box

Related To -J

\N

Select Error Control Mode

Description   AT\N*n*

\N0   NORMAL mode. The modem buffers data and honors flow control. No error control or data compression is used between modems. (Same as &Q6.)

\N1   DIRECT mode. The modem does not buffer data and ignores flow control. No error control or data compression is used between modems. The serial port speed is adjusted to match the speed of the data link. (Same as &Q0.) [AT&T, Dallas, Microcom, Sierra, Zoom]

Reserved. [Prometheus, Rockwell, Twincom]

\N2   MNP RELIABLE mode. The modem uses MNP protocols to implement error control over the data link. Flow control is in effect between modems. The local mode will disconnect if it fails to establish an MNP RELIABLE data link with the remote modem immediately after establishing a connection.

\N3   AUTO RELIABLE mode. The modem can establish a data link both with modems that support MNP and LAPM error correction and with modems that do not support error correction. The modem attempts to establish a LAPM RELIABLE or MNP RELIABLE data link with the remote modem immediately after establishing a connection. If the attempt fails, the modem will revert to a NORMAL link. [Microcom, Prometheus]

MNP AUTO RELIABLE mode. The modem can establish a data link both with modems that support MNP error correction and modems that do not support error correction. The modem attempts to establish an MNP RELIABLE data link with the remote modem immediately after establishing a connection. If the attempt fails, the modem will revert to a NORMAL link. [AT&T, Black Box, Dallas, Practical, Rockwell, Sierra, Twincom, Zoom]

\N4   LAPM RELIABLE mode. The modem uses LAPM protocols to implement error control over the data link. Flow control is in effect between modems. The local modem will disconnect if it fails to establish a LAPM RELIABLE data link with the remote modem immediately after establishing a connection. [AT&T, Black Box, Dallas, Microcom, Prometheus]

\N5   LAPM AUTO RELIABLE mode. The modem attempts to establish a LAPM RELIABLE data link with the remote modem immediately after establishing a connection. If the attempt fails, the modem will revert to a NORMAL link. [AT&T, Black Box, Dallas, Microcom]

     MNP AUTO RELIABLE mode. The modem can establish a data link both with modems that support MNP error correction and modems that do not support error correction. The modem attempts to establish an MNP RELIABLE data link with the remote modem immediately after establishing a connection. If the attempt fails, the modem will revert to a NORMAL link. [Prometheus]

\N6   RELIABLE mode. The modem attempts to establish a LAPM RELIABLE data link with the remote modem immediately after establishing a connection. If the attempt fails, the modem will then attempt to establish an MNP RELIABLE link. If that fails, the modem will disconnect. [AT&T, Black Box, Prometheus, Microcom]

\N7   AUTO RELIABLE mode. The modem can establish a data link both with modems that support MNP and LAPM error correction and with modems that do not support error correction. The modem attempts to establish a LAPM RELIABLE or MNP RELIABLE data link with the remote modem immediately after establishing a connection. If the attempt fails, the modem will revert to a NORMAL link. [AT&T, Black Box]

Defaults

     \N1 [Dallas, Practical, Sierra]

     \N3 [Dallas, Microcom, Prometheus, Rockwell, Twincom]

     \N7 [AT&T, Black Box]

This command selects the operating mode that the local modem will use to make a link with the remote modem.

Application   AT&T, Dallas, Microcom, Practical, Prometheus, Rockwell, Sierra, Twincom

Related To %C, \O, \U, \Y, S36, S46, S48

Notes

1. V.42 error correction is not supported for Bell 103, V.21, and V.23 links.

2. Selecting the connection type with this command disables the use of V.42 and V.42bis. [Sierra]

3. Dial modifiers can also be used to set the operating mode for a single call. [Microcom]

4. The escape sequence is disabled in DIRECT mode if \J0 is set. [Microcom]

5. The default for this command is \N0, but is set to \N3 by configuration switches. [Microcom]

\O

Initiate MNP RELIABLE Connection

Description   AT\O

After a NORMAL or DIRECT link has been established, the \O command may be used to convert to an MNP RELIABLE link.

The \O command may be sent regardless of whether the local modem originated or answered the call. The remote DTE must issue the \U command to the remote modem within 5 seconds after the \O command is issued. The local modem attempts to establish an MNP RELIABLE connection twice, then returns to the original connection type.

Issuing this command when the local modem is not connected returns NO CARRIER. Commands that appear on the command line after \O are ignored.

Application   Black Box, Dallas, Practical, Prometheus, Rockwell, Sierra, Twincom, Zoom

Related To   O, \N, \U, \Y, \Z

Notes   **1.** This command is not supported in fax modes.

\P

Store Telephone Number

Description AT\P*ns*

n = telephone directory entry

0–3 [Dallas, Practical, Sierra]

01–20 [Microcom]

s = dial string to be saved

s≤30 characters [Dallas, Sierra]

s≤36 characters [Practical]

s≤39 characters [Microcom]

This command stores a telephone dial string in the modem's telephone number directory. The string may contain any valid dial character, including dial modifiers. Strings stored with this command should be dialed using the D*n* command.

Application Dallas, Microcom, Practical, Sierra

Related To D*n*, &V, &Z

\Q

Select Serial Port Flow Control

Description AT\Q*n*

\Q0   Disable DTE flow control.

\Q1   Bidirectional XON/XOFF flow control. Both the modem and the DTE suspend data transfer when they receive the XOFF character and resume when they receive the XON character.

\Q2   Unidirectional CTS flow control. The modem uses the CTS line to control data transfer from the DTE. The DTE cannot control data transfer from the modem.

\Q3   Bidirectional RTS/CTS flow control. The modem uses the CTS line to control data transfer from the DTE. The DTE uses the RTS line to control data transfer from the modem.

\Q4   Unidirectional XON/XOFF flow control. The modem uses the XOFF character to suspend and the XON character to resume data transfer from the DTE. The DTE cannot control data transfer from the modem. [Microcom, Sierra]

\Q5   CTS is off until a connection is established, then unidirectional CTS flow control is enabled. [Microcom]

Unidirectional XON/XOFF flow control. The DTE uses the XOFF character to suspend and the XON character to resume data transfer from the modem. The modem cannot control data transfer from the DTE. [AT&T]

\Q6   CTS is off and RTS is ignored until a connection is established, then bidirectional RTS/CTS flow control is enabled. [Microcom]

Unidirectional RTS flow control. The DTE uses the RTS line to control data transfer from the modem. The modem cannot control data transfer from the DTE. [AT&T]

Default

Q0 [Dallas, Sierra]

\Q1 [Black Box, Prometheus]

\Q2 [AT&T]

\Q3 [Dallas, Microcom, Practical, Prometheus]

This command selects the type of flow control, if any, that will be used between the DTE and the modem.

If the serial port data transfer speed is faster than the effective speed of the data link between modems, the modem will buffer data from the DTE and request that it stop sending data. This situation is common during RELIABLE connections when retransmissions reduce the effective data link transfer rate.

Hardware flow control overrides the &C and \D settings for CTS operation.

Application AT&T, Dallas, Microcom, Practical, Prometheus, Sierra

Related To &K, *F, \X

Notes

1. The default setting for this command is \Q0, but is set to \Q3 by hardware configuration switches. [Microcom]

2. \Q4 is available only during a LAPM link. [Dallas, Sierra]

\R

Serial Port Ring Indicator Control

Description　AT\R*n*

\R0　　RI signal is kept ON for the duration of the telephone call.

\R1　　RI signal is turned off after the call is answered.

Default

　　\R1

This command controls the ring indicator (RI) signal on the serial port connection.

Application　Black Box, Microcom

\S

Display Modem Status

Description   AT\S

This command displays the current value of selected options and S registers, the active connection type, and the duration of the current or previous connection.

Application   Dallas, Microcom, Practical, Prometheus, Sierra

Notes   1. The output from this command occupies several screens. Press any key to advance to the next screen. Press Ctrl-X or send a BREAK to cancel the display. [Microcom]

\T

Set Inactivity Timer

Description   AT\Tn

n = 0–90 minutes, default = 0 (disabled) [Black Box, Dallas, Microcom, Practical, Prometheus, Sierra]

n = 0–42 minutes, default = 0 (disabled) [Rockwell, Twincom, Zoom]

n = 0–255 minutes, default = 60 minutes. [AT&T]

This command instructs the modem to break an established connection if no data transfer occurs for the specified amount of time. The n option represents the number of minutes of idle time that must pass before the connection is severed. Setting n to 0 disables the timer.

The inactivity timer is available during NORMAL and RELIABLE connections only. In NORMAL mode, the inactivity timer is reset when data is transmitted. In RELIABLE mode, the inactivity timer is reset when data is transmitted or received. The timer is ignored during DIRECT and synchronous connections.

Application   AT&T, Black Box, Dallas, Microcom, Practical, Prometheus, Rockwell, Sierra, Twincom, Zoom

\U

Accept MNP RELIABLE Link

Description   AT\U

After a normal or direct connection has been established, the \U command may be used to accept an MNP reliable link.

The \U command may be sent regardless of whether the local modem originated or answered the call. The remote DTE must issue the \O command to the remote modem within 5 seconds after the \U command is issued. The local modem may wait up to 12 seconds for a reliable connection to be established, then return to the original connection type.

Issuing this command when the local modem is not connected returns NO CARRIER. Commands that appear on the command line after \U are ignored.

Application   Black Box, Dallas, Practical, Prometheus, Rockwell, Sierra, Twincom, Zoom

Related To   \O, \Y, \Z

\V

Select RELIABLE Link Responses

Description AT\V*n*

\V0 Use long form CONNECT responses without error-control information.

\V1 Use long form CONNECT responses indicating error- control. (Typically /REL or \ARQ.)

\V2 Use long form CONNECT responses with error-control type (MNP, LAPM, or CELLULAR) specified. [Microcom]

\V3 Append /REL to long form CONNECT responses. Display Hayes compatible short form (numeric) result codes. [Microcom]

\V4 Use long form CONNECT responses with error control type (MNP, LAPM, or CELLULAR) specified. (Same as \V2.) [Microcom]

Default

\V0 [Dallas, Sierra]

\V1 [Black Box, Prometheus]

\V2 [Microcom]

This command enables the expanded CONNECT messages that contain error-control and data compression information. The text of the messages returned is manufacturer-dependent.

Application Black Box, Dallas, Microcom, Practical, Prometheus, Sierra

Related To Q, V, W, X, S95

Notes

1. The default setting for this command is \V0, but is set to \V2 by hardware configuration switches. [Microcom]

\W

Split Serial Port Speed

Description AT\W*n*

\W0   Disable split speed.

\W1   Enable split speed.

Default

\W0

This command determines whether the serial port will use the split transmit and receive operation when either %F1 or %F2 is set. The DTE must support split speed operation.

When set to \W1, the serial port speed automatically adjusts to match the split transmit/receive speed set for the data link by the %F command. If %F1 is in effect, the modem accepts data from the DTE at 75 bps on the transmit data line, and outputs data to the DTE at 1200 bps on the receive data line. If %F2 is in effect, the modem accepts data from the DTE at 1200 bps on the transmit data line, and outputs data to the DTE at 75 bps on the receive data line.

Application Microcom

Related To \C, \J, %F

\X

Select XON/XOFF Pass-Through Flow Control

Description AT\X*n*

\X0 The local modem will honor XON/XOFF flow-control characters received from thc local DTE, but will not pass them to the remote modem.

\X1 The local modem will honor XON/XOFF flow-control characters received from the local DTE, and will pass them to the remote modem.

Default

\X0

This command determines whether the XON/OFF flow-control characters will be passed to the remote DTE through the modem link.

This command is effective only during a NORMAL buffered connection when XON/XOFF flow control has been enabled using the \Q command.

Application AT&T, Black Box, Dallas, Microcom, Practical, Prometheus, Sierra

Related To *F, &K, \Q

Notes
1. If \X1 is enabled, local flow-control characters will pass through to the remote system. These flow-control characters may turn on the flow of data from the remote system before the local modem is ready to receive them, resulting in data loss.

\Y

Convert to MNP RELIABLE Link

Description   AT\Y

After a NORMAL or DIRECT connection has been established, the \Y command may be used to convert to an MNP RELIABLE link.

If the local modem originated the call, this command initiates an MNP RELIABLE link. If the local modem answered the call, this command accepts an MNP RELIABLE link.

The \Y command must be sent first to the answering modem, then to the originating modem. The commands must be received by both modems within 5 seconds of each other. If the link attempt fails the modems return to the original connection type.

Issuing this command when the local modem is not connected returns NO CARRIER. Commands that appear on the command line after \Y are ignored.

Application   Black Box, Dallas, Practical, Prometheus, Rockwell, Sierra, Twincom, Zoom

Related To   \O, \U, \Z

\Z

Convert to NORMAL Link

Description   AT\Z

After an MNP RELIABLE link has been established, the \Z command can be used to convert to a NORMAL link.

The \Z command can be sent regardless of whether the local modem originated or answered the call. If the remote modem does not respond to the command, the local modem will disconnect and return NO CARRIER.

Application   Black Box, Dallas, Practical, Prometheus, Rockwell, Sierra, Twincom, Zoom

Related To   \O, \U, \Y

Notes   **1.** Issuing this command when a LAPM RELIABLE link is established will cause the local modem to disconnect and return NO CARRIER. [Sierra]

%A

Set AUTO RELIABLE Fallback Character

Description   AT%A*n*

n = 0–127

Default

&A0 [Black Box, Dallas, Microcom, Practical, Prometheus, Sierra]

&A13 [AT&T, Dallas]

This command sets the ASCII character that will be recognized as the AUTO RELIABLE fallback character by the answering modem. Selecting 0 disables fallback character recognition.

When the modem is in AUTO RELIABLE mode and \C2 is in effect, receiving the fallback character causes the modem to switch to NORMAL mode and pass the character through to the DTE. Fallback character recognition stops if the modem receives a SYN (ASCII 22) character.

Application   AT&T, Black Box, Dallas, Microcom, Practical, Prometheus, Sierra

Related To   \C

Notes

1. Do not set the fallback character to 63 or 126; these settings interfere with V.42 protocol negotiations.

2. With this command \N3\C2 must also be set. [Microcom]

%B

Select Data Link Speed

Description AT%B*n*

  n = 75, 300, 600, 1200, 2400, 4800, 7200, 9600, 14400 [Microcom]

  n = 00, 1200, 2400, 4800, 9600, 9600C [Black Box]

  n = 300, 1200, 2400, 4800, 9600, 12000, 14400 [AT&T]

  AT%BT*n*

  n = 12000 [Microcom]

Default

  14400 [AT&T, Microcom]

  9600C [Black Box]

This command is issued to the local modem to set the initial data link speed in bps as specified by the *n* argument. Downshifting may still occur. If this command is issued while a connection is established, the new rate does not take effect until the current connection ends.

Application AT&T, Black Box, Microcom

Related To $B, %F, %G, \N

Notes

1. 9600C represents 9600 bps with trellis coding. [Black Box]

2. During asynchronous operation at data link speeds of 7200, 12000, or 14400 bps, the modem supports only LAPM RELIABLE or MNP RELIABLE connections. If the modem is configured for AUTO RELIABLE (\N3) or LAPM RELIABLE (\N5) and connects at one of these speeds but does not establish a RELIABLE connection, the modem disconnects.

   If the modem is configured for \N0 or \N1, a data link speed setting of 12000 or 14400 bps will result in a connection at 9600 bps, and a data link speed of 7200 bps will result in a connection at 4800 bps.

If %G0 is set, an AT command issued locally causes the data link speed to match the serial port speed, regardless of any previous %B setting. If %G1 is set, the data link speed is changed only when a %B command is entered. If a %F1, %F2, or %F3 command is issued, the modem changes to either split speed or 1200 bps. [Microcom]

%B

Set Serial Port Speed

Description   AT%B*n*

%B0   Set serial port speed to 110 bps.

%B1   Set serial port speed to 300 bps.

%B2   Set serial port speed to 600 bps.

%B3   Set serial port speed to 1200 bps.

%B4   Set serial port speed to 2400 bps.

%B5   Set serial port speed to 4800 bps.

%B6   Set serial port speed to 9600 bps.

%B7   Set serial port speed to 19200 bps.

%B8   Set serial port speed to 38400 bps.

%B9   Set serial port speed to 57600 bps.

This command sets the serial port speed during a remote access session.

Application   USRobotics

%C

Select Data Compression Mode

Description   AT%C*n*

%C0   Disable data compression.

%C1   Enable data compression. [AT&T, Dallas, Prometheus, Rockwell, Twincom, Zoom]

Enable MNP 5 data compression only. [Dallas, Microcom, Practical, Sierra, Zoom]

%C2   Enable V.42bis data compression only. [Microcom, Zoom]

%C3   Enable both MNP 5 and V.42bis data compression. [Microcom, Zoom]

Default

%C0 [Sierra]

%C1 [AT&T, Practical, Prometheus, Rockwell, Twincom, Zoom]

%C3 [Microcom, Zoom]

This command determines whether the modem will attempt to use data compression during a RELIABLE connection. If the remote modem does not support data compression or has data compression disabled, the modem can establish a connection without data compression, regardless of the %C setting.

Application   AT&T, Dallas, Microcom, Practical, Prometheus, Rockwell, Sierra, Twincom, Zoom

Related To   \J, \N, *E, "H, S36, S46, S48

%C

Configuration Control

Description   AT%C*n*

%C0   Configuration changes do not take place until the remote session is terminated.

%C1   Configuration changes made during the remote session are ignored.

%C2   Configuration changes made during the remote session take effect immediately.

Default

%C0

This command determines when configuration changes made during a remote session take effect.

Application   USRobotics

%C

Select Data Compression Mode

Description   AT%C*n*

%C0   Disable compression.

%C1   Enable V.42bis or MNP 5 compression during transmit and receive.

%C2   Enable V.42bis transmit compression only.

%C3   Enable V.42bis receive compression only.

Default

%C1

This command globally enables V.42bis or MNP 5 compression, or selectively enables V.42bis compression.

Application   Black Box

%D

Set V.42bis Dictionary Size

AT%D*n*

%D0	Set dictionary size to 512 bytes.
%D1	Set dictionary size to 1024 bytes.
%D2	Set dictionary size to 2048 bytes.
%D3	Set dictionary size to 4096 bytes if one-way compression is selected (%M3). If two-way compression is selected, set the dictionary size to 2048 bytes.

Default

%D2

This command sets the size of the dictionary used during V.42bis compression and decompression.

Application Dallas, Rockwell, Twincom, Zoom

Related To %M, %P, %S

%D

Set Disconnect Buffer Delay

Description AT%D*n*

n = 0–255 seconds, default = 0

This command establishes a time period of n seconds during which the modem attempts to process data in its transmit or receive buffer before acknowledging a disconnect.

When the disconnect is local, DTR is lowered or the ATH command is issued, the modem attempts for n seconds to empty its transmit buffer before disconnecting. If the carrier drops, the modem will attempt to empty its receive buffer to the DTE before acknowledging the disconnect. If its buffers are empty or n=0, the modem disconnects immediately.

Application Black Box, Microcom

%D

Set DTMF Attenuation

Description   AT%D*n*

n = 0–7, default = 0

This command sets the attenuation level for transmission of dialing tones. The *n* argument specifies the amount of attenuation in units of 2 dB. %D0 sets 0 dB attenuation, while %D7 sets 14 dB attenuation.

Application   Infotel, Rockwell, Twincom

Related To   %L

Notes

1. This command is implemented in the Rockwell RC224ATF and RC224ATL modem chips.

%E

Enable Auto-Retrain

Description AT%E*n*

%E0   Disable auto-retrain.

%E1   Enable auto-retrain at 2400 bps or higher.

%E2   Enable auto-fallback. [Black Box]

Default

%E0 [Dallas, Prometheus, Rockwell, Sierra, Twincom]

%E1 [Black Box, Microcom, Prometheus, Zoom]

When auto-retrain is enabled, the modem monitors the line quality. If the line quality is too poor to sustain communications, the modem will try to retrain (resynchronize) the modems up to three times (a total of 6 seconds). The ATO1 command can be used to force the retrain sequence when %E0 is set. This command is effective only for data links of 2400 bps and higher.

Application Black Box, Dallas, Microcom, Prometheus, Rockwell, Sierra, Twincom, Zoom

Related To O, &B, *Q

Notes **1.** The %E setting is ignored during V.32 and V.32bis connections. *See the &B command.*

%F

V.23 Mode Control

Description   AT%F*n*

%F0   Allows multiprotocol answering; disables V.23 mode on originate modem.

%F1   75 bps transmit, 1200 bps receive (split speed) V.23 operation.

%F2   1200 bps transmit, 75 bps receive (split speed) V.23 operation.

%F3   1200 bps transmit, 1200 bps receive (half-duplex) V.23 operation.

Default

%F0

This command determines the V.23 mode that will be used at 1200 bps. Enabling V.23 disables all other protocols.

Application   Microcom

Related To   %B

Notes

1. Issuing the %B*n* command forces %F0.

2. %G1 must be set before issuing %F1, %F2, or %F3.

%F

Select Data Format

Description AT%F*n*

%F0   8 data bits, no parity.

%F1   7 data bits, MARK parity.

%F2   7 data bits, ODD parity.

%F3   7 data bits, EVEN parity.

This command selects the data format during a remote session.

Application USRobotics

%F

Enable V.32 Fast Train

Description AT%F*n*

%F0   Disable V.32 fast train.

%F1   Enable V.32 fast train.

Default

%F0

Selecting the %F1 command reduces the time required for the modem to complete a connection at 4800 or 9600 bps.

Application Black Box

%G

Select Serial Port/Data Link Speed Tracking

Description   AT%G*n*

%G0   The serial port speed establishes the data link speed.

%G1   The %B command establishes data link speed.

Default

%G0

This command selects whether the data link speed is updated to match the serial port speed each time an AT command is issued. When %G1 is set, the data link speed may be changed only by the %B or %F command.

Application   Microcom, Prometheus

Related To   %B, %F

%G

Auto-Fall-Forward/Auto-Fallback

Description   AT%G*n*

%G0   Disable auto-fall-forward/auto-fallback.

%G1   Enable auto-fall-forward/auto-fallback.

Default

%G0

This command enables the auto-fall-forward/auto-fallback function of the modem. This speed adjustment is effective during V.22bis and V.32 connections only.

Application   Dallas

%H

Select V.54 and Busy-Out Control

Description   AT%H*n*

%H0   Disable V.54 control by circuit.

%H1   Enable busy out when pin 18 is high.

%H2   Enable V.54 control by circuit (local analog loopback when pin 18 is high or remote digital loopback when pin 21 is high).

Default

%H0

This command determines whether the modem will respond to circuit inputs to control V.54 and busy-out testing.

When %H0 is set, pins 18 and 21 are ignored.

When %H1 is set and pin 18 goes high, the modem busies out the phone line by going off-hook. If DTR is high, the modem also performs a local analog loopback test. Pin 21 is ignored.

When %H2 is set and pin 18 goes high, the modem goes on-hook and performs a local analog loopback test. If %H2 is set and pin 21 goes high when the modem is connected, the modem performs a remote digital loopback test.

Application   Microcom

%I

Set Connection Security Password

Description AT%I

Default

no password

This command sets a new password or changes an existing password. The modem prompts for the old and new passwords as appropriate. Use &W or *W to save the password.

To clear an existing password, press <CR> at both NEW PASSWORD: prompts. Alternately, the command AT&F&W erases the password from the stored configuration.

Application Microcom

Related To %P

%J

Select Secondary Defaults

Description AT%J

This command resets all S registers and commands to the default values specified by the &F command with the following exceptions:

Command/S Register	%J Default
%D	2 dB
%L	6 dB
S6	3 seconds
S11	95 milliseconds

Application Infotel, Rockwell, Twincom

Related To %D, %L, S6, S11

%L

Report Received Signal Level

Description   AT%L

This command returns a value that identifies the received signal level in dBm. Possible values range from 009 (-9 dBm) to 043 (-43 dBm). If the received level is greater than -9 dBm, 009 will be returned. Similarly, if the received level is less than -43 dBm, 043 will be returned.

This command is used during an established connection. Issue the escape sequence followed by the %L command to read the received signal level. Then return to the data mode with the O or \O command.

Application   Dallas, Prometheus, Rockwell, Twincom, Zoom

Related To   %Q

%L

Select Speed Matching

Description AT%L*n*

%L0   Provide partial speed matching.

%L1   Enable speed matching.

%L2   Disable speed matching.

%L3   Enable CCITT V.32 automode.

Default

%L1

This command selects whether the modem will use speed matching to establish a data link. When set to %L3, the modem complies with the proposed annex to CCITT V.32 for automoding when interworking with V.22 and V.22bis modems.

Application Microcom

Related To :T13

%L

Set Transmit Attenuation

Description AT%L*n*

n = 0–7, default = 0

This command sets the attenuation level for data transmission. The *n* argument specifies the amount of attenuation in units of 2 dB. %D0 sets 0 dB attenuation, while %D7 sets 14 dB attenuation.

Application Infotel, Rockwell, Twincom

Related To %D

Notes

1. This command is implemented in the Rockwell RC224ATF and RC224ATL modem chips.

%M

Select One-Way/Two-Way Compression

Description   AT%M*n*

%M0   Disable compression in both directions.

%M1   Enable transmit compression only.

%M2   Enable receive decompression only.

%M3   Enable both transmit compression and receive decompression.

Default

%M3

This command selects whether data compression will be used on transmitted data only, received data only, or both.

Application   Dallas, Rockwell, Twincom, Zoom

%O

V.23 Equalizer Control

Description AT%O*n*

%O0   Disable equalizers in V.23 half-duplex mode.

%O1   Enable equalizers in V.23 half-duplex mode.

Default

%O1

This command determines if the modem's equalizers are active during V.23 half-duplex operation. To avoid transmission errors, equalizer settings must be the same on both modems.

Application Microcom

%P

Clear V.42bis Encoder Dictionary

Description   AT%P

This command clears the local modem's V.42bis encoder dictionary and sends a command code to the remote modem to clear the remote V.42bis dictionary. This command would typically be issued between files in a multifile transfer and is only effective during V.42bis operations.

Application   Dallas, Prometheus, Rockwell, Twincom, Zoom

Related To   %D

%P

Set Remote Access Password

Description   AT%P=*n*

n = numeric access password

AT%P?   View remote access password

This command allows you to set or view the password that will be required to establish a remote access session. The password must consist of the characters 0–9 and may be up to eight characters in length. Setting the password to D disables remote access.

Application   Black Box

Related To   %T, $V

%Q

Report Line Signal Quality

Description AT%Q

This command returns the high-order byte of the calculated eye quality monitor (EQM) value. The high-order byte can range from 0 to 127.

If the EQM value is 70 ± 10 (depending on the line speed) or greater, the modem will automatically retrain if enabled by the %E1 command. The value for a normal connection ranges from about 0 to 15 and approaches 60 for a progressively poorer connection.

This command is used during an established connection. Issue the escape sequence followed by the %Q command to read the received signal level. Then return to the data mode with the O or \O command.

Application Dallas, Prometheus, Rockwell, Twincom, Zoom

Related To %L

%R

Display Modem Registers

Description AT%R

This command displays the values of all S registers in tabular form. Values are displayed in both decimal and hexadecimal formats.

Application Dallas, Microcom, Practical, Sierra

Notes

1. This command is not available in Sierra send/receive fax modem boards. [Sierra]

2. The :T registers are also displayed. [Microcom]

%R

Enable Rack Controller Unit Access

Description   AT%R*n*

%R0   Normal operation. RCU access is disabled.

%R1   Enable RCU access.

Default

%R0

This command determines if rack controller unit (RCU) access to the modem is permitted. This command is used with USRobotics Total Control Modem Management systems.

Application   USRobotics

%S

Select Maximum V.42bis String Length

Description A%S*n*

n = 6–250 characters, default = 32 characters

This command sets the maximum number of characters that can be compressed into a single code word.

Application Dallas, Rockwell, Twincom, Zoom

Related To %D, %M, "O

%S

Display Switch Settings

Description AT%S*n*

%S0   Display front switch settings.

%S1   Display rear switch settings.

%S2   Display internal switch settings.

This command displays the current configuration switch settings.

Application Microcom

%T

Enable Touch-Tone Recognition

Description   AT%T

This command enables the recognition of DTMF dialing tones.

Application   USRobotics

%T

Initiate Remote Configuration Session

Description AT%T

This command allows the local modem to change the configuration of an identical remote modem. The modems must be connected in NORMAL, DIRECT, or MNP RELIABLE mode. In MNP mode, the modem will fallback to NORMAL when this command is entered. After exiting remote configuration, restoration of the MNP link is not automatic.

Application Black Box

Related To %P, $V

%U

Clear Serial Port Speed

Description AT%U*n*

%U0   Serial port speed can be changed.

%U1   Serial port speed is constant.

%U2   Serial port speed can be changed.

Default

%U0

This command determines whether the serial port speed can be changed. If %U1 is selected, you must issue %U1 each time you change the serial port speed.

It is not necessary to use this command when the automatic bps rate adjustment changes the serial port speed during a connection. You must issue %U0 when changing from 11-bit characters to 11-bit or 10-bit characters.

Application Microcom

%U

Reset Serial Port Speed

Description AT%U

This command instructs the modem to adjust its serial port speed based on the speed of the next AT command prefix received.

Application Black Box

%V

Display Firmware Revision

Description AT%V

This command displays the firmware (ROM) revision level.

Application Dallas, Microcom, Practical, Sierra

Related To I

Notes **1.** The %V command is equivalent to the I3 command.

%W

Pulse Digit Command

Description   AT%W*n*

%W0   *n* pulses are produced when dialing digit *n*.

%W1   *n*+1 pulses are produced when dialing digit *n*.

%W2   10-*n* pulses are produced when dialing digit *n*.

Default

%W0

When pulse dialing is in effect, this command determines whether each number *n* in a dial string is dialed with *n*, *n*+1, or 10-*n* pulses.

When %W0 or %W2 is set, the digit 0 is dialed with 10 pulses. If %W1 is set, the digit 0 is dialed with 1 pulse.

Application   Microcom

Related To   DP, &P

*A

Request Remote Access

Description   AT*A

This command initiates a request for remote access. The requesting modem waits 10 seconds for a response from the answering modem. If denied, the requesting modem displays an error message.

This command automatically sends the character set by the *S command. The *S character and register S12 (guard time) should be set to the same value on both modems.

Application   Microcom

Related To   *E, *S, S12

Notes   **1.** Remote access is available only during a NORMAL or MNP RELI-ABLE connection without data compression.

*E

Set Error Correction Mode

Description   **1.** AT*E*n*

*E0   Disable error control and data compression.

*E1   MNP 5 AUTO RELIABLE mode.

*E2   MNP 5 RELIABLE mode.

*E3   MNP 4 AUTO RELIABLE mode.

*E4   MNP 4 RELIABLE mode.

*E5   V.42 AUTO RELIABLE mode with detection phase.

*E6   V.42 RELIABLE mode with detection phase.

*E7   V.42 AUTO RELIABLE mode without detection
        phase.

*E8   V.42 RELIABLE mode without detection phase.

*E9   V.42bis AUTO RELIABLE mode.

*E10   V.42bis RELIABLE mode.

This command sets the modem's error control mode and determines whether the modem will use a detection phase to negotiate protocols.

This command is provided primarily for compatibility purposes. Changing the *E command setting will change the settings of the \N, %C, "H, and -J commands.

The following equivalences are typically in effect:

Command	Equivalent
*E0	\N0 %C0
*E1	\N5 %C1
*E2	\N2 %C1
*E3	\N5 %C0
*E4	\N2 %C0

Command	Equivalent
*E5	\N3 "H0 -J1
*E6	\N4 "H0 -J1
*E7	\N3 "H0 -J0
*E8	\N4 "H0 -J0
*E9	\N3 "H3 -J1
*E10	\N4 "H3 -J1

Application   Prometheus

Related To   \N, %C, "H, -J

*E

Select Remote Access

Description AT*E*n*

*E0   Disable remote access.

*E1   Enable remote access.

This command determines how the modem responds to a request for remote access. Remote access is available only during a NORMAL or MNP RELI-ABLE connection without data compression.

Default

*E0

Application Microcom

Related To *A

*F

Select Serial Port Flow Control

Description   AT*F*n*

     *F0   Disable serial port flow control.

     *F1   Bidirectional XON/XOFF flow control. Both the modem and the DTE suspend data transfer when they receive the XOFF character and resume when they receive the XON character.

     *F2   Bidirectional XON/XOFF flow control. Both the modem and the DTE suspend data transfer when they receive the XOFF character and resume when they receive the XON character.

     *F3   Bidirectional RTS/CTS flow control. The modem uses the CTS line to control data transfer from the DTE. The DTE uses the RTS line to control data transfer from the modem.

Default

     *F3

This command selects the type of flow control, if any, that will be used between the DTE and the modem.

If the serial port data transfer speed is faster than the effective speed of the data link between modems, the modem will buffer data from the DTE and request that it stop sending data. This situation is common during RELIABLE connections when retransmissions reduce the effective data link transfer rate. The following equivalences are typically in effect:

Command	Equivalent
*F0	\Q0\X0
*F1	\Q1\X1
*F2	\Q1\X0
*F3	\Q3\X0

Application   Prometheus

Related To   \Q, \X, *F

*H

Set Link Negotiation Speed

Description   AT*H*n*

*H0   Link negotiation occurs at the highest supported speed.

*H1   Link negotiation occurs at 1200 bps.

*H2   Link negotiation occurs at 4800 bps.

Default

*H0

This command sets the initial connection speed for link negotiation between two MNP 10 modems. After the connection has been established, speed up-shifting can occur.

Application   Microcom

*I

Set Modem Identifier

Description　AT*I

This command causes the modem to prompt for the identifier that appears as part of the remote access session banner. Up to 25 characters may be entered. The modem identifier can also be displayed by the \S command.

Application　Microcom

*M

Modify Remote Access Level

Description AT*M

This command initiates a request to move up from a level 0 to a level 1 remote access session. If a password is set, the modem will prompt for a valid password.

Application Microcom

*P

Set Remote Access Passwords

Description AT⋆P*n*

*P0   Set level 0 remote access password.

*P1   Set level 1 remote access password.

Allows you to set a password that will be required to establish a remote access session. The modem will prompt for passwords.

Application Microcom

*Q

Select Auto-Retrain

Description AT*Qn

*Q0   Disable auto-retrain.

*Q1   Enable auto-retrain at 2400 bps or higher.

Default

*Q1

When auto-retrain is enabled, the modem monitors the line quality. If the line quality is too poor to sustain communications, the modem will try to retrain (resynchronize) the modems up to 3 times (a total of 6 seconds).

Application Prometheus

Related To &B, %E

Notes

1. This command is linked to the setting of the %E command.

2. The *Q setting is ignored during V.32 and V.32bis connections. *See the &B command.*

*Q

Recover Remote Access Configuration

Description   AT*Q

Discards configuration changes made during a level 1 remote access session that have not been saved with *U.

Application

Related To   *U

*R

Select Remote Access Security

Description   T*R*n*

*R0   Disables remote access security.

*R1   Enables remote access security.

Default

   *R0

This command controls the remote access security feature. Remote access is available only during a NORMAL or MNP RELIABLE connection without data compression.

Application   Microcom

*S

Serial Port Speed Conversion

Description AT*S*n*

*S0   The serial port (DTE/DCE interface) speed is reduced to match the modem communications speed.

*S1   The serial port (DTE/DCE interface) speed remains constant, regardless of the DCE communications speed.

Default

*S1

When the *S1 command is in effect, the serial port connection speed is independent of the rate of the communications channel connection. If *S0 is selected, the serial port speed of the modem is changed to match the bps rate of the communications channel connection.

When *S1 is selected and the serial port and data link rates differ, flow control should be used on the serial port connection.

This command is provided for compatibility purposes and is linked to \J. Changing the setting of this command will change the setting of the \J command.

Application Prometheus

Related To &K, \J, \Q, *F

*S

Set Remote Access Attention Character

Description AT*S*n*

$n = 0–126$, default $= 42$

This command sets the attention character that is sent four times in succession to request a remote access session. The *A command sends this sequence automatically. This command is available only during a NORMAL or MNP RELIABLE connection without data compression.

Application

Related To *A

*U

Update Remote Access Configuration

Description   AT*U

This command saves the configuration changes made during a level 1 remote access session. To save changes even after the modem is reset, use the &W or *W command.

Application   Microcom

Related To   &W, *W

*W

Store Complete Configuration

Description AT*W*n*

n = 0–3, default = 0

This command stores all active commands and registers that are stored by the &W command as well as additional restricted registers to the specified profile.

Application Microcom

Related To &W, &Y, Z

*X

Exit Remote Access

Description AT*X

Moves remote access down one level. If issue during a level 1 session, access is moved to level 0. When issued during a level 0 session, the session is terminated and the originating modem returns to the data mode.

Application Microcom

"H

Select V.42bis Compression Mode

Description AT"H*n*

"H0   Disable compression.

"H1   Compress transmitted data. Do not expand received data.

"H2   Expand received data. Do not compress transmitted data.

"H3   Enable bidirectional compression/expansion.

Default

    "H3

This command enables or disables V.42bis data compression. Compression can be enabled in one or both directions. Both modems must be configured compatibly.

Application AT&T, Dallas, Prometheus

Related To %C, \N, *E, -J

"O

Set Maximum V.42bis String Length

Description AT%S*n*

n = 6–250 characters, default = 250 characters

This command sets the maximum number of characters that can be compressed into a single coded word.

Application Prometheus

Related To %S

-A

Set Auto-Retrain Limit

Description   AT-A*n*

$n = 0–255$, default $= 0$

This command sets the maximum number of times that the modem can auto-retrain.

Application   Microcom

-D

Repeat Dial

Description AT-D*s*

s = dial string, ≤ 39 characters

This command causes the modem to redial a telephone number up to nine times until a connection is made.

If the modem is in RELIABLE mode and the remote system answers, but fails to establish a RELIABLE connection, the redial sequence is terminated.

Application Microcom

-E

Set Serial Port Word Length

Description   AT-E*n*

-E0   Enable 10-bit data during NORMAL mode connec-
         tions.

-E1   Enable 11-bit data during NORMAL mode connec-
         tions.

Default

-E0

This command sets the number of data bits that will be used on the serial port during NORMAL mode connections when 11-bit serial characters are exchanged. This setting must be the same on both modems.

Application   Microcom

Related To   -O, \N

Notes

1. The modems will not be able to pass data if a RELIABLE connection falls back to a NORMAL connection and 11-bit data characters are enabled on both modems.

-F

Description AT-F*n*

-F0   Disables secondary flow-control characters.

-F1   Enables secondary flow-control characters.

Default

-F0

This command controls whether secondary flow-control characters are sent or received on the serial port. When -F1 is selected and primary flow control is enabled on the serial port, two flow control characters (one primary and one secondary) are sent to the host for flow-control processing.

Application Microcom

-H

Select Smart Mode

Description AT-H*n*

-H0   Modem is configured as a smart modem.

-H1   Modem is configured as a dumb modem.

Default

-H0

This command is used to configure the modem to ignore commands and not send result codes. This setting can be cleared only by a power on/off cycle.

Application Microcom

-J

Select V.42 Error Control Detection Phase

Description AT-J*n*

-J0   Disable error control detection phase.

-J1   Enable error control detection phase.

Default

-J1

This command determines whether the originating modem will send the V.42 control sequence to the answering modem to determine the type of error correction it supports. If disabled, both modems must be set to use identical protocols before attempting a connection.

Application Dallas, Microcom, Prometheus

Related To %C, \N, *E, "H

-K

Select MNP Extended Services

Description　AT-K*n*

-K0　　Disable MNP extended services.

-K1　　Enable MNP extended services.

-K2　　Enable MNP extended services without MNP indication during the answer detect phase.

Default

-K1

MNP extended services allow two compliant modems to use MNP data services (Class 10, for example) that are not available when operating with LAPM.

Application　Microcom

-M

Select MNP Class Connect Messages

Description AT-M*n*

-M0   Disable MNP class connect messages.

-M1   Enable MNP class connect messages.

Default

-M0

This command determines whether MNP class connect messages are displayed. The -M1 setting overrides the \V and W command settings.

Application Microcom

-O

Set Serial Port Parity

Description   AT-On

-O0   7 data bits, ODD parity

-O1   7 data bits, EVEN parity

-O2   7 data bits, MARK parity

-O3   7 data bits, SPACE parity

-O4   8 data bits, no parity

-O5   8 data bits, ODD parity

-O6   8 data bits, EVEN parity

-O7   8 data bits, MARK parity

This command is used to change the serial port parity to a different setting than is automatically detected by decoding the AT sequence.

Application   Microcom

-P

Check Parity

Description   AT-P*n*

-P0   Ignores parity of special characters

-P1   Processes special characters only if their parity matches the parity of the serial port.

-P2   Processes special characters only if their parity matches the parity of the serial port. Data link flow control characters are recognized regardless of whether their parity matches the serial port.

Default

-P0

This command controls checking of parity for XON, XOFF, the escape code sequence, and HP ACK characters. In command state, all command echoes and modem responses are sent to the DTE with parity that matches the serial port parity.

The -P command is used only for 10-bit data; it is ignored when the modem is set for 11-bit data.

Application   Microcom

-Q

Select Fallback Modulation Speeds

Description   AT-Q*n*

-Q0   Disables fallback from a V.32 or V.32bis MNP RELIABLE connection to an MNP RELIABLE 2400 or 1200 bps connection.

-Q1   Enables fallback from a V.32 or V.32bis MNP RELIABLE connection to an MNP RELIABLE 2400 bps connection.

-Q2   Enables fallback from a V.32 or V.32bis MNP RELIABLE connection to an MNP RELIABLE 2400 or 1200 bps connection.

Default

   -Q2

This command controls whether the modem can fall back from a V.32 or V.32bis MNP RELIABLE connection to an MNP RELIABLE 2400 or 1200 bps connection. Fallback may occur when poor telephone lines cause excessive MNP retransmissions.

Fallback from a V.32 or V.32bis MNP RELIABLE connection to a 4800 bps V.32 or V.32bis MNP RELIABLE is always enabled. V.22 is always used at 1200 bps, regardless of the B command setting.

Application   Microcom

-V

Split Serial Port Speed with Multiprotocol Auto-Answer

Description AT-V*n*

-V0   Enable V.23 split serial port speed within the multiprotocol auto-answer feature.

-V1   Disable V.23 split serial port speed within the multiprotocol auto-answer feature.

Default

-V0

This command determines whether the serial port uses split transmit-and-receive speed operation when using the multiprotocol auto-answer feature. %F0 must also be set.

Application Microcom

Related To %F

-X

Display Command Default Modification Switch Settings

Description   AT-X

This command displays the switch settings that were in effect the last time the modem was reset with switches 2 and 3 down.

Application   Microcom

$B

Set Serial Port Speed

Description AT$B*n*

n = 75, 300, 600, 1200, 2400, 4800, 9600, 19200, 38400, 57600, default = 38400

This command is issued to the local modem to set the serial port speed in bps as specified by the *n* argument.

Application Microcom

$D

Power-On Diagnostics

Description AT$D

This command resets the modem and initiates the power-on diagnostic test sequence.

Application Microcom

$G

Description AT$G*n*

$G0   Disables dial access security.

$G1   Enables dial access security.

Default

$G0

This command controls whether dial access security is used during logon operation.

Application Microcom

$H

Edit Dial Access Security Database

Description AT$H*n*

n = 1–20

This command allows the security administrator to enter valid users and passwords. The *n* parameter indicates a position in the dial access security database.

Application Microcom

$H

Help

Description AT$H

This command displays a multipage summary of all commands and registers used by the modem.

Application Practical

$I

Display Dial Access Security Database

Description   AT$I

This command displays the dial access security database.

Application   Microcom

$J

Clear Security Database and Telephone Numbers

Description   AT$J*n*

$J0   Clear the dial access security database and restore the default auto-logon sequences $L1–$L4.

$J0   Clear the dial access security database and restore the default auto-logon sequences $L1–$L4. The stored telephone numbers are also cleared.

Application   Microcom

Related To $L

$K

Select Configuration Switches

Description AT$K*n*

$K0   Enable all switch banks.

$K1   Disable all switch banks.

Default

$K0

This command controls whether the modem's configuration switches are enabled.

Application Microcom

$L

Description   AT$L*n*

n = 0–9

This command allows you to edit the logon sequences that will be used during NORMAL or RELIABLE connections.

Application   Microcom

Related To $P

$O

Originate/Answer Control

Description   AT$0*n*

$O0   Originate/answer mode selected by configuration switch.

$O1   Select originate mode.

$O2   Select answer mode.

Default

$O0

This command instructs the modem to determine its operating mode from an external switch or from software control.

Application   Microcom

$P

Set Logon Sequence Password

Description AT$P

Default

No password required

This command prompts you to enter the password that will be required to edit the logon sequences.

Application Microcom

$S

Asynchronous/Synchronous Switch Control

Description   AT$S*n*

$S0   Enable A/S switch.

$S1   Disable A/S switch, force asynchronous operation.

$S2   Disable A/S switch, force synchronous operation.

Default

$S0

This command enables or disables a configuration switch. The type of connection can be determined under software control or by using the switch.

Application   Microcom

$T

Talk/Data Switch Control

Description AT$T*n*

> $T0   Enable T/D switch.
>
> $T1   Disable T/D switch.
>
> $T2   Simulate T/D switch.
>
> **Default**
>
> > $T0

This command controls the talk/data (T/D) switch. The $T2 command toggles the hook setting of the modem.

Application Microcom

Related To $O

$V

Select Logon View Modem

Description AT$V*n*

$V0   Disables the passing through of data during the logon sequence.

$V1   Enables the passing through of data during the logon sequence.

Default

$V1

This command determines whether data is passed through from the remote system to the locate DTE during the logon sequence.

Application Microcom

$V

Display Remote Configuration ID

Description AT$V

This command displays a remote configuration identification code assigned at the factory.

Application Black Box

)B

Force a Leased Line Restoral

Description   AT)B

This command forces an attempted restoral of the leased line connection by the originating modem only during a dial backup connection. The)L1 command must be set.

Application   Microcom

Related To   )L

)C

Select Dial Backup in Answer Mode

Description   AT)C*n*

)C0   Disable dial backup in answer mode.

)C1   Enable dial backup in answer mode.

Default

)C0

This command allows the answering modem to dial the first stored telephone number while connected or attempting to establish a connection on a leased line.

When)C1 is selected, :N1 must also be set. The originating modem is able to answer an incoming ring when auto-answer is on and &V0 is set.

Application   Microcom

Related To   :N, &V

)E

Select Leased Line Compromise Equalizer

Description AT)E*n*

)E0   Disable the compromise equalizer for leased line connections when in V.32 or V.32bis mode.

)E1   Enable the compromise equalizer for all leased line connections.

Default

)E0

This command determines if the compromise equalizer will be used when the modem connects in V.32 or V.32bis mode on a leased line.

Application Microcom

)F

Display Leased Line EQM Values

Description AT)F

This command displays the maximum EQM (eye quality monitor) value. Possible return values range from 0 to 65535. The lower the quality of the phone line, the higher the number that is returned.

The modem continuously monitors the phone line connection and reports the poorest line condition value. The saved value is cleared when a new connection is made, or it may be cleared with the :Y command.

Application Microcom

Related To %L, %Q, :Y

)H

Set Automatic Dial Connection Restoral Time

Description   AT)H*n*

n = 0–255 minutes, default = 0

If a connection fails, this command specifies how long the local modem will attempt to reestablish the data line with the remote modem. This command is valid only during MNP RELIABLE connections.

Application   Microcom

)L

Leased Line Restoral

Description AT)L*n*

)L0   Do not attempt to restore the leased line connection.

)L1   Do attempt to restore the leased line connection.

Default

)L1

This command selects whether the modem will attempt to restore the leased line connection after the time specified by the)X command expires during a dial backup connection or if forced by the)B command. Both modems should have the save)L setting.

Application Microcom

Related To)B,)X

)M

Set Cellular Power Level Adjustment

Description   AT)M*n*

)M0   For central site modems: auto-adjustment (adjusts power level if remote modem is set to)M1). Use for MNP Class 10 modems that will connect to both cellular and noncellular modems.

)M1   For cellular site modems: forces adjustment of power level.

Default

)M0

This command enables power level adjustment during link negotiation for RELIABLE connections to accommodate the signalling requirements of cellular telephone equipment.

Application   Microcom

)P

MNP Leased Line Restoral

Description   AT)P*n*

)P0   Disabled.

)P1   Prevents data loss during leased line restoral.

Default

)P1

When this command is set, it enables two modems connected by leased line to establish a dial backup connection without data loss if the leased line connection fails. Both modems must have)P1, :N1, and)L1 set. Data loss is also prevented if the leased line connection is reestablished.

Application   Microcom

Related To   :N1,)L1

)W

Set Leased Line Carrier Time

Description AT)W*n*

n = 0–255 seconds, default = 20

If leased line restoral is enabled, this command sets the amount of time that the modem waits for a carrier while attempting a leased line restoral. If the restoral fails, the modem then attempts to reestablish the dial-backup connection.

Application Microcom

)X

Set Leased Line Retry Timer

Description   AT)X*n*

n = 0–60 minutes, default = 0

If leased line restoral is enabled, this command sets how long the originate modem will wait after a dial-backup connection is established before monitoring the leased line. If the leased line is usable, the modem attempts to reestablish the leased line connection.

Application   Microcom

)Y

Dial Backup Retry Timer

Description   AT)Y*n*

n = 0–255 seconds, default = 40

If the restoral of a leased line connection fails, this command sets how long the modem will wait for a carrier while trying to reestablish the dial-backup connection. If the timer expires, the modem hangs up and redials the first stored telephone number.

Application   Microcom

@C

CTS, DSR, CD Connect Message Control

Description AT@C*n*

@C0 Turns CTS, DSR, and CD on after the connect message is displayed.

@C1 Turns CTS, DSR, and CD on before the connect message is displayed.

Default

@C0

This command controls whether the modem activates the CTS, DSR, and CD control signals before or after the connect message is sent to the DTE. This command should be used in conjunction with the :T14 register.

Application Microcom

Related To :T14

:D

Manual Dial

Description AT:D*n*

:D0   Modem does not go off-hook when DTR is raised.

:D1   Modem goes off-hook in originate modem when DTR is raised. &D*n* must be set to 1, 2, or 3.

:D2   Modem goes off-hook in originate mode and dials the first stored telephone number when DTR is raised. &D*n* must be set to 1, 2, or 3.

Default

:D0

This command determines the action taken by the modem when the DTR signal is raised.

Application Microcom

Related To &D, :T18

Notes   **1.** When :D1 or :D2 is set, register :T18 must be 0.

:E

Select Compromise Equalizer

Description AT:E*n*

:E0   Disables the compromise equalizer only when the modem is in V.32 or V.32bis mode.

:E1   Enables the compromise equalizer.

Default

:E1

This command controls equalizer operation when the modem connects in V.32 or V.32bis mode. The :E0 setting is useful for direct line connections or PBX-to-PBX connections. The :E1 setting is useful for outside line-to-outside line or PBX-to-outside line connections.

Application Microcom

:G

Set Leased Line Auto-Retrain Counter

Description AT:G*n*

n = 0–255, default = 0

This command sets the maximum number of times the modem can retrain within the time specified by the :H command. If the retrain limit is reached and the originate modem has :N1 set and &V set to a value greater than 0, it attempts a dial-backup connection. Otherwise, the modem is forced on-hook.

Application Microcom

Related To :H, :N, &V

:H

Set Leased Line Auto-Retrain Window

Description   AT:H*n*

n = 0–255 minutes, default = 0

This command sets the maximum amount of time that the modem can perform retrains. If the retrain limit is reached and the originate modem has :N1 set and &V set to a value greater than 0, the modem attempts a dial-backup connection.

Application   Microcom

Related To   :G, :N, &V

:K

Select Kermit/UUCP Protocol Spoofing

Description　AT:K*n*

:K0　Disable Kermit and UUCP spoofing asynchronous protocols.

:K1　Enable Kermit spoofing asynchronous protocol.

:K2　Enable UUCP spoofing asynchronous protocol.

Default

:K0

This command selects the Kermit or UUCP spoofing asynchronous protocol. Both modems must use the same :K setting. These protocols are effective only during an MNP RELIABLE connection (with or without data compression), and are unavailable during DIRECT, NORMAL, or synchronous operation.

Application　Microcom

Related To　:Q

:N

Select Leased Line Dial Backup

Description AT:N*n*

:N0   Disables leased line dial backup
         mode.

:N1   Enables leased line dial backup mode.

Default

   :N1

This command determines whether the modem dials a stored telephone number to establish a connection when a leased line connection fails. Both modems should have the same :N setting.

Application Microcom

Related To)C

:Q

Set Kermit Mark Character

Description   AT:Q*n*

n = 0–31, default = 1

This command sets the mark character that the modem will use when the Kermit spoofing asynchronous protocol is enabled.

Application   Microcom

Related To   :K

:Y

Clear Maximum EQM

Description AT:Y

This command clears the saved maximum eye quality monitor (EQM) recorded during the connection and restarts the monitoring process.

Application Microcom

Related To %L, %O,)F

~H

Help

Description   AT~H*n*

$n = 0-9$

~H0   Enters interactive help mode.

~H*n*   Displays page *n* of the help text.

This command displays brief descriptions of all commands and registers used by the modem. All commands on the command line after ~H are ignored.

Application   Telebit

~L

Display Stored Telephone Numbers

Description   AT~L

This command displays the two telephone numbers stored in the modem's nonvolatile memory.

Application   Telebit

Related To   ~N, ~V

~M

Modify Stored Profile

Description　AT~M*n*

~M0　　Modify stored profile 0.

~M1　　Modify stored profile 1.

This command modifies the specified profile without affecting the current profile. Commands that follow ~M on the same command line are written directly to the specified profile.

Application　Telebit

~N

Store Telephone Number

Description AT~N*n*=*s*

n = telephone number memory location to use

s = dial string to be saved

~N*n*=*s* Write dial strings to telephone number memory *n*

n = 0–1, *s* ≤ 38 characters

This command stores a telephone dial string in nonvolatile memory. The string may contain any character that is valid in a normal dial string. It must be the last command on the command line. Nondial characters are removed before the string is stored.

Application Telebit

Related To ~L, ~V

~U

Update System Password

Description   ATU

This command is used to change the system callback security password. The modem will prompt for the current and new passwords.

Application   Telebit

Related To   U, S46

~V

View Configuration Profiles

Description AT~V*n*

n = 0–1, number of configuration profile

&V*n*   Display profile *n*

This command instructs the modem to return the values of selected configuration parameters and S registers in the current and stored profiles. Stored telephone numbers are also displayed.

After receiving this command, the modem will return the current profile parameters. Modems equipped with nonvolatile memory will additionally return stored profiles. The format and contents of the information displayed vary, depending on the modem model.

Application Telebit

Related To ~L, ~N

#A

Select Fax Modem Answer Mode

Description   AT#A*n*

#A0   Answer as a data modem only.

#A1   Answer as a fax modem only.

#A2   Automatically detect data and fax calls and answer appropriately.

Default

#A2

This command selects the default answer mode for the modem. It is not supported in Sendfax modems.

Application   Sierra-based fax modems

#B

Select Initial Fax Transmission Speed

Description   AT#B*n*

#B4	Set initial fax transmission speed to 2400 bps.
#B5	Set initial fax transmission speed to 4800 bps.
#B6	Set initial fax transmission speed to 7200 bps.
#B7	Set initial fax transmission speed to 9600 bps.

Default

   #B7

This command selects the highest initial fax transmission speed that will be proposed by the sending modem. The final transmission speed may be lower, depending on the capabilities of the receiving fax terminal.

Application   Sierra-based fax modems

#D

Fax Transmitter Control

Description AT#D*n*

#D0   Turn transmitter off.

#D1   Turn on fax V.21 transmitter.

#D2   Turn on fax 2400 bps transmitter. (V.27 BAK)

#D3   Turn on fax 4800 bps transmitter. (V.27 BAK)

#D4   Turn on fax 9600 bps transmitter. (V.29 BAK)

Default

#D0

This command turns the fax transmitter on or off.

Application Sierra-based fax modems

Notes   **1.** This command is not supported on Sierra internally-coded controllers.

#E

Select Received HDLC Frame Display

Description   AT#E*n*

#E0   Disable the display of received HDLC frames.

#E1   Display received HLDC frames in binary format.

#E2   Display received HLDC frames as 2-digit ASCII hexadecimal numbers.

Default

#E0

This command determines the format in which HDLC frames received from the remote fax terminal are displayed.

Application   Sierra-based fax modems

#F

Select Fax Modem Operating Mode

Description AT#F*n*

#F0   Configure modem for operation as a data modem.

#F1   Configure modem for operation as a fax modem. Serial port speed must be 19200 bps.

Default

#F0

This command initiates and terminates fax operation. It must appear as the last command in a command line.

Application Sierra-based fax modems

Related To +FCLASS

#K

Select Serial Port Flow Control

Description AT#K*n*

#K0   Disable serial port flow control.

#K3   Unidirectional CTS flow control. Thc modem uses the CTS line to control data transfer from the DTE. The DTE cannot control data transfer from the modem.

#K4   Unidirectional XON/XOFF flow control. The modem uses the XOFF character to suspend and the XON character to resume data transfer from the DTE. The DTE cannot control data transfer from the modem.

Default

#K3

This command selects the type of flow control that will be used on the DTE-to-modem serial port connection.

Application Sierra-based fax modems

#P

Set Transmitted Page Count

Description AT#T*n*

n = 1–255, number of pages to transmit

This command specifies the number of pages that are to be transmitted.

Application Sierra-based fax modems

#R

Set Outgoing Fax Resolution

Description AT#R*n*

    #R0   Transmit document using normal resolution.

    #R1   Transmit document using fine resolution.

Default

    #R0

This command determines the resolution that is used when documents are transmitted to a remote fax machine.

Application Sierra-based fax modems

#T

Select Fax Test Mode

Description   AT#T*n*

#T0   End the test in progress.

#T1   Start test mode 1.

Default

#T0

In test mode 1, the modem dials a remote fax terminal and automatically sends a message stored in EPROM. Received HLDC frames are displayed in hexadecimal format as 2-digit ASCII characters.

Application   Sierra-based fax modems

+FAA

Select Fax Auto Answer Mode

Description AT+FAA=*n*

+FAA=0   Answer as a fax modem only using the mode set by the
+FCLASS command.

+FAA=1   Automatically detect data and fax calls and answer appropriately.

Default

+FA A=0

This command determines whether the modem will answer an incoming call
and automatically determine how it should configure itself. If the DTE
switches modes, it will modify the +FCLASS parameter appropriately.

Application SP-2388-A Class 2, SP-2388-B Class 2.0.

+FAE

Select Fax Auto Answer Mode

Description   AT+FAE*n*

+FAE=0   Answer as a Class 1 fax modem only.

+FAE=1   Automatically detect data and fax calls and answer appropriately.

This command determines whether the modem will answer an incoming call and automatically determines how it should configure itself. If the DTE switches modes, it will modify the +FCLASS parameter appropriately.

Application   Zoom

+FAXERR

Fax T.30 Error Response

Description   AT+FAXERR=*n*

n = hang-up status code

This message indicates the cause of a hang up and is set by the modem at the conclusion of each session. The modem resets this parameter to 0 at the beginning of each session. Values for *n* are listed in the entry for the +FHNG response.

Application   SP-2388-A Class 2

+FBADLIN

Bad Line Threshold

Description AT+FBADLIN=*n*

$n = 0–255$

This command sets one of the parameters in the algorithm used by the modem to determine if the copy quality is acceptable. If the number of lines received with a bad pixel count exceeds this number, the error rate is deemed to be too high. Setting this to 0 disables this form of error checking.

Application SP-2388-A Class 2

Related To +FBADMUL, +FRQ

+FBADMUL

Error Threshold Multiplier

Description   AT+FBADMUL=n

$n = 0–255$

This command sets one of the parameters in the algorithm used by the modem to determine if the copy quality is acceptable. The number of lines received with a bad pixel count is multiplied by this number. If the result exceeds the number of lines in the page, then the error rate is deemed to be too high. Setting this to 0 disables this form of error checking.

Application   SP-2388-A Class 2

Related To   +FBADLIN, +FRQ

+FBO

Select Data Bit Order

Description   AT+FBO=*n*

+FBO=0   Direct bit order for phases B, C, and D.

+FBO=1   Reversed bit order for phase C. Direct bit order for phases B and D.

+FBO=2   Direct bit order for phase C. Reversed bit order for phases B and D.

+FBO=3   Reversed bit order for phases B, C, and D.

Default

+FBO=0

This command selects the bitmapping between the data sent between the DTE and the modem and the data sent over the communications channel.

With direct bit order, the first bit of each byte transferred from the DTE to the modem corresponds to the first bit of each byte transferred over the data link. With reversed bit order, the first bit of each byte transferred from the DTE to the modem corresponds to the last bit of each byte transferred over the data link.

The setting of this parameter does not affect the bit order of the control and framing characters generated by the modem.

Application   SP-2388-B Class 2.0

Related To   +FBO

+FBOR

Select Data Bit Order

Description AT+FBOR=*n*

+FBOR=0   Direct bit order for phases B, C, and D.

+FBOR=1   Reversed bit order for phase C. Direct bit order for phases B and D.

+FBOR=2   Direct bit order for phase C. Reversed bit order for phases B and D.

+FBOR=3   Reversed bit order for phases B, C, and D.

Default

+FBOR=0

This command selects the bitmapping between the data sent between the DTE and the modem and the data sent over the communications channel.

With direct bit order, the first bit of each byte transferred from the DTE to the modem corresponds to the first bit of each byte transferred over the data link. With reversed bit order, the first bit of each byte transferred from the DTE to the modem corresponds to the last bit of each byte transferred over the data link.

The setting of this parameter does not affect the bit order of the control and framing characters generated by the modem.

Application SP-2388-A Class 2

Related To +FBO

+FBS

Query Buffer Size

Description AT+FBS?

This read-only command allows the DTE to query the modem to determine the size of its data buffers. The values are reported in the form *tbs,rbs*, where *tbs* is the size of the transmit buffer and *rbs* is the size of the receive buffer. The size is reported in hexadecimal. No minimum size is mandated.

Application SP-2388-B Class 2.0

Related To +FBUF

+FBU

Select HDLC Frame Reporting

Description AT+FBU=*n*

+FBU= 0   Disable HDLC frame reporting.

+FBU= 1   Enable HDLC frame reporting.

Default

+FBU–0

This command enables the reporting of phase B and D frames to the DTE as they are sent and received.

Application SP-2388-B Class 2.0

Related To +FBUG

+FBUF

Query Buffer Size

Description   AT+FBUF?

This read-only command allows the DTE to query the modem to determine the size of its data buffer. The response is in the form *bs,xoft,xont,bc*, where *bs* is the size of the buffer, *xoft* represents the number of bytes required to trigger an XOFF, *xont* represents the number of bytes at which XON will be issued after an XOFF, and *bc* is the current buffer byte count. No minimum size is mandated.

Application   SP-2388-A Class 2

Related To   +FBS

+FBUG

Select HDLC Frame Reporting

Description   AT+FBUG=*n*

+FBUG=0   Disable HDLC frame reporting.

+FBUG=1   Enable HDLC frame reporting.

Default

+FBUG=0

This command enables the reporting of phase B and D frames to the DTE as they are sent and received.

Application   SP-2388-A Class 2

Related To   +FBU

+FCERROR

Class 1 Error Code Response

Description   AT+FCERROR (verbose)

AT+F4 (numeric)

If the modem detects a data carrier other than that specified by the +FRM or +FRH command, it sends this response to the DTE.

Application   EIA/TIA-578 Class 1

+FCC

Set DCE Fax Capabilities

Description AT+FCC=*s*

s = T.30 session subparameter codes

This command allows the DTE to sense and constrain the capabilities of the fax modem from the choices defined in CCITT T.30. When the DTE modifies +FDCC, the modem will copy this into the +FDIS command. The T.30 session subparameter codes are defined in the entry for the +FDCC command.

Application SP-2388-B Class 2.0

Related To +FIS, +FDCC, +FDIS

+FCFR

Confirmation to Receive Response

Description   AT+FCFR

The local modem sends this response to the DTE after receiving an acceptable TCF training signal and a valid DCS signal from the remote fax terminal.

Application   SP-2388-A Class 2

+FCI

Report Received CSI Response

Description   +FCI:"*s*"

  s = called station ID

  This response reports the CSI response received from the called station.

Application   SP-2388-B Class 2.0

Related To   +FCSI

+FCIG

Set Local Polling ID String

Description   AT+FCIG=*s*

s = 20 ASCII characters

This command sets the local polling ID string if the specified string is not null. The string is blank-padded to fill 20 characters.

Application   SP-2388-A Class 2

Related To   +FPI

+FCIG

Report Remote ID Response

Description   AT+FCIG:"*s*"

s = called station ID

This command reports the CIG response received from the called station.

Application   SP-2388-A Class 2

Related To   +FPI

+FCLASS

Service Class Identification and Control

Description

AT+FCLASS?

Query current class.

AT+FCLASS=?

Query modem class capabilities.

AT+FCLASS=n

Set modem class.

This command is used to set and query the fax modem's operating mode and capabilities. The modem will respond as follows:

1   EIA/TIA-578 Class 1

2   Reserved for manufacturers. (SP-2388-A Class 2)

2.0   TIA/EIA-592 Class 2.0

Application   EIA/TIA-578 Class 1, SP-2388-A Class 2, SP-2388-B Class 2.0

+FCO

Fax Connection Response

Description   +FCO

This response is issued by the modem to indicate that a link has been established with the remote fax terminal. It is sent by the local modem to the DTE after the first HDLC flags in the first HDLC frame are received.

Application   SP-2388-B Class 2.0

Related To   +FCON

+FCON

Fax Connection Response

Description +FCON

This response is issued by the modem to indicate that a link has been established with the remote fax terminal. It is sent by the local modem to the DTE after the first HDLC flags in the first HDLC frame are received.

Application SP-2388-A Class 2

Related To +FCO

+FCQ

Set Quality Checking

Description AT+FCQ=*n*

+FCQ=0   The modem performs no quality checking.

+FCQ=1   The modem checks one-dimensional phase C data.

+FCQ=2   The modem checks one- and two-dimensional phase C data and makes line substitutions.

This command enables both copy quality checking and bad line regeneration.

Application SP-2388-A Class 2

+FCQ

Enable Quality Checking and Correction

Description   `AT+FCQ=r,t`

r,t as defined below.

r   **Action**

0   Disable received data quality checking.

1   Receive quality checking is enabled. The modem determines the post-page message and stores it in the +FPS parameter.

2   Receive quality correction is enabled. The modem determines the post-page message and stores it in the +FPS parameter. The modem will detect and correct errors in received data.

t   **Action**

0   Disable transmit data quality checking.

1   Transmit quality checking is enabled. The modem will verify T.4 or T.6 compliance and return a CAN to the DTE if errors are detected.

2   Transmit quality correction is enabled. The modem will detect and correct errors in data before transmission.

Default

+FCQ=1,0

This command enables both copy quality checking and bad line regeneration. The *r* argument determines the action taken on data the modem receives from the remote fax terminal and sends to the DTE. The *t* argument determines the action taken on data the modem receives from the DTE and sends to the remote fax terminal.

Application   SP-2388-B Class 2.0

Related To   +FCQ

+FCR

Set Capability to Receive

Description AT+FCR=*n*

+FCR=0 The modem will not receive message data and will not be able to poll a remote device. This can be used when the modem has insufficient buffer space.

+FCR=1 The modem can receive message data.

This command specifies the modem's capability to receive. This parameter is examined during phase A and phase D.

Application SP-2388-A Class 2, SP-2388-B Class 2.0

+FCS

Report Current Session Response

Description   AT+FCS:s

s = T.30 session subparameter codes

The modem sends this response to report the negotiated parameters for the current session. The session subparameter codes are shown in the table listed for the +FDCC response.

Application   SP-2388-B Class 2.0

Related To   +FDCS

+FCSI

Report Received CSI Response

Description +FCSI:"*s*"

s = called station ID

This response reports the CSI response received from the called station.

Application SP-2388-A Class 2

Related To +FCI

+FCT

Set Phase C Response Timeout

Description   AT+FCT=*n*

n = 0–FFh, time in 1-second increments. Default = 1Eh (30 seconds)

This command sets the length of time the modem will wait for a command after the end of data when transmitting in phase C, or the length of time it will wait for data after a +FDT command. If the timeout expires, the modem will send EOP to the remote fax terminal.

Application   SP-2388-B Class 2.0

Related To   +FPHCTO

+FCTCRTY

ECM Retry Count

Description AT+FCTCRTY=*n*

n = 0–255, units of 4 retries, default = 0

This command sets the number of retries that will be performed during error-control mode operations.

Application SP-2388-A Class 2

Related To +FRY

+FDCC

Set DCE Fax Capabilities

Description AT+FDCC=*s*

s = T.30 session subparameter codes

This command allows the DTE to sense and constrain the capabilities of the fax modem from the choices defined in CCITT T.30. When the DTE modifies +FDCC the modem will copy this into the +FDIS command. The T.30 session subparameter codes are shown in the following table.

Label	Function	Values	Description
VR	Vertical resolution	0	Normal, 98 lpi
		1	Fine, 196 lpi
BR	Data transfer speed[2]	0	2400 bps, V.27ter
		1	4800 bps, V.27ter
		2[1]	7200 bps, V.29 or V.17
		3[1]	9600 bps, V.29 or V.17
		4[1]	12000 bps, V.33 or V.17
		5[1]	14400 bps, V.33 or V.17
WD	Page width	0	1728 pixels in 215 mm
		1[1]	2048 pixels in 255 mm
		2[1]	2432 pixels in 303 mm
		3[1]	1216 pixels in 151 mm
		4[1]	864 pixels in 107 mm
LN	Page length	0	A4, 297 mm
		1[1]	B4, 364 mm
		2[1]	Unlimited length
DF	Data compression format	0	1-dimensional, modified Huffman

Label	Function	Values	Description
		1^1	1-dimensional, modified Read
		2^1	2-dimensional, uncompressed
		3^1	2-dimensional, modified Read
EC	Error correction	0	Disable ECM
		1^1	Enable error correction mode, 64 bytes/frame
		2^1	Enable error correction mode, 256 bytes/frame
BF	Binary file transfer	0	Disable binary file transfer
		1^1	Enable binary file transfer
ST	Scan time per line	0	0 ms
		1	5 ms
		2	10 ms normal, 5 ms fine
		3	10 ms
		4	20 ms normal, 10 ms fine
		5	20 ms
		6	40 ms normal, 20 ms fine
		7	40 ms

[1] Optional

[2] The encoding specified for the DIS frame in CCITT T.30 does not allow all speeds to be specified exactly. The identification of some BR speeds will therefore be manufacturer-specific.

Application SP-2388-A Class 2

Related To +FDIS, +FCC, +FIS

+FDCS

Set Current Session Parameters

Description   AT+FDCS=*s*

s = T.30 session subparameter codes

Default

All session subparameter codes set to 0.

This command is used to set the negotiated parameters for the current session. All session subparameter codes are set to 0 during initialization. Allowable session subparameter codes are shown in the table listed for the +FDCC response.

Application   SP-2388-A Class 2, SP-2388-B Class 2.0

Related To   +FCS

+FDCS

Report Current Session Parameters Response

Description   AT+FDCS:*s*

s = T.30 session subparameter codes

The modem sends this response to report the negotiated parameters for the current session. The session subparameter codes are shown in the table listed for the +FDCC response.

Application   SP-2388-A Class 2

Related To   +FCS

+FDFFC

Data Compression Format Conversion Error Handling

Description AT+FDFFC=*n*

+FDFFC=0   Disable mismatch checking.

+FDFFC=1   Enable mismatch checking.

This command enables mismatch checking during data compression format conversion. If +FDFFC=1 and a mismatch is found, the modem acts as if a +FK command has been issued.

Application SP-2388-A Class 2

Related To +FFC, +FLNFC, +FVRFC, +FWDFC

+FDIS

Set Current Session Negotiation Parameters

Description   AT+FDIS=*s*

s = T.30 session subparameter codes

This command allows the DTE to sense and constrain the capabilities used for the current session. The DCE uses the specified parameters to generate DIS or DTC messages directly. Allowable session subparameter codes are shown in the table listed for the +FDCC response.

Application   SP-2388-A Class 2

Related To   +FIS

+FDIS

Remote Fax Capabilities Response

Description AT+FDIS:s

s = T.30 session subparameter codes

This response reports the T.30 session parameter frames as directed by the session parameter codes shown in the table listed for the +FDCC response.

Application SP-2388-A Class 2

Related To +FIS

+FDM

Transition to Data Mode

Description AT+FDM

The modem issues this response to indicate that the calling device is a data modem.

Application SP-2388-B Class 2.0

+FDR

Receive Phase C Data

Description AT+FDR

This command initiates or continues the reception of phase C data. The modem will report the negotiated T.30 parameters with the remote ID and NSS frame data if available.

Application SP-2388-A Class 2, SP-2388-B Class 2.0

+FDT

Transmit Phase C Data

Description   AT+FDT[=]n

n = DF, VR, WD, LN subparameters

In phase B, the +FDT command instructs the modem to proceed with negotiation and to send the DCS message to the remote fax terminal. In phase C, this command begins or continues the transmission of phase C data. The subparameter codes are defined in the table listed for the +FDCC response.

Application   SP-2388-A Class 2

+FDT

Transmit Phase C Data

Description AT+FDT

This command instructs the modem to transmit a phase C page. It is issued at the beginning of each page, either in phase B or phase D. When the modem is ready to accept the phase C data from the DTE, it will send negotiation responses and the CONNECT message to the DTE.

Application SP-2388-B Class 2.0

+FDTC

Remote Capabilities Response

Description   +FDTC: *s*

s = T.30 session subparameter codes

This response reports the T.30 session parameter frames as directed by the session parameter codes shown in the table listed for the +FDCC response. This response is used when the remote fax terminal wants to poll.

Application   SP-2388-A Class 2

Related To   +FTC

+FEA

Set Phase C Receive EOL Alignment

Description   AT+FEA=*n*

+FEA=0   EOL patterns are bit-aligned as received.

+FEA=1   EOL patters are byte-aligned by the modem with the necessary zero fill bits inserted.

Default

+FEA=0

This command determines whether EOL patterns will be bit-aligned as received or zero-filled and byte-aligned per T.30.

Application   SP-2388-B Class 2.0

Related To   +FREL

+FECM

Enable Error Corretion Mode

Description   AT+FECM=*n*

AT+FECM=0   Disable error control.

AT+FECM=1   Enable error correction, 64 bytes/frame.

AT+FECM=2   Enable error correction, 256 bytes/frame.

This command enables the error correction mode to be used during the fax session.

Application   SP-2388-A Class 2

+FET

End the Page or Document

Description   AT+FET=*n*

n = 0–15

This command ends the page or document that has been transmitted. For a non-error-control operation, this command causes the modem to append RTC as needed and enter phase D by sending the selected T.30 post-page message code.

Application   SP-2388-A Class 2

+FET

Post-Page Message Response

+FET:*n*

n = as shown in table

PPM Code	T.30 Mnemonic	Description
0	[PPS-]MPS	Another page next, same document
1	[PPS-]EOM	Another document next
2	[PPS-]EOP	No more pages or documents
3	PPS-NULL	Another partial page next
4	[PPS-]PRI-MPS	Another page, procedure interrupt
5	[PPS-]PRI-EOM	Another document, procedure interrupt
6	[PPS-]PRI-EOP	All done, procedure interrupt

This response is generated by the local fax modem after the end of phase C reception upon receipt of the post-page message from the remote fax terminal. The +FET:*n* message is generated when the command +FDR is executed.

SP-2388-B Class 2.0 modems return only PPM codes 0–2. PRI codes are converted to their non-PRI equivalents.

SP-2388-A Class 2, SP-2388-B Class 2.0

+FFC

Format Conversion

Description　AT+FFC=*vrc,dfc,lnc,wdc*

vrc,dfc,lnc,wdc values defined in table.

vrc	Definition
0	Disable vertical resolution checking
1	Enable vertical resolution checking.
2	Enable vertical resolution conversion for one-dimensionally encoded data.
3	Enable vertical resolution conversion for two-dimensionally encoded data.
dfc	**Definition**
0	Disable data format checking.
1	Enable data format checking.
2	Enable data format conversion.
lnc	**Definition**
0	Disable page length format checking.
1	Enable page length checking.
2	Enable page length conversion for one-dimensionally encoded data.
3	Enable page length conversion for two-dimensionally encoded data.
wdc	**Definition**
0	Disable page width data format checking.
1	Enable page width checking.
2	Enable page width conversion.

This command sets the modem's response to a mismatch between the format of the phase C data received and the format preferred by the DTE.

Application   SP-2388-B Class 2.0

Related To   +FDFFC, +FLNFC, +FVRFC, +FWDFC

+FHNG

Call Termination Status Response

Description +FHNG: *n*

n=hang up code from table.

n	Class 1 Definition
	Call Placement and Termination
0	Normal and proper end of connection
1	Ring detect without successful handshake
2	Call aborted from +FK or <CAN>
3	No loop current
	Transmit Phase A and Miscellaneous Errors
10	Unspecified phase A error
11	No answer (T.30 T1 timeout)
	Transmit Phase B Hangup Codes
20	Unspecified phase B error
21	Remote cannot receive or send
22	Command received error in transmit phase B
23	Command received invalid command received
24	Response received error
25	DCS sent three times without response
26	DIS/DTC received three times; DCS not recognized
27	Failure to train
28	Response received invalid response
	Transmit Phase C Hangup Codes
40	Unspecified phase C error
43	DTE to DCE data underflow

n	Class 1 Definition
	Transmit Phase D Hangup Codes
50	Unspecified phase D error
51	Response received error
52	No response to MPS repeated three times
53	Invalid response to MPS
54	No response to EOP repeated three times
55	Invalid response to EOP
56	No response to EOM repeated three times
57	Invalid response to EOM
58	Unable to continue after PIN or PIP
	Receive Phase B Hangup Codes
70	Unspecified receive phase B error
71	Response received error
72	Command received error
73	T.30 T2 timeout, expected page not received
74	T.30 T1 timeout after EOM received
	Receive Phase C Hangup Codes
90	Unspecified receive phase C error
91	Missing EOL after 5 seconds
92	Unused code
93	DCE to DTE buffer overflow
94	Bad CRC or frame (ECM or BFT modes)
	Receive Phase D Hangup Codes
00	Unspecified receive phase D error
01	Response received invalid response received
02	Command received invalid response received
03	Unable to continue after PIN or PIP

This response is sent to the DTE by the modem to indicate the status of call termination. The response is also stored in the +FAXERR parameter.

The hangup codes returned by SP-2388-B Class 2.0 modems are specified in the entry for the +FHS command.

Application   SP-2388-A Class 2

Related To   +FHS

+FHR

Report Received HDLC Frame Response

Description   +FHR:

This response reports the HDLC frame received. The frame is returned as a series of two-character ASCII character pairs representing the bytes in hex notation. Flags are removed.

Application   SP 2388-A Class 2, SP-2388-B Class 2.0

+FHS

Call Termination Status Response

Description   AT+FHS?

This read-only parameter indicates the cause of a hangup. The +FHS parameter is set by the modem at the conclusion of a fax session. The modem resets this parameter to 0 when a new session begins. The value returned is interpreted according to the table shown here. (All values are in hexadecimal.)

n	Definition
	Call Placement and Termination
00h	Normal and proper end of connection
01h	Ring detect without successful handshake
02h	Call aborted from +FK or AN
03h	No loop current
04h	Ringback detected, no answer (timeout)
05h	Ringback detected, answer without CED
	Transmit Phase A and Miscellaneous Errors
10h	Unspecified phase A error
11h	No answer (T.30 T1 timeout)
	Transmit Phase B Hangup Codes
20h	Unspecified phase B error
21h	Remote cannot receive or send
22h	Command received error in transmit phase B
23h	Invalid command received
24h	Response received error
25h	DCS sent three times without response
26h	DIS/DTC received three times; DCS not recognized
27h	Failure to train

n	Definition
28h	Invalid response
	Transmit Phase C Hangup Codes
40h	Unspecified phase C error
41h	Unspecified image format error
42h	Image conversion error
43h	DTE to DCE data underflow
44h	Unrecognized transparent data
45h	Image error, line length wrong
46h	Image error, page length wrong
47h	Image error, wrong compression code
	Transmit Phase D Hangup Codes
50h	Unspecified phase D error
51h	Response received error
52h	No response to MPS repeated three times
53h	Invalid response to MPS
54h	No response to EOP repeated three times
55h	Invalid response to EOP
56h	No response to EOM repeated three times
57h	Invalid response to EOM
58h	Unable to continue after PIN or PIP
	Receive Phase B Hangup Codes
70h	Unspecified receive phase B error
71h	Response received error
72h	Command received error
73h	T.30 T2 timeout, expected page not received
74h	T.30 T1 timeout after EOM received
	Receive Phase C Hangup Codes
90h	Unspecified receive phase C error
91h	Missing EOL after 5 seconds

n	Definition
92h	Bad CRC or frame (ECM or BFT modes)
93h	DCE to DTE buffer overflow
	Receive Phase D Hang-Up Codes
A0h	Unspecified receive phase D error
A1h	Response received invalid response received
A2h	Command received invalid response received
A3h	Unable to continue after PIN or PIP

Application SP-2388-B Class 2.0

Related To +FHNG

+FHT

Report Transmitted HDLC Frame

Description   +FHT: s

This response reports the transmitted HDLC frame. The frame is returned as a series of two-character ASCII character pairs representing the bytes in hex notation. Flags are removed.

Application   SP-2388-A Class 2, SP-2388-B Class 2.0

+FIE

Procedure Interrupt Enable

Description   AT+FIE=*n*

+FIE=0   Procedure interrupt requests from the remote fax terminal are ignored.

+FIE=1   Procedure interrupt requests from the remote fax terminal are accepted.

Default

+FIE=0

This command enables the local modem's response to a procedure interrupt request from the remote fax terminal.

Application   SP-2388-B Class 2.0

+FIP

Initialize Fax Parameters

Description   `AT+FIP[=n]`

n = optional profile number

This command causes the modem to reset all Class 2 fax parameters to their manufacturer default settings. This command does not affect the +FCLASS setting.

The *n* argument may be used to select from more than one manufacturer-defined default profile.

Application   SP-2388-B Class 2.0

+FIS

Set Current Session Negotiation Parameters

Description   AT+FIS=*s*

s = T.30 session subparameter codes

This command allows the DTE to sense and constrain the capabilities used for the current session. The DCE uses the specified parameters to generate DIS or DTC messages directly. Allowable session subparameter codes are shown in the table listed for the +FDCC response.

Application   SP-2388-B Class 2.0

Related To   +FDIS

+FIS

Remote Fax Capabilities Response

Description   AT+FIS:*s*

s = T.30 session subparameter codes

This response reports the T.30 session parameter frames as directed by the session parameter codes shown in the table listed for the +FDCC response.

Application   SP-2388-B Class 2.0

Related To   +FDIS

+FK

Terminate Fax Session

Description AT+FK

This command instructs the modem to terminate the session in an orderly manner. The modem sends a DCN message at the next opportunity, then hangs up.

Application SP-2388-A Class 2

Related To +FKS

+FKS

Terminate Fax Session

Description   AT+FKS

This command instructs the modem to terminate the session in an orderly manner. The modem sends a DCN message at the next opportunity, then hangs up.

Application   SP-2388-B Class 2.0

Related To   +FK

+FLI

Set Local ID String

Description AT+FLI="*s*"

s = 20-character ASCII string

Sets the local ID string that will be used in the TSI/CSI frames.

Application SP-2388-B Class 2.0

Related To +FLID

+FLID

Set Local ID String

Description   AT+FLID="*s*"

s = 20-character ASCII string

Sets the local ID string that will be used in the TSI/CSI frames.

Application   SP-2388-A Class 2

Related To   +FLI

+FLNFC

Page Length Format Conversion

Description AT+FLNFC=*n*

+FLNFC=0 Disable mismatch checking.

+FLNFC=1 Enable mismatch checking.

+FLNFC=2 Enable mismatch checking for two-dimensionally encoded data. One-dimensionally encoded data is automatically converted to a compatible format.

This command determines the modem's response to a mismatch between the page length negotiated for the session and the page length desired by the DTE.

If checking is disabled, a mismatch will require clipping or scaling. If +FLNFC=1 is enabled, a mismatch will cause the modem to act as if a +FK command has been received. If +FLNFC=2 is enabled, a mismatch in two-dimensionally encoded data will cause the modem to act as if a +FK command has been received.

Application SP-2388-A Class 2

Related To +FFC, +FDFFC, +FVRFC, +FWDFC

+FLO

Select Flow Control

Description AT+FLO=*n*

+FLO=0   Disable XON/XOFF and RTS/CTS flow control.

+FLO=1   Enable bidirectional XON/XOFF flow control.

+FLO=2   Enable bidirectional hardware flow control using the RTS/CTS (133/106).

This command enables the type of flow control that will be used locally between the DTE and the modem.

Application SP-2388-B Class 2.0

+FLP

Indicate Document to Poll

Description AT+FLP=*n*

+FLP=0   The DTE has no document to poll.

+FLP=1   The DTE has a document ready for polling.

Default

+FLP=0

This command informs the modem if the DCE has a document ready for polling. If so, the modem reports this to the remote fax terminal in the DIS frame. After a polled document is sent, the modem automatically resets this parameter to 0.

Application SP-2388-B Class 2.0

Related To +FSP, +FLPL, +FSPL

+FLPL

Indicate Document to Poll

Description   AT+FLPL=*n*

+FLPL=0   The DTE has no document to poll.

+FLPL=1   The DTE has a document ready for polling.

Default

+FLPL=0

This command informs the modem if the DCE has a document ready for polling. If so, the modem reports this to the remote fax terminal in the DIS frame. After a polled document is sent, the modem will automatically reset this parameter to 0.

Application   SP-2388-A Class 2

Related To   +FSPL, +FLP, +FSP

+FMDL

Request Modem Model

Description `AT+FMDL?`

This command requests the modem to return its product identification. The modem responds with text information as determined by the manufacturer. The total number of characters returned will not exceed 2048.

Application SP-2388-A Class 2

Related To +FMM

+FMFR

Request Modem Manufacturer

Description   AT+FMFR?

This command requests the modem to return its manufacturer identification. The modem responds with text information as determined by the manufacturer. The total number of characters returned will not exceed 2048.

Application   SP-2388-A Class 2

Related To   +FMI

+FMI

Request Modem Manufacturer

Description   AT+FMI?

This command requests the modem to return its manufacturer identification. The modem responds with text information as determined by the manufacturer. The total number of characters returned will not exceed 2048.

Application   SP-2388-B Class 2.0

Related To   +FMI

+FMINSP

Set Minimum Phase C Speed

Description   AT+FMINSP=*n*

n = speed as defined for the BR subparameter codes

0   2400 bps, V.27ter

1   4800 bps, V.27ter

2   7200 bps, V.29 or V.17

3   9600 bps, V.29 or V.17

Default

+FMINSP=0

This command sets the lowest negotiable speed that will be permitted for a session.

Application   SP-2388-A Class 2

Related To   +FMS

+FMM

Request Modem Model

Description AT+FMM?

This command requests the modem to return its product identification. The modem responds with text information as determined by the manufacturer. The total number of characters returned will not exceed 2048.

Application SP-2388-B Class 2.0

Related To +FMDL

+FMR

Request Modem Revision

Description AT+FMR?

This command causes the modem to return its revision identification to the DTE. The total number of characters returned will not exceed 2048.

Application SP-2388-B Class 2.0

Related To +FREV

+FMS

Set Minimum Phase C Speed

Description   AT+FMS=*n*

n = speed as defined for the BR subparameter codes

0	2400 bps, V.27ter
1	4800 bps, V.27ter
2	7200 bps, V.29 or V.17
3	9600 bps, V.29 or V.17
4	12000 bps, V.33 or V.17
5	14400 bps, V.33 or V.17

Default

+FMS=0

This command sets the lowest negotiable speed that will be permitted for a session.

Application   SP-2388-B Class 2.0

Related To   +FMINSP

+FNC

Report NSC Response

Description   AT+FNC:*s*

s = NSC string

This command returns the nonstandard command (NSC) facsimile information field. The field is returned as a series of two-character ASCII character
pairs representing the bytes in hex notation. Flags are removed.

Application   SP-2388-B Class 2.0

Related To   +FNSC

+FNF

Report NSF Response

Description AT+FNF:*s*

s = NSF string

This command returns the nonstandard facilities (NSF) facsimile information field. The field is returned as a series of two-character ASCII character pairs representing the bytes in hex notation. Flags are removed.

Application SP-2388-B Class 2.0

Related To +FNSF

+FNR

Negotiation Message Reporting Control

Description `AT+FNR=rpr,tpr,idr,nsr`

rpr,tpr,idr,nsr values defined in table.

rpr	Definition
0	Received parameters are not reported. +FIS: and +FTC reports are suppressed.
1	Received parameters are reported. +FIS: and +FTC reports are generated.
tpr	**Definition**
0	Transmit parameters are not reported. +FCS: reports are suppressed. (+FCS parameter is still loaded.)
1	Transmit parameters are reported. +FCS: reports are generated.
idr	**Definition**
0	ID strings are not reported. +FTI:, +FCI:, and +FPI reports are suppressed.
1	ID strings are reported. +FTI:, +FCI:, and +FPI reports are generated.
nsr	**Definition**
0	Nonstandard frames are not reported. +FNF:, +FNS:, and +FNC: reports are suppressed.
1	Nonstandard frames are reported. +FNF:, +FNS:, and +FNC: reports are generated.

This command controls the reporting of messages that are generated during T.30 phase B negotiations.

Application SP-2388-B Class 2.0

+FNS

Set Nonstandard Frame FIF String

Description AT+FNS="*s*"

s = string of 0–90 hexadecimally-coded bytes

This command sets the facsimile information field for the next nonstandard frame that is sent. The string set with this command may be used with the DIS, DCS, and DTC frames.

Application SP-2388-B Class 2.0

+FNSC

Report NSC Response

Description   AT+FNSC:*s*

s = NSC string

This command returns the nonstandard command (NSC) facsimile information field. The field is returned as a series of two-character ASCII pairs representing the bytes in hex notation. Flags are removed.

Application   SP-2388-A Class 2

Related To   +FNC

+FNSF

Description   AT+FNSF:*s*

s = NSF string

This command returns the nonstandard facilities (NSF) facsimile information field. The field is returned as a series of two-character ASCII pairs representing the bytes in hex notation. Flags are removed.

Application   SP-2388-A Class 2

Related To   +FNF

+FNS

Report NSS Response

Description   AT+FNS:*s*

s = NSF string

This command returns the nonstandard setup (NSS) facsimile information field. The field is returned as a series of two-character ASCII pairs representing the bytes in hex notation. Flags are removed.

Application   SP-2388-B Class 2.0

Related To   +FNSS

+FNSS

Report NSS Response

Description AT+FNSS:*s*

s = NSF string

This command returns the nonstandard setup (NSS) facsimile information field. The field is returned as a series of two-character ASCII pairs representing the bytes in hex notation. Flags are removed.

Application SP-2388-A Class 2

Related To +FNS

+FPHCTO

Set Phase C Response Timeout

Description   AT+PHCTO=*n*

n = 0–255, time in 100 millisecond increments. Default = 30

This command sets the length of time the modem will wait for a command after the end of data when transmitting in phase C, or the length of time it will wait for data after a +FDT command. If the timeout expires, the modem will send EOP to the remote fax terminal.

Application   EIA/TIA-578 Class 1, SP-2388-A Class 2

Related To   +FCT

+FPI

Set Local Polling ID String

Description   AT+FPI=*s*

s = 20 ASCII characters

This command sets the local polling ID string if the specified string is not null. The string is blank-padded to fill 20 characters.

Application   SP-2388-B Class 2.0

Related To   +FPI

+FPI

Report Remote ID Response

Description   AT+FPI:"*s*"

s = called station ID

This response reports the CIG response received from the called station.

Application   SP-2388-B Class 2.0

Related To   +FCIG

+FPO

Polling Request Response

Description AT+FPO

This response indicates that the remote fax terminal has a document to poll and invites the DTE to poll it. This message reports bit 9 of the received DIS frame.

Application SP-2388-B Class 2.0

Related To +FPOLL

+FPOLL

Polling Request Response

Description   AT+FPOLL

This response indicates that the remote fax terminal has a document to poll and invites the DTE to poll it. This message reports bit 9 of the received DIS frame.

Application   SP-2388-A Class 2

Related To   +FPO

+FPP

Enable Packet Protocol

Description AT+FPP=*n*

+FPP=0   Disable DTE-to-modem packet protocol.

+FPP=1   Enable DTE-to-modem packet protocol.

This command enables the DTE-to-modem packet protocol. All multicharacter messages from the modem are sent to the DTE using a simple packet protocol data link to ensure reliable delivery of data.

Application SP-2388-B Class 2.0

+FPPR

Partial Page Report Response

Description   +FPPR:

This response is generated in error correction mode only. It indicates that the previous page has been received with errors.

Application   SP-2388-A Class 2

+FPR

Set Serial Port Speed

Description   AT+FPR=*n*

+FPR=0   Automatic DTE rate detection.

+FPR=*n*   Serial port speed is fixed at *n* * 2400 bps.

Default

+FPR=0 or 8 (19200 bps)

This command allows the modem to fix the serial port speed during fax operations. This command takes effect after the final result code is issued for the command line containing this command.

Application   SP-2388-B Class 2.0

+FPS

Set Page Transfer Status

Description   AT+FPTS=*ppr*

ppr = 1–5, default = 1

Value	Mnemonic	Definition
1	MCF	Page good
2	RTN	Page bad. Retrain requested.
3	RTP	Page good. Retrain requested.
4	PIN	Page bad. Interrupt requested.
5	PIP	Page good. Interrupt requested.

This command sets the post-page response value. The DTE determines this value based on its copy-checking or signal quality-monitoring functions.

Application   SP-2388-B Class 2.0

Related To   +FPTS

+FPS

Receive Page Transfer Status Response

Description   +FPTS:*ppr*,*lc*,*blc*,*cblc*,*lbc*

ppr   post-page message value as defined for the +FPTS set page transfer status command

lc   line count

blc   bad line count

cblc   consecutive bad line count

blc   lost byte count

This response is sent from the fax modem to the DCE at the end of phase C data reception to report the status of the page transfer.

Application   SP-2388-B Class 2.0

Related To   +FPTS

+FPTS

Set Page Transfer Status

Description   AT+FPTS=*ppr*

ppr = 1–5, default = 1

Value	Mnemonic	Definition
1	MCF	Page good
2	RTN	Page bad. Retrain requested.
3	RTP	Page good. Retrain requested.
4	PIN	Page bad. Interrupt requested.
5	PIP	Page good. Interrupt requested.

This command sets the post-page response value. The DTE determines this value based on its copy-checking or signal quality-monitoring functions.

Application   EIA/TIA-578 Class 1

Related To   +FPS

+FPTS

Receive Page Transfer Status Response

Description   +FPTS:*ppr,lc[,blc,cblc[,lbc]]*

    ppr   post-page message value as defined for the +FPTS set page transfer status command

    lc   line count

    blc   bad line count

    cblc   consecutive bad line count

    blc   lost byte count

This response is sent from the fax modem to the DCE at the end of phase C data reception to report the status of the page transfer.

Application   SP-2388-A Class 2

Related To   +FPS

+FPTS

Transmit Page Transfer Status Response

Description +FPTS:*ppr*

ppr post-page message value as defined for the +FPTS set page transfer status command

The modem sends this response to the DTE to indicate the copy quality and related post-page message responses from the remote fax terminal.

Application SP-2388-A Class 2

+FRBC

Set Phase C Receive Block Size

Description AT+FTBC=*n*

n = 0–65535 bytes, default = 0

This command sets the size of the blocks that will be sent during block mode phase C data transfer.

Application SP-2388-A Class 2

+FREL

Set Phase C Receive EOL Alignment

Description   AT+FREL=*n*

+FREL=0   EOL patterns are bit-aligned as received.

+FREL=1   EOL patters are byte-aligned by the modem with the necessary zero fill bits inserted.

Default

+FREL=0

This command determines whether EOL patterns will be bit-aligned as received or zero filled and byte-aligned per T.30.

Application   SP-2388-A Class 2

Related To   +FEA

+FREV

Description AT+FREV?

This command causes the modem to return its revision identification to the DTE. The total number of characters returned will not exceed 2048.

Application SP-2388-A Class 2

Related To +FMR

+FRH

Receive HDLC Frame

Description   AT+FRH=*n*

n = modulation type as defined in table

n	Data rate	Modulation type
3	300	V.21 channel 2
24	2400	V.27ter
48	4800	V.27ter
72	7200	V.29
73	7200	V.17
74	7200	V.17 with short training
96	9600	V.29
97	9600	V.17
98	9600	V.27 with short training
121	12000	V.17
122	12000	V.17 with short training
145	14400	V.17
146	14400	V.17 with short training

This command tells the fax modem to receive a data framed per the HDLC protocol using specified modulation. The modem will connect to the remote fax terminal and receive the frame. If the HDLC flags are not detected, the modem will return the +FCERROR (connect error) response.

The modem strips flags, receives and buffers frames in this mode. The modem manages HDLC transparency and verifies the frame-check sequence (FCS) in this mode. The FCS is passed to the DTE, but may be ignored.

Application   EIA/TIA-578 Class 1

Related To   +FRM, +FRS, +FTH, +FTM, +FTS

+FRM

Receive Fax Data

Description AT+FRM=*n*

n = modulation type

This command instructs the fax modem to enter receive mode using the specified modulation. The modem will connect to the remote fax terminal and receive the data. If the modulation types do not match, the modem will return the +FCERROR (connect error) response.

Valid modulation types are listed in the entry for the +FRH.

Application EIA/TIA-578 Class 1

Related To +FRH, +FRS, +FTH, +FTM, +FTS

+FRQ

Receive Quality Threshold

Description   AT+FRQ=*pgl*,*cbl*

pgl = 0–64h

cbl = 0–FFh

This command sets the parameters in the algorithm used by the modem to determine if the copy quality is acceptable. The *pgl* parameter specifies the percentage of good lines required for a page to be considered acceptable. The *cbl* parameter specifies the maximum number of consecutive bad lines a page can have and be considered acceptable.

Application   SP-2388-B Class 2.0

Related To   +FBADLIN, +FBADMUL

+FRS

Receive Silence

Description   AT+FRS=*n*

n = 0–255, time in 10-millisecond increments

This command causes the modem to listen and report back an OK result code when silence has been present on the data link for the specified amount of time. The time is specified in multiples of 10 milliseconds. Sending any character to the modem cancels this command.

Application   EIA/TIA-578 Class 1

Related To   +FRH, +FRM, +FTH, +FTM, +FTS

+FRY

ECM Retry Count

Description   AT+FRY=*n*

n = 0–FFh, units of four retries, default = 0

This command sets the number of retries that will be performed during error control mode operations.

Application   SP-2388-B Class 2.0

Related To   +FRY

+FSP

Request to Poll

Description   AT+FSP=*n*

+FSP=0   DTE does not want to poll.

+FSP=1   DTE can receive a polled document.

Default

+FSP=0

This command instructs the modem whether a polled document should be received. If set to 1, the modem will reset automatically to 0 after the polled document is received.

Application   SP-2388-B Class 2.0

Related To   +FLP, +FSPL, +FLPL

+FSPL

Request to Poll

Description AT+FSPL=*n*

+FSPL=0   DTE does not want to poll.

+FSPL=1   DTE can receive a polled document.

Default

+FSPL=0

This command informs the modem about whether a polled document can be received. If set to 1, the modem will reset automatically to 0 after the polled document is received.

Application SP-2388-A Class 2

Related To +FLPL, +FSP, +FLP

+FTBC

Set Phase C Transmit Block Size

Description   AT+FTBC=n

n = 0–65535 bytes, default = 0

This command sets the size of the blocks that will be sent during block mode phase C data transfer.

Application   SP-2388-A Class 2

+FTC

Remote Capabilities Response

Description   +FTC:*s*

s = T.30 session subparameter codes

This response reports the T.30 session parameter frames as directed by the session parameter codes shown in the table listed for the +FDCC response. This response is used when the remote fax terminal wants to poll.

Application   SP-2388-B Class 2.0

Related To   +FDTC

+FTH

Transmit HDLC Frame

Description   AT+FTH=*n*

n = modulation type

This command tells the fax modem to transmit data framed per the HDLC protocol using specified modulation. The modem buffers data in this mode. The modem manages HDLC transparency and frame check sequence (CRC) generation in this mode.

Valid modulation types are listed in the entry for the +FRH.

Application   EIA/TIA-578 Class 1

Related To   +FRH, +FRM, +FRS, +FTM, +FTS

+FTI

Report Received TSI Response

Description   +FTI:"*s*"

   s = transmitting station ID

   This response reports the TSI response received from the calling station.

Application   SP-2388-B Class 2.0

Related To   +FTSI

+FTM

Transmit Fax Data

Description AT+FTM=*n*

n = modulation type

This command tells the fax modem to transmit data using the specified modulation. The modem buffers data in this mode.

Valid modulation types are listed in the entry for the +FRH.

Application EIA/TIA-578 Class 1

Related To +FRH, +FRM, +FRS, +FTH, +FTS

+FTS

Stop Transmission and Wait

Description   AT+FTS=*n*

n = 0–255, time in 10-millisecond increments

This command causes the modem to stop any transmission and wait for the specified amount of time. The time is specified in multiples of 10 milliseconds.

Application   EIA/TIA-578 Class 1

Related To   +FRH, +FRM, +FRS, +FTH, +FTM

+FTSI

Report Received TSI Response

Description   +FTSI:"*s*"

s = transmitting station ID

This response reports the TSI response received from the calling station.

Application   SP-2388-A Class 2

Related To   +FTI

+FVO

Transition to Voice Response

Description AT+FVO

This response is sent by the modem to indicate that a procedure interrupt has been negotiated and the fax session is suspended.

Application SP-2388-B Class 2.0

Related To +FVOICE

+FVOICE

Transition to Voice Response

Description AT+FVOICE

This response is sent by the modem to indicate that a procedure interrupt has been negotiated and the fax session is suspended.

Application SP-2388-A Class 2

Related To +FVO

+FVRFC

Vertical Resolution Format Conversion

Description   AT+FVRFC=*n*

+FVRFC=0   Disable mismatch checking.

+FVRFC=1   Enable mismatch checking.

This command determines the modem's response to a mismatch between the vertical resolution negotiated for the session and the vertical resolution desired by the DTE.

If checking is disabled, a mismatch will require conversion. If +FLNFC=1 is enabled, a mismatch will cause the modem to act as if a +FK command has been received. If +FLNFC=2 is enabled, a mismatch will cause the modem to act as if a +FK command has been received for two-dimensionally encoded data.

Application   SP-2388-A Class 2

Related To   +FFC, +FDFFC, +FLNFC, +FWDFC

+FWDFC

Page Width Format Conversion

Description   AT+FWDFC=*n*

+FWDFC=0   Disable mismatch checking.

+FWDFC=1   Enable mismatch checking.

This command determines the modem's response to a mismatch between the page width negotiated for the session and the page width desired by the DTE. If checking is disabled, clipping or scaling will have to be performed. If checking is enabled, a mismatch will cause the modem to act as if a +FK command has been received.

Application   SP-2388-A Class 2

Related To   +FFC, +FDFFC, +FLNFC, +FVRFC

APPENDIX B

S REGISTER REFERENCE

The S registers documented by a variety of modem manufacturers are presented first in tabular form: Table B.1 lists all the registers described in the reference and provides a short description of their purpose. This table can be used as a quick reference to check a register's purpose or validity.

TABLE B.1

S Registers in Numerical Order

S0	Auto-Answer Ring Number
S1	Incoming Ring Counter
S2	Escape Character
S3	End-of-Line Character
S4	Line Feed Character
S5	Backspace Character
S6	Blind Dial Pause
S7	No Carrier Timeout
S8	Comma Modifier Pause Time
S9	Carrier Detect Time Threshold
S10	Carrier Loss Disconnect Time
S11	DTMF Tone Duration and Spacing
S12	Escape Sequence Guard Time
S13	Configuration Bitmap
S14	Configuration Bitmap
S15	Configuration Bitmap
S16	Configuration Bitmap
S18	Modem Self-Test Timeout
S19	Inactivity Timeout
S19	Autosync Bitmap
S20	HDLC Address/BSC Sync Character

TABLE B.1

S Registers in Numerical Order (Continued)

S21	Configuration Bitmap
S21	ARQ BREAK Length
S22	Configuration Bitmap
S22	XON Character
S23	Configuration Bitmap
S23	XOFF Character
S24	DSR Signal Duration
S25	DTR Detection Delay and Transition Threshold
S26	RTS to CTS Delay
S27	Configuration Bitmap
S27	Configuration Bitmap
S27	Configuration Bitmap
S28	Configuration Bitmap
S28	V.32 Answer Tone Duration
S29	V.21 Answer Tone Duration
S29	Configuration Bitmap
S30	Inactivity Timeout
S30	Programmable/Permissive Transmit Level
S32	Voice/Data Switch Function
S32	Configuration Bitmap
S33	AFT Options
S34	Configuration Bitmap
S36	Error-Control Negotiation Failure Action
S36	Configuration Bitmap
S37	AUTO RELIABLE Fallback Character
S37	Maximum Data Link Speed
S38	Forced Disconnect Buffer Delay
S38	Configuration Bitmap
S39	MNP Inactivity Timeout
S39	Flow Control
S40	Configuration Bitmap
S40	Configuration Bitmap
S40	Auto Make Busy

TABLE B.1

S Registers in Numerical Order (Continued)

S41	Configuration Bitmap
S41	Dial-up Link Speed
S41	Remote Access Login Attempt Limit
S41	Inactivity Timeout
S42	Remote Access Character
S43	Current Data Link Speed
S43	Remote Access Guard Time
S43	V.32bis Train
S44	Framing Technique
S44	Leased Line Link Speed
S45	Report Framing Technique Status
S45	Leased Line Transmit Level
S45	Remote Access
S46	Error-Control/Compression Selection
S46	Auto Dial Backup
S46	Modem Security
S47	Report Error-Control/Compression Status
S47	Auto Dial Standby
S47	DSR/DCD Delay
S48	Feature Negotiation
S48	Leased Line Carrier Threshold
S48	Control Character Mask
S49	Forced Disconnect Buffer Delay
S49	Buffer Lower Threshold
S49	Product Identification String
S50	Buffer Upper Threshold
S50	RAM Status
S50	Set Data Link Speed
S51	DTE Remote Loopback
S51	Serial Port Speed
S52	DTE Local Loopback
S52	Leased Line Transmit Level
S52	DTR Interpretation

TABLE B.1

S Registers in Numerical Order (Continued)

S53	Global PAD Configuration
S53	V.54 Address
S54	V.54 Device Type
S54	BREAK Handling
S54	Configuration Bitmap
S55	AutoStream Protocol Request
S55	Access From Remote
S55	Escape Handling
S56	AutoStream Protocol Status
S56	XON Character
S56	Remote Access Password
S57	Network Options
S57	XOFF Character
S57	Remote Access Password
S58	MNP Inactivity Timeout
S58	Serial Port Flow Control
S58	Remote Access Password
S59	BREAK control
S59	Prompt Character
S59	CONNECT Suffix Bitmap
S59	Remote Access Password
S60	Configuration Bitmap
S60	Serial Port Data Format
S61	CT111 Rate Control
S61	Set Serial Port Speed
S61	Local BREAK Action
S61	Speaker Volume
S62	V.25bis Coding
S62	Forced Disconnect Buffer Delay
S62	BREAK Length
S63	Leased Line Transmit Level
S63	V.25bis Idle Character
S63	MNP block size

TABLE B.1

S Registers in Numerical Order (Continued)

S63	Link Layer BREAK Action
S63	Command Mode
S64	V.25bis New Line Character
S64	AUTO RELIABLE Fallback Character
S64	Dial/Answer Sequence Abort
S65	Line Current Disconnect
S65	XON/XOFF Failsafe
S66	NMS Call Messages
S66	Serial Port Speed Conversion
S67	Callback Security
S67	CTS Action
S68	Serial Port Flow Control
S69	Data Link Speed
S69	Link Layer Window Size (K)
S69	XON/XOFF Signal Handling
S70	Maximum Number of Retransmissions (N2)
S70	Protocol Bitmap
S70	Instantaneous Transmit Rate
S71	Link Layer Propagation Delay (T2)
S71	Transmit Channel Size
S72	Loss of Flag Idle Timeout (T3)
S72	Instantaneous Receive Rate
S73	No Activity Timeout (T4)
S73	Receive Channel Size
S74	Network Positive Identification
S74	Received Packet Retransmission Count
S74	Packet Transmission Status
S74	Minimum Incoming Logical Channel Number
S75	Network Management Address
S75	Packets Accepted
S75	Minimum Incoming Logical Channel Number
S76	Set Dial Line V.32bis Autorate
S76	Equivalent Line Noise Profile

TABLE B.1

S Registers in Numerical Order (Continued)

S76	Maximum Incoming Logical Channel Number
S77	Frequency Offset
S77	Maximum Incoming Logical Channel Number
S78	Set V.32bis Automode
S78	Line Quality
S78	Outgoing Logical Channel Number
S79	Outgoing Logical Channel Number
S80	Restart Request Limit (N20)
S81	Acknowledgment Wait Timeout (T20)
S82	BREAK Signaling Technique
S82	Set Leased Line V.32bis Autorate
S83	MI/MIC Dialing
S84	AT Command Mode
S84	Adaptive Start-Up Negotiation
S85	Fast Disconnect
S85	Adaptive Start-Up Report
S86	Connection Failure Report
S87	AT Command High Speed
S90	Communications Protocol
S90	DSRS Behavior
S91	Leased Line Transmit Level
S91	Guard Tone
S92	MI/MIC Options
S92	Answer Sequence
S93	V.25bis Serial Port Speed
S93	V.32 Probe Transmit Time
S94	V.25bis Mode Selection
S94	Transmission Speed Negotiation
S95	Negotiation Message Options
S95	MNP Error Control
S96	MNP Data Compression
S97	V.32 Automode Probe Timing
S97	LAPM Error Control

TABLE B.1

S Registers in Numerical Order (Continued)

S98	V.42bis Data Compression
S100	Answer/Originate Mode
S101	Continuous Answer/Originate
S102	Set Pulse Dial Make/Break Ratio
S102	Auxiliary Phone Leads
S104	Automatic Dialing
S105	Link Layer Frame Size
S105	T/D Switch Enable
S106	V.42 Detection
S107	Error-Control Detection Timeout
S108	Signal Quality Requirement
S108	V.42 Match Count
S109	V.32bis Carrier Speed
S110	V.32/V.32bis Selection
S110	PEP Mode Data Compression
S111	File Transfer Protocol Spoofing
S112	Set Serial Port Speed
S112	Set Kermit Mark Character
S118	LCD Scroll Rate
S119	LCD Message Display Options
S121	Echo Suppressor Compensation
S130	DSR Options
S131	DCD Options
S150	Asynchronous/Synchronous Mode
S151	SDLC Interface Speed
S152	SDLC Switched/Nonswitched
S153	SDLC Full/Half-Duplex
S154	Synchronous Transmit Clock Source
S155	NRZ/NRZI Data Encoding
S157	SDLC Disconnect Delay
S158	SDLC DSR Delay
S160	SDLC Frame Retransmit Limit
S161	SDLC Device Timeout

TABLE B.1

S Registers in Numerical Order (Continued)

S162	SDLC Nonproductive Timeout
S163	SDLC Retransmit Timeout
S164	SDLC Primary Poll Rate
S169	Synchronous Dialing Command Set
S180	Feature Negotiation
S181	Error Control Fallback
S183	Error Control Detection Timeout
S190	Data Compression
S191	LZ Compression
S222	Enhanced Command Mode Character
S253	Select Smart Mode
S254	&F0 Configuration
S255	Configuration Select
:T0	V.32 Probe Timing
:T1	V.23 Probe Timing
:T2	V.21 Probe Timing
:T3	V.21/V.23 Answer Tone Time
:T4	Line Turnaround Delay
:T5	V.23 Intercharacter Delay
:T6	CD Detection Delay
:T7	False Answer Abort Timeout
:T9	Primary XON Character
:T10	Primary XOFF Character
:T11	Secondary XON Character
:T12	Secondary XOFF Character
:T13	Automode Timeout
:T14	Connect Message Delay
:T15	V.24 Control Bitmap
:T16	CTS Delay
:T17	V.32/V.32bis Training
:T18	Busy Out Timer
:T19	MNP Link Control

Details on each S register are presented in this appendix in numerical order. The entry for each S register includes a description of how it is used by the modem, the actions or parameters it controls, notes on inconsistencies, and a list of modem types on which the command is applicable.

Where one register is used to implement more than one function (from different manufacturers, for example), a separate entry appears for each application. The S41 register, for example, can be used to specify the dial-up link speed, set a limit on remote access logins, specify the maximum amount of time the modem can remain idle, or hold a configuration bitmap—it all depends on the particular manufacturer.

S register definitions for S0 through S12 tend to be relatively consistent between modems. The definitions for S13 through S255, however, vary widely between manufacturers, between different modems from the same manufacturer, and even between different versions of the same modem! Because of this, some S register entries will list more than one definition, range, or default value for the same manufacturer.

Example Register Listing

Each entry in the S register reference follows the same basic format, an example of which is shown in Figure B.1. An explanation of each element in a reference entry is given below.

1. *Title*. S register number and a short description of the register's function.

2. *Description*. The syntax of the register is given, including replaceable parameters in italics where applicable. Unless otherwise specified, all S registers may be read. As such, the ATSn? syntax is not shown except for read-only registers.

   The parameters for writable S registers may appear in one of three possible forms. For S registers that specify a quantity (length of time, number of bytes, and so on), the legal values are given as a range as shown here:

   ```
   ATS0=n
   ```

   Set ring to answer after.

   ```
   n = 0–255
   ```

   When the parameter identifies an action, each possible action is listed separately, as shown here:

   ```
   ATS43=n
   ```

   0   Use long training sequence.

   1   Use short training sequence.

FIGURE B.1
Reference listing example

S3

End-of-Line Character

Description ATS3=*n*

Set end-of-line character ASCII value.

n = 0–127 [AT&T, Black Box, Dallas, Hayes, Infotel, Microcom, Motorola, Prometheus, Rockwell, Sierra, Telebit, Twincom]

n = 0–255 [Practical, USRobotics]

n = 0–96, 123–127 [Telebit]

Default

13 (<CR>)

This register holds the ASCII value of the character that will be recognized as the end-of-line character. The character selected by this register will be used by the modem to determine the end of a command line and to terminate responses sent to the DTE.

Related To S4, S5

Application AT&T, Black Box, Dallas, Hayes, Infotel, Microcom, Motorola, Practical, Prometheus, Rockwell, Sierra, Telebit, Twincom, USRobotics, Zoom

Notes **1.** The documentation for many modems lists multiple values for the legal range of this register.

Finally, some S registers are used as bitmaps and control multiple options. Each bit or group of bits represents a single action parameter. Bitmapped registers are displayed in graphical form as shown here:

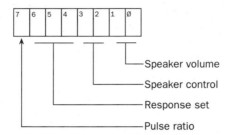

Explanations of each field and enumerations of possible values are presented in tables that follow the graphic.

The default value for the register (if any) appears at the end of the description.

Not all options or parameter values are supported by all modem manufacturers, and the same value may perform a different function on a different modem. When manufacturer-specific forms must be indicated, the command is followed by the application enclosed in square brackets, as shown here:

ATS89=*n*

0   Attempt to connect at the highest data link speed that does not exceed the speed of the last AT command issued.

1   Attempt a data link at 75 bps. [Hayes]

   Attempt a data link at 300 bps. [AT&T]

   Reserved. [Hayes, Microcom, Zoom]

2   Attempt a data link at 110 bps. [Hayes]

   Reserved.

In this example, S89=0 is valid for all modems listed in the Application block. The S89=1 command means "Attempt a data link at 75 bps" for Hayes modems only, "Attempt a data link at 300 bps" for AT&T modems only, and is reserved for Hayes, Microcom, and Zoom modems. (The fact that Hayes appears after two different options means that the implementation varies among different Hayes modems or modem versions.) Finally, the S89=2 command means "Attempt a data link at 110 bps" for Hayes modems and is reserved for all other modems listed in the Application block.

3. *Related To*. Where other commands or registers affect the behavior or effectiveness of a command, they will appear in this listing. Not all cross-referenced commands and registers are supported by all manufacturers.

4. *Application*. This section lists the modem types that support this command. A manufacturer appears in this listing if at least one modem from that manufacturer supports the command. In other words, not all commands are supported by all modems made by a single manufacturer.

5. *Notes*. This section contains additional information that is applicable to the command including limitations, interactions, and so on.

S0

Auto-Answer Ring Number

Description

ATSØ=*n*

Set ring to answer after.

n = 0–255

Default

0   [Black Box, Dallas, Hayes, Microcom, Motorola, Practical, Prometheus, Rockwell, Sierra, Telebit, Twincom, USRobotics]

1   [AT&T, Infotel, Telebit]

The S0 register determines the number of times the phone must ring before the modem automatically answers the call.

Assigning a nonzero value to this register places the modem in auto-answer mode. The value in this register specifies how many rings must occur before the modem goes off-hook to answer the incoming call. Setting S0=0 turns off the auto-answer feature.

Related To S1

Application AT&T, Black Box, Dallas, Hayes, Infotel, Microcom, Motorola, Practical, Prometheus, Rockwell, Sierra, Telebit, Twincom, USRobotics, Zoom

S1

Incoming Ring Counter

Description   S1?

Return current ring count (0–255).

When the modem is in command mode and the phone rings, this register is incremented to reflect the count value.

When the value in this register equals the (nonzero) value in S0, the modem automatically answers the telephone. Approximately 8 seconds after the last ring occurs, this register resets itself to 0. S1 is a read-only register.

Related To   S0

Application   Black Box, Dallas, Hayes, Infotel, Microcom, Motorola, Practical, Prometheus, Rockwell, Sierra, Telebit, Twincom, USRobotics, Zoom

S2

Escape Character

Description ATS2=*n*

Set escape character ASCII value.

n = 0–255

Default

43 (+)

This register holds the ASCII value of the character that will be recognized in the escape sequence. Setting S2 to a value between 128 and 255 disables escape sequence recognition.

Related To S12, S48, S55, &D

Application AT&T, Black Box, Dallas, Hayes, Infotel, Microcom, Motorola, Practical, Prometheus, Rockwell, Sierra, Telebit, Twincom, USRobotics, Zoom

S3

End-of-Line Character

Description ATS3=*n*

Set end-of-line character ASCII value.

n = 0–127 [AT&T, Black Box, Dallas, Hayes, Infotel, Microcom, Motorola, Prometheus, Rockwell, Sierra, Telebit, Twincom]

n = 0–255 [Practical, USRobotics]

n = 0–96, 123–127 [Telebit]

Default

13 (<CR>)

This register holds the ASCII value of the character that will be recognized as the end-of-line character. The character selected by this register will be used by the modem to determine the end of a command line and to terminate responses sent to the DTE.

Related To S4, S5

Application AT&T, Black Box, Dallas, Hayes, Infotel, Microcom, Motorola, Practical, Prometheus, Rockwell, Sierra, Telebit, Twincom, USRobotics, Zoom

Notes **1.** The documentation for many modems lists multiple values for the legal range of this register.

S4

Line Feed Character

Description ATS4=*n*

Set line feed character ASCII value.

n = 0–127 [AT&T, Black Box, Dallas, Hayes, Infotel, Microcom, Motorola, Prometheus, Rockwell, Sierra, Telebit, Twincom]

n = 0–255 [Practical, Telebit, USRobotics]

Default

> 10 (<LF>)

This register holds the ASCII value of the character that will be used as the line feed character.

The character selected by this register will be used by the modem in verbose responses sent to the DTE. If a line feed character in responses is not desired, set S4 to the null character (0). The line feed character cannot be totally disabled.

Related To S3, S5

Application AT&T, Black Box, Dallas, Hayes, Infotel, Microcom, Motorola, Practical, Prometheus, Rockwell, Sierra, Telebit, Twincom, USRobotics, Zoom

Notes

1. The documentation for many modems lists multiple values for the legal range of this register.

S5

Backspace Character

Description ATS5=*n*

Set backspace character ASCII value.

n = 0–32 [Dallas, Microcom, Practical, Rockwell, Twincom, Zoom]

n = 0–32, 127 [Dallas, Hayes, Infotel, Prometheus, Sierra]

n = 0–96, 123–127 [Telebit]

n = 0–127 [AT&T, Black Box, Dallas, Hayes, Motorola, Telebit]

n = 0–255 [Telebit, USRobotics]

Default

8 (<BS>)

This register holds the ASCII value of the character that will be recognized as the backspace character.

The character selected by this register is used by the modem to implement a destructive backspace. When command echo is enabled (E1), the modem responds to this character by sending three characters to the DTE: a backspace, a space (ASCII 32), and another backspace.

Related To S3, S4

Application AT&T, Black Box, Dallas, Hayes, Infotel, Microcom, Motorola, Practical, Prometheus, Rockwell, Sierra, Telebit, Twincom, USRobotics, Zoom

Notes
1. documentation for many modems lists multiple values for the legal range of this register.
2. Setting S5 to a value between 128 and 255 will disable backspace recognition. [USRobotics]
3. Setting S5 to a value greater than 32 will disable backspace recognition. [Rockwell, Twincom]
4. Setting S5 to a value other than 0–32 or 127 will disable backspace recognition. [Motorola]

S6

Blind Dial Pause

Description ATS6=*n*

Set pause before blind dial time in seconds.

n = 0–255 [Practical, Prometheus, USRobotics]

n = 1–255 [Motorola]

n = 2–255 [AT&T, Black Box, Dallas, Hayes, Infotel, Microcom, Rockwell, Sierra, Telebit, Twincom, Zoom]

Default

2

The S6 register determines the amount of time that the modem will wait after going off-hook before it begins to process the dial string. This delay allows for the normal period of time that elapses between an off-hook condition and the provision of a dial tone by the GSTN central office.

The value in S6 is used only when the X0, X1, or X3 command is in effect. Other values for the X command enable dial tone detection and disable blind dialing.

The wait specified by this register applies only to the first dial tone. Subsequent wait periods and dial tones may be enabled using the W dial modifier and are independent of any S register setting.

Related To D, X

Application AT&T, Black Box, Dallas, Hayes, Infotel, Microcom, Motorola, Practical, Prometheus, Rockwell, Sierra, Telebit, Twincom, USRobotics, Zoom

Notes

1. The documentation for many modems lists multiple values for the legal range of this register.

S7

No Carrier Timeout

Description ATS7=*n*

Set timeout in seconds.

n = 1–60 [Dallas, Hayes, Sierra]

n = 1–255 [Black Box, Dallas, AT&T, Infotel, Motorola, Practical, Prometheus, Rockwell, Telebit, Twincom, Zoom]

n = 0–255 [Microcom, USRobotics]

Default

> 30 [Black Box, Dallas, Hayes, Infotel, Motorola, Practical, Prometheus, Sierra, Telebit, Zoom]
>
> 40 [Telebit]
>
> 45 [AT&T]
>
> 50 [Dallas, Hayes, Rockwell, Twincom]
>
> 60 [Dallas, Microcom, Prometheus, USRobotics]

The S7 register tells the modem the maximum time that it may wait after dialing to detect an incoming carrier. If the modem does not detect a carrier before the specified time has elapsed, it hangs up and returns the NO CARRIER message.

The complex negotiation process of speed, error-correction protocol, and compression protocol that may occur between two modems can easily exceed the default value for this register.

Application AT&T, Black Box, Dallas, Hayes, Motorola, Practical, Prometheus, Rockwell, Sierra, Telebit, Twincom, USRobotics, Zoom

S8

Comma Modifier Pause Time

Description   ATS8=n

Set comma pause value in seconds.

$n = 0$–255

Default

> 2

This command sets the time that the modem will pause when it encounters the comma dial modifier while processing a dial string.

Related To   D

Application   AT&T, Black Box, Dallas, Hayes, Infotel, Microcom, Motorola, Practical, Prometheus, Rockwell, Sierra, Telebit, Twincom, USRobotics, Zoom

Notes

     1. The documentation for many modems contains conflicting information about the lower limit for this register.

S9

Carrier Detect Time Threshold

Description ATS9=*n*

Set carrier detect time threshold in increments of 0.1 second.

n = 1–255 [AT&T, Black Box, Dallas, Hayes, Infotel, Practical, Prometheus, Rockwell, Sierra, Telebit, Twincom, USRobotics, Zoom]

n = 0–255 [Microcom]

Default

6

The S9 register specifies the amount of time the carrier signal from the remote modem must be present before the local modem issues a carrier detect.

The value of S9 is referenced only if the X3 or X4 command has been selected. In addition, S9 is ignored when the modem is operating in half-duplex mode.

Related To X

Application AT&T, Black Box, Dallas, Hayes, Infotel, Microcom, Practical, Prometheus, Rockwell, Sierra, Telebit, Twincom, USRobotics, Zoom

Notes
1. Accessing this register does not produce an error, but has no effect on modem operation. [AT&T]

S10

Carrier Loss Disconnect Time

Description ATS10=*n*

Set carrier loss time threshold in increments of 0.1 second.

n = 1–255 [Black Box, Dallas, Hayes, Infotel, Motorola, Practical, Prometheus, Rockwell, Sierra, Telebit, Twincom, Zoom]

n = 0–255 [AT&T, Microcom, USRobotics]

Default

7 [Telebit]

14 [Black Box, Dallas, Hayes, Infotel, Practical, Prometheus, Rockwell, Sierra, Telebit, Twincom, USRobotics, Zoom]

15 [Motorola]

20 [AT&T]

30 [Microcom]

The S10 register sets the maximum time that a remote modem's carrier may disappear from the telephone line without causing the local modem to assume that it has been disconnected. This feature provides some compensation for noisy telephone lines and call-waiting interference.

Setting this register to 255 makes the modem ignore the data carrier detect signal and behave as if the remote modem's carrier is always present.

Application AT&T, Black Box, Dallas, Hayes, Infotel, Microcom, Motorola, Practical, Prometheus, Rockwell, Sierra, Telebit, Twincom, USRobotics, Zoom

Notes
1. When operating in half-duplex synchronous mode, S10 specifies the amount of time that a carrier may be continuously present or absent before causing the modem to disconnect. [Hayes]

S11

DTMF Tone Duration and Spacing

Description   ATS11=*n*

Set DTMF tone duration and spacing in milliseconds.

n = 50–255 [AT&T, Dallas, Hayes, Infotel, Microcom, Motorola, Practical, Prometheus, Rockwell, Sierra, Telebit, Twincom, Zoom]

n = 0–255 [USRobotics]

Default

50 [AT&T]

70 [Dallas, Prometheus, Telebit, USRobotics]

72 [Motorola]

75 [Microcom]

95 [Dallas, Hayes, Infotel, Practical, Rockwell, Sierra, Telebit, Twincom, Zoom]

100 [Prometheus]

The S11 register controls the duration of the DTMF tones used during tone dialing and the spacing between adjacent tones.

Default times for this command are manufacturer-dependent, but 50 milliseconds is the minimum value that is reliably recognized by the GSTN. This command has no effect on the pulse dialing speed, which is nominally 10 pulses per second.

Application   AT&T, Dallas, Hayes, Infotel, Microcom, Motorola, Practical, Prometheus, Rockwell, Sierra, Telebit, Twincom, USRobotics, Zoom

S12

Escape Sequence Guard Time

Description ATS12=*n*

Set guard time in increments of 20 milliseconds.

n = 0–255

Default

50

This register sets the duration of the guard time that must occur immediately before and after the escape code sequence.

During the guard time, no data may flow from the DTE to the modem. If the escape code sequence is detected and is bracketed by two valid guard times, the modem switches from data mode to command mode without disconnecting.

Indirectly, this register also specifies the maximum time that can elapse between the individual characters of the escape code without resetting the escape code detection sequence. To be effective, S12 must not specify a time that is less than the time required to exchange one character between the DTE and the modem.

If S12 is set to 0 or to a value that is less than one character transmission time, guard time detection is effectively disabled.

Related To S2

Application AT&T, Black Box, Dallas, Hayes, Infotel, Microcom, Motorola, Practical, Prometheus, Rockwell, Sierra, Telebit, Twincom, USRobotics, Zoom

Notes

   1. This register has no effect when the TIES escape sequence is being used.

S13

Configuration Bitmap

Description ATS13=*n*

n = decimal value of byte determined by bitmap.

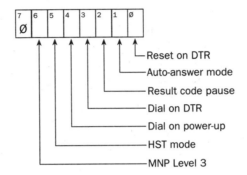

Bit	Default	Definition
0	0	Reset on DTR 0 Disabled. 1 Reset modem after ON-to-OFF DTR transition.
1	0	Auto-answer mode 0 Auto-answer with answer tone. 1 Auto-answer with originate tone.
2	0	Result code pause 0 Insert 250-millisecond pause before sending result code. 1 Disable pause.
3	0	Dial on DTR 0 Disabled. 1 Dial first stored number after OFF-to-ON DTR transition.
4	0	Dial on power-up 0 Disabled. 1 At power-up, dial first stored number.

Bit	Default	Definition
5	0	HST mode 0 Enabled. 1 Disabled.
6	0	MNP Level 3 0 Enabled. 1 Disabled.
7	0	Reserved

Default

> 0

S13 is a bitmapped register that controls or reports a variety of modem parameters.

Application   USRobotics

S14

Configuration Bitmap

Description ATS14=*n*

n = decimal value of byte determined by bitmap.

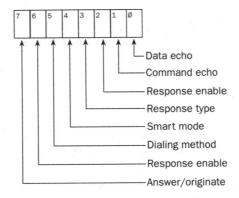

Bit	Default	Definition
0	0	Data echo [Dallas, Rockwell, Twincom, Zoom] 0 Do not echo data. Same as F0. 1 Echo data. Same as F1. Reserved [Black Box, Infotel, Microcom, Practical, Prometheus, Sierra]
1	1	Command echo 0 Do not echo commands. Same as E0. 1 Echo commands. Same as E1.
2	0	Response enable 0 Send responses. Same as Q0. 1 Do not send responses. Same as Q1.
3	1	Response type 0 Use numeric responses. Same as V0. 1 Use text responses. Same as V1.

Bit	Default	Definition
4	0	Smart mode [Dallas, Infotel, Microcom, Sierra] 0 Smart mode. Accept AT commands. 1 Dumb mode. Do not accept AT commands. Reserved [Black Box, Practical, Prometheus, Rockwell, Twincom, Zoom]
5	1	Dialing method 0 Tone dialing. Same as T. 1 Pulse dialing. Same as P.
6	0	Response enable [Dallas, Rockwell, Twincom, Zoom] 0 Set by Q0 and Q1. 1 Set by Q2. Reserved [Black Box, Infotel, Microcom, Practical, Prometheus, Sierra]
7	1	Answer/Originate 0 Answer mode. Same as A and DR. 1 Originate mode. Same as D.

Default

170 (10101010b)

S14 is a bitmapped register that controls a variety of modem parameters. Where appropriate, equivalent commands have been given for bit settings. The bitmap and corresponding command states are linked; changing one changes the other.

Related To   A, D, E, F, P, T, Q

Application   Black Box, Dallas, Infotel, Microcom, Practical, Prometheus, Rockwell, Sierra, Twincom, Zoom

Notes

1. Bit 4 (smart mode) is usually reserved in internal modems because a dumb modem must be physically reset to return to smart mode.

S15

Configuration Bitmap

Description   ATS15=*n*

n = decimal value of byte determined by bitmap.

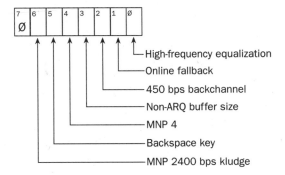

Bit	Default	Definition
0	0	High-frequency equalization 0 Enabled. 1 Disabled.
1	0	Online fallback 0 Enabled. 1 Disabled.
2	0	450 bps backchannel 0 Enabled. 1 Disabled.
3	0	Non-ARQ buffer size 0 1536 bytes. 1 128 bytes.
4	0	MNP 4 0 Enabled. 1 Disabled.

Bit	Default	Definition
5	0	Backspace key 0 Destructive backspace. 1 Delete.
6	0	MNP 2400 bps kludge 0 Standard MNP protocol. 1 Kludged MNP protocol.
7	0	Reserved

Default

> 0

S15 is a bitmapped register that controls a variety of modem parameters.

Application   USRobotics

S16

Configuration Bitmap

Description ATS16=*n*

n=decimal value of byte determined by bitmap.

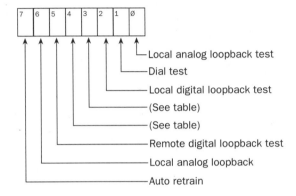

Bit	Default	Definition
0	0	Local analog loopback test 0 Inactive. See &T0. 1 Active. See &T1.
1	0	Dial test [USRobotics] 0 Inactive. 1 Active. Reserved [Black Box, Dallas, Infotel, Microcom, Prometheus, Rockwell, Sierra, Twincom, Zoom]
2	0	Local digital loopback test 0 Inactive. See &T0. 1 Active. See &T3.

Bit	Default	Definition
3	0	Initiate remote digital loopback test [Dallas, Infotel, Prometheus, Rockwell, Sierra, Twincom, USRobotics, Zoom] 0 Inactive. See &T0. 1 Active. See &T6. Remote digital loopback test status [Black Box, Dallas, Microcom] 0 Loopback not in progress. See &T0. 1 Loopback test started by remote modem in progress. See &T7.
4	0	Remote digital loopback test status [Dallas, Infotel, Prometheus, Rockwell, Sierra, Twincom, USRobotics, Zoom] 0 Loopback not in progress. See &T0. 1 Loopback test started by remote modem in progress. See &T7. Initiate remote digital loopback test [Black Box, Dallas, Microcom] 0 Inactive. See &T0. 1 Active. See &T6. Reserved [USRobotics]
5	0	Remote digital loopback test [Black Box, Dallas, Infotel, Microcom, Prometheus, Rockwell, Sierra, Twincom, Zoom] 0 Inactive. See &T0. 1 Loopback test will use test pattern and count errors. See &T7. Reserved [USRobotics]
6	0	Local analog loopback test [Black Box, Dallas, Infotel, Microcom, Prometheus, Rockwell, Sierra, Twincom, Zoom] 0 Inactive. See &T0. 1 Loopback test will use test pattern and count errors. See &T8. Reserved [USRobotics]

Bit	Default	Definition
7	x	Auto retrain [Dallas, Sierra] 0 Disable. See %E0. 1 Enable. See %E1. Reserved [Black Box, Infotel, Microcom, Prometheus, Rockwell, Twincom, USRobotics, Zoom]

Default

0 (00000000b) [Black Box, Dallas, Infotel, Microcom, Prometheus, Rockwell, Twincom, USRobotics, Zoom]

128 (10000000b) [Dallas, Sierra]

S16 is a bitmapped register that provides equivalents for some of the self-test configurations provided by the &T command. The modem can perform only one of the indicated tests at a time.

This register may also be used to enable the modem's auto retrain option. [Sierra]

Related To   &T, %E

Application   Black Box, Dallas, Infotel, Microcom, Prometheus, Rockwell, Sierra, Twincom, USRobotics, Zoom

S18

Modem Self-Test Timeout

Description ATS18=*n*

Set timeout in seconds.

n = 0–255

Default

0

This register sets the maximum length of time for which the modem's self-test can execute. If a self-test has been active for a time equal to this limit, the modem automatically terminates the test.

Setting S18 to 0 disables the timer; self-testing will not be automatically terminated.

Related To &T

Application AT&T, Black Box, Dallas, Hayes, Infotel, Microcom, Motorola, Practical, Prometheus, Rockwell, Sierra, Telebit, Twincom, USRobotics, Zoom

S19

Inactivity Timeout

Description ATS19=*n*

Set timeout in minutes.

n = 0–255

Default

0

This register sets the maximum time that the modem will maintain a connection in the absence of any data transfer. If the connection is inactive for a time equal to this limit, the modem automatically terminates the connection.

Setting S19=0 disables the timer. Inactivity checking is enforced only for asynchronous modes; it is not enabled for any synchronous mode.

Application USRobotics

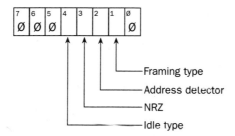

S19

Autosync Bitmap

Description ATS19=*n*

n = decimal value of byte determined by bitmap.

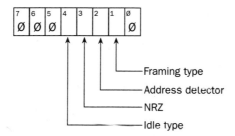

Bit	Default	Definition
0	0	Reserved
1	0	Framing type 0 BSC (binary synchronous communications). 1 HDLC (high-level data link control).
2	0	Address detector 0 Disabled. 1 Enabled (HDLC only).
3	0	NRZ 0 NRZI (NRZ inverted). 1 NRZ (non return to zero).
4	0	Idle type 0 MARK idle. 1 Flag (sync) idle.
7-5	000	Reserved

Default

0

S19 is a bitmapped register that controls options for autosync operation.

Related To   S20

Application   Hayes

S20

HDLC Address/BSC Sync Character

Description ATS2Ø=*n*

Set address or character ASCII value.

n = 0–255

Default

0

If the modem is operating in HDLC (high-level data link control) mode, S20 contains the HDLC address. If in BSC (binary synchronous communications) mode, S20 contains the BSC sync character.

Related To S19

Application Hayes

S21

Configuration Bitmap

Description ATS21=*n*

n = decimal value of byte determined by bitmap.

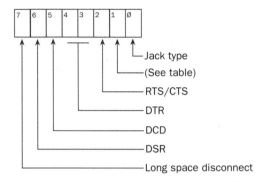

Bit	Default	Definition
0	0	Telephone jack type [Black Box, Dallas, Infotel, Microcom, Practical, Rockwell, Sierra, Twincom, Zoom] 0 RJ-11, RJ-41S, RJ-45S. Same as &J0. 1 RJ-12, RJ-13. Same as &J1. Reserved [Prometheus]
1	x	Interface type [Dallas, Sierra] 0 Serial. 1 Parallel. Default user profile [Dallas, Rockwell, Twincom] 0 User profile 0. Same as &Y0. 1 User profile 1. Same as &Y1. Reserved [Black Box, Infotel, Practical, Prometheus, Zoom]
2	x	RTS/CTS [Black Box, Dallas, Infotel, Practical, Prometheus, Rockwell, Sierra, Twincom, Zoom] 0 CTS tracks RTS. Same as &R0. 1 RTS ignored. CTS on in data mode. Same as &R1.

Bit	Default	Definition
2-1	xx	RTS/CTS [Microcom] 00 CTS tracks RTS. Same as &R0. 01 RTS ignored. CTS on in data mode. Same as &R1. 10 CCITT V.13 emulates half-duplex on a full-duplex line. Same as &R2.
4-3	xx	DTR 00 DTR is ignored. Same as &D0. 01 Go to command mode after ON-to-OFF DTR transition. Same as &D1. 10 Hang up after an ON-to-OFF DTR transition. Same as &D2. 11 Reset after an ON-to-OFF DTR transition. Same as &D3.
5	x	DCD 0 DCD always active. Same as &C0. 1 DCD reflects true carrier status. Same as &C1.
6	x	DSR [Black Box, Dallas, Microcom, Prometheus, Rockwell, Sierra, Twincom, Zoom] 0 DSR always active. Same as &S0. 1 DSR active when handshake begins. Same as &S1. Reserved [Infotel, Practical]
7	0	Long space disconnect 0 Disable. Same as Y0. 1 Enable. Same as Y1.

Default

0 (00000000b) [Dallas, Sierra (serial interface), Practical]

2 (00000010b) [Dallas, Sierra (parallel interface)]

4 (00000100b) [Black Box]

20 (00010100b) [Rockwell, Twincom]

48 (01001000b) [Dallas, Prometheus]

56 (00111000b) [Infotel]

176 (10110000b) [Microcom]

S21

S21 is a bitmapped register that controls a variety of modem parameters. Where appropriate, equivalent commands have been given for bit settings. The bitmap and corresponding command states are linked; changing one changes the other.

Related To   Y, &C, &D, &J, &R, &S, &Y

Application   Black Box, Dallas, Infotel, Microcom, Practical, Prometheus, Rockwell, Sierra, Twincom, Zoom

S21

ARQ BREAK Length

Description   ATS21=*n*

Set length in increments of 10 milliseconds.

n = 0–255

Default

10

This register sets the length of the BREAK sent from the modem to the DTE in ARQ mode.

Application   USRobotics

S22

Configuration Bitmap

Description ATS22=*n*

n = decimal value of byte determined by bitmap.

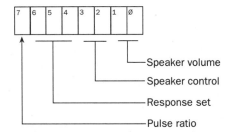

Bit	Default	Definition
1-0	10	Speaker volume 00 Low volume. Same as L0. 01 Low volume. Same as L1. 10 Medium volume. Same as L2. 11 High volume. Same as L3.
3-2	01	Speaker control 00 Always off. Same as M0. 01 On until carrier. Same as M1. 10 Always on. Same as M2. 11 Off during dialing, on until carrier. Same as M3.

Bit	Default	Definition
6-4	xxx	Response set [Black Box, Dallas, Microcom, Practical, Prometheus, Sierra, Zoom] 000 Same as X0. 001 Reserved. 010 Reserved. 011 Reserved. 100 Same as X1. 101 Same as X2. 110 Same as X3. 111 Same as X4. Response set [Dallas, Infotel, Rockwell, Twincom, Zoom] 000 Same as X0. 001 Same as X1. 010 Same as X2. 011 Same as X3. 100 Same as X4. 101 Reserved. 110 Reserved. 111 Reserved.
7	0	Pulse dial make/break ratio 0 39/61 for U.S. and Canada. Same as &P0. 1 33/67 for UK and Hong Kong. Same as &P1.

Default

6 (00000110b) [Infotel]

70 (01000110b) [Dallas, Rockwell, Twincom, Zoom]

118 (01110110b) [Black Box, Dallas, Microcom, Practical, Prometheus, Sierra, Zoom]

S22 is a bitmapped register that controls a variety of modem parameters. Where appropriate, equivalent commands have been given for bit settings. The bitmap and corresponding command states are linked; changing one changes the other.

Related To L, M, X, &P

Application Black Box, Dallas, Infotel, Microcom, Practical, Prometheus, Rockwell, Sierra, Twincom, Zoom

S22

XON Character

Description　ATS22=*n*

Set XON character ASCII value.

n = 0–255

Default

17 (<DC1>)

This register holds the ASCII value of the character that will be recognized as the XON character during software flow-control operations.

Related To　S23

Application　USRobotics

S23

Configuration Bitmap

Description ATS23=*n*

n = decimal value of byte determined by bitmap.

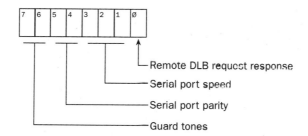

Bit	Default	Definition
0	x	Remote digital loopback (DLB) request response 0 Ignore request. Same as &T5. 1 Grant request. Same as &T4.
3-1	xxx	Serial port speed 000 0-300 bps. [Black Box, Dallas, Infotel, Microcom, Practical, Prometheus, Rockwell, Twincom, Zoom] 110 bps. [Dallas, Sierra] 001 300 bps. [Dallas, Sierra] 600 bps. [Dallas, Microcom, Zoom] 1200 bps. [Dallas, Prometheus] 010 1200 bps. [Black Box, Dallas, Infotel, Microcom, Practical, Prometheus, Rockwell, Sierra, Twincom, Zoom] 2400 bps. [Dallas, Prometheus] 011 2400 bps. [Black Box, Dallas, Infotel, Microcom, Practical, Prometheus, Rockwell, Sierra, Twincom, Zoom] 4800 bps. [Dallas, Prometheus] 100 4800 bps. [Black Box, Dallas, Microcom, Rockwell, Sierra, Twincom, Zoom] 7200 bps. [Dallas] 101 9600 bps. [Black Box, Dallas, Microcom, Prometheus, Rockwell, Sierra, Twincom, Zoom]

Bit	Default	Definition
3-1	xxx	Serial port speed (Continued) 110 19200 bps. [Dallas, Microcom, Prometheus, Rockwell, Sierra, Twincom, Zoom] 9600 bps with trellis coding. [Black Box] 111 38400 [Dallas, Microcom, Prometheus, Rockwell, Twincom, Zoom]
5-4	xx	Serial port parity 00 Even. 01 SPACE. 10 Odd. 11 MARK or none.
7-6	00	Guard tones 00 Disabled. Same as &G0. 01 550 Hz guard tone. Same as &G1. 10 1800 Hz guard tone. Same as &G2. 11 Reserved.

Default

5 (00000101b) [Dallas, Prometheus]

7 (00000111b) [Dallas, Microcom, Practical, Prometheus, Rockwell, Sierra, Twincom, Zoom]

13 (00001101b) [Black Box]

54 (00110110b) [Infotel]

S23 is a bitmapped register that controls a variety of modem parameters. Where appropriate, equivalent commands have been given for bit settings. The bitmap and corresponding command states are linked; changing one changes the other.

Related To &G, &T

Application Black Box, Dallas, Infotel, Microcom, Practical, Prometheus, Rockwell, Sierra, Twincom, Zoom

S23

XOFF Character

Description ATS23=*n*

Set XOFF character ASCII value.

n = 0–255

Default

19 (<DC3>)

This register holds the ASCII value of the character that will be recognized as the XOFF character during software flow-control operations.

Related To S22

Application USRobotics

S24

Description   `ATS24=n`

Set duration in increments of 20 milliseconds.

Default

150

This register sets the time that will elapse between pulsed DSR signals when the modem has been configured with the &S2 or &S3 command.

Related To   &S

Application   USRobotics

S25

DTR Detection Delay and Transition Threshold

Description   ATS25=*n*

Sets value for delay (seconds) and threshold (increments of 10 milliseconds).

$n = 0–255$

Default

> 5

The S25 register serves two different purposes, depending on the operating mode of the modem.

If the modem is configured for synchronous mode 4, the value in S25 represents the number of seconds the modem will wait after a connection is established before examining the data terminal ready (DTR) circuit. During this interval, the modem will ignore an ON-to-OFF DTR transition, giving the user sufficient time to disconnect the modem from the asynchronous terminal and attach it to a synchronous terminal.

In all other modes, and after the synchronous connection has been established in synchronous mode 4, S25 is interpreted as a time value in increments of 10 milliseconds. Under these conditions, a change in the state of the DTR signal that persists for less than the value specified by S25 will be ignored.

Related To   &M, &Q

Application   AT&T, Black Box, Dallas, Hayes, Infotel, Microcom, Motorola, Practical, Prometheus, Rockwell, Sierra, Telebit, Twincom, Zoom

Notes

1. Accessing this register does not produce an error, but has no effect on modem operation. [AT&T]

2. Telebit documentation states the lower limit of this register variously as 0, 1, and 5. [Telebit]

S26

RTS to CTS Delay

Description ATS26=*n*

Set value for delay in increments of 10 milliseconds.

n = 0–255

Set value for delay in increments of .1 second. [Telebit]

n = 0–255

Default

0 [AT&T, Infotel, Telebit]

1 [Black Box, Dallas, Hayes, Microcom, Motorola, Practical, Prometheus, Rockwell, Sierra, Telebit, Twincom, USRobotics, Zoom]

The S26 register specifies the amount of time to delay before the modem turns CTS ON in response to an OFF-to-ON DTR transition.

The RTS to CTS delay is used only during synchronous modes 1, 2, and 3 when the &R0 command has been selected.

Related To &R, S67

Application AT&T, Black Box, Dallas, Hayes, Infotel, Microcom, Motorola, Practical, Prometheus, Rockwell, Sierra, Telebit, Twincom, USRobotics, Zoom

S27

Configuration Bitmap

ATS27=*n*

n = decimal value of byte determined by bitmap.

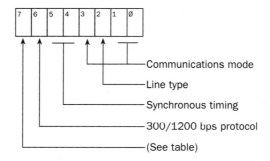

Bit	Default	Definition
3,1-0	xxx	Communications mode 000 Asynchronous mode. Same as &M0 or &Q0. 001 Synchronous mode 1. Same as &M1 or &Q1. 010 Synchronous mode 2. Same as &M2 or &Q2. 011 Synchronous mode 3. Same as &M3 or &Q3. 100 Synchronous mode 3. Same as &Q4. [Dallas, Rockwell, Twincom, Zoom] Invalid. [Dallas, Prometheus, Sierra] 101 Asynchronous error control mode. Same as &Q5. [Dallas, Rockwell, Sierra, Twincom, Zoom] 110 Asynchronous buffered mode. Same as &Q6. [Dallas, Rockwell, Sierra, Twincom, Zoom] 111 No effect. Same as &Q7. [Dallas, Rockwell, Twincom, Zoom] Invalid. [Dallas, Prometheus, Sierra] Reserved [Practical]

Bit	Default	Definition
2	0	Line type [Black Box, Dallas, Infotel, Rockwell, Sierra, Twincom, Zoom] 0 Dial-up line. Same as &L0. 1 Leased line. Same as &L1. Reserved [Practical, Prometheus]
5-4	00	Synchronous timing 00 Modem provides transmit clock. Same as &X0. 01 Modem accepts external clock. Same as &X1. 10 Receive clock. Same as &X2. 11 Reserved. Reserved [Practical]
6	x	300/1200 bps protocol 0 Use CCITT V.22/V.22bis. Same as B0. 1 Use Bell 212A. Same as B1. Reserved [Black Box]
7	0	V.23 [Dallas, Sierra] 0 Disabled. 1 Use V.23 standard. Same as B2. Trellis coding [Black Box] 0 Trellis coding enabled at 9600 bps. 1 Trellis coding disabled at 9600 bps. Reserved [Infotel, Prometheus, Rockwell, Twincom, Zoom]

Default

0 (00000000b) [Black Box]

64 (01000000b) [Dallas, Infotel, Practical, Prometheus, Rockwell, Sierra, Twincom]

69 (01000101b) [Dallas, Rockwell, Twincom, Zoom]

S27 is a bitmapped register that controls a variety of modem parameters. Where appropriate, equivalent commands have been given for bit settings. The bitmap and corresponding command states are linked; changing one changes the other.

Related To   B, &L, &M, &Q, &X

Application   Black Box, Dallas, Infotel, Prometheus, Rockwell, Sierra, Twincom, Zoom

Notes   **1.** Synchronous mode, timing, and line type selections are valid only on modems that support leased line and synchronous connections.

S27

Configuration Bitmap

Description   ATS27=*n*

n = decimal value of byte determined by bitmap.

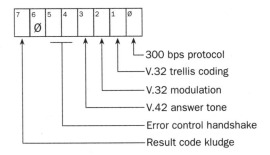

Bit	Default	Definition
0	0	300 bps protocol 0 Use Bell 103 at 300 bps. 1 Answer both Bell 103 and V.21 calls; originate only V.21.
1	0	V.32 trellis coding 0 Enable V.32 trellis coding. 1 Disable V.32 trellis coding.
2	0	V.32 modulation 0 Enable V.32 modulation. 1 Disable V.32 modulation.
3	0	V.42 answer tone 0 Enable 2100 Hz answer tone. 1 Disable 2100 Hz answer tone to enable two V.42 modems to connect more quickly.
5-4	00	Error control handshake 00 Complete handshaking sequence: V.42 detection, LAPM, MNP. 01 Disable MNP. 10 Disable V.42 detection and LAPM. 11 Disable V.42 detection.

Bit	Default	Definition
6	0	Reserved
7	0	Result code kludge 0 Report actual link speed. 1 Report link speed as 9600 if 9600 bps or higher.

Default

    0

S27 is a bitmapped register that controls and reports a variety of modem parameters.

Application   USRobotics

S27

Configuration Bitmap

Description ATS27=*n*

n=decimal value of byte determined by bitmap.

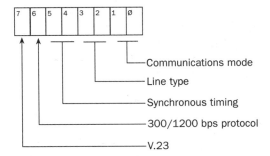

Bit	Default	Definition
1-0	00	Communications mode 00 Asynchronous mode. Same as &M0 or &Q0. 01 Synchronous mode 1. Same as &M1 or &Q1. 10 Synchronous mode 2. Same as &M2 or &Q2. 11 Synchronous mode 3. Same as &M3 or &Q3.
3-2	00	Leased line operation 00 Dial-up line. Same as &L0. 01 Two-wire leased line. Same as &L1 or &L3. 10 Four-wire leased line. Same as &L2 or &L4.
5-4	00	Synchronous timing 00 Modem provides transmit clock. Same as &X0. 01 Modem accepts external clock. Same as &X1. 10 Receive clock. Same as &X2. 11 Reserved.
6	1	300/1200 bps protocol 0 Use CCITT V.22/V.22bis. Same as B0. 1 Use Bell 212A. Same as B1.
7	0	Reserved

Default

    64 (01000000b)

S27 is a bitmapped register that controls a variety of modem parameters. Where appropriate, equivalent commands have been given for bit settings. The bitmap and corresponding command states are linked; changing one changes the other.

Related To B, &L, &M, &Q, &X

Application Microcom

S28

Configuration Bitmap

Description ATS28=*n*

n = decimal value of byte determined by bitmap.

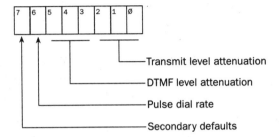

Bit	Default	Definition
2-0	000	Transmit level attenuation 000 0 dB 001 2 dB 010 4 dB 011 6 dB 100 8 dB 101 10 dB 110 12 dB 111 14 dB
5-3	000	DTMF level attenuation 000 0 dB 001 2 dB 010 4 dB 011 6 dB 100 8 dB 101 10 dB 110 12 dB 111 14 dB
6	0	Pulse dial rate 0 10 pulses per second. 1 20 pulses per second.

Bit	Default	Definition
7	0	Secondary defaults 0 Use &F defaults. 1 Use %J defaults.

Default

> 0

S28 is a bitmapped register that controls a variety of modem parameters. Where appropriate, equivalent commands have been given for bit settings. The bitmap and corresponding command states are linked; changing one changes the other.

Related To   %D, %J, %L, %F

Application   Rockwell, Twincom

S28

V.32 Answer Tone Duration

Description ATS28=*n*

Set duration in increments of .1 second.

$n = 0–255$

Default

8

This register sets the duration of the extra 3000 Hz and 600 Hz answer tones sent during V.32 handshaking.

Application USRobotics

S29

V.21 Answer Tone Duration

Description ATS29=*n*

Set duration in increments of .1 second.

n = 0–255

Default

20

This register sets the duration of the answer tones sent during V.21 handshaking.

Application USRobotics

S29

Configuration Bitmap

Description ATS29=*n*

n = decimal value of byte determined by bitmap.

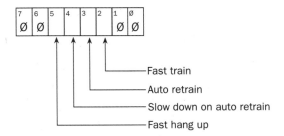

Bit	Default	Definition
1-0	00	Reserved
2	0	Fast train 0 Enabled. Same as %F0. 1 Disabled. Same as %F1.
3	1	Auto retrain 0 Enabled. same as %E0. 1 Disabled. Same as %E1.
4	0	Slow down on auto retrain 0 Enabled. Same as %E0. 1 Disabled. Same as %E2.
5	0	Fast hang up 0 Enabled. Same as H2. 1 Disabled. Same as H3.
7-6	00	Reserved

Default

8 (00001000b)

S29 is a bitmapped register that controls a variety of modem parameters.

Application   Black Box

S30

Inactivity Timeout

Description   ATS3Ø=*n*

Set timeout value in increments of 10 seconds.

n = 0–255 [Hayes, Motorola, Practical, Rockwell, Twincom, Zoom]

Set timeout value in seconds.

n = 0–90 [Dallas, Practical]

Default

0

This register sets the maximum time that the modem will maintain a connection in the absence of any data transfer. If the connection is inactive for a time equal to this limit, the modem automatically terminates the connection.

When S30 is set to 0, the inactivity timeout is disabled. Inactivity checking is enforced only for asynchronous modes; it is not enabled for any synchronous mode.

Application   Dallas, Hayes, Motorola, Practical, Rockwell, Twincom, Zoom

S30

Programmable/Permissive Transmit Level

Description ATS3Ø=*n*

0   Set transmit level for programmable dial-up line. (RJ-41S or RJ-45S).

9   Set transmit level for permissive dial-up line. (RJ-11, RJ-12, or RJ-13.)

Default

9

This register sets the dial-up line transmit level for programmable or permissive operation.

Related To &L

Application Black Box

S32

Voice/Data Switch Function

Description ATS32=*n*

0   Disabled.

1   Voice/data, originate mode.

2   Voice/data, answer mode.

3   Redial last number.

4   Dial first stored number.

5   Auto-answer on/off toggle.

6   Reset modem.

7   Initiate remote digital loopback.

8   Busy out phone line toggle.

Default

1

This register sets the function for the voice/data panel switch.

Application USRobotics

S32

Configuration Bitmap

Description ATS32=*n*

n = decimal value of byte determined by bitmap.

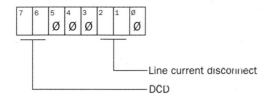

Bit	Default	Definition
0	0	Reserved
2-1	11	Line current disconnect 00 Disabled. Same as Y2. 01 Reserved. 10 8 millisecond line current disconnect. Same as Y4. 11 90 millisecond line current disconnect. Same as Y3.
5-3	000	Reserved
7-6	00	DCD 00 DCD follows register S21 bit 5. 01 Same as 00. 10 DCD pulses low at disconnect. Same as &C2. 11 Reserved.

Default

6 (00000110b)

S32 is a bitmapped register that controls a variety of modem parameters.

Related To Y, &C

Application Black Box

S33

AFT Options

Description ATS33=*n*

0   No transparency options required.

1   Flow control transparency. XON and XOFF characters sent from the DTE to the modem are replaced by substitute characters before transmission over the data link.

2   Control character transparency.

4   8-bit data transparency.

5   Flow control and 8-bit data transparency.

6   Control character and 8-bit data transparency.

Default

0

This register selects the options to be used with Hayes's asynchronous framing technique (AFT) protocol and is effective only for communications using a V-series enhancer and a Smartmodem 1200 with an asynchronous serial port connection to the DTE.

AFT transmission allows two compliant modems to exchange all 256 8-bit data values, even if intervening equipment restricts transmission of those values. If feature negotiation is enabled, the transparency option selected by one modem is used by both modems.

Related To S44

Application Hayes

S34

Configuration Bitmap

Description ATS34=*n*

n=decimal value of byte determined by bitmap

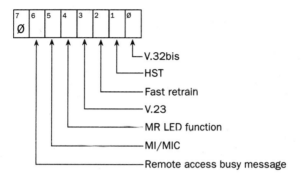

Bit	Default	Definition
0	0	V.32bis 0 Enabled. 1 Disabled.
1	0	HST 0 Enabled. 1 Disabled.
2	0	Fast retrain 0 Enabled. 1 Disabled.
3	0	V.23 0 Disabled. 1 Enabled.
4	0	MR (modem ready) LED function 0 MR LED shows modem ready. 1 MR LED shows DSR.

Bit	Default	Definition
5	0	MI/MIC (mode indicate/mode indicate common) 0 Disabled. 1 Enabled.
6	0	Remote access busy message 0 Enabled. 1 Disabled.
7	0	Reserved

Default

0

S34 is a bitmapped register that controls a variety of modem parameters.

Application USRobotics

S36

Error-Control Negotiation Failure Action

Description

ATS36=*n*

0   Hang up.

1   Attempt a DIRECT link (Q0).

2   Reserved.

3   Attempt a NORMAL link using buffering (Q6).

4   Attempt a V.42 alternative protocol (MNP 2-4) link. Disconnect if negotiation fails.

5   Attempt a V.42 alternative protocol (MNP 2-4) link. If negotiation fails, attempt a DIRECT link.

6   Reserved.

   Attempt a V.42 alternative protocol (MNP 2-4) link. Disconnect if negotiation fails. [Hayes]

7   Attempt a V.42 alternative protocol (MNP 2-4) link. If negotiation fails, attempt a NORMAL buffered link.

Default

   5 [Hayes, Rockwell, Twincom]

   7 [Dallas, Hayes, Practical, Prometheus, Sierra, Zoom]

When an attempt to establish a data link using an error-control protocol fails, the setting of this register determines the subsequent action taken by the modem.

The setting of this register is examined only when an error-control mode has been selected with the &Q command and this mode cannot be negotiated.

Related To   S46, S48, &Q

Application   Dallas, Hayes, Practical, Prometheus, Rockwell, Sierra, Twincom, Zoom

1. This register definition is valid for the SC11091 and SC11095 2400 bps universal modem advanced controllers only. The SC11095 does not support V.42bis. [Sierra]

S36

Configuration Bitmap

Description ATS36=*n*

n = decimal value of byte determined by bitmap

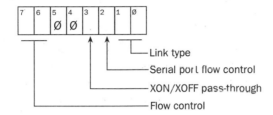

Bit	Default	Definition
1-0	01	Link type 00 NORMAL buffered data link. Same as \N0. 01 DIRECT data link. Same as \N1. 10 MNP RELIABLE link. 11 MNP AUTO RELIABLE link.
2	0	Data link flow control 0 Disabled. Same as \G0. 1 Enabled. Same as \G1.
3	0	XON/XOFF pass-through 0 Honor XON/XOFF, don't pass through. Same as \X0. 1 Honor XON/XOFF, pass through. Same as \X1.
5-4	00	Reserved
7-6	00	Flow control 00 Disabled. Same as \Q0. 01 XON/XOFF flow control. Same as \Q1. 10 CTS unidirectional hardware flow control. Same as \Q2. 11 RTS/CTS bidirectional flow control. \Q3.

Default

> 1 (00000001b)

S36 is a bitmapped register that controls a variety of modem parameters. Where appropriate, equivalent commands have been given for bit settings. The bitmap and corresponding command states are linked; changing one changes the other.

Related To   \G, \N, \Q, \X

Application   Dallas, Sierra

Notes   **1.** This register definition is valid for the SC11061 2400 bps fast modem advanced controller only. [Sierra]

S37

AUTO RELIABLE Fallback Character

Description ATS37=*n*

Set fallback character ASCII value.

n = 0–127.

Default

0

This register holds the ASCII value of the character that will be recognized as the AUTO RELIABLE fallback character by the answering modem. Setting S37=0 disables fallback character recognition. Values greater than 127 are treated as 0.

Related To %A

Application Dallas, Sierra

Notes
1. This register definition is valid for the SC11061 2400 bps fast modem advanced controller only. [Sierra]

S37

Maximum Data Link Speed

Description   ATS37=*n*

0   Attempt to connect at the highest data link speed that does not exceed the speed of the last AT command issued.

1   Attempt a data link at 75 bps. [Hayes]

     Attempt a data link at 300 bps. [Dallas, Rockwell, Twincom, Zoom]

     Reserved. [Hayes, Practical, Prometheus]

2   Attempt a data link at 110 bps. [Hayes]

     Attempt a data link at 300 bps. [Dallas, Rockwell, Twincom, Zoom]

     Reserved. [Practical, Prometheus]

3   Attempt a data link at 300 bps.

4   Attempt a data link at 600 bps. (Not supported.) [Hayes]

5   Attempt a data link at 1200 bps.

6   Attempt a data link at 2400 bps.

7   Attempt a data link at 4800 bps. [Dallas, Hayes, Practical, Prometheus]

     Attempt a V.23 data link at 75/1200 bps. [Zoom]

     Reserved. [Rockwell, Twincom]

8   Attempt a data link at 7200 bps. [Dallas, Hayes, Prometheus, Rockwell, Twincom]

     Attempt a data link at 4800 bps. [Zoom]

     Reserved. [Practical]

9   Attempt a data link at 9600 bps.

10   Attempt a data link at 12000 bps. [Dallas, Hayes, Practical, Prometheus, Zoom]

11   Attempt a data link at 14400 bps. [Dallas, Hayes, Practical, Prometheus, Zoom]

12   Attempt a data link at 7200 bps. [Dallas, Zoom]

Default

0

The modem will attempt to establish a data link at the highest supported speed that does not exceed the value specified by this register. If S37 is set to a speed not supported by the modem, the modem will attempt to connect at the next lowest supported speed.

Related To S93

Application Dallas, Hayes, Practical, Prometheus, Rockwell, Twincom, Zoom

Notes

1. If S37=0 and the speed of the last AT command was greater than 9600 bps, the modem will attempt to connect at 9600 bps. [Rockwell, Twincom]

2. If the modem supports MNP 5, the class that is negotiated is determined by S46. MNP 5 negotiation results if bit 2 of S46 is 1; MNP 4 negotiation results if bit 2 of S46 is 0. [Hayes]

S38

Forced Disconnect Buffer Delay

Description ATS38=*n*

Set delay in seconds.

n = 0–255

Default

    0 [Telebit, USRobotics]

    5 [Motorola]

    20 [Dallas, Hayes, Practical, Prometheus, Rockwell, Telebit, Twincom, Zoom]

This register specifies the amount of time that may expire between the modem's receipt of a hang-up command or an ON-to-OFF DTR transition and the actual disconnect operation.

This timeout function is useful when forcing a disconnect during an error-control link. If S38 is set between 0 and 254, the modem will wait the indicated number of seconds before disconnecting. This provides time for the local modem to send all data in its buffers and for the remote modem to acknowledge receipt of the data.

If the S38 time limit expires before all data is sent and acknowledged, the modem returns NO CARRIER. Otherwise, it returns OK.

If S38 is set to 255, the modem does not timeout, but will continue to send data and receive acknowledgments until the connection is lost or all data has been delivered.

Application Dallas, Hayes, Motorola, Practical, Prometheus, Rockwell, Telebit, Twincom, USRobotics, Zoom

Notes **1.** If the modem receives an ATH command, it ignores this register and disconnects immediately. [USRobotics]

S38

Configuration Bitmap

Description ATS38=*n*

n = decimal value of byte determined by bitmap.

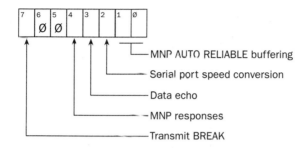

Bit	Default	Definition
1-0	00	MNP AUTO RELIABLE buffering 00 Data not buffered. Same as \C0. 01 Data buffered until 200 non-SYN characters are received or a SYN character is detected within 3 seconds. Same as \C1. 10 Data not buffered. Switches to NORMAL link when fallback character is received. Same as \C2. 11 Reserved.
2	0	Serial port speed conversion 0 Speed remains constant. Same as \J0. 1 Speed set to match link speed. Same as \J1.
3	0	Data echo 0 Data not echoed. Same as \E0. 1 Data echoed. Same as \E1.
4	0	MNP responses 0 Disabled. Same as \V0. 1 Enabled. Same as \V1.
6-5	00	Reserved

Bit	Default	Definition
7	0	Transmit BREAK 0 Normal operation. 1 Send BREAK. Same as \B. Bit resets automatically.

Default

    0 (00000000b)

S38 is a bitmapped register that controls a variety of modem parameters. Where appropriate, equivalent commands have been given for bit settings. The bitmap and corresponding command states are linked; changing one changes the other.

Related To   \B, \C, \E, \J, \V

Application   Dallas, Sierra

Notes   **1.** This register definition is valid for the SC11061 2400 bps fast modem advanced controller only. [Sierra]

S39

MNP Inactivity Timeout

Description ATS39=*n*

Set timeout value in minutes.

n = 0–90

Default

0

This register sets the maximum amount of time that the modem will maintain an MNP connection in the absence of any data transfer. If the connection is inactive for a time equal to this limit, the modem automatically terminates the connection.

When S39 is set to 0, the inactivity timeout is disabled. Inactivity checking is enforced only for asynchronous modes; it is not enabled for any synchronous mode.

Application Dallas, Sierra

Notes
1. This register definition is valid for the SC11061 2400 bps fast modem advanced controller only. [Sierra]

S39

Flow Control

Description   ATS39?

Return current setting.

0   No flow control.

3   RTS/CTS flow control.

4   XON/XOFF flow control.

5   Transparent XON/XOFF flow control.

The value in this register indicates the current flow-control method. This register reflects the state of the &K command and is read-only.

Related To   &K

Application   Hayes

S40

Configuration Bitmap

Description ATS40=*n*

n = decimal value of byte determined by bitmap.

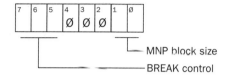

MNP block size
BREAK control

Bit	Default	Definition
1-0	11	MNP block size 00 Maximum block size is 64 characters. Same as \A0. 01 Maximum block size is 128 characters. Same as \A1. 10 Maximum block size is 192 characters. Same as \A2. 11 Maximum block size is 256 characters. Same as \A3.
4-2	000	Reserved
7-5	101	BREAK control 000 Same as \K0. 001 Same as \K1. 010 Same as \K2. 011 Same as \K3. 100 Same as \K4. 101 Same as \K5. 110 Reserved. 111 Reserved.

Default

163 (10100011b)

S40 is a bitmapped register that controls a variety of modem parameters. Where appropriate, equivalent commands have been given for bit settings.

The bitmap and corresponding command states are linked; changing one changes the other.

Related To \A, \K

Application Dallas, Sierra

Notes

1. This register definition is valid for the SC11061 2400 bps fast modem advanced controller only. [Sierra]

S40

Configuration Bitmap

Description ATS4Ø=*n*

n = decimal value of byte determined by bitmap

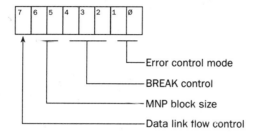

Error control mode
BREAK control
MNP block size
Data link flow control

Bit	Default	Definition
1-0	11	Error control mode 00 NORMAL mode. Same as \N0. 01 Reserved. 10 MNP RELIABLE mode. Same as \N2. 11 MNP AUTO RELIABLE mode. Same as \N3.
4-2	101	BREAK control 000 Same as \K0. 001 Same as \K1. 010 Same as \K2. 011 Same as \K3. 100 Same as \K4. 101 Same as \K5.
6-5	xx	MNP block size 00 Maximum block size is 64 characters. Same as \A0. 01 Maximum block size is 128 characters. Same as \A1. 10 Maximum block size is 192 characters. Same as \A2. 11 Maximum block size is 256 characters. Same as \A3.
7	0	Data link flow control 0 Disabled. Same as \G0. 1 Enabled. Same as \G1.

Default

119 (01110111b) [Rockwell, Twincom, Zoom]

87 (01010111b) [Dallas]

S40 is a bitmapped register that controls a variety of modem parameters. Where appropriate, equivalent commands have been given for bit settings. The bitmap and corresponding command states are linked; changing one changes the other.

Related To   \A, \G, \K, \N

Application   Dallas, Rockwell, Twincom, Zoom

S40

Auto Make Busy

Description   ATS4Ø=*n*

    0   Disable.

    1   Enable.

Default

    0

The setting of this register determines if the modem goes off-hook automatically under certain conditions. This register should be enabled only when the modem is located behind a user's PBX (private branch exchange).

Application   AT&T

S41

Configuration Bitmap

Description ATS41=*n*

n = decimal value of byte determined by bitmap.

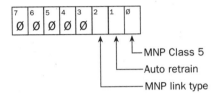

Bit	Default	Definition
0	x	MNP Class 5 0 Disabled. Same as %C0. 1 Enabled. Same as %C1.
1	0	Auto retrain [Rockwell, Twincom] 0 Disable. Same as %E0. 1 Enable. Same as %E1. Reserved [Dallas, Sierra]
2	0	MNP Link Type 0 Use stream mode. Same as \L0. 1 Use block mode. Same as \L1. Reserved [Dallas, Sierra]
7-3	00000	Reserved

Default

0 (00000000b) [Dallas, Sierra]

1 (00000001b) [Dallas, Rockwell, Twincom, Zoom]

S41 is a bitmapped register that controls a variety of modem parameters.
Where appropriate, equivalent commands have been given for bit settings.

The bitmap and corresponding command states are linked; changing one changes the other.

Related To   % C

Application   Dallas, Rockwell, Sierra, Twincom, Zoom

Notes

1. This register definition is valid for the SC11061 2400 bps fast modem advanced controller only. [Sierra]

S41

Dial-Up Link Speed

Description   ATS41=*n*

0   Link at 14400 bps using V.32bis modulation.

1   Same as S41=0.

2   Link at 12000 bps using V.32bis modulation.

3   Link at 9600 bps using V.32bis or V.32 modulation.

4   Link at 7200 bps using V.32 modulation.

5   Link at 4800 bps using V.32bis or V.32 modulation.

6   Link at 2400 bps using V.22bis modulation.

7   Link at 1200 bps using V.22 modulation.

8   Link at 1200 bps using Bell 212A modulation.

10   Link at 0-300 bps using V.21 modulation.

11   Link at 0-300 bps using Bell 103J modulation.

12   Link at 1200/75 bps (transmit/receive) using V.23 modulation.

13   Link at 75/1200 bps (transmit/receive) using V.23 modulation.

Default

1 [AT&T]

This register determines the protocol and data link rate that the modem will use for operation on dial-up lines.

For settings 0–5, the modem can be forced by the remote modem to connect at a lower data rate within the V.32bis protocol. For settings 8–11, the modem does not support V.42 or MNP error control.

Related To   S78

Application   AT&T

S41

Remote Access Login Attempt Limit

Description   ATS41=*n*

Set number of attempts.

n = 0–255

Default

   0

This register sets the number of remote access attempts that will be allowed during a single connection. The default setting of 0 disables remote access.

Application   USRobotics

S41

Inactivity Timeout

Description   ATS41=n

Set timeout value in increments of 6 minutes.

$n = 0$–255

Default

   0

This register sets the maximum amount of time that the modem will maintain a connection in the absence of any data transfer. If the connection is inactive for a time equal to this limit, the modem automatically terminates the connection. The limit is specified in multiples of 6 minutes (one-tenth hour).

When S41 is set to 0, the inactivity timeout is disabled. Inactivity checking is enforced only for asynchronous modes; it is not enabled for any synchronous mode.

Application   Telebit

S42

Remote Access Character

Description ATS42=*n*

Set remote access character ASCII value.

n = 0–255

Default

126 (~)

This register holds the ASCII value of the character that will be recognized as the remote access character. By default, S42 holds the ASCII value for the tilde (~).

Related To S43

Application USRobotics

S43

Current Data Link Speed

Description ATS43?

Return the speed of the last data link.

0   No connection.

1   Reserved.

2   110 bps. [Hayes]

3   300 bps.

4   600 bps. (Not supported.) [Hayes]

5   1200 bps.

6   2400 bps.

7   4800 bps.

8   7200 bps.

9   9600 bps.

10   12000 bps.

11   14400 bps.

12   14400 bps.

The value in register S43 indicates the speed of the last data link that was established successfully. S43 is a read-only register.

Application Hayes, Practical

S43

Remote Access Guard Time

Description ATS43=*n*

Set time in increments of 20 milliseconds.

Default

100

The S43 register sets the duration of the guard time that must surround the remote access sequence (~~~~ by default).

Related To S42

Application USRobotics

S43

V.32bis Train

Description   ATS43=*n*

0   Use long training sequence.

1   Use short training sequence.

Default

0

The S43 register determines whether the minimum or maximum times are used for the V.32bis and V.32 training sequences. The long train is typically required for satellite links or other signal paths that have long delays. The short train allows the modems to handshake faster.

Application   AT&T

S44

Framing Technique

Description ATS44=*n*

0   No error-control connection will be negotiated.

1   Negotiate synchronous only.

2   Negotiate asynchronous only. Required if the data link passes through asynchronous-only equipment.

3   Negotiate either synchronous (preferred) or asynchronous (fallback).

Default

3

S44 determines whether Hayes's asynchronous framing technique (AFT) will be used.

Normally, connections to a packet-switched network or between two error-control modems using LAPB or X.25 are synchronous. In some environments, asynchronous-to-synchronous conversion may be required. The setting of this register is examined only during communications using a V-series Modem Enhancer with a Smartmodem 1200.

Related To S33, S45

Application Hayes

S44

Leased Line Link Speed

Description ATS44=*n*

1   Link at 14400 bps using V.32bis modulation.

2   Link at 12000 bps using V.32bis modulation.

3   Link at 9600 bps using V.32bis or V.32 modulation.

4   Link at 7200 bps using V.32 modulation.

5   Link at 4800 bps using V.32bis or V.32 modulation.

11   Link at 14400 bps using V.33 modulation.

12   Link at 12000 bps using V.33 modulation.

13   Link at 9600 bps using V.29 modulation.

14   Link at 7200 bps using V.29 modulation.

15   Link at 4800 bps using V.29 modulation.

Default

1

This register determines the protocol and data link rate that the modem will use for operation on leased lines.

Application AT&T

S45

Report Framing Technique Status

Description   ATS45?

Return current framing type.

0   Reserved.

1   Synchronous. (V.32 half-duplex only.)

2   Asynchronous.

3   Either synchronous or asynchronous; not limited by intervening hardware.

The value in register S45 indicates the framing type that was negotiated for the last successful connection. S45 is a read-only register.

Related To   S44

Application   Hayes

S45

Leased Line Transmit Level

Description   ATS45=*n*

Set current leased line transmit level in -dBm.

$n = 0$–15

Default

0

This register selects the nominal transmit power level in dBm that will be used during leased line operation.

Application   AT&T

S45

Remote Access

Description ATS45=*n*

  0 Disabled.

  254 Request remote access (MNP only).

  255 Enabled.

  Default

    0

When S45=1, a remote modem is able to access the control functions of the local modem.

Related To S180, S181

Application Telebit

Notes **1.** Remote access in non-PEP connections is not supported in all firmware versions.

S45

Access Security Tone Duration

Description ATS45=*n*

Set duration in seconds.

n = 0–255

Default

5

This register specifies the duration of the prompt tone when access security is enabled.

Related To S46

Application Motorola

S46

Error-Control/Compression Selection

Description ATS46=*n*

0 LAPM with fallback to LAPB. No compression. [Hayes]

1 LAPB only. No compression. [Hayes]

2 LAPM with fallback to LAPB. Attempt V.42bis data compression with fallback to adaptive (MNP) data compression. [Hayes]

3 LAPB with V.42bis data compression or fallback to adaptive (MNP) data compression. [Hayes]

6 X.25 with fallback to LAPB. If LAPB, attempt data compression. [Hayes]

134 X.25 only. No compression. [Hayes]

136 LAPM only. No compression.

138 LAPM with V.42bis data compression.

Default

2 [Hayes]

138 [Dallas, Practical, Prometheus, Rockwell, Sierra, Twincom, Zoom]

This register specifies the error-control method that will be used for subsequent data links.

Related To S36, S47, S48

Application Dallas, Hayes, Practical, Prometheus, Rockwell, Sierra, Twincom, Zoom

Notes

1. This register definition is valid for the SC11091 and SC11095 2400 bps universal modem advanced controllers only. The SC11095 does not support V.42bis. [Sierra]

2. On some modems, the definition of this register has been generalized to enable error control (S46=136) and to enable error control with

compression (S46=138). LAPM/V.42bis or MNP 2–4/MNP 5 may be selected. [Rockwell, Twincom]

3. Some documentation lists the values 0 (equivalent to 136) and 2 (equivalent to 138) as the only legal values for this register. [Practical]

S46

Auto Dial Backup

Description ATS46=*n*

0   Disabled.

1   Enabled.

Default

0

This register determines if the modem performs an automatic dial backup if a leased line connection fails.

Related To S47

Application AT&T

S46

Modem Security

Description ATS46=*n*

0 Callback security disabled.

1 Callback security enabled.

2 Callback security enabled with password reverification.

3 Pass-through security enabled; no callback occurs.

Default

0

The S46 register determines the type of security used when the modem answers an incoming call.

Related To ~L, ~N, ~U

Application Telebit

S46

Access Security Lead Digit Timeout

Description ATS46=*n*

Set duration in seconds.

n = 0–255

Default

12

This register specifies the lead digit delay timeout when the access security tone option is enabled.

Related To S45

Application Motorola

S47

Report Error-Control/Compression Status

Description   ATS47?

Return current status.

0   LAPM with fallback to LAPB. No compression.

1   LAPB only. No compression.

2   LAPM with fallback to LAPB. Attempt V.42bis data compression with fallback to adaptive (MNP) data compression.

3   LAPB with V.42bis data compression or fallback to adaptive (MNP) data compression.

6   X.25 with fallback to LAPB. If LAPB, attempt data compression.

134   X.25 only. No compression.

136   LAPM only. No compression.

138   LAPM with V.42bis data compression.

The value in register S47 indicates the framing type that was negotiated. S47 is a read-only register.

Related To   S36, S46, S48

Application   Hayes

S47

Auto Dial Standby

Description ATS47=*n*

0   Disabled.

1   Evaluate line once every 15 min-
     utes.

2   Evaluate line once every hour.

3   Evaluate line once every 4 hours.

Default

0

When the modem is operating on dial lines, the S47 register sets the time interval at which the modem will evaluate the quality of the leased line, and if it
is good, it will switch to a leased line connection.

Related To S46

Application AT&T

S47

DSR/DCD Delay

Description   ATS47=*n*

Set delay in increments of 50 milliseconds.

n = 0–255

Default

4

The S47 register specifies the amount of time that the data set ready (DSR) and data carrier detect (DCD) signals are pulsed when the carrier is lost and the &C2 or &S2 command is in effect.

Related To   &C, &S, S130, S131

Application   Telebit

S48

Feature Negotiation

Description ATS48=*n*

0   Negotiation (detection and XID) is disabled. Connect only with the configuration specified by S46.

1   Enable detection, disable XID. (Unpublished) [Hayes]

2   Disable detection, enable XID. (Unpublished) [Hayes]

3   Negotiation (detection and XID) is enabled, but the originating modem remains silent during the detection phase. Use this setting for connections with MNP modems only as it defeats the V.42 negotiation sequence. [Hayes, Prometheus]

7   Negotiation (detection and XID) is enabled.

128   Negotiation (detection and XID) is disabled. The fallback options specified by S36 are performed immediately.

Default

7 [Dallas, Hayes, Practical, Prometheus, Rockwell, Twincom, Zoom]

128 [Dallas, Practical, Sierra]

Feature negotiation has two phases: detection and negotiation using XID frames. This register selects how feature negotiation is performed or whether it is bypassed entirely.

Related To S36, S46

Application Dallas, Hayes, Practical, Prometheus, Rockwell, Sierra, Twincom, Zoom

Notes

1. This register definition is valid for the SC11091 and SC11095 2400 bps universal modem advanced controllers only. The SC11095 does not support V.42bis. [Sierra]

S48

Leased Line Carrier Threshold

Description ATS48=*n*

0   -43 dBm.

1   -26 dBm.

Default

0

This register sets the minimum acceptable level for a leased line carrier. Below the specified level, the modem will automatically disconnect.

Application AT&T

S48

Control Character Mask

Description ATS48=*n*

0   Use only the low-order 7 bits.

1   Use all 8 bits.

Default

0

The setting of this register determines if the modem uses 7 or 8 bits when comparing each character to the values in the S2, S56, and S57 registers to detect the escape, XON, and XOFF characters, respectively.

If the local DTE is using a data format of 7 data bits plus parity, S48 should be set to 0 to mask the eighth bit. This permits end-to-end parity checking for data and allows the modem to recognize escape, XON, and XOFF characters.

Related To S2, S56, S57

Application Telebit

S49

Forced-Disconnect Buffer Delay

Description ATS49=*n*

Set buffer disconnect delay in seconds.

n = 0–255

Default

10

This register specifies the time that may expire between the modem's receipt of a hangup command from the local DTE and the actual disconnect operation.

This timeout function is useful when forcing a disconnect during an error-control link. The modem will wait the number of seconds indicated in S49 before disconnecting. This provides time for the local modem to send all data in its buffers and for the remote modem to acknowledge receipt of the data.

If the S38 time limit expires before all data is sent and acknowledged, the modem returns NO CARRIER. Otherwise, it returns OK. Setting S49 to 0 forces an immediate response to a disconnect request.

Related To H

Application AT&T

S49

Buffer Lower Threshold

Description ATS49=*n*

Set buffer lower threshold in bytes.

n = 1–249

Default

8

The S49 register sets the buffer lower threshold size that will be used during a
NORMAL buffered asynchronous connection. If data transfer from the DTE
to the modem is disabled and the buffer empties to this level, the modem will
restart data flow.

Related To &Q6, S36, S50

Application Hayes, Prometheus

S49

Product Identification String

Description ATS49=*n*

0   I0 returns true model number.

1   I0 returns 123 as the model number.

2   I0 returns 965 as the model number.

Default

0

The S49 register controls the product identification number returned by the I0 command. This can be altered to ensure software compatibility.

Related To I

Application Telebit

S50

Buffer Upper Threshold

Description ATS5Ø=*n*

Set buffer upper threshold in bytes.

n = 2–250

Default

16

The S50 register sets the buffer upper threshold size that will be used during a NORMAL buffer asynchronous connection. If data transfer from the DTE to the modem is enabled and the buffer fills to this level, the modem will act to stop data flow from the DTE.

Related To &Q6, S36, S49

Application Hayes, Prometheus

S50

RAM Status

Description   ATS5Ø?

Return RAM status.

0   RAM tested good at power-up.

1   RAM failed self-test.

This register holds the result of the power-on self test the modem performs on its internal RAM.

Application   Black Box

S50

Set Data Link Speed

Description   ATS50=*n*

0   Automatic speed determination. Attempt a link at a speed determined by S94.

1   Attempt a link at 300 bps using Bell 103 or V.21.

2   Attempt a link at 1200 bps using Bell 212A or V.22.

3   Attempt a link at 2400 bps using V.22bis.

4   Attempt a link at 300 bps using Bell 103.

5   Attempt a link at 1200/75 bps using V.23.

6   Attempt a link at 9600 bps using V.32.

7   Attempt a link at 14400 bps using V.32bis.

254   Attempt a link at the speed of the last AT command (non-PEP).

255   FAST operation (PEP mode).

Default

0, 254

If S94=0, the modem connects only at the speed specified by S50. If S94=1, the modem attempts to connect at any speed up to the maximum specified by S50.

If S50 is 1 or 2, use the B command to select between Bell and CCITT standards.

Related To   B, S90, S91, S92, S94

Application   Telebit

S51

DTE Remote Loopback

Description ATS51=*n*

0   Disabled.

1   Enabled.

Default

0

The S51 register determines whether the modem performs a remote digital loopback test if it receives a V.24 CT140 signal from the DTE.

Related To   S52, S61

Application   AT&T

S51

Serial Port Speed

Description   ATS51=*n*

0	300 bps.
1	1200 bps.
2	2400 bps.
3	4800 bps.
4	9600 bps.
5	19200 bps.
6	38400 bps.
7	57600 bps.
8	76800 bps.
9	115200 bps.
35	7200 bps.
43	12000 bps.
46	14400 bps.
252	Autobaud; type-ahead not permitted. Default to speed of last &W command.
253	Autobaud; type-ahead permitted. Default to 38400 bps.
254	Autobaud; type-ahead permitted. Default to 19200 bps.
255	Autobaud; type-ahead permitted. Default to 9600 bps.

Default

   252, 255

The S51 register sets the serial port speed that will be used between the DTE and the modem.

Autobauding (automatic speed selection based on the last AT command) requires that you use either 8 data bits with no parity or 7 data bits with 1 parity bit. Autobauding does not support speeds of 57600, 76800, or 115200 bps.

Related To   S51, S181

Application   Telebit

S52

DTE Local Loopback

Description   ATS52=*n*

0	Disabled.
1	Enabled.
Default	
	0

The S52 register determines whether the modem performs a local analog loopback test if it receives a V.24 CT141 signal from the DTE.

Related To   S51, S61

Application   AT&T

S52

Leased Line Transmit Level

Description ATS52=*n*

Set current leased line transmit level in -dBm.

$n = 0{-}15$

Default

9

This register selects the nominal transmit power level in dBm that will be used during leased line operation.

Application Black Box

S52

DTR Interpretation

Description ATS52=*n*

0   Modem assumes DTR is always ON.

1   Modem disconnects and enters command mode following an ON-to-OFF DTR transition. Auto-answer is disabled while DTR is OFF.

2   Modem performs a hard reset and enters command mode following an ON-to-OFF DTR transition. Auto-answer is disabled while DTR is OFF.

3   Modem switches to command mode (if in data mode) following an ON-to-OFF DTR transition.

4   Modem disconnects, enters command mode, and disables auto-answer following an ON-to-OFF DTR transition. Auto-answer is enabled when DTR is turned ON.

Default

0

The S52 register determines how the modem will interpret the data terminal ready (DTR) signal from the DTE.

Related To S25

Application Telebit

S53

Global PAD Configuration

Description   ATS53=*n*

n = decimal value of byte determined by bitmap.

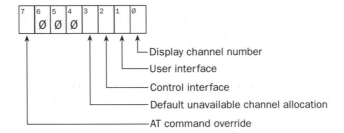

Bit	Default	Definition
0	0	Display channel number 0 Disabled. 1 Precede PAD prompt with channel number.
1	1	User interface 0 CCITT user interface. 1 Fixed user interface.
2	0	Control interface 0 CCITT control interface. 1 Fixed control interface.
3	0	Default unavailable channel allocation 0 Disabled. 1 Reset national parameter 108 each time a PAD profile is loaded.
6-4	000	Reserved
7	0	AT command override 0 Disabled. 1 Enable echo and set Ctrl+H as backspace character.

Default

   2 (00000010b)

The S53 register defines a set of behavior switches that controls the PAD (packet assembler/disassembler) and all four channels in V-series products.

The default prompt character is an asterisk (*). If a fixed user interface or control interface is selectcd, the prompt changes to a hyphen (-).

Application Hayes

S53

V.54 Address

Description ATS53=*n*

Set modem address.

$n = 0, 1–34$

Default

0

The S53 register identifies the address of the modem to be placed in a loop-back test. Setting the register to 0 disables this feature.

Related To S54

Application AT&T

S54

V.54 Device Type

Description ATS54=n

0   Peripheral.

1   Intermediate.

Default

0

This register identifies the physical location of the modem within the network.

Related To S53

Application AT&T

S54

BREAK Handling

Description ATS54=*n*

0   Switch to command mode.

1   Reserved.

2   The modem immediately sends a BREAK to the remote DTE.

3   If in data mode, the modem sends the BREAK to the remote modem in sequence with the data. If in command mode, the modem sends the BREAK immediately.

4   BREAK is ignored.

Default

0, 3

The S54 register determines the modem's response to a BREAK signal sent by the local DTE.

The responses shown above apply when the modem is operating in PEP mode. If the modem is operating in V.32 or a lower speed mode and S54 is set to either 0 or 4, the modem responds as shown. If not, the modem sends the BREAK to the remote modem. In PEP mode, the remote modem empties its buffers when it receives a BREAK.

Related To S62

Application Telebit

S54

Configuration Bitmap

Description　ATS54=*n*

n = decimal value of byte determined by bitmap.

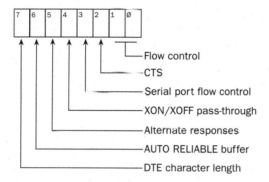

Bit	Default	Definition
1-0	01	Flow control 00 Disabled. Same as \Q0. 01 XON/XOFF flow control. Same as \Q1. 10 CTS unidirectional hardware flow control. Same as 　　\Q2. 11 RTS/CTS bidirectional flow control. \Q3.
2	0	CTS 0 Always on. Same as \D0. 1 Follows DCD. Same as \D1.
3	0	Serial port flow control 0 Disabled. Same as \G0. 1 Enabled. Same as \G1.
4	0	XON/XOFF pass-through 0 Disabled. Same as \X0. 1 Enabled. Same as \X1.

Bit	Default	Definition
5	0	Alternate responses 0 Same as Q3. 1 Same as Q4.
6	0	AUTO RELIABLE buffer 0 Disabled. Same as \C0. 1 Enabled. Same as \C1.
7	0	DTE character length 0 10 bits. 1 11 bits.

Default

1 (00000001b)

S34 is a bitmapped register that controls a variety of modem parameters.

Related To   Q, \C, \D, \G, \Q, \X

Application   Black Box

S55

AutoStream Protocol Request

Description ATS55=*n*

0 No AutoStream.

1 Request AutoStream Level 1: Allows multiplexing of multiple virtual channels on the DTE.

2 Request AutoStream Level 2: Allows transparent control over one PAD at a time, nonsimultaneously.

3 Request AutoStream Level 3: Allows transparent control over all PADs simultaneously.

Default

0

This register allows the selection of the AutoStream level. To query the current level, see the S56 register.

Related To S56

Application Hayes

S55

Access From Remote

Description ATS55=*n*

0   Enabled.

1   Disabled.

Default

0

The S55 register determines if a modem's diagnostic control panel can be accessed by a remote modem.

Application AT&T

S55

Escape Handling

Description ATS55=*n*

0   Enter command mode after receipt of proper escape sequence. Send escape characters to remote modem.

1   Empty local buffers, remain in data mode, and send escape characters to remote modem.

2   Remain in data mode and send escape characters to remote modem.

3   Remain in data mode and send escape characters to remote modem in sequence with data stream. If in command mode, send the escape characters immediately.

Default

0

This register determines the modem's response to the escape sequence entered from the local DTE.

Related To S2, S12

Application Telebit

S56

AutoStream Protocol Status

Description　ATS56?

0　　No AutoStream.

1　　AutoStream Level 1: Allows multiplexing of multiple virtual channels on the DTE.

2　　AutoStream Level 2: Allows transparent control over one PAD at a time, nonsimultaneously.

3　　AutoStream Level 3: Allows transparent control over all PADs simultaneously.

This register reports the status of the current AutoStream level. The S56 register is read-only.

Related To　S55

Application　Hayes

S56

XON Character

Description ATS56=*n*

Set XON character ASCII value.

n = 0 255

Default

17 (<DC1>)

This register holds the ASCII value of the character that will be recognized as the XON character during software flow control operations.

Related To S48, S57, S58, S68

Application Telebit

S56–S59

Remote Access Password

Description   ATS56=*n*

Set first pair of digits of a remote password.

ATS57=*n*

Set second pair of digits of a remote password.

ATS58=*n*

Set third pair of digits of a remote password.

ATS59=*n*

Set fourth pair of digits of a remote password.

$n = 00\text{–}99$

These four registers are used to set an 8-digit remote access password. Each register can hold a decimal value from 00 to 99, yielding a composite password from 00000000 to 99999999.

For example, the password 12345678 could be entered using the following command:

AT S56=12 S57=34 S58=56 S59=78

Application   AT&T

S57

Network Options

Description ATS57=*n*

0   In call accept or clear request packets, the address length is set to 0, but the facility and data fields may be present.

1   In call accept or clear request packets, the address, facility, or data fields may be present.

2   In call accept or clear request packets, no fields may be sent.

3   Same as S57=2.

Default

0

The setting of this register, effective only on modems that support X.25 and AutoStream, allows configuration of the packet layer for operation with different networks.

Application Hayes

S57

XOFF Character

Description   ATS57=*n*

Set XOFF character ASCII value.

n = 0–255

Default

19 (<DC3>)

This register holds the ASCII value of the character that will be recognized as the XOFF character during software flow-control operations.

Related To   S48, S56, S58, S68

Application   Telebit

S58

MNP Inactivity Timeout

Description ATS58=*n*

Set timeout value in minutes.

n = 0–90

Default

0

This register sets the maximum amount of time that the modem will maintain an MNP connection in the absence of any data transfer. If the connection is inactive for a time equal to this limit, the modem automatically terminates the connection.

When S58 is set to 0, the inactivity timeout is disabled. Inactivity checking is enforced only for asynchronous modes; it is not enabled for any synchronous mode.

Application Black Box

S58

Serial Port Flow Control

Description   ATS58=*n*

0   Disabled.

1   CTS flow control. The modem uses the CTS line to control data transfer from the DTE.

2   RTS flow control. The DTE uses the RTS line to control data transfer from the modem.

3   XON/XOFF flow control. The DTE uses the XOFF character to suspend and the XON character to resume data transfer from the modem.

4   RTS and XON/XOFF flow control. The DTE uses the RTS line and XON/XOFF characters to control data transfer from the modem.

5   Use HP ENQ/ACK protocol.

6   Use HP ENQ/ACK protocol and XON/XOFF flow control.

7   Transparent XON/XOFF flow control. The local modem ignores XON/XOFF flow-control characters received from the local DTE, but passes them to the remote modem.

Default

2, 3

Related To   S48, S56, S57, S66, S68, S180, S181

Application   Telebit

S59

BREAK control

Description ATS59=*n*

0   Same as \K0.

1   Same as \K1.

2   Same as \K2.

3   Same as \K3.

4   Same as \K4.

5   Same as \K5.

Default

5

This register selects the modem's response when it receives a BREAK or the transmit BREAK (\B) command from the DTE or a BREAK from the remote modem.

Related To \K

Application Black Box

S59

Prompt Character

Description ATS59=*n*

Set prompt character ASCII value.

n = 0–255

Default

0

This register holds the ASCII value of the character that will be used as a prompt when in command mode. Setting S59 to 0 disables the prompt.

Application Telebit

S59

CONNECT Suffix Bitmap

Description ATS59=*n*

n=decimal value of byte determined by bitmap.

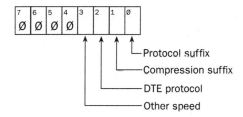

Bit	Default	Definition
0	0	Protocol 0 Disabled. 1 Enabled.
1	0	Compression 0 Disabled. 1 Enabled.
2	0	DTE protocol 0 Disabled. 1 Enabled.
3	0	Other speed 0 Disabled. 1 Enabled.
7–4	0000	Reserved.

Default

S59 is a bitmapped register that determines the suffixes that will be applied to the CONNECT message in verbose mode.

Bit 3 determines whether an additional speed is displayed. If X1 or X2 is set, this option displays the serial port speed. If X4 is set, the data link speed is displayed.

Related To   Q, V, X

Application   Telebit

S60

Configuration Bitmap

Description   ATS6Ø=*n*

n = decimal value of byte determined by bitmap.

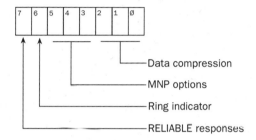

Bit	Default	Definition
2-0	111	Data compression 000 Disabled. Same as %C0. 011 V.42bis transmit compression enabled. Same as %C2. 101 V.42bis receive compression enabled. Same as %C3. 111 V.42bis or MNP 5 compression during transmit and receive. Same as %C1.
5-3	000	MNP options 000 Mode selected from S70. 001 Same as 000. 010 Same as 000. 011 Same as 000. 100 Convert to NORMAL Link. Same as \Z. 101 Convert to MNP RELIABLE Link. Same as \Y. 110 Accept MNP RELIABLE Link. Same as \U. 111 Initiate MNP RELIABLE Link. Same as \O.
6	1	Serial port ring indicator control 0 Ring and off-hook indication. Same as \R0. 1 Ring indication. Same as \R1.

Bit	Default	Definition
7	1	RELIABLE link responses 0 Protocol result codes off. Same as \V0. 1 Protocol result codes on. Same as \V1.

Default

199 (11000111b)

S60 is a bitmapped register that controls a variety of modem parameters.

Related To % C, \O, \R, \U, \V, \Y, \Z

Application Black Box

S60

Serial Port Data Format

Description ATS60=*n*

0   8 data bits, no parity. (10-bit word size.)

1   8 data bits, odd parity. (11-bit word size.)

2   8 data bits, even parity. (11-bit word size.)

3   8 data bits, MARK parity. (11-bit word size.)

4   8 data bits, SPACE parity. (11-bit word size.)

Default

0

The S60 register defines the format of the data exchanged between the local DTE and the local modem.

Application Telebit

S61

CT111 Rate Control

Description   ATS61=*n*

0   Disabled.

1   Fallback rate 1.

2   Fallback rate 2.

Default

0

This register determines the effect that the V.24 CT111 DTE rate control signal (EIA-232-D pin 23) will have on the modem. It is valid only in the asynchronous DIRECT and synchronous modes.

Related To   S51, S52

Application   AT&T

S61

Set Serial Port Speed

Description ATS61=*n*

0	Reserved.
1	Reserved.
2	300 bps.
3	Reserved.
4	Reserved.
5	1200 bps.
6	2400 bps.
7	4800 bps.
8	9600 bps.
9	19200 bps.
10	38400 bps.

Default

8

The S61 register is used to lock the serial port speed. All commands from the DTE must arrive at the designated speed.

Application Black Box

S61

Local BREAK Action

Description   ATS61=*n*

0   BREAK is processed as defined by S63.

1   Enter command mode.

Default

1

The S61 register determines how the modem reacts to a BREAK signal that it receives from the local DTE.

Related To   S63

Application   Telebit

S61

Description ATS61=*n*

Set speaker volume.

n = 0–255

Default

150

The value specified in this register determines the speaker volume. A value of 255 represents maximum volume; 0 disables the speaker.

Related To L, M

Application Telebit

S62

Description   ATS62=*n*

0	ASCII coding.
1	EBCDIC coding.

Default

0

The S62 register identifies for the modem the type of coding being used by the DTE when operating in V.25bis mode.

Related To   S63, S64

Application   AT&T

S62

Forced Disconnect Buffer Delay

Description　ATS62=*n*

Set buffer disconnect delay in seconds.

n = 0–255

Default

0

This register specifies the amount of time that may expire between the modem's receipt of a hangup command from the local DTE and the actual disconnect operation when operating in MNP mode.

This timeout function is useful when forcing a disconnect during an error-control link. The modem will wait the number of seconds indicated in S62 before disconnecting. This provides time for the local modem to send all data in its buffers and for the remote modem to acknowledge receipt of the data.

If the S62 time limit expires before all data is sent and acknowledged, the modem returns NO CARRIER. Otherwise, it returns OK. Setting S62 to 0 forces an immediate response to a disconnect request.

Application　Black Box

S62

BREAK Length

Description ATS62=*n*

Set length in increments of 10 milliseconds.

n = 0–255

Default

15

Set length in increments of 50 milliseconds.

n = 2–255

Default

3

The S62 register sets the length of the BREAK signal sent to the local DTE when the local modem receives a BREAK from the remote modem during an error-control link.

Application Telebit

Notes
1. The units used for this parameter vary among different modems from this manufacturer. [Telebit]

S63

Leased Line Transmit Level

Description ATS63=n

Set current leased line transmit level in -dBm.

$n = 0–15$

Default

0

This register selects the nominal transmit power level in dBm that will be used during leased line operation.

Application Hayes, Practical

S63

V.25bis Idle Character

Description   ATS63=*n*

0   MARK idle.

1   Flag idle.

Default

0

The S63 register determines the type of idle signal that is transmitted by the modem during V.25bis connections.

Related To   S62, S64

Application   AT&T

S63

MNP Block Size

Description ATS63=*n*

63   Maximum block size is 64 characters. Same as \A0.

127   Maximum block size is 128 characters. Same as \A1.

191   Maximum block size is 192 characters. Same as \A2.

255   Maximum block size is 256 characters. Same as \A3.

Default

255

The S63 register sets the maximum size of the data blocks transmitted by the modem during MNP stream link operations. The value in the register is one less than the desired block size. Only the specified values are permitted.

This command affects only MNP 4 and MNP 5 operations. MNP 3 and lower protocols fix the block size at 64 characters.

Related To \A

Application Black Box

S63

Link Layer BREAK Action

Description   ATS63=*n*

0   BREAK sent in sequence with the data.

1   BREAK sent immediately.

2   Reserved.

3   BREAK ignored.

Default

0

The S63 determines the modem's response when it receives a BREAK from the local DTE.

Application   Telebit

S63

Command Mode

Description ATS63=*n*

0   Enhanced command mode. AT prefix not allowed.

1   Enhanced command mode. AT prefix required.

2   Conventional command mode. AT prefix required.

Default

1, 2

The S63 selects either conventional or enhanced command mode and disables the requirement for the AT attention code.

This register can be accessed only in enhanced command mode or if prefixed by a tilde (~) in conventional mode.

Related To S222

Application Telebit

S64

V.25bis New Line Character

Description   ATS64=*n*

0   Carriage return and line feed.

1   Carriage return.

2   Line feed.

Default

0

The S64 register sets the type of line terminator that will be used by the DTE when communicating in V.25bis mode.

Related To   S62, S63

Application   AT&T

S64

AUTO RELIABLE Fallback Character

Description ATS64=*n*

Set fallback character ASCII value.

n = 0–127

Default

0

This register holds the ASCII value of the character that will be recognized as the AUTO RELIABLE fallback character when the modem is answering a call. Selecting 0 disables fallback character recognition. Values greater than 127 are treated as equivalent to 0.

Related To %A

Application Black Box

S64

Dial/Answer Sequence Abort

Description ATS64=*n*

0   Abort the dialing or answering sequence if the local DTE sends a character before a connection is established.

1   Ignore characters from the DTE while dialing or answering a call.

Default

0

The S64 register determines the modem's reaction to characters received from the DTE while dialing or answering a call.

Application Telebit

S65

Line Current Disconnect

Description ATS65=*n*

0   Enable 8-millisecond disconnect.

1   Enable 90-millisecond disconnect.

2   Disabled.

Default

0

The setting of this register determines if the modem will disconnect after receiving an interruption in loop (telephone line) current of the specified duration.

Application AT&T

S65

XON/XOFF Failsafe

Description ATS65=*n*

0   Use normal XON/XOFF flow control.

1   Use failsafe XON/XOFF flow control.

Default

0

The S65 register allows the modem to reissue one or more XOFF characters over the serial interface if the local DTE continues to transmit data after a single XOFF has been issued. In failsafe mode, the modem issues an XOFF when the flow-control threshold is reached and once again for every five characters sent by the DTE.

Related To S58, S68

Application Telebit

S66

DNMS Call Messages

Description ATS66=n

0   Send call connect and progress messages.

1   Disabled.

2   Send call connect messages only.

3   Send progress messages only.

Default

0

The S66 register determines if the modem sends information regarding status (call progress) and/or sends summarized call statistics (call connect) to the dial network management system (DNMS).

Application AT&T

S66

Serial Port Speed Conversion

Description ATS66=n

0   Change serial port speed to match data link speed and disable flow control when a connection is established.

1   Lock serial port speed and use flow control.

2   Lock serial port speed and use flow control if an MNP data link is established. In non-MNP modes, identical to S66=0.

Default

0, 2

The S66 register determines if the modem will change the serial port speed and use flow control when establishing a connecting using V.32 or a lower speed mode.

Application Telebit

S67

Callback Security

Description   ATS67=*n*

    0   Disabled.

    1   Enabled.

Default

    0

This register enables the modem's callback security feature.

Application   AT&T

S67

CTS Action

Description $ATS67=n$

0   If RTS/CTS flow control is enabled, CTS controls DTE data flow as described for S68. If not, CTS is always ON.

1   CTS is OFF when no carrier is present. When a carrier is present, CTS follows RTS with a fixed 200-millisecond delay. If RTS/CTS flow control is enabled, CTS controls DTE data flow.

2   CTS is turned ON after an OFF-to-ON RTS transition with the delay specified by S26.

Default

0

The S67 register defines how the modem interprets the clear-to-send (CTS) signal in combination with the request-to-send (RTS) and carrier signals.

Related To   S26, S58, S68

Application   Telebit

S68

Serial Port Flow Control

Description ATS68=*n*

0   Disabled.

2   CTS flow control. The modem uses the CTS line to control data transfer from the DTE.

3   XON/XOFF flow control. The modem uses the XOFF character to suspend and the XON character to resume data transfer from the DTE.

4   Use both CTS and XON/XOFF flow control.

5   Use HP ENQ/ACK protocol.

6   Use HP ENQ/ACK protocol and XON/XOFF flow control.

255 Use the flow control specified by S58.

Default

255

The S68 register determines the method of flow control used by the modem to control data flow from the local DTE.

Related To S48, S56, S57, S58, S180, S181

Application Telebit

S69

Data Link Speed

Description   ATS69=*n*

0   Data link speed matches serial port speed. Same as %B0 and \J1.

1   300 bps. Same as %B300.

2   Reserved.

3   1200 bps. Same as %B1200.

4   2400 bps. Same as %B2400.

5   4800 bps. Same as %B4800.

6   9600 bps. Same as %B9600.

7   9600 bps with trellis coding. Same as %B9600C.

Default

7

The S69 register sets the maximum data link speed. When S69 is not 0, this speed is set independent of the speed of the serial port connection.

Application   Black Box

S69

Link Layer Window Size (K)

Description   ATS69=*n*

Set link layer window size in packets.

n = 1–15

Default

15

This register sets the number of packets (frames) that can be sent without being acknowledged by the remote system; this is known as the link layer K parameter.

LAPM connections can use a window size of 1 to 15 packets. LAPB and X.25 can use a window size of 1 to 8; values of S69 greater than 8 are equivalent to 8.

Related To   S70, S71, S72, S73, S80, S81, S105

Application   Hayes

S69

XON/XOFF Signal Handling

Description ATS69=*n*

0 The local modem will honor XON/XOFF flow-control characters received from the local DTE, but does not pass them to the remote modem.

1 The local modem will honor the XON flow-control character received from the local DTE, but does not pass it to the remote modem.

2 If the modem has received an XOFF character, it process the next XON character locally. If not, it passes it to the remote modem.

Default

0

Application Telebit

S70

Maximum Number of Retransmissions (N2)

Description ATS7Ø=*n*

n = 0–255

Default

10

The S70 register specifies the maximum number of times the modem will retransmit a packet if requested; this is known as the link layer N2 parameter.

During poor connection conditions, raising this limit may prevent the modem from disconnecting, although throughput will be reduced.

Related To S69, S71, S72, S73, S80, S81, S105

Application Hayes, Prometheus

S70

Protocol Bitmap

Description　ATS7Ø=n

n = decimal value of byte determined by bitmap.

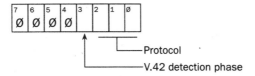

Bit	Default	Definition
2-0	111	Protocol 000 NORMAL. Same as \N0. 001 DIRECT. Same as \N1. 010 MNP RELIABLE. Same as \N2. 011 MNP AUTO RELIABLE. Same as \N3. 100 LAPM RELIABLE. Same as \N4. 101 LAPM AUTO RELIABLE. Same as \N5. 110 RELIABLE. Same as \N6. 111 AUTO RELIABLE. Same as \N7
3	1	V.42 detection phase 0 Disabled. Same as \M0. 1 Enabled. Same as \M1.
7-4	0000	Reserved

Default

15 (00001111b)

S70 is a bitmapped register that controls the data link protocol and detection options for error-control connections.

Application　Black Box

S70

Instantaneous Transmit Rate

Description ATS70?

Return current rate.

Reading the S70 register causes the modem to report the instantaneous rate at which data is being transmitted to the remote modem in bits per second. This value represents the present data transmission capacity of the dial-up lines.

S70 is a read-only register and reports either the current rate or the last rate that was sampled during an active connection. Any new connection attempt clears this register.

Related To S72

Application Telebit

S71

Link Layer Propagation Delay (T2)

Description ATS71=*n*

Set the delay inflation in increments of 10 milliseconds.

n = 1–255

Default

2

This register sets the amount of time the modem will allow for propagation delay. When the link layers transmits a packet, it starts an internal timer. If the remote end does not respond before the timer expires, the link layer will re-transmit the packet. The timeout value is calculated automatically using the following formula:

```
Timeout (milliseconds) = 2 * (maximum packet size + 11) * (8 / bits per second)
+ S71 + 500
```

By setting the value of S71 (link layer T2 parameter), the value of the calculated timeout can be increased.

Related To S69, S70, S72, S73, S80, S81, S105

Application Hayes

Notes **1.** Some documentation indicates that this parameter is set in milliseconds with a range of 0–255. [Hayes]

S71

Transmit Channel Size

Description ATS71?

Return current size.

Reading S71 causes the modem to display the number of transmit bits assigned to each channel at 511 frequency points in the current connection. All 511 values are displayed when S71 is accessed. S71 is a read-only register.

Related To S73, S76

Application Telebit

S72

Loss of Flag Idle Timeout (T3)

Description ATS72=*n*

Set loss of flag idle timeout in seconds.

n = 0–255

Default

30

Normally, a transmitter that is not sending data will send a repeating flag idle pattern. The local modem monitors the link to make sure it is receiving either data or a flag idle at all times. If the modem is not receiving data or a flag idle, the S72 register determines how long the modem will wait before disconnecting (link layer T3 parameter).

Some systems occasionally transmit periods of mark idle (all 1s instead of the flag idle pattern). It may be necessary to increase the setting of the S72 register to accommodate these systems.

Setting S72=0 disables the flag idle monitoring function.

Related To S69, S70, S71, S73, S80, S81, S105

Application Hayes

S72

Instantaneous Receive Rate

Description ATS72?

Return current rate.

Reading S72 causes the modem to report the instantaneous rate at which data is being transmitted to the remote modem in bits per second and represents the present data transmission capacity of the dial-up lines.

S72 is a read-only register and reports either the current rate or the last rate that was sampled during an active connection. Any new connection attempt clears this register.

Related To S70

Application Telebit

S73

No Activity Timeout (T4)

Description   ATS73=*n*

Set no activity timeout in seconds.

$n = 1$–255

Default

    5

During a good connection, when the local modem is receiving a good carrier and flag idle from the remote modem, a period of no activity may occur during which no data is received. If the duration of this no activity period exceeds the value held in S73 (link layer T4 parameter), the local modem will query the remote modem by sending a receiver ready (RR) packet. If, after several retries, the local modem receives no reply to its RR packet, it disconnects. Lower values of *n* cause the modem to test more frequently for remote malfunctions.

Related To   S69, S70, S71, S72, S80, S81, S105

Application   Hayes

S73

Receive Channel Size

Description   ATS73?

Return current size.

Reading S73 causes the modem to report the number of receive bits assigned to each channel at 511 frequency points in the current connection. All 511 values are displayed when S73 is accessed. S73 is a read-only register.

Related To   S71, S76

Application   Telebit

S74

Network Positive Identification

Description ATS74=*n*

0   Tributary.

1   Control.

Default

0

This register identifies the local modem as either a tributary or control modem within the network.

Application AT&T

S74

Received Packet Retransmission Count

Description   ATS74?

Return current count.

Reading the S74 register causes the modem to return a count of received packets requiring retransmission since the current connection was made. The count is retained until the next connection attempt. S74 is a read-only register.

Related To   S75

Application   Telebit

S74

Packet Transmission Status

Description   ATS74?

Return current count statistics.

Reading S74 causes the modem to return the counts of MNP or LAPM packets transmitted, received, retransmitted, and received with errors and is used to retransmit data after an error is detected. S74 retains this information until the next connection attempt. S74 is a read-only register.

Application   Telebit

S74, S75

Minimum Incoming Logical Channel Number

Description   `ATS74=n`

Set high portion of channel number.

$n = 0–40$

Default

0

`ATS75=n`

Set low portion of channel number.

$n = 0–99$

Default

1

The S74 and S75 registers, taken together, specify the lowest incoming logical channel number (LCN) that the packet layer will report or accept. The values in the two registers are combined to produce an LCN according to the following formula:

`S74*100+S75`

Valid channel numbers are 0–4095. Channel numbers greater than 4095 are interpreted as 4095.

Packet-switched networks can support up to 4096 channels (numbered 0–4095). They are often set up so that all incoming calls are assigned channels within one numeric range and outgoing calls are within another range. These registers allow the modem to be configured to meet specific system requirements.

Related To   S76, S77, S78, S79

Application   Hayes

S75

Network Management Address

Description ATS75=*n*

Set address.

n = 0–255

Default

0

This register sets the modem's network management address. This address is used when accessing the modem from the dial network management system. S75 may be set to a value from 0 (network address 001) to 255 (network address 256).

Application AT&T

S75

Packets Accepted

Description ATS75?

Return current count.

Reading S75 returns a count of the number of packets accepted since the current connection was made. The count is maintained until the next connection attempt. S75 is a read-only register.

Related To S74

Application Telebit

S76

Set Dial Line V.32bis Autorate

Description   ATS76=*n*

0   Autorate enabled.

1   Autorate disabled.

Default

0

The S76 register determines if the modem can adjust the data link speed (autorate) on dial-up lines when operating in the V.32bis mode.

After a connection is established, the modem will automatically lower the data link rate (fallback) if line conditions are poor. If conditions improve, the modem will increase the data link rate (fall-forward). Data link speed adjustment is effective only during V.32bis/V.32 connections and can shift between 4800 bps and 14400 bps.

Related To   S78, S82

Application   AT&T

S76

Equivalent Line Noise Profile

Description   ATS76?

Return current noise level.

Reading S76 causes the modem to return the noise level in dBm to the nearest tenth observed at 511 frequency points during the current connection. All 511 values are displayed when S76 is accessed. S76 is a read-only register.

Related To   S71, S73

Application   Telebit

S76, S77

Maximum Incoming Logical Channel Number

Description ATS76=n

Set high portion of channel number.

n = 0–40

Default

40

ATS77=n

Set low portion of channel number.

n = 0–99

Default

95

The S76 and S77 registers, taken together, specify the highest incoming logical channel number (LCN) that the packet layer will report or accept. The values in the two registers are combined to produce an LCN according to the following formula:

S76*100+S77

Valid channel numbers are 0-4095. Channel numbers greater than 4095 are interpreted as 4095.

Packet-switched networks can support up to 4096 channels (numbered 0–4095). They are often set up so that all incoming calls are assigned channels within one numeric range and outgoing calls are within another range. These registers allow the modem to be configured to meet specific system requirements.

Related To S74, S75, S78, S79

Application Hayes

S77

Frequency Offset

Description   ATS77?

Return current offset.

Reading S77 causes the modem to return the observed frequency offset in Hz to the nearest sixteenth for the current connection. Frequency offset is reported in 1200 bps, 2400 bps, and PEP modes.

Application   Telebit

S78

Set V.32bis Automode

Description   ATS78=*n*

0   Enabled.

1   Disabled.

Default

0

The S76 register enables the automode function, permitting the modem to connect to a remote modem using any supported modulation scheme.

When automode is enabled, S41 determines the maximum data link rate. If disabled, the modem will only support the modulation scheme specified by S41.

Related To   S41, S76

Application   AT&T

S78

Line Quality

Description ATS78?

Return current setting.

Reading S78 causes the modem to report its estimate of the quality of the current connection. This register is valid only when in 212A, V.22, V.22bis, or V.32 mode. Quality is represented on a scale from 0 to 100, with higher numbers representing higher quality.

A value greater than 50 is considered acceptable for communications. Values lower than 30 will incur an unacceptably high error rate.

Application Telebit

S78, S79

Outgoing Logical Channel Number

Description   ATS78=*n*

Set high portion of channel number.

n = 0–40

Default

0

ATS79=*n*

Set low portion of channel number.

n = 0–99

Default

16

The S78 and S79 registers, taken together, specify the logical channel number (LCN) that the packet layer will use to place a call. The values in the two registers are combined to produce an LCN according to the following formula:

S78*100+S79

Valid channel numbers are 0–4095. Channel numbers greater than 4095 are interpreted as 4095.

Packet-switched networks can support up to 4096 channels (numbered 0–4095). They are often set up so that all incoming calls are assigned channels within one numeric range and outgoing calls are within another range. These registers allow the modem to be configured to meet specific system requirements.

Related To   S74, S75, S76, S77

Application   Hayes

S80

Restart Request Limit (N20)

Description   ATS8Ø=*n*

Set maximum retry count.

n = 0–255

Default

1

The S80 register sets the maximum number of times a restart request can be retransmitted (packet layer N20 parameter).

Related To   S69, S70, S71, S72, S73, S81, S105

Application   Hayes

S81

Acknowledgment Wait Timeout (T20)

Description   ATS81=*n*

Set timeout in increments of 10 seconds.

$n = 0$–255

Default

18

The S81 register sets the maximum amount of time that the transmitter will wait for acknowledgment of a restart request packet before initiating a recovery procedure (packet layer T20 parameter).

Related To   S69, S70, S71, S72, S73, S80, S105

Application   Hayes

S82

BREAK Signaling Technique

Description ATS82=*n*

1 In-sequence signaling. Send timed BREAK to remote modem in sequence with transmitted data. [Hayes, Practical]

2 In-sequence signaling. Send untimed BREAK to remote modem in sequence with transmitted data. [Hayes, Practical]

3 Expedited signaling. Immediately send timed BREAK to remote modem. Data in transmit buffers is preserved.

4 Expedited signaling. Immediately send untimed BREAK to remote modem. Data in transmit buffers is preserved. [Hayes, Practical]

7 Destructive signaling. Empty transmit buffers. Immediately send timed BREAK to remote modem.

8 Destructive signaling. Empty transmit buffers. Immediately send untimed BREAK to remote modem. [Hayes, Practical]

128 In-sequence signaling. Send timed BREAK to remote modem in sequence with transmitted data.

Default

128

The S82 register selects the method of BREAK handling used during a V.42 error-control link.

Related To \K

Application Dallas, Hayes, Practical, Rockwell, Sierra, Twincom, Zoom

Notes
1. This register definition is valid for the SC11091 and SC11095 2400 bps universal modem advanced controllers only. The SC11095 does not support V.42bis. [Sierra]

S82

Set Leased Line V.32bis Autorate

Description ATS82=*n*

0 Autorate enabled.

1 Autorate disabled.

Default

0

The S82 register determines if the modem can adjust the data link speed (autorate) on leased lines when operating in the V.32bis mode.

After a connection is established, the modem will automatically lower the data link rate (fallback) if line conditions are poor. If conditions improve, the modem will increase the data link rate (fall-forward). Autorate is effective only during V.32bis/V.32 connections and can shift between 4800 bps and 14400 bps.

Related To S76

Application AT&T

S83

MI/MIC Dialing

Description   ATS83=*n*

0   Disabled.

1   Enabled.

Default

0

The S83 register selects the MI/MIC (mode indicate/mode indicate common) interface and determines whether it can be used to force the modem to generate the originate signal after first dialing a call.

Application   AT&T

S84

AT Command Mode

Description   ATS84=*n*

0   Normal AT mode. The modem acts upon all valid AT commands and issues the ERROR message for invalid AT commands. AT command line processing stops at the first invalid command.

1   No error mode. The modem acts upon all valid AT commands. Invalid commands do not produce the ERROR message. Instead, they are ignored and the OK message is issued. An invalid command does not stop processing of the command line.

2   No strap or error mode. The modem ignores all AT commands that would change a configuration option. Only nonconfiguration commands (ATD, ATA, and so on) are executed. Invalid commands do not produce the ERROR message.

231   Normal AT mode. (Same as S84=0.)

232   No error mode. (Same as S84=1.)

233   No strap or error mode. (Same as S84=2.)

Default

0 or 231

The setting of S84 determines how the modem will respond to valid and invalid AT commands.

Application   AT&T

S84

Adaptive Start-Up Negotiation

Description ATS84=*n*

0   ASU negotiation disabled.

126   Negotiate ASU with fixed start-up.

129   Negotiate ASU with fast start-up on both sides.

130   Negotiate ASU with smooth start-up on both sides.

131   Negotiate ASU with configuring modem using fast start-up and the other modem using smooth start-up.

132   Negotiate ASU with configuring modem using smooth start-up and the other modem using fast start-up.

Default

129

The S84 register sets the adaptive start-up (ASU) method to be negotiated for subsequent connections.

Related To S85

Application Hayes

S85

Fast Disconnect

Description ATS85=*n*

0 Disable fast disconnect.

1 Enable fast disconnect.

Default

0

When fast disconnect is enabled (S85=1), the modem does not issue the clear-down sequence or send a long space to the remote modem to disconnect. Instead, it goes immediately on-hook.

Application AT&T

S85

Adaptive Start-Up Report

Description   ATS85?

Return the negotiated ASU method.

0   ASU not negotiated; fixed start-up in use.

126   ASU negotiated with fixed start-up.

129   ASU negotiated with fast start-up on both sides.

130   ASU negotiated with smooth start-up on both sides.

131   ASU negotiated with configuring modem using fast start-up and the
        other modem using smooth start-up.

132   ASU negotiated with configuring modem using smooth start-up and
        the other modem using fast start-up.

The modem sets this register to report the adaptive start-up (ASU) method (if
any) that was negotiated for the current connection. S85 is a read-only register.

Related To   S84

Application   Hayes

S86

Connection Failure Report

Description   ATS86?

Return the failure cause.

0   Normal hang up. No error.

4   Physical carrier loss.

5   Feature negotiation failed to detect the presence of another error-control modem at the remote end.

6   The remote modem did not respond to the feature negotiation message sent by the local modem. [Hayes, Practical, Prometheus]

7   The local modem is asynchronous-only while the remote modem is synchronous-only. [Hayes, Practical, Prometheus]

8   The modems could not negotiate a common framing technique. [Hayes, Practical, Prometheus]

9   The modems could not negotiate a common protocol.

10   The feature negotiation message sent by the remote modem was incorrect. [Hayes, Practical, Prometheus]

11   The local modem waited 30 seconds without receiving synchronous information (data or flags) from the remote modem. [Hayes, Practical, Prometheus]

12   A normal disconnect was initiated by the remote modem. [Dallas, Hayes, Practical, Prometheus, Rockwell, Twincom, Zoom]

13   The local modem repeated the same message ten times without a response from the remote modem.

14   A protocol violation occurred.

15   A compression protocol failure occurred. [Dallas, Hayes, Practical, Prometheus, Sierra]

When the modem returns the NO CARRIER response, it sets the S86 register to indicate the first incident that caused the connection failure.

Application   Dallas, Hayes, Practical, Prometheus, Rockwell, Sierra, Twincom, Zoom

Notes   **1.** This register definition is valid for the SC11091 and SC11095 2400 bps universal modem advanced controllers only. The SC11095 does not support V.42bis. [Sierra]

S87

AT Command High Speed

Description ATS87=*n*

14   Accept AT commands at 19200 bps.

28   Accept AT commands at 38400 bps.

The modem will always accept AT commands from the DTE at speeds of 9600 bps and lower and automatically detect the correct speed. The S87 register determines the one additional speed that will be available for automatic detection.

Application Hayes

S90

Communications Protocol

Description ATS9Ø=*n*

0   Use Bell 103 protocol during 300 bps operation and Bell 212A proto-
       col during 1200 bps operation. Same as B1.

1   Use CCITT V.21 protocol during 300 bps operation and CCITT
       V.22/V.22bis protocol during 1200 bps operation. Same as B0.

Default

0

Related To B, S50, S91

Application Telebit

S90

DSRS Behavior

Description ATS9Ø=*n*

0   Disable DTE/DSRS input.

1   Enable DTE/DSRS input on the serial port interface.

Default

0

The S90 register enables the DTE-source data signal rate selector (DSRS) signal on the RS-232 serial port interface. If the S94 register conflicts with the DTE/DSRS line, the DTE/DSRS line takes precedence if it specifies a fallback speed.

Application Telebit

S91

Leased Line Transmit Level

Description   ATS91=*n*

Set transmit level in -dBm.

n = 0–15

Default

0 [Hayes]

0 [Dallas, Rockwell, Twincom, Zoom (for US)]

15 [Dallas, Rockwell, Twincom, Zoom (for Japan)]

This register selects the maximum carrier power level that will be used during leased line operation. Selecting S91=15, for example, sets the transmit level to -15 dBm.

Application   Dallas, Hayes, Rockwell, Twincom, Zoom

S91

Guard Tone

Description ATS91=*n*

    0   Disable guard tone. Same as &G0.

    1   Enable 1800 Hz guard tone. (Required in United Kingdom and some Commonwealth countries.) Same as &G2.

    2   Enable 550 Hz guard tone. (Required in some European countries.) Same as &G1.

Default

    0

The S91 register determines whether the modem will transmit guard tones when transmitting in the high band (answer mode) during CCITT operation.

Related To &G, S50, S90

Application Telebit

S92

MI/MIC Options

Description ATS92=*n*

0   MI/MIC interface disabled.

1   Level triggered, originate mode, RI pulse enabled.

3   Edge triggered, originate mode, RI pulse enabled.

5   Level triggered, answer mode, RI pulse enabled.

7   Edge triggered, answer mode, RI pulse enabled.

9   Level triggered, originate mode, RI pulse disabled.

11   Edge triggered, originate mode, RI pulse disabled.

13   Level triggered, answer mode, RI pulse disabled.

15   Edge triggered, answer mode, RI pulse disabled.

Default

0

The S92 register selects the MI/MIC (mode indicate/mode indicate common) interface. The settings available for this register support various combinations of edge and level detection, originate and answer mode, and RI pulse enabled or disabled.

Setting this register to a nonzero value overrides the current &J command setting.

Related To &J

Application Hayes

S92

Answer Sequence

Description   ATS92=*n*

0   Use normal sequence specified by S50.

1   Issue the PEP answer tones at the end of the sequence rather than at the beginning.

2   Use the S50 sequence, but precede with a 3-second V.25 answer tone.

Default

0

This register specifies the sequence that will be used by an answering modem when attempting to establish a connection in automatic speed determination mode (S50=0). This accommodates slower modems that are adversely affected by PEP tones.

Related To   S50

Application   Telebit

S93

V.25bis Serial Port Speed

Description ATS93=*n*

2   110 bps.

3   300 bps.

4   600 bps. (Not supported.)

5   1200 bps.

6   2400 bps.

7   4800 bps.

8   7200 bps.

9   9600 bps.

10   12000 bps.

11   14400 bps.

12   19200 bps.

13   38400 bps.

Default

0

The S93 register sets the serial port speed used between the DTE and the modem when the modem is configured for V.25bis mode.

Related To S37, S94

Application Hayes

S93

V.32 Probe Transmit Time

Description ATS93=*n*

Set time in increments of .1 second.

n = 3–255 [Telebit]

n = 0–255 [Telebit]

Default

8

If the modem is in answer mode and S50 is set to 0 or 6, this register sets the amount of time the modem will wait for a V.32 originate sequence before abandoning this mode.

For manual or late-connecting V.32 modems, increase the value of this register.

Related To S50

Application Telebit

S94

V.25bis Mode Selection

Description   ATS94=*n*

n = value from table.

n	Signal	Command	Access	Framing	Character Set
0	Asynchronous	AT	n/a	n/a	n/a
1	Asynchronous	V.25bis	Addressed	n/a	n/a
2	Synchronous	V.25bis	Addressed	HDLC	ASCII
3	Synchronous	V.25bis	Addressed	BSC	ASCII
4	Asynchronous	AT	n/a	n/a	n/a
5	Asynchronous	V.25bis	Direct	n/a	n/a
6	Synchronous	V.25bis	Direct	HDLC	ASCII
7	Synchronous	V.25bis	Direct	BSC	ASCII
8	Asynchronous	AT	n/a	n/a	n/a
9	Asynchronous	V.25bis	Addressed	n/a	n/a
10	Synchronous	V.25bis	Addressed	HDLC	EBCDIC
11	Synchronous	V.25bis	Addressed	BSC	EBCDIC
12	Asynchronous	AT	n/a	n/a	n/a
13	Asynchronous	V.25bis	Direct	n/a	n/a
14	Synchronous	V.25bis	Direct	HDLC	EBCDIC
15	Synchronous	V.25bis	Direct	BSC	EBCDIC

Default

0

The S94 register is provided as an alternative to setting configuration switches. The various settings of this command select between the standard AT command mode and the various CCITT V.25bis command modes.

Related To   S93

Application   Hayes

S94

Transmission Speed Negotiation

Description ATS94=*n*

0 Negotiation disabled. Connect at the speed set by S50.

1 Connect at the highest supported speed that does not exceed S50.

2 Connection and fallback is limited within the protocol specified by S50.

3 Same as S94=2.

Default

1

The S94 register determines the speed and protocol choices that the modem many negotiate.

Related To S50, S90

Application Telebit

S95

Negotiation Message Options

ATS95=*n*

n = decimal value of byte determined by bitmap.

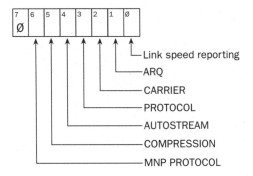

Bit	Default	Definition
0	0	Link speed reporting 0 CONNECT message do not indicate link speed. 1 Verbose CONNECT messages will indicate the link speed rather than the serial port speed. Numeric codes will also be different.
1	0	ARQ 0 /ARQ not appended. 1 /ARQ appended to the CONNECT message when an error control link is made.
2	0	CARRIER 0 CARRIER message not displayed. 1 CARRIER message displayed.
3	0	PROTOCOL 0 PROTOCOL message not displayed. 1 PROTOCOL message displayed.

Bit	Default	Definition
4	0	AUTOSTREAM [Hayes] 0 AUTOSTREAM message not displayed. 1 AUTOSTREAM message displayed. Reserved [Dallas, Practical, Prometheus, Rockwell, Twincom, Zoom]
5	0	COMPRESSION 0 COMPRESSION message not displayed. 1 COMPRESSION message displayed.
6	0	MNP PROTOCOL [Dallas, Prometheus] 0 PROTOCOL message not displayed for MNP connections. 1 PROTOCOL message displayed for MNP connections. Reserved [Dallas, Hayes, Practical, Rockwell, Twincom, Zoom]
7	0	Reserved

Default

   0 (00000000b)

The S95 register enables variants of the basic CONNECT result code that is sent to the DTE by the modem. The setting of this register does not affect the negotiation of the connection, it simply changes the way it is reported to the DTE.

Setting a bit to 1 enables the corresponding message enhancement. Clearing a bit to 0 disables the additional message information. All bit permutations are valid.

Related To   W, X

Application   Dallas, Hayes, Practical, Prometheus, Rockwell, Twincom, Zoom

Notes
   1. The settings in this register override the actions of the W command. Changing the W command does not affect this register.

S95

MNP Error Control

Description ATS95=*n*

0 NORMAL mode. MNP is disabled.

1 MNP RELIABLE mode.

2 MNP AUTO RELIABLE mode.

Default

0, 2

S95 determines how the modem establishes an MNP connection when operating in V.32 and slower modes.

Related To \N, S66, S96, S97, S98

Application Telebit

S96

MNP Data Compression

Description ATS96=*n*

0   Disabled.

1   Enabled.

Default

0

S96 determines if the modem will attempt to negotiate MNP 5 data compression during an MNP error control connection.

Related To S95, S97, S98

Application Telebit

S97

V.32 Automode Probe Timing

Description ATS97=*n*

Set timeout in increments of 0.1 second.

n = 15–70

Default

30

If the local modem is in the answer mode and is configured for V.32 automode operation, the S97 register sets the duration of the signal used to determine if the calling modem is using V.22 or V.22bis. S97 is also used to determine the length of time that the local modem will reject the V.22/V.22bis problem signal when executing a V.32 automode handshake in the originate mode.

The default value of 30 (3 seconds) provides the timing necessary to connect to most V.22bis modems. When compatibility with V.32 late connecting modems is a primary requirement, S97 should be set to 15.

Application Hayes, Practical

S97

LAPM Error Control

Description   ATS97=*n*

0   Disabled.

1   Enabled.

Default

0

S97 determines if the modem will attempt to negotiate a LAPM error-control link when operating in V.42 mode (S106=1).

Related To   S95, S96, S98, S106

Application   Telebit

S98

V.42bis Data Compression

Description ATS98=*n*

0 Disabled.

1 Data compression in transmit direction only.

2 Data compression in receive direction only.

3 Data compression in both directions.

Default

3

S98 determines if the modem will use data compression while operating in LAPM mode.

Related To S97, S106

Application Telebit

S100

Answer/Originate Mode

Description `ATS100=`*n*

0   Normal mode. Use originate mode when dialing and answer mode when answering.

1   Reverse mode. Use answer mode when dialing and originate mode when answering.

Default

0

The S100 register determines whether the modem reverses the answer/originate protocol used to establish a connection. Regardless of the setting of this register, the R dial modifier causes the dialing modem to issue the answer tones.

Related To D

Application Telebit

S101

Continuous Answer/Originate

Description ATS101=*n*

0   Disabled. Normal operation.

1   Attempt to connect as an answer modem every 20 seconds whenever a carrier is absent.

2   Attempt to connect as an originate modem every 20 seconds whenever a carrier is absent.

3   If carrier is lost, wait 20 seconds before attempting to establish a connection as an answer modem. If carrier is absent, attempt to establish a connection immediately.

4   If carrier is lost, wait 20 seconds before attempting to establish a connection as an originate modem. If carrier is absent, attempt to establish a connection immediately.

Default

0

The S101 register is used to configure the modem to continuously attempt to establish a connection in either answer or originate mode. Values from 1–4 are intended for leased line operation.

Application Telebit

S102

Set Pulse Dial Make/Break Ratio

Description ATS102=*n*

0   Select a make/break ratio of 39%/61% at 10 pulses per second (United States and Canada). Same as &P0.

1   Select a make/break ratio of 33%/67% at 10 pulses per second (United Kingdom, Europe, and Hong Kong). Same as &P1.

Default

0

Related To   &P

Application   Telebit

S102

Auxiliary Phone Leads

Description ATS102=*n*

0　　Ignore the auxiliary leads. Disregard hardware jumpers.

1　　The modem uses the A/A1 leads to inform the switching equipment that it is using the line.

2　　The modem uses the MI/MIC leads to inform the switching equipment that it is using the line.

Default

0

This register must be set to match the A/A1 or MI/MIC (mode indicate/mode indicate common) jumper connection on the modem board.

Related To S158

Application Telebit

S104

Automatic Dialing

Description   ATS104=*n*

0   Disable.

1   Enable automatic dialing after an OFF-to-ON DTR transition.

2   Reserved.

3   Enable automatic dialing using the T/D (talk/data) switch.

4   Following an OFF-to-ON transition, enter the originate mode if S1=0. Otherwise, enter answer mode.

The S104 register enables automatic dialing. The S100 register setting determines the whether answer or originate tones will be used unless overridden by the R dial modifier.

Default

0

Related To   S100, S105

Application   Telebit

S105

Link Layer Frame Size

Description   `ATS105=n`

4   Maximum frame size is 16 bytes.

5   Maximum frame size is 32 bytes.

6   Maximum frame size is 64 bytes.

7   Maximum frame size is 128 bytes.

8   Maximum frame size is 256 bytes.

9   Maximum frame size is 512 bytes.

Default

7

The S105 register selects the maximum frame size to be used by the link layer (N401 in V.42, N1 in X.25).

The frame size is determined from the value n according to the following formula:

```
frame size = 2^n
```

Related To   S71, S73, S76, S77, S78, S80, S81

Application   Hayes

S105

T/D Switch Enable

Description ATS105=*n*

0   Disabled.

1   Enabled.

2   Enabled when modem is off-hook.

Default

1

The S105 register enables the T/D (talk/data) switch function.

Related To S104

Application Telebit

S106

V.42 Detection

Description `ATS106=n`

0   Disabled.

1   Enabled.

Default

0

When S106=1, the modem performs the V.42 detection phase. LAPM, MNP, or no error control is established based on the settings of the S95 and S97 registers.

Related To S95, S97, S107, S108

Application Telebit

S107

Error Control Detection Timeout

Description ATS1Ø7=*n*

Set timeout factor.

n = 0–255

Default

20

S107 determines the amount of time that the modem will wait for the LAPM or MNP mode staring pattern according to the following formula:

```
timeout = 1ØØ * S1Ø7 + 8ØØ milliseconds
```

Related To S183

Application Telebit

S108

Signal Quality Requirement

Description   ATS108=*n*

0   Signal quality requirement disabled.

1   Low or better signal quality required.

2   Medium or better signal quality required.

3   High signal quality required.

Default

1

The setting of S108 determines the minimum signal quality required for the modem to handshake at the highest designated V.32bis speed. The same criterion is used to determine when automatic rate renegotiation will occur.

If, during a V.32bis handshake or connection, the modem determines that the signal quality is less than the value specified by S108, the modem will attempt to fall back to the next lower carrier speed specified by S109. If the N0 command has been selected, however, fallback will not occur and only the speed specified by S37 will be used.

Related To   N, S37, S109, S110

Application   Dallas, Hayes, Practical, Prometheus

S108

V.42 Match Count

Description   ATS108=*n*

0   Match count is 4. (CCITT V.42 standard and current Microcom implementation.)

1   Match count is 1. (Current Hayes implementation.)

Default

0

The S108 register sets the V.42 pattern match count that is required to successfully satisfy the V.42 detection algorithm.

Related To   S106

Application   Telebit

S109

V.32bis Carrier Speed

Description   ATS109=*n*

n = decimal value of byte determined by bitmap.

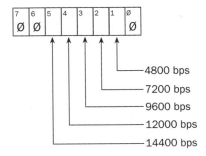

The speeds available for a V.32bis connection handshake, retrain, and rate renegotiation are specified by S109. Each speed may be enabled or disabled independently.

S37 selects the highest carrier speed. If the N0 command is selected, the speed specified by S37 must be enabled in the S109 bitmap and the modem will connect only at that speed. If not, the modem will not connect.

If the modem is operating in V.32bis mode, the N0 and S37 settings do not affect the modem speed during retrain or rate renegotiation.

Default

62 (00111110b)

Related To   N, S37, S108, S110

Application   Dallas, Hayes, Practical, Prometheus

S110

V.32/V.32bis Selection

Description ATS110=*n*

0   V.32 enabled.

1   V.32bis enabled.

2   V.32bis and automatic rate renegotiation enabled.

Default

2

The S110 register can be used to disable the automatic rate renegotiation that is part of the V.32bis protocol or to limit handshake options to that specified by V.32.

Rate renegotiation may be initiated by the remote modem either manually (in response to the O3 command) or when the signal quality or frame error rate indicate that a lower or higher speed should be used. When in V.32bis mode, the modem always responds to a rate renegotiation request.

Automatic rate renegotiation is always disabled when the &X1 command is selected (&Q1, &Q2, or &Q3) and the modem is in synchronous mode, or if the modem is in asynchronous mode (&Q0).

Related To S108, S109, B, O, Q, X

Application Dallas, Hayes, Practical, Prometheus

S110

PEP Mode Data Compression

Description   ATS11Ø=*n*

0   Disabled.

1   Enabled for PEP mode connection if remote modem has S110=1 or 255.

255   Enabled for PEP mode connection if remote modem has S110=1.

Default

255

Data compression is negotiated between the two modems during the PEP initialization sequence. Changing S110 after a connection is established does not change the data compression setting for the session unless the &R1 command is issued.

Related To   &R

Application   Telebit

S111

File Transfer Protocol Spoofing

Description   ATS111=*n*

0	Disabled.
10	Kermit with no parity.
11	Kermit with odd parity.
12	Kermit with even parity.
13	Kermit with MARK parity.
14	Kermit with SPACE parity.
20	XMODEM/YMODEM.
30	UUCP g protocol.
40	ENQ/ACK host (negotiated).
41	ENQ/ACK terminal (negotiated).
42	ENQ/ACK host (not negotiated).
43	ENQ/ACK terminal (not negotiated).
50	Selects the SDLC accelerator. (&Q6 must be set for this selection.)
255	Use protocol specified by remote modem.

Default

255

The S111 register determines the file transfer protocol that will be spoofed during a communications session. Both modems must agree on the protocol, otherwise spoofing is disabled.

Normal file transfer protocol implementations use end-to-end confirmation. Spoofing is the process by which the local modem provides confirmation immediately to its local DTE, eliminating the delay incurred in end-to-end confirmation. The modem then assumes responsibility for ensuring that the data is transferred successfully.

Related To   &Q, S112

Application   Telebit

S112

Set Serial Port Speed

Description ATS112=*n*

0   Use the speed of the last AT command issued.

1   Reserved.

2   300 bps.

3   1200 bps.

4   2400 bps.

5   4800 bps.

6   7200 bps.

7   9600 bps.

8   12000 bps.

9   14400 bps.

10   16800 bps.

11   19200 bps.

12   38400 bps.

13   57600 bps.

14   600 bps.

Default

0

The S112 register can be used to lock the serial port speed. All commands from the DTE must arrive at the designated speed.

Application Dallas, Prometheus

S112

Set Kermit Mark Character

Description   ATS112=*n*

Set mark character ASCII value.

$n = 0–255$

Default

   1

This command sets the mark character that the modem will use when Kermit protocol spoofing is enabled.

Related To   S111

Application   Telebit

S118

LCD Scroll Rate

Description　ATS118=*n*

Set scroll rate in seconds.

n = 1–10

Default

1

When two or more LCD status messages await display, S118 specifies the amount of time each message is displayed sequentially.

Related To　S119

Application　Practical

S119

LCD Message Display Options

Description   ATS119=*n*

0   Display disabled.

1   Display enabled.

Default

1

The S119 register enables the LCD display.

Related To   S118

Application   Practical

S121

Echo Suppressor Compensation

Description ATS121=*n*

0   Disabled.

1   Enabled.

Default

0

The S121 register enables compensation for the effects of echo supressors (part of the GSTN equipment) that may be interfering with data transmission. When compensation is enabled, throughput decreases by about 5 percent.

Application Telebit

S130

DSR Options

Description   ATS130=*n*

0   DSR is always ON.

1   DSR is turned ON at the start of handshaking and remains on during the connection.

2   DSR is ON when the modem is ready to accept commands or data.

3   DSR is ON when the modem is ready to accept commands or data except momentarily at disconnect.

4   DSR is ON when the modem is off-hook.

5   DSR in ON only when a carrier is present.

6   DSR follows DTR.

Default

     0, 2

S130 determines whether the data set ready (DSR) signal generated by the modem operates in accordance with the EIA-232-D and later specification.

Related To   &S

Application   Telebit

S131

DCD Options

Description ATS131=*n*

0   DCD is always ON.

1   DCD indicates the true state of the remote carrier.

2   DCD is on when the modem is ready to accept commands or data.

3   DCD is always ON except momentarily at disconnect.

4   DCD is the inverse of the clear-to-send (CTS) signal.

Default

0, 2

The S131 register determines how the modem controls the data carrier detect (DCD) signal that is sent to the DTE.

Related To &C

Application Telebit

S150

Asynchronous/Synchronous Mode

Description   ATS150=*n*

0   Asynchronous mode.

1   PEP SDLC mode.

2   Transparent synchronous mode.

3   Asynchronous/synchronous mode.

Default

0

The S150 register determines the initial mode for the modem following power up or a Z or &T command.

When S150=1, registers S151-S164 configure the modem for SDLC operation.

Related To   S151–S164

Application   Telebit

S151

SDLC Interface Speed

Description ATS151=*n*

0   300 bps.

1   1200 bps.

2   2400 bps.

3   4800 bps.

4   9600 bps.

5   19200 bps.

35   7200 bps.

43   12000 bps.

46   14400 bps.

Default

4

The S151 register specifies the data rate between the DTE and the local modem when operating in synchronous command modes and when the SDLC accelerator is in use.

Related To S151–S164

Application Telebit

S152

SDLC Switched/Nonswitched

Description ATS152=*n*

0   Nonswitched mode. DSR is ON when modem is ready. DTR must be ON for the modem to exchange data.

1   Switched mode. DSR is held OFF until DTR is turned ON and a link is established.

2   Special switched mode. DSR is ON when the modem is ready.

Default

1

This register defines how the modem interprets the data set ready (DSR) signal in SLDC mode.

Related To S52, S151–S164

Application Telebit

S153

SDLC Full/Half Duplex

Description ATS153=*n*

0   Full duplex. DCD and CTS are ON when the modem is ready.

1   Half duplex. DCD is ON and CTS is OFF when the modem is sending data to the DTE. CTS follows RTS.

Default

1

The data transfer between the modem and the local DTE in SLDC mode is controlled by S153.

Related To S151–S164

Application Telcbit

S154

Synchronous Transmit Clock Source

Description ATS154=*n*

0   The DCE transmit signal element timing (pin 15) and receive signal element timing (pin 17) signals from the modem.

1   The DTE transmit signal element timing (pin 24) signal from the local DTE.

2   The DCE transmit signal element timing (pin 15) is derived from the incoming data stream. Valid only in transparent synchronous mode.

Default

0

S154 determines the RS-232 signals that will be used to control the timing of the transmitted and received data stream when operating in SDLC or transparent synchronous mode.

Related To   &X, S151–S164

Application   Telebit

S155

NRZ/NRZI Data Encoding

Description ATS155=*n*

0   NRZ (nonreturn to zero) encoding. A "1" is represented by a high
        level and a "0" is represented by a low level.

1   NRZI (NRZ inverted) encoding. A "0" is represented by no change in
        the level and a "1" is represented by a level transition.

Default

0

S155 specifies the encoding method that will be used when operating in SDLC
mode.

Related To S151–S164

Application Telebit

S157

SDLC Disconnect Delay

Description ATS157=*n*

Specify time in .1-second increments.

n = 0–255

S157 specifies the time that the modem will wait before disconnecting after one of the following events occurs:

- The DTR is dropped by the local DTE when S52=1.
- An SDLC DISC command is received from the local or remote DTE.
- The carrier from the remote DTE is lost.

The modem will wait until its buffers are empty or until this time expires, whichever occurs first.

Default

0

Related To S52, S151–S164

Application Telebit

S158

SDLC DSR Delay

Description ATS158=*n*

Set delay in seconds.

n = 0–255

Default

0

S158 holds the amount of time that the modem will wait before asserting DSR after detecting a contact closure on the MI/MIC (mode indicate/mode indicate common) auxiliary phone leads when S102=2.

Related To S102, S151–S164

Application Telebit

S160

SDLC Frame Retransmit Limit

Description ATS160=*n*

Set retry limit.

n = 0–255

Default

10

The S160 register specifies the maximum number of times any one frame can be retransmitted without receiving an acknowledgement from the DTE. It also limits the number of SDLC polls that can go unanswered by the DTE. If the limit is exceeded, the modem disconnects.

Related To S151–S164

Application Telebit

S161

SDLC Device Timeout

Description ATS161=*n*

Set timeout in seconds.

n = 0–255

Default

20

This register specifies the length of time the SDLC link can be idle before the modem disconnects. Setting S161 to 0 disables this function.

Related To S151–S164

Application Telebit

S162

SDLC Nonproductive Timeout

Description   ATS162=*n*

Set timeout in seconds.

n = 0–255

Default

2

This register specifies the length of time the modem waits before generating an SDLC frame to maintain the link in an active status. Setting S162 to 0 disables this function.

Related To   S151–S164

Application   Telebit

S163

SDLC Retransmit Timeout

Description ATS162=*n*

Set timeout in seconds.

n = 0–255

Default

> 3

This register specifies the length of time the modem waits for the DTE to acknowledge an SDLC frame before retransmitting the frame. Setting S163 to 0 disables this function.

Related To S151–S164

Application Telebit

S164

SDLC Primary Poll Rate

Description ATS164=*n*

Set number of polls per second.

n = 1–32

Default

7

S164 sets the number of SDLC polls per second that will be generated by the modem while operating as a primary link station when an idle condition exists.

Related To S151–S164

Application Telebit

S169

Synchronous Dialing Command Set

Description ATS169=*n*

0   Disable synchronous dialing.

1   Enable IBM 4941 synchronous dialing.

2   Enable V.24bis synchronous dialing.

Default

0

The S169 register determines if the IBM 4941 or V.25bis dialing command set is enabled during SDLC or transparent synchronous mode operation.

Related To S151–S164, S253

Application Telebit

S180

Feature Negotiation

Description ATS180=*n*

0   Error control disabled.

1   V.42 without detection phase.

2   V.42 with detection phase.

3   MNP.

Default

2

The S180 register determines whether an error-control connection should be attempted and determines the type.

Related To S181

Application Telebit

S181

Error Control Fallback

Description   ATS181=*n*

0   DIRECT mode; flow control disabled.

1   NORMAL mode; flow control enabled.

2   Disconnect.

Default

1

If error control cannot be negotiated, S181 determines the alternative connection type the modem will attempt to establish.

Related To   S180, S183

Application   Telebit

S183

Error Control Detection Timeout

Description ATS183=*n*

Set timeout in increments of 0.1 second.

n = 8–255

Default

25, 28,30

S183 determines the amount of time that the modem will wait for the LAPM or MNP mode starting pattern.

Related To S180, S181

Application Telebit

S190

Data Compression

Description ATS190=*n*

0   Disallowed in both directions.

1   Allowed in both directions.

2   Required in receive, allowed in transmit.

3   Allowed in receive, required in transmit.

4   Required in both directions.

5   Disallowed in receive, allowed in transmit.

6   Disallowed in receive, required in transmit.

7   Allowed in receive, disallowed in transmit.

8   Required in receive, disallowed in transmit.

Default

1

S190 determines how data compression is implemented during a connection. If the two modems cannot satisfy the requirements of this register, the local modem disconnects.

Application   Telebit

S191

LZ Compression

Description ATS191=*n*

6   Disabled.

7   Enabled.

Default

7

The S191 register determines if the modem will attempt to negotiate Telebit's proprietary Lempel-Ziv (LZ) data compression for PEP connections with data compression enabled. LZ compression is negotiated along with V.42bis, with V.42bis as the preferred method.

Related To S190

Application Telebit

S222

Enhanced Command Mode Character

Description ATS222=*n*

Set access character ASCII code.

n = 0–255

Default

126 (~)

The value contained in this register is interpreted as the prefix character required to access enhanced commands when the modem is in conventional command mode.

Related To S63

Application Telebit

S253

Select Smart Mode

Description ATS253=n

0   Modem is configured as a dumb modem.

10   Modem is configured as a smart modem.

32   LPDA bit-synchronous dialing.

Default

10

This register configures the modem to ignore commands and not send result codes. This setting becomes effective the next time the modem is reset.

Related To S169

Application Telebit

S254

&F0 Configuration

Description `ATS254=n`

0   Load configuration A.

1   Load configuration B.

255   Load factory defaults.

Default

255

The S254 register defines the configuration that is recalled by the &F0 command.

Related To &F

Application Telebit

S255

Configuration Select

Description ATS255=*n*

0   Load configuration A after power-up or reset. Disable A/B switch. [Telebit]

Load configuration specified by A/B switch after power-up or reset. [Telebit]

1   Load configuration B after power-up or reset. Disable A/B switch. [Telebit]

Load configuration A after power-up or reset. Disable A/B switch. [Telebit]

255   Load configuration specified by A/B switch after power-up or reset. [Telebit]

Load configuration B after power-up or reset. Disable A/B switch. [Telebit]

Default

0 [Telebit]

255 [Telebit]

The S255 register determines the configuration that will be loaded when 0 is specified for the Z and &W commands. The setting of this register is not affected by the &F command.

Related To Z, &W

Application Telebit

:T0

V.32 Probe Timing

Description   AT:T0=*n*

Set time in increments of 0.1 second.

n = 0–255

Default

40

The :T0 register determines how long the modem attempts to establish a V.32, V.22bis, or V.22 connection before falling back to a V.23 split speed or V.21 connection.

Related To   :T1, :T2, :T3

Application   Microcom

:T1

V.23 Probe Timing

Description

`AT:T1=`*n*

Set time in increments of 0.1 second.

n = 0–255

Default

30

The :T1 register determines how long the modem attempts to establish a V.23 split-speed connection before dropping back to a V.21 or V.23 half-duplex connection.

Related To :T0, :T2, :T3

Application Microcom

:T2

V.21 Probe Timing

Description AT:T2=*n*

Set the time in increments of 0.1 second.

n = 0–255

Default

0

The :T2 register determines how long the modem attempts to establish a V.21 connection before dropping back to a V.23 half-duplex connection.

Related To :T0, :T1, :T3

Application Microcom

:T3

V.21/V.23 Answer Tone Time

Description AT:T3=*n*

Set the time in increments of 0.1 second.

n = 0–33

Default

33

When the answering modem is set for V.21 or V.23, the :T3 register determines the duration of the V.25 answer tone sent to the originating modem. When the originating modem is set for V.21 or V.23, the :T3 register determines how long the modem waits after detecting the answer tone before establishing the connection.

Related To :T0, :T1, :T2

Application Microcom

:T4

Line Turnaround Delay

Description AT:T4=*n*

Set the time in increments of 12.5 milliseconds.

n = 0–255

Default

20

This register determines the amount of time the modem waits before turning its carrier on when shifting from receive to transmit mode during V.23 half-duplex connections.

Related To :T5

Application Microcom

:T5

V.23 Intercharacter Delay

Description   AT:T5=*n*

Set delay in increments of 12.5 milliseconds.

n = 0–255

Default

7

This register sets the amount of time the modem waits after transmitting the last character in its buffer before turning its carrier off.

Related To   :T4

Application   Microcom

:T6

CD Detection Delay

Description AT:T6=*n*

Set delay in milliseconds.

n = 0–255

Default

200

This register sets the amount of time the modem waits after receiving the remote carrier before it begins looking for data.

Application Microcom

:T7

False Answer Abort Timeout

Description AT:T7=*n*

Set timeout in seconds.

$n = 0$–255

Default

60

The :T7 register sets the amount of time the modem will wait before hanging up when no data is received from the DTE after a connection is established. Setting :T7=0 disables the timer.

Application Microcom

:T9

Primary XON Character

Description AT:T=*n*

Set XON character ASCII value.

n = 0–255

Default

17 (<DC1>)

This register holds the ASCII value of the character that will be recognized as the primary XON flow-control character.

Related To \Q, \G, :T10, :T11, :T12

Application Microcom

:T10

Primary XOFF Character

Description AT:T1Ø=*n*

Set XOFF character ASCII value.

n=0–255

Default

19 (<DC3>)

This register holds the ASCII value of the character that will be recognized as the primary XOFF flow-control character.

Related To \Q, \G, :T9, :T11, :T12

Application Microcom

:T11

Secondary XON Character

Description   AT:T=*n*

Set XON character ASCII value.

n = 0–255

Default

> 249

This register holds the ASCII value of the character that will be recognized as the secondary XON flow-control character.

Related To   \Q, \G, :T9, :T10, :T12

Application   Microcom

:T12

Secondary XOFF Character

Description   AT:T1Ø=*n*

Set XOFF character ASCII value.

n = 0–255

Default

     251

This register holds the ASCII value of the character that will be recognized as the secondary XOFF flow-control character.

Related To   \Q, \G, :T9, :T10, :T11

Application   Microcom

:T13

Automode Timeout

Description AT:T=*n*

Sets the timeout in increments of 0.1 second.

n = 0–255

Default

15

This register sets the time that the modem will attempt to automatically negotiate a compatible mode before abandoning a connection attempt.

Application Microcom

:T14

Connect Message Delay

Description AT:T=*n*

Set delay in increments of 0.1 second.

n = 0–255

Default

0

The :T14 register specifies how long the modem will wait before or after issuing a CONNECT message before setting CTS, DSR, and CD high.

Related To @C

Application Microcom

:T15

V.24 Control Bitmap

Description AT:T=*n*

n = decimal value of byte determined by bitmap.

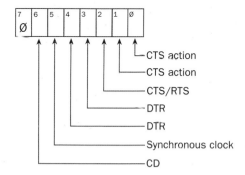

Bit	Default	Definition
0	1	CTS action on synchronous and direct mode retrains 0 CTS is not affected. 1 CTS is lowered.
1	1	CTS action on leased line restoral or dial backup operation 0 CTS is not affected. 1 CTS is lowered.
2	1	CTS/RTS 0 RTS ignored while not connected when &R0 or &R2 is set. 1 CTS follows RTS when not connected if &R1 or &R3 is set.
3	1	DTR operation on leased lines 0 DTR controlled by &D. 1 DTR ignored.

Bit	Default	Definition
4	1	DTR action on leased lines when modem is idle 0 Raising DTR forces the modem off hook when the modem is idle if &D1 or &D2 is set. 1 DTR ignored.
5	0	Synchronous clock 0 Off until connection established. 1 Always on.
6	0	CD status 0 CD follows link negotiation connection status. 1 CD follows true carrier status when &C1 is set.
7	0	Reserved

Default

31 (00011111b)

:T15 is a bitmapped register that controls a variety of modem parameters.

Related To   &R

Application   Microcom

:T16

CTS Delay

Description   AT:T=*n*

Set delay in increments of 12.5 milliseconds.

n = 0–255

Default

0

This register determines how long the modem waits after CD (carrier detect) and/or DSR (data set ready) have been turned ON before turning its CTS (clear-to-send) signal ON.

Application   Microcom

:T17

V.32/V.32bis Training

Description   AT:T17=*n*

$n = 0, 1, 5\text{--}28$

Default

1

The :T17 register controls the length of the training sequences exchanged during V.32 and V.32bis connections. Setting :T17=1 enables dynamic training. Setting :T17=0 is equivalent to setting :T17=28 and enables the default training sequences. Lower settings reduce connection time but increase the modem's sensitivity to line noise.

Application   Microcom

:T18

Busy Out Timer

Description   AT:T18=*n*

Set the time in seconds.

$n = 0$–255

Default

0

When DTR is OFF, the modem goes off-hook and busies out the line after the time set by :T18 expires. When DTR is subsequently raised, the modem enters command mode. Setting :T18=0 disables the timer. This option is effective only when &D1, &D2, or &D3 is set.

Application   Microcom

:T19

MNP Link Control

Description AT:T19=*n*

0 Modem will establish a 1200 bps connection regardless of MNP detection.

1 Modem will refuse a 1200 bps connection if MNP is not detected within 2 minutes.

Default

1

This register determines the modem's response to 1200 bps connections without MNP protocols.

Application Microcom

APPENDIX C
SELECTED COMMUNICATIONS STANDARDS

ANSI (American National Standards Institute)

X3.4–1986

> "Coded Character Set—7-Bit American National Standard Code for Information Interchange (ASCII)"

CCITT (International Telegraph and Telephone Consultative Committee)

Blue Book Volume VII Fascicle 3 (BB 7.3)

> "Terminal Equipment and Protocols for Telematic Services"

> Contains the complete text of the CCITT specifications T.1 through T.63, which were approved and current as of November 1988. Since publication, revised editions of several key specifications have been released as noted in descriptions that follow.

Blue Book Volume VIII Fascicle 1 (BB 8.1)

> "Data Communications Over the Telephone Network"

> Contains the complete text of the CCITT specifications V.1 through V.230 that were available and current as of November 1988. Several key standards not present in this volume include V.17, V.32bis, and V.42bis. Since publication, revised editions of several key specifications have been released as noted in descriptions that follow.

T.2 (BB 7.3, 1988)

> "Standardization of Group 1 Facsimile Apparatus for Document Transmission"

> Provides a minimal definition of some terms and parameters used for G1 fax operations.

T.3 (BB 7.3, 1988)

> "Standardization of Group 2 Facsimile Apparatus for Document Transmission"

> Provides definitions of the protocols and signals used during G2 fax operations.

T.4 (BB 7.3, 1988)

"Standardization of Group 3 Facsimile Apparatus for Document Transmission"

Provides definitions of the protocols and signals used during G3 fax operations including supported resolutions, one- and two-dimensional encoding, and optional error-control and error limiting modes. The version of T.4 that appears in the 1988 Blue Book 7.3 is incomplete without the 1990 revision sheet.

NOTE: A draft revision is currently pending for this standard. Proposed changes include support for higher resolutions, binary file transfer, and character and mixed mode transmissions.

T.6 (BB 7.3, 1988)

"Facsimile Coding Schemes and Coding Control Functions for Group 4 Facsimile Apparatus"

Provides a brief definition of the line encoding schemes and control functions that are to be used in the G4 fax service.

T.10 (BB 7.3, 1988)

"Document Facsimile Transmissions on Leased Telephone-Type Circuits"

T.10bis (BB 7.3, 1988)

"Document Facsimile Transmissions in the General Switched Telephone Network"

T.20 (BB 7.3, 1988)

"Standardized Test Chart for Facsimile Transmissions"

T.21 (BB 7.3, 1988)

"Standardized Test Charts for Document Facsimile Transmissions"

T.30 (1988)

"Procedures for Document Facsimile Transmission in the General Switched Telephone Network"

Describes the procedures and signals used when operating G1, G2, and G3 fax service. Descriptions of the HDLC framing system, fax information control fields, and set-up procedures are described. A current copy of T.30 is essential to fax programming. The version of T.30 that appears in the 1988 Blue Book 7.3 is incomplete without the 1990 revision sheet.

NOTE: A draft revision is currently pending for this standard. Proposed changes include support for passwords, selective polling, additional modulation schemes, and higher resolutions.

T.50 (1988)

"International Alphabet A5"

NOTE: A draft revision is currently pending for this standard.

T.434

"Binary File Transfer Protocol for the Telematic Services"

T.503 (1990)

"A Document Application Profile for the Interchange of Group 4 Facsimile Documents"

Provides a brief outline of the formats that are used to interchange fax documents that contain only graphics.

T.563 (1991)

"Terminal Characteristics for Group 4 Facsimile Apparatus"

V.4 (BB 8.1, 1988)

"General Structure of Signals of International Alphabet Number 5 Code for Data Transmission over Public Telephone Networks"

V.17 (1991)

"A 2-Wire Modem for Facsimile Application with Rates Up to 14400 bit/s"

Defines the half-duplex modulation methods and operating sequences for fax operation at speeds of 7200, 9600, 12000, and 14400 bps. (This specification is not included in the CCITT 1989 Blue Book 8.1.)

V.21 (BB 8.1, 1988)

"300 Bits per Second Duplex Modem Standardized for Use in the General Switched Telephone Network"

V.22 (BB 8.1, 1988)

"1200 Bits per Second Duplex Modem Standardized for Use in the General Switched Telephone Network and on Point-to-Point 2-Wire Leased Telephone-Type Circuits"

V.22bis (BB 8.1, 1988)

"2400 Bits per Second Duplex Modem Using the Frequency Division Technique Standardized on the General Switched Telephone Network and on Point-to-Point 2-Wire Leased Telephone-Type Circuits"

V.23 (BB 8.1, 1988)

"600/1200-Baud Modem Standardized for Use in the General Switched Telephone Network"

V.24 (BB 8.1, 1988)

"List of Definitions for Interchange Circuits between Data Terminal Equipment (DTE) and Data Circuit-Terminating Equipment (DCE)"

V.25bis (BB 8.1, 1988)

"Automatic Answering Equipment and/or Parallel Automatic Calling Equipment on the General Switched Telephone Network including Procedures for Disabling of Echo Control Devices for both Manually and Automatically Established Calls"

V.27ter (BB 8.1, 1988)

"4800/2400 Bits per Second Modem with Automatic Equalizer Standardized for Use on Leased Telephone-Type Circuits"

Defines an early standard supported by G3 fax.

V.29 (BB 8.1, 1988)

"9600 Bits per Second Modem Standardized for Use on Point-to-Point 4-Wire Leased Telephone-Type Circuits"

Defines a standard used by G3 fax and some nonstandard data modems.

V.32 (1988)

"A Family of 2-Wire, Duplex Modems Operating at Data Signaling Rates of up to 9600 bit/s for Use on the General Switched Telephone Network and on Leased Telephone-Type Circuits"

Describes the modulation methods used for communications up to 9600 bps, speed negotiation options, echo cancellation, and trellis coding.

V.32bis (1991)

"A Duplex Modem Operating at Data Signaling Rates of Up to 14400 bit/s for Use on the General Switched Telephone Network and on Leased Point-to-Point 2-Wire Telephone-Type Circuits"

This specification is a self-contained extension of the CCITT V.32 specification. V.32bis defines modulation speeds up to 14400 bps with fallback speeds of 12000, 9600, 7200, and 4800 bps. (This specification is not included in the CCITT 1989 Blue Book volume 8.1.)

V.33 (1988)

"14400 Bit/s Modem Standardized for Use on Point-to-Point 4-Wire Leased Telephone-Type Circuits"

V.42 (1988)

"Error-Correcting Procedures for DCEs Using Asynchronous-to-Synchronous Conversion"

Describes an error-control procedure that provides for error detection and automatic retransmission of data. The standard describes the LAPM (link access procedure for modems) as the primary method and the MNP 2-4 protocols as an alternate.

NOTE: The V.42 specification that appears in the CCITT 1989 Blue Book 8.1 is incomplete without the errata sheet dated August 1990.

V.42bis (1990)

"Data Compression Procedures for DCEs Using Error Correcting Procedures"

Defines the data compression method that can be provided during a LAPM error-control link. V.42bis is not a tutorial on data compression. (This specification does not replace the V.42 specification, and is not included in the CCITT 1989 Blue Book volume 8.1.)

V.FAST

A working title for the proposed standard providing modulation methods up to 28800 bps. Approval of the standard is expected after January 1994.

Bell System Specifications

Bell 103/113

Frequency division multiplexed full-duplex asynchronous signaling at speeds from 0 to 300 bps using frequency shift keying.

Bell 201

Full-duplex (201B) and half-duplex (201B/C) synchronous signaling at speeds up to 2400 bps using 4-state differential phase-shift keying (DPSK-4).

Bell 202

Half-duplex asynchronous signaling at speeds up to 1200 bps using frequency shift keying and an on-off keyed backchannel.

Bell 212A

Frequency division multiplexed full-duplex synchronous signaling at speeds up to 1200 bps using 4-state differential phase-shift keying (DPSK-4).

EIA/TIA Standards

EIA/TIA-232-E (July 1991)

"Interface between Data Terminal Equipment and Data Circuit-Terminating Equipment Employing Serial Binary Data Interchange"

Provides an electrical and functional description of the signals present in a serial port interface. This revision of the specification also includes a mechanical description of the standard DB-25 serial port connector and an alternate 26-pin connector.

EIA/TIA-465-A

"Group 3 Facsimile Apparatus for Document Transmission"
See CCITT T.4.

EIA/TIA-466-A

"Procedures for Document Facsimile Transmission"
See CCITT T.30.

EIA/TIA-578 (November 1990)

"Asynchronous Facsimile DCE Control Standard, Service Class 1"

Defines the AT+F commands that the DTE issues to a fax modem and the possible modem responses during a Class 1 fax session. The command descriptions are terse and provide little insight into Group 3 and 4 fax protocols.

TIA/EIA-592 (Proposed)

"Asynchronous Facsimile DCE Control Standard, Service Class 2.0"

Currently under development as standards proposal SP-2388-B, this standard will define the AT+F commands that a DTE issues to a fax modem and the possible modem responses during a Class 2.0 fax session. For Class 2 compatibility see SP-2388-A.

TIA/EIA-602 (June 1992)

"Data Transmission Systems and Equipment—Serial Asynchronous Automatic Dialing and Control"

Simply documents the basic set of AT commands and S registers that were found to be in common on a large number of modems. It defines no new commands and serves only to state that the "+F" prefix is reserved for fax operations.

SP-2388-A (August 1991)

"Asynchronous Facsimile DCE Control Standard (Service Class 2)"

SP-2388-A is a draft of TIA/EIA-592. This proposed standard was issued for review in August 1991. On the basis of this draft, a number of manufacturers built conforming modems that implemented the proposed command set.

The comment period for this draft was closed in October 1991. Subsequently, draft B was released which differed markedly from draft A. Recognizing the large installed base of draft A-compatible fax modems, this standard has been given the "Class 2" designation. The designation "Class 2.0" will be used for the final release of TIA/EIA-592.

SP-2388-B (March 1992)

"Asynchronous Facsimile DCE Control Standard (Service Class 2.0)"

SP-2388-B is the most recent draft of TIA/EIA-592. This proposed standard was issued for review and comments in March 1992 and is expected to closely match the final standard. Its most significant difference from SP-2388-A is that nearly all the fax control commands and responses have been changed. It also assigns the designation "2" to equipment compatible with SP-2388-A, reserving "2.0" for TIA/EIA-592 compatibility.

ISO (International Organization for Standardization) Standards

ISO 646

"7-bit Coded Character Set for Information Processing Interchange"

ISO 1177

"Information Processing—Character Structure for Stop/Start and Synchronous Transmission"

ISO 2111

(1972) "Data Communication—Basic-Mode Control Procedures— Code Independent Information Transfer"

ISO 2382-9

"Information Technology—Vocabulary—Part 9, Data Communications"

ISO 3309

"Data Communications—High-Level Data Link Control Procedures— Frame Structure"

Additional Standards

DCA/Intel Communicating Applications Specification (CAS)

Describes the DCA/Intel CAS high-level programming interface for communications applications. Documents the interrupt-level interface to CAS-compliant software servers.

FaxBios

Describes the FaxBios application program interface for computer based facsimile operations. Documents the C-based interface to Fax-Bios-compliant software servers.

Sierra Modem Command and S-Registers User's Guide

Describes the AT commands and S registers for Sierra Semiconductor modem chips. It includes a description of the Sierra Sendfax instruction set.

USRobotics High Level Fax Interface

Describes the software interface for the USRobotics Worldport fax modem with T.30 firmware.

APPENDIX D

BIBLIOGRAPHY AND MANUFACTURER REFERENCE

Periodicals

Bunton, Suzanne, and Gaetano Borriello. "Practical Dictionary Management for Hardware Data Compression (for the Second Ziv-Lempel Data Compression Scheme)." *Communications of the ACM,* January 1992.

Fiala, E., and D. Greene. "Data Compression with Finite Windows." *Communications of the ACM,* April 1989.

Hamming, R.W. "Error Detecting and Correcting Codes." *The Bell System Technical Journal,* April 1950.

Kodis, John. "Fletcher's Checksum: Error Correction at a Fraction of the Cost." *Dr. Dobb's Journal,* May 1992.

Koksal, F. Zeynep, and Melek D. Yucel. "Comments on the Decoding Algorithms of DBEC-TBEC Reed-Solomon Codes." *IEEE Transactions on Computers,* February 1992.

Nelson, Mark R. "LZW Data Compression." *Dr. Dobb's Journal,* October 1989.

Nelson, Mark R. "File Verification Using CRC (Cyclical Redundancy Check)." *Dr. Dobb's Journal,* May 1992.

Poor, Alfred. "Looking at the TIFF Specification from the Inside. (Tagged Image File Format)." *PC Magazine,* December 17, 1991.

Ramabadran, Tenkasi V., and Sunil S. Gaitonde. "A Tutorial on CRC Computations." *IEEE Micro,* August 1988.

Ritter, Terry. "The Great CRC Mystery." *Dr. Dobb's Journal of Software Tools,* February 1986.

Welch, T. "A Technique for High-Performance Data Compression." *IEEE Computer,* June 1984.

Ziv, J., and A. Lempel. "A Universal Algorithm for Sequential Data Compression." *IEEE Transactions on Information Theory,* 1977.

Ziv, J., and A. Lempel. "Compression of Individual Sequences via Variable-Rate Coding." *IEEE Transactions on Information Theory,* September 1978.

Books

Apostolico A., and Z. Galil, Eds. *Combinatorial Algorithms on Words*. New York, NY: Springer-Verlag, 1985.

Campbell, Joe. *C Programmer's Guide to Serial Communications*. Indianapolis, IN: Howard W. Sams, 1987.

Green, James H. *Business One Irwin Handbook of Telecommunications*. Homewood, IL: Business One Irwin, 1991.

Nelson, Mark R. *The Data Compression Book*. San Mateo, CA: M&T Books, 1991.

Storer, James A. *Data Compression: Methods and Theory* (Principles of Computer Science Serial). Rockville, MD: W.H. Freeman, 1988.

Sources for Standards Publications

Electronic Industries Association
2001 Pennsylvania Avenue, NW
Washington, DC 20006
202–457–4966
    EIA and TIA standards.

Global Professional Publications
A Division of Global Engineering Documents
3130 South Harbor Boulevard
Suite 330
Santa Ana, CA 92704
800–854–7179
    CCITT, ANSI, and ISO standards.

Omnicom
Philips Publishing, Inc.
7811 Montrose Road
Potomac, MD 20854
301–424–3338
    CCITT, ANSI, and ISO standards.

Aldus Corp.
411 First Avenue South
Seattle, WA 98104
206–628–2320
    TIFF Developer's Toolkit.

Intel Corporation (technical support)
5200 N.E. Elam Young Parkway
Hillsboro, OR 97124
503–629–7000 (inside US and Canada)
503–629–7354 (outside US and Canada)
>DCA/Intel Communicating Applications Specification. DCA/Intel. Intel Part Number 301812-005.

>Programmer's Toolkit for CAS and the Phonebook. DCA/Intel. Intel Part Number 302638-001A.

FaxBios Specification
WordPerfect Corporation
1555 North Technology Way
Orem, UT 84057-2399
800-321-4566
>Describes the FaxBios application program interface. (The FaxBios Association has been dissolved and all distribution responsibility has been assumed by WordPerfect Corp.)

IBM Technical Publications
P.O. Box 2009
Racine, WI 53404
800–426–7282
>IBM Options and Adapters Technical Reference. Part Number 6322509. Describes asynchronous and bisynchronous communications adapters.

>IBM Options and Adapters Technical Reference: Personal Computer AT. Part Number 6280134. Describes serial/parallel adapter.

>IBM Options and Adapters Technical Reference: IBM Dual Async Adapter/A. Part Number 68X2315.

Manufacturers:
Modems and Communication Products

AT&T Paradyne Corporation
8545 126th Avenue, North
P.O. Box 2826
Largo, FL 34649
813–530–2000

Black Box
P.O. Box 12800
Pittsburgh, PA 15241
412–746–5500

Hayes Microcomputer Products, Inc.
P.O. Box 105203
Atlanta, GA 30348
404–840–9200

Intel Corporation
5200 N.E. Elam Young Parkway
Hillsboro, OR 97124
503–629–7000 (inside US and Canada)
503–629–7354 (outside US and Canada)

Microcom Systems, Inc.
500 River Ridge Drive
Norwood, MA 02062
617–551–1000

Motorola Codex Corporation
20 Cabot Boulevard
Mansfield, MA 02048
508–261–4000

National Semiconductor Corporation
2900 Semiconductor Drive
P.O. Box 58090
Santa Clara, CA 95052-8090
408–721–5000

Practical Peripherals
375 Conejo Ridge Avenue
Thousand Oaks, CA 91361
805–497–4774

Prometheus Products, Inc.
9524 SW Tualatin-Sherwood Road
Tualatin, OR 97062
503-692-9601

Rockwell International
Digital Communications Division
4311 Jamboree Road
P.O. Box C
Newport Beach, CA 92658
714–833–4655

Sierra Semiconductor Corporation
2075 North Capitol Avenue
San Jose, CA 95132
408–263–9300

SilverSoft, Inc.
1100 Centennial Boulevard
Suite 240
Richardson, TX 75081
214-669-1426

Telebit Corporation
1315 Chesapeake Terrace
Sunnyvale, CA 94089-1100
408–734–4333

Twincom
A Division of Target Technologies, Inc.
6714 Netherlands Drive
Wilmington, NC 28405
919-395–6100

USRobotics
8100 North McCormick Boulevard
Skokie, Illinois 60076
800–342–5877
800–982–5151 (technical support line)

Yamaha Corporation of America
981 Ridder Park Drive
San Jose, CA 95131
408–437–3133

Zoom Telephonics, Inc.
207 South Street
Boston, MA 02111
617–423–1072

Manufacturers: Communication Software

Datastorm Technologies, Inc.
P.O. Box 1471
Columbia, MO 65205
314–443–3282
314–875–0530 (technical support)

Smith Micro Software, Inc.
51 Columbia
Aliso Viejo, CA 92656
714–362–5800

Traveling Software, Inc.
18702 North Creek Parkway
Bothell, WA 98011
206–483–8088

APPENDIX E
UART REGISTER QUICK REFERENCE

Programming a UART can be confusing. Sometimes it's difficult to remember the offset of the interrupt enable register or the interpretation of the bit settings in the line status register. This appendix is a quick-reference guide that identifies each of the registers and their individual bit fields. Registers for both the 8250 and 16550 families of UARTs are shown in the same table. Register fields or alternate definitions that apply only to the 16550 are shaded gray.

TABLE E.1

UART Register Quick Reference Guide

Register Address (DLAB=0)	Register Name	Bit 7	Bit 6	Bit 5	Bit 4	Bit 3	Bit 2	Bit 1	Bit 0
0	Receiver Buffer (read only)	d_7	d_6	d_5	d_4	d_3	d_2	d_1	d_0
0	Transmitter Buffer (write only)	d_7	d_6	d_5	d_4	d_3	d_2	d_1	d_0
1	Interrupt Enable	0	0	0	0	Modem Status	Receiver Line Status	Transmitter Holding Register Empty	Received Data Available
2	Interrupt Identification (read only)	0 / FIFOs Enabled	0 / FIFOs Enabled	0	0	0 / Interrupt Identifier 000 = Modem Status 001 = THR Empty 010 = Received Data Available 011 = Line Status 110 = Receiver FIFO Timeout	Interrupt Identifier 00 = Modem Status 01 = THR Empty 10 = Received Data Available 11 = Line Status		Interrupt Pending 0 = Interrupt Pending
2	FIFO Control Register (write only)	Receiver FIFO Interrupt Trigger Level 00 = 1 byte 01 = 4 bytes 10 = 8 bytes 11 = 14 bytes		Reserved		DMA Mode Select	Clear Transmit FIFO	Clear Receiver FIFO	Enable FIFO Mode
3	Line Control	Divisor Latch Access Bit	Set Break	Parity Type 00 = ODD 01 = EVEN 10 = MARK 11 = SPACE		Parity Enable 1 = parity on	Number of STOP bits 0 = 1 bit 1 = 2 bits ($1\frac{1}{2}$ bits for char len = 5)	Character Length 00 = 5 bits 01 = 6 bits 10 = 7 bits 11 = 8 bits	

TABLE E.1

UART Register Quick Reference Guide (Continued)

Register Address (DLAB=0)	Register Name	Bit 7	Bit 6	Bit 5	Bit 4	Bit 3	Bit 2	Bit 1	Bit 0
4	Modem Control	0	0	0	Loop	General Purpose Output 2	General Purpose Output 1	Request To Send	Data Terminal Ready
5	Line Status	0 / Receiver FIFO Error	Transmitter Shift Register Empty	Transmitter Holding Register Empty	Break Interrupt	Framing Error	Parity Error	Overrun Error	Data Ready
6	Modem Status	Data Carrier Detect	Ring Indicator	Data Set Ready	Clear To Send	Delta Data Carrier Detect	Trailing Edge Ring Indicator	Delta Data Set Ready	Delta Clear To Send
7	Scratch Pad	d_7	d_6	d_5	d_4	d_3	d_2	d_1	d_0

Register Address (DLAB=1)	Register Name	Bit 7	Bit 6	Bit 5	Bit 4	Bit 3	Bit 2	Bit 1	Bit 0
0	Divisor Latch - Least Significant Byte	d_7	d_6	d_5	d_4	d_3	d_2	d_1	d_0
1	Divisor Latch - Most Significant Byte	d_{15}	d_{14}	d_{13}	d_{12}	d_{11}	d_{10}	d_9	d_8

A INDEX